I0868074

Forms of Mobility

FLASHPOINTS

The FlashPoints series is devoted to books that consider literature beyond strictly national and disciplinary frameworks and that are distinguished both by their historical grounding and by their theoretical and conceptual strength. Our books engage theory without losing touch with history and work historically without falling into uncritical positivism. FlashPoints aims for a broad audience within the humanities and the social sciences concerned with moments of cultural emergence and transformation. In a Benjaminian mode, FlashPoints is interested in how literature contributes to forming new constellations of culture and history and in how such formations function critically and politically in the present. Series titles are available online at http://escholarship.org/uc/flashpoints.

A complete list of titles begins on page 314.

Forms of Mobility

Genre, Language, and Media in African Literary Cultures

Stephanie Bosch Santana

NORTHWESTERN UNIVERSITY PRESS | EVANSTON, ILLINOIS

Northwestern University Press
www.nupress.northwestern.edu

Printed in the United States of America

10 9 8 7 6 5 4 3 2 1

Library of Congress Cataloging-in-Publication Data

Names: Bosch Santana, Stephanie, author.
Title: Forms of mobility : genre, language, and media in African literary cultures / Stephanie Bosch Santana.
Other titles: FlashPoints (Evanston, Ill.)
Description: Evanston : Northwestern University Press, 2024. | Series: Flashpoints | Includes bibliographical references and index.
Identifiers: LCCN 2024023381 | ISBN 9780810147690 (paperback) | ISBN 9780810147706 (cloth) | ISBN 9780810147713 (ebook)
Subjects: LCSH: African fiction—History and criticism. | Residential mobility—Africa, Sub-Saharan. | Street literature—Africa, Sub-Saharan—History and criticism. | Electronic publications—Africa, Sub-Saharan—History and criticism. | Africans in literature.
Classification: LCC PR9340 .B67 2024 | DDC 823.900996—dc23/eng/20240520
LC record available at https://lccn.loc.gov/2024023381

Contents

Acknowledgments

Researching and writing this book has been an enormous privilege that would not have been possible without the support, guidance, wisdom, and patience of a great many people. I am thankful to Beulah Thumbadoo, who, in hiring me to work on her national short story competition in South Africa in 2006, changed the course of my life and work. The stories from this competition, and the dazzling forms they took, were the inspiration for this project. I am grateful to my former housemates at 30 Kingston and colleagues at Creative Media, who made living in Joburg such a joy. Don Thomas introduced me to his many friends in Malawi, among them Luzu Gondwe and his family and Rachel and Claus Fiedler, who opened their home and Lydia Foundation school to me. I thank the girls at Lydia who inspired the Malawian Girls' Literary competition, several stories from which are discussed here, and Kasuzi Mbaluko, who helped to make the competition a reality. Mike Mvona, former president of the Malawi Writers Union (MAWU), has been exceedingly generous with his time and connected me to many writers over the years. Many thanks are also owed to MAWU's Women's Desk for facilitating the 2007 and 2012 girls' competitions. Special thanks to Rhoda Zulu, for welcoming me into her home many times, and to Carolyn Zulu, for sending me stories from the *Malawi News*. Hope Ndhlovu assisted me in accessing materials from the Zimbabwe National Archives and translating several Shona stories from *African Parade*. Thanks also to Natalie Jackson and Holo Hachonda for being such wonderful hosts in Lusaka and to Dov and Kim Green for giving me a home in Joburg when I no longer lived there.

The writers and critics whom I have interviewed over the years in southern Africa are too many to name, but I thank especially Shadreck Chikoti, Lawrence Kadzitche, Norah Lungu, D. D. Phiri, Mike Kamwendo, Juniah Ngwira, Steve Chimombo, Stanley Kenani, Bill Saidi, Memory Chirere, Thulani Lupondwana, Mike Maphoto, Ekari Mbvundula, Muthi Nhlema, and Shaun Swingler. To my many Chichewa teachers and interlocutors, including Chidzero Nkumba, Evelyn Kachaje, Shadreck Chikoti, and Charity Gondwe, zikomo kwambiri.

This book began in the Department of African and African American Studies at Harvard and would not have taken the shape it did without the guidance and support of my many mentors there. Biodun Jeyifo pushed me to be the best scholar and thinker I can be. Glenda Carpio, who asks the most important questions, steered the project into some of its most fruitful territories. Karen Thornber was willing to dive into the field of African literature with me, lending me her keen eye and wonderful professional advice. I am also grateful to John Mugane, Caroline Elkins, Achille Mbembe, and the late Abiola Irele for their guidance and friendship. My former colleagues and friends at the University of Michigan were wonderful interlocutors and supporters in my brief time there. I thank especially Frieda Ekotto, Derek Peterson, Valerie Traub, Walter Cohen, Lucy Hartley, Tung-Hui Hu, Aliyah Khan, Madhumita Lahiri, Scott Lyons, David Porter, Michael Schoenfeldt, Omolade Adunbi, Antoine Traisnel, and Anna Watkins Fisher. The Department of Comparative Literature at UCLA has been, and continues to be, a tremendous source of support, mentorship, and friendship. My warm appreciation goes to Nouri Gana, Eleanor Kaufman, Kathy Komar, Efraín Kristal, Tamara Levitz, David MacFadyen, Kirstie McClure, Aamir Mufti, Anjali Prabhu, Michael Rothberg, Shu-mei Shih, Zrinka Stahuljak, and Whitney Arnold, with special thanks to Nouri Gana and Efraín Kristal for commenting on draft chapters of the manuscript and book proposal, respectively. I also thank Yogita Goyal, Ali Behdad, David Kim, David Schaberg, and Ed Keller for their intellectual support over the years.

I am indebted to Stephanie Newell for her generous mentorship and for reading portions of the current manuscript. Isabel Hofmeyr, Derek Peterson, and the other participants at the 2016 African Print Networks conference provided encouragement and feedback on an early iteration of chapter 2. Many thanks to Louise Bethlehem for inviting me to participate in the "APARTHEID-STOPS" conference at WiSER, where I presented parts of chapter 1, and to Nathan Suhr-Sytsma, Clifton Crais, Subha Xavier, and the other participants in the research seminar at Emory's Institute of African Studies for their incisive comments on a draft of chapter 3. I was also lucky to have the opportunity to present portions of the current manuscript at Uppsala University and Stockholm University thanks to Ashleigh Harris, Lynda Gichanda Spencer, Nicklas Hållén, and Stefan Helgesson. I am grateful to Moradewun Adejunmobi, Carli Coetzee, and Olakunle George for their mentorship and keen editorial eyes on portions of this and other projects. This book has also benefited enormously from Katelyn Knox's workshops and talented readers and editors such as Allison Van Deventer and Erin Mosely. I would also like to express my sincerest thanks to Faith Wilson Stein, the FlashPoints editors, the Northwestern University Press staff, and the anonymous readers who provided invaluable feedback to help improve the manuscript.

The writing and research for this book was made possible through the generous support of a Mellon/ACLS fellowship, a Hellman Fellowship, and a grant from the UCLA Center for the Study of Women. An earlier version of chapter 1 was published in 2014 as "Migrant Forms: *African Parade*'s New Literary Geographies" in a special issue of *Research in African Literatures* (45, no. 3) edited by Yogita Goyal. Several pages of chapter 5 were originally published in my essay "Navigating Digital Worlds" in *A Companion to African Literatures* (Wiley Blackwell, 2021). I am grateful to Dale Halvorsen for granting me permission to reproduce his artwork on the cover of *Jungle Jim* issue 16 and to Chimurenga for allowing me to reproduce an image of the cover of the *Chimurenga Chronic*, *Chimurenga* 16. Rumbi Katedza, who happens to be a former winner of Beulah's competition, kindly connected me to Peter Churu of Padare reNhau, who granted permission to reproduce the cover of *African Parade* magazine included here. Sam Banda Jr. has been enormously helpful in facilitating access to the *Malawi News* archives and photographing the two images in chapter 3, which are reproduced with permission from Pilirani Kachinziri. I am also beyond thankful to Franco K. Mbilizi for generously granting me permission to include an image of one of his stunning paintings on the book's cover.

I have been lucky to find myself among many inspirational scholars and friends in the African literary field, who are too many to name here. Special thanks to those whom I have collaborated with in various ways, including Duncan Yoon, Rhonda Cobham-Sander, Shola Adenekan, Kwabena Opoku-Agyemang, Madhu Krishnan, Bhakti Shringarpure,

Dina Ligaga, James Yékú, Adwoa Opoku-Agyemang, Susanna Sacks, Meg Arenberg, Lowell Brower, Monica Popescu, Toby Warner, Wendy Belcher, Mukoma wa Ngũgĩ, Grace Musila, and Matthew Christensen. I am also grateful to Stéphane Robolin, Nathan Suhr-Sytsma, Ranka Primorac, Lindsey Green-Simms, Tsitsi Jaji, Shane Graham, Akin Adesokan, Ester de Bruijn, Jeanne-Marie Jackson, John Nimis, Ainehi Edoro, and Lily Saint for their advice over the years. Special thanks to my friends and fellow editors at *Africa in Words* for their support and inspiration: Katie Reid, Kate Wallis, Rebecca Jones, Kristen Stern, Doseline Kiguru, Temitayo Olofinlua, and Joanna Woods.

Undertaking a more than decade-long project would have been impossible without the unconditional love and support of my family. To Don, Susan, and Matthew Bosch: thank you for making me who I am. Thank you to the entire Santana family, in South Africa and beyond, for making me one of your own. And to the friends who have become family—Erin Mosely and Giovanna Micconi—thank you for always being there, no matter the time of day or night.

To Peter Santana and Madeline Bosch Santana, who joined us for the last, but most important part of this journey: thank you from the bottom of my heart. Without you, none of this would have been possible.

I dedicate this book to Luzu Gondwe (1964–2022), my first guide and friend along the roads of Malawi. Pitani bwino, mzanga.

Forms of Mobility

INTRODUCTION

Reading in Motion

In 2013, Mike Maphoto's *Diary of a Zulu Girl* (*DOAZG*) blog went viral. In fast-paced prose that Maphoto composed on his mobile phone, *DOAZG* tells a genre-bending story of twenty-first-century South Africa through the eyes of Thandeka, who moves from rural KwaZulu-Natal to Johannesburg to study law at Wits University. A classic story of migration to the city with elements of chick lit, soap operas, American TV shows like *Gossip Girl*, and viral blogs like *Fifty Shades of Grey*, as well as the "Jim Comes to Joburg" stories that have been ubiquitous in print for the past century, *DOAZG* appealed to millions of readers not only in South Africa but also across the African continent and in the diaspora. As recorded in the thousands of comments posted on the blog, readers were hungry for entertaining stories that reflected contemporary African life in megacities such as Johannesburg, including ties to rural areas like Thandeka's home in Mooi River, the blending of English and African languages in everyday speech, and the coexistence of traditional food and culture alongside McDonald's and shopping malls. For many, this was a story that was neither stuck in the "apartheid stories" of the past nor reliant on the reductive tropes of Africa common in Western media.[1] As one young writer, Thulani Lupondwana, who was inspired by Maphoto to write her own blog on Facebook, told me, "It was nice actually reading about South Africans in South Africa doing things that you only see in the movies."[2]

In many ways, *DOAZG* epitomizes the kind of hypermobility that is frequently associated with new media literature. As soon as Maphoto posted a chapter, readers from anywhere in the world could respond almost instantly, and they often competed to see who would comment first. The portability of mobile platforms meant that Maphoto was able to write his chapters while on the move—he apologized once for a late chapter that he uploaded from the side of the road—and his readers, in turn, read the blog on their phones from just about anywhere: taxis, workplaces, and even public restrooms at the mall. As one reader noted, because she always had her phone with her, she never had to worry about leaving her "book" at home.[3] Some readers even likened the experience of reading the blog to a form of travel. "ZEE," who read the first hundred chapters in just three days, suggested that having to wait for Maphoto to post the next chapter was "like getting off a jet to go on a public plane."[4] Although this reader would have clearly preferred to zoom ahead on their own rather than wait with other readers in frustration, their comment captures the idea of the blog as a communal vehicle, with its readers reading together in motion.

This community was not traveling through a global, placeless cyberspace, as the digital world is so often imagined.[5] Rather, *DOAZG* inspired different kinds of place-based affiliations among its diverse, geographically dispersed audience, many of whom were located in Gauteng province, home to major cities like Johannesburg and Pretoria.[6] While the diary afforded these readers the pleasure of recognizing their local environments in intimate detail—eliciting debates about the particularities of the Zulu language in Mooi River and whether one could walk between certain landmarks in Johannesburg—readers from across South Africa embraced it as a new national narrative for the postapartheid generation. To others still, it was a pan-African story of Black life and culture that resonated with their lived experiences in other parts of the continent and the diaspora. Maphoto anticipated and encouraged such comparisons, and in the diary, Thandeka likens her experience of moving to Johannesburg to that of Zimbabweans relocating to London, Nigerians going to America, and Xhosas to Cape Town.[7] And just as Maphoto wrote these comparisons between intra- and extracontinental migration into the diary, *DOAZG* itself traveled nimbly across the same geographies.

In this respect, *DOAZG*'s mobility is neither as new nor as medium specific as it first appears. In its ability to forge connections across multiple spatial scales, the diary closely resembles the literary forms published in African newspapers and magazines in the twentieth century, the new media of their day.[8] Like *DOAZG*, these print publications' readerships were densest at the local level, but they traveled widely enough—both actually and imaginatively—to create networks across regional, continental, and global geographies. The literary forms published in these periodicals were also, like Maphoto's blog, characterized by formal and linguistic border crossing. Writers and editors experimented with a variety of forms, including poetry, short stories, and serialized fiction, as well as hybrid forms that did not fit neatly into Western generic categories. Many of these publications from Anglophone Africa were also multilingual, appearing in English and one or more African languages, and the heated debates over language on their pages bear an uncanny resemblance to those that took place in the comments section of Maphoto's blog. In both cases, some readers questioned the use of vernacular languages in internationally circulating publications, while others defended the cultural importance of their inclusion. Such debates, which often unfolded in the letters to the editor sections of print periodicals, demonstrate that even the interactivity and sociality that seem so unique to online literatures have earlier precedents.[9]

Maphoto attributed some of *DOAZG*'s wide-ranging relatability to the fact that it is a story of migration. And in this sense, too, it is a very old story. South Africa's iconic *Drum* magazine made a strikingly similar claim in the early 1950s when presenting its first fictional work, Alfred Mbeba's "Rhodesia Road," about a group of men from Nyasaland (Malawi) who travel to Southern Rhodesia (Zimbabwe) to find work. *Drum*'s editor suggested that the story "may have a wider appeal, for it tells of an experience common to all Africans."[10] Despite the omnipresence of such narratives, however, stories of intra-African migration have been largely absent from the African literary field's recent "migration turn."[11] From Chimamanda Adichie's *Americanah* to Helon Habila's *Travelers*, the African migration stories that still tend to receive the most popular and scholarly consideration focus overwhelmingly on journeys to and from the Global North. In a 2016 blog post on Okayafrica, Motswana writer Siyanda Mohutsiwa contrasts *DOAZG* with what she calls "African immigrant literature" of the "'Afropolitan' variety," stories set in Europe or America that, to Mohutsiwa, feel very far away from her own day-to-day experiences.[12] Why should it be, she asks, that her "first encounter with Alain Mabanckou's work was a foot-chase in a Paris subway station" or that so many stories ended "with the African protagonist being whisked away to America"? Additionally, the narratives Mohutsiwa refers to have taken a limited number of literary forms, in particular the novel, and are usually written in former colonial languages. In the years since Mohutsiwa's post was published, new African fiction, especially in its genre and speculative iterations, has increasingly gained international attention with a range of real and imagined settings.[13] Nevertheless, stories of the "Afropolitan variety" continue to have an outsized role in discussions of African migration narratives, resulting in an incomplete, and potentially misleading, vision of the many forms of African mobility and the spatial affiliations they have mapped.

To tell a different story about African imaginations of mobility since the mid-twentieth century, this book turns to a different archive: the ubiquitous but still largely unstudied literary forms in Africa-based periodical print and digital media, from magazines and newspapers to blogs and Facebook. These mass-circulated publications and platforms have served as vital outlets for African-language fiction and local literary forms as well as criticism, often by figures such as Mohutsiwa, who straddle the creative and critical divide. *Forms of Mobility* examines the ways writers from Malawi, Zimbabwe, Zambia, and South Africa experiment with literary form in periodical media to chart new geographies of interconnection and belonging. Because these forms are current and iterative and tend to circulate faster and farther than traditionally published books, they also generate affiliations that are local, national, regional, pan-African, global, and sometimes even interplanetary in scale—envisioning outer space as a refuge from racial oppression on Earth. I argue that motion is an essential feature of these media-based literary forms across space and genre, and that they both contest and are constrained by colonial and neocolonial literary categories and spatial formations. Based on a corpus of texts in English and Chichewa/Nyanja—one of southern Africa's most widely spoken indigenous languages—from publications such as *African Parade*, *Africa!*, the *Malawi News*, the *Chimurenga Chronic*, *Jungle Jim*, and Facebook, I propose a set of categories with which to grasp the scope and range of southern African fiction: migrant forms, township tales, weekend stories, pan African time machines, and digital diaries. These categories correspond to forms of mobility, and they suggest complex ideas of movement, space, and belonging in relation to Africanness and Blackness.

This book contends that in order to map and theorize the many nuanced geographies envisioned by African writers, it is necessary to consider this wide set of forms and languages. Literary forms not only reflect the world but are powerful space-making and world-making tools.[14] And yet, as Christopher Ouma and Madhu Krishnan remind us, the African literary canon, as it was constructed at seminal conferences such as the 1962 Makerere University Conference of African Writers of English Expression, is fundamentally "exclusionary," comprised primarily of the genres of the (realist) novel and poetry.[15] Similarly, Ashleigh Harris calls for "deconstruct[ing] the novel's hold on the field" in order to "realize a more inclusive canon for the future of African literary studies."[16] Compared to the novel, media-based forms, including the many genres found in African newspapers and digital platforms, have received significantly less scholarly attention. However, recent interventions by Ouma, Krishnan, and Harris as well as many others have built on foundational work by Karin Barber, Isabel Hofmeyr, and Stephanie Newell to read such forms as central to African literary history.[17] While less has been written about periodical forms in African languages, important work in this area reveals forms of public-making that precede, run alongside, and sometimes counter the ways reading publics were envisioned in former colonial languages.[18] In proposing an expanded set of media-based forms through which to approach southern African literatures, *Forms of Mobility* continues this work of augmenting and disrupting the canons, revealing a different map of African literary production on the continent and beyond. The forms that I consider here illuminate geographies of belonging that cut across hegemonic spatial formations at various scales—from the colonial township to the nation and the world—producing new, though not inherently liberational, geographies.[19] These include utopian ideas of "Central Africa" (today's Zimbabwe, Malawi, and Zambia) as a national and transnational space that contested South African literary domination in the region as well as a twenty-first-century pan Africanism that recenters Africa in global space and history.

The mobility of media-based forms is an important part of their world making. Most of the forms considered in this book were published in commercial venues with enough capital to seek out wide audiences, unlike the many "little magazines" with national circulations and "limited mobility."[20] Such forms were therefore more likely to be read widely at the local level—a single copy of a newspaper in Africa is read not by one but by approximately ten to twenty people—and to cross international borders.[21] The hypermobility of such forms is also significant because it unsettles traditional categorizations of postcolonial and world literatures. The way these forms circulate is inherently relational, with multiple languages, fictional and nonfictional material, and local and international writers appearing side by side. While the literatures of Malawi, Zimbabwe, Zambia, and South Africa are usually studied as distinct national projects or are merged into larger studies where South African texts constitute the central corpus, the popular media forms examined here reveal the interconnective tissue between these different literary traditions, as well as important patterns of regional influence and broader global affiliations. For example, chapter 2 follows a series of adaptations of Langston Hughes's Here to Yonder column that traveled swiftly across southern Africa in the 1950s and '60s: from Casey Motsisi's Johannesburg-focused On the Beat to similar stories by Bill Saidi and Daniel Dlamanzi rooted in Harare, Bulawayo, and Lusaka. From the decolonization period to the present, my analysis finds southern African writers consistently experimenting with forms like this to convey a sense of belonging to spaces both smaller and larger than the nation, from the township to the galaxy, as they envision traveling to the moon or Mars to escape Earth's color line. Indeed, it is by centering periodical literary media—forms that are too often elided in studies of postcolonial and world literatures as a result of narrow conceptions of literariness and literary mobility—that I demonstrate how writers from southern Africa have been and continue to be connected to regional, pan-African, global, and interplanetary imaginaries. I also show that these sub- and supranational affiliations have operated from an earlier moment than previously understood.

Although an account of the circulation of texts is central to this book, *Forms of Mobility* is also concerned with motion as a defining feature of literary form itself. How these texts travel and imagine travel is essential to their form, which in turn shapes depictions of motion and space. Each of the forms I consider in this book envisions mobility differently. In some cases, travel takes the form of unfettered migration across the region, while in others, the newspaper is used as a time-traveling machine in order to reanimate earlier forms of pan-African solidarity. While largely secular, some of these forms also address mobility in spiritual terms, equating journeys to outer space with heavenly respite.[22] Across its chapters, this book considers literary forms that are structured by different kinds of mobilities, each of which facilitates the imagination and reimagination of communities. Each form is associated most readily with one particular space—the region, township, nation, continent, or world—that serves as a vantage point from which to appreciate how southern African writers have continuously navigated these entangled geographies and affiliations. Each chapter is based on a large archive of material from various periodical publications, and many chapters consider materials in both English and Chichewa/Nyanja, mirroring the way African-language materials and former colonial languages often circulated together in these popular publications.

To work across this vast archive, I use a method I call "reading in motion," which entails reading individual stories closely while situating them within particular publications and in the networks through which they traveled, including anthologies, other periodicals, websites, and so on. This method is not new: scholars of African periodicals, among others, have read sources in similar ways, producing a rich body of work that attends to the material conditions under which these literatures were produced and the multiple publics they convened.[23] What this book suggests is that reading in motion is a useful strategy for reading across both print and digital forms, and that doing so reveals a form of literary mobility and space making that is occluded by current models of world literature. Reading in motion across genres, languages, publications, and broad print and digital networks, moreover, is a process in which African readers, critics, and editors are deeply engaged as they adapt, theorize, and curate materials from a transnational, and especially regional, textual field for their own newspapers, magazines, and digital platforms.[24] Attending to these print and digital publications, which have traditionally been seen as nonscholarly, thus expands our understanding of African literary criticism as well as production. The literary categories that emerge from such publications showcase a wide range of southern African forms of mobility and belonging. These mobile forms, in turn, shift the axis along which we read African literatures in other contexts.

NEW LITERARY GEOGRAPHIES: FORMS IN MOTION

In 1938, T. Cullen Young, a Scottish missionary in Northern Nyasaland, today's Malawi, warned other would-be publishers of "'native' newspaper[s]" of the necessity of creating an open forum for African contributors in their papers, citing the utter failure of several such endeavors that did not do so.[25] Across the region, the earliest newspapers and magazines aimed at Africans were published by missionaries like Young.[26] These publications were often multilingual, appearing in one or several African languages in addition to English, but were authored and edited by Europeans. Sometimes jointly produced and financed by colonial governments with the general aim of "educating" Africans, many such newspapers left little space for African contributions or opinions.[27] Young was not surprised that the mission's first magazine in English—whose articles focused on tsetse flies, "various carnivora," and mission stations—drew few African readers.[28] But another attempt, *Makani* ("News"), which appeared in English and Tumbuka from 1906 to 1908, was also a dud, despite his and others' best efforts to write "helpful" articles.[29] (One issue printed on "primrose"-colored paper received a particularly poor response; eventually, the editors realized that this may have been because the color is known locally as "calf's excrement."[30]) In 1928, Young finally found success with a newspaper that actively sought out African contributions, in the form of first letters to the editor and eventually full articles and translations. He notes that many contributors began their letters with "May I be allowed to speak at the *mphara*?" or the "talking-place of the village," which leads him to the conclude that the newspaper could play an essential role as the talking-place of modern Africa.[31]

Young was right about the future of the newspaper as a central site for African discourse. But what I wish to point out here is the geographic scope of this particular newspaper and its "talking-place." Though one might imagine the *mphara* to be the epitome of a local space, embedding the paper in village affairs, this was anything but the case. Young realized that *Vyaro na Vyaro*, or "Here and Beyond," needed to appeal to Nyasalanders at home as well as to a Nyasa diaspora that was already widely dispersed across southern and eastern Africa.[32] Those living abroad were concerned with what was happening at home and vice versa, with interests ranging from Clements Kadalie's Industrial and Commercial Workers' Union in South Africa to the life story of the Indian Christian missionary Sadhu Sundar Singh, which was translated by a Nyasalander in Tanganyika and serialized in the newspaper. Five years after it began publication, *Vyaro na Vyaro* had enough subscribers that it no longer needed to be subsidized.

While *Vyaro na Vyaro* did not carry fiction, its multilingual, transnational forum was an early iteration of the kinds of border-crossing forms and publications considered in this book.[33] *Vyaro na Vyaro* was missionary run and edited, while the publications in my corpus, the earliest of which dates to 1953, are African authored and edited. Nevertheless, the writers and editors of these later publications were still often constrained by the colonial and imperial structures embedded in these media, both formally and institutionally, something we see replicated today on neo-imperialist platforms like Facebook. And yet many of these publications thrived because they worked within such structures, which were financed variously by white "liberal" capital and newly established African governments, some of which, like Hastings Kamuzu Banda's single-party state in Malawi, were clearly antidemocratic.[34] What this commercial and governmental support gave such publications, despite the many compromises it necessitated, was visibility and mobility—something that many smaller literary journals from the region have lacked.[35]

Vyaro na Vyaro provides an important illustration of what such mobility could afford—in this case, the opportunity to provide African perspectives on the question of mobility itself. A letter by a Nyasa man who had emigrated to Northern Rhodesia (Zambia), which originally appeared in *Vyaro na Vyaro*, was republished in the *Manchester Guardian* in 1937 as part of an ongoing conversation about the issue of migration in what was then the British protectorate of Nyasaland. The discovery of diamonds and gold in South Africa and copper in Northern Rhodesia in the late nineteenth and early twentieth centuries, respectively, led to a substantial migration of workers from across the region into these industries.[36] Labor migration was presented in the British press as a "tragic exodus" that was destroying African village and family life, a view held by colonial officials and missionaries in the region, and the letter is presented (in English translation) as an alternative African point of view.[37] The unnamed author immediately points to a problematic assumption underlying the British perspective: that Nyasalanders at "home" in the village had always been there and were not themselves from elsewhere. The idea that rural Africans are static and immobile—reinforced in countless colonial narratives—is quickly dismissed by the writer, who evokes the chief of his own village, an immigrant from an unnamed country who "style[d] himself 'The one who crossed over.'" The letter also demonstrates that the region's long history of migration was not only a response to colonial intervention, as the British account so often assumed. In the early 1800s, various indigenous groups, including the Ngoni of today's Malawi, scattered across the region as they fled an increasingly militarized Zulu kingdom under Shaka in what is known as the Mfecane—just one example of the intra-African migration that shaped southern Africa.[38] The author's other central argument in the letter is that the desire to emigrate in search of a better life elsewhere is hardly an African phenomenon; indeed, it is what brought countless immigrants, including Europeans, to southern Africa. This letter—itself symbolic of the mobility of print—encapsulates periodical forms' ability to illuminate the complexity of migrant geographies and to reflect on African mobilities.

This letter resonates across the decades with an idea that gained critical purchase relatively recently: the concept of Afropolitanism, or "African cosmopolitanism." In an interview in the *Chimurenga Chronic*, one of the publications I consider in chapter 4, Achille Mbembe describes how African societies have long "constituted themselves through circulation and mobility."[39] Southern Africa is exemplary of the kind of community forming through movement that Mbembe describes as Afropolitan, though it is not always recognized as such. As the above letter in *Vyaro na Vyaro* attests, intra-African labor migration was often understood in cosmopolitan terms by those who engaged in it. However, as Afropolitanism has been taken up and applied in literary criticism in recent years, it has been used primarily to theorize extracontinental circulations. In other words, scholars have tended to recognize only half of Mbembe's original formulation of Afropolitanism as Africa-in-the world and the world-in-Africa.

Afropolitanism may be the most buzzworthy term to emerge in African studies in the past decade, but it is indicative of the longer trend toward literary transnationalism and the remapping of the African literary field in relation to more expansive geographic networks. One of the oldest of these projects has been the charting of Black Atlantic literatures, which has situated African literary production in the context of the wider African diaspora in Europe and the Americas.[40] More recent studies have extended their comparative lenses across different oceans, such as the Indian Ocean and the "Global South Atlantic," or charted interconnectivity along the continent's coasts.[41] In contrast, far less attention has been given to the intra-African circulation of texts and to forms of mobility that do not fit the Afropolitan model of unfettered global travel.[42] Without discounting these other significant geographies, it is necessary to understand them in relation to the literary routes and diasporic spaces within the African continent itself and to consider how this movement has, in turn, impacted global literary transmission and form. Intra-African literary circulation is particularly visible when we turn to periodical culture and to writing in indigenous languages. Recent work in this area, for example, has drawn attention to the pan-African circulations and imaginaries of Anglophone and Francophone magazines such as *Drum*, *Transition*, *Black Orpheus*, *Bingo*, *La Vie Africaine*, and *Awa*.[43]

In this book, I focus on literary mobility within a particular part of Anglophone southern Africa, namely Malawi, Zimbabwe, Zambia, and South Africa.[44] This part of the region is connected through its intertwined material, political, and literary histories, all of which have been profoundly shaped by movement. The Mfecane, for example, created an Nguni diaspora across the region, a key feature of which has been the retention of various traditions of oral praise poetry, or *izibongo*.[45] Zoe Groves observes that while the region was "highly mobile" in the precolonial period, with significant connections between parts of the region and East Africa in the nineteenth century, "the nature and intensity of colonial-era labour migration was a new development" that served to reorient Africans in early twentieth-century Nyasaland toward the south.[46] Indeed, from the late nineteenth century onward, the region has been characterized by southward-moving labor migration, especially to the gold mines on South Africa's Witwatersrand.[47] Numerous studies have considered the historical and contemporary impacts of this system of labor migration, which Jonathan Crush and others describe as "the single most important factor tying together all of the various colonies and countries of the sub-continent into a single regional labor market during the twentieth century."[48] Nevertheless, an overwhelming focus on migration to South Africa has obscured other significant migrant itineraries, such as between Malawi and Zimbabwe.[49]

From 1953 to 1963, the region was formally integrated through the formation of the Central African Federation from the British protectorates of Northern Rhodesia (Zambia) and Nyasaland (Malawi) and the self-governing colony of Southern Rhodesia (Zimbabwe), a space-making project that had important implications for mobilities in the region. Contested by African nationalists throughout southern Africa, and particularly in Nyasaland and Northern Rhodesia, the federation brought to fruition a political and economic union long desired by Southern and Northern Rhodesian white settlers.[50] In 1948, the same year that the National Party came to power in South Africa and introduced racial apartheid, a group of settlers from both Rhodesias formed the United Central Africa Association (UCAA) to advocate for federation.[51] The UCAA's 1951 pamphlet, whose innermost page is a map of the desired federation (fig. 1), is an example of colonial space making par excellence. Published by the London Committee of the UCAA, the pamphlet frames its argument for a federation based on interracial cooperation, or "Partnership," as a means to prevent apartheid's "sinister shadow" from spreading northward.[52] However, its map—which highlights the region's "single railway system," Wankie coalfields, and the increasingly lucrative Copperbelt—belies its underlying economic rationale for linking the territories' "complementary and interdependent" economies.[53] The territories were "complementary," in large part, in terms of "their supply of and demand for labour," with Northern Rhodesia, and especially Nyasaland, serving as labor reserves for Southern Rhodesia's growing industries. Due to lobbying efforts from groups like the UCAA (which from 1949 was funded by international mining corporations)[54] and its own desire to recoup wartime losses, Britain finally acceded to the federation, justifying its formation with some of the same arguments regarding the need to "counterbalance" South African apartheid contained in this pamphlet.[55] In practice, Partnership was so loosely defined as to be largely meaningless, resulting in little political advancement for Africans and de facto "social apartheid," as one British member of Parliament described it.[56]

Despite the many aspects of South African history that resonate with similar, if distinct, experiences of British colonialism and white supremacy in Zimbabwe, Zambia, and Malawi, South Africa's literature, like its history, is considered to be "exceptional." In most cases, South African literature is given pride of place in studies of the region, with the countries to South Africa's north treated as its "peripheries."[57] This is due to a number of not insignificant factors, including South Africa's longer history of fiction in print and earlier "visibility" on the global literary stage.[58] The first African-run newspapers in South Africa date to the late 1800s, and S. E. K. Mqhayi published a novel in isiXhosa, *Ityala lamawele* (*The Lawsuit of the Twins*), in 1914.[59] In comparison, most of the earliest Afrophone novels from Zimbabwe, Zambia, and Malawi were published in the 1950s by colonial literary bureaus, whose paternalistic advice on writing is captured in magazines like *Look Up: The Magazine of the Publications Bureau of Northern Rhodesia and Nyasaland*.[60] The first African-authored novels in English from these countries did not appear until the 1960s. This was the beginning of the postindependence period in Malawi and Zambia and a time of intensifying repression in white-ruled Southern Rhodesia, which resulted in the first Zimbabwean novels in English being published in exile.[61] Following independence, Zambian literature is perceived by many critics to have stagnated, despite the efforts of Kenneth Kaunda's single-party state to promote the arts. In contrast, in Malawi, "President for Life" Banda censored the media and jailed writers, which, counter to Banda's aims, produced a literary tradition rich with subversive symbolism.

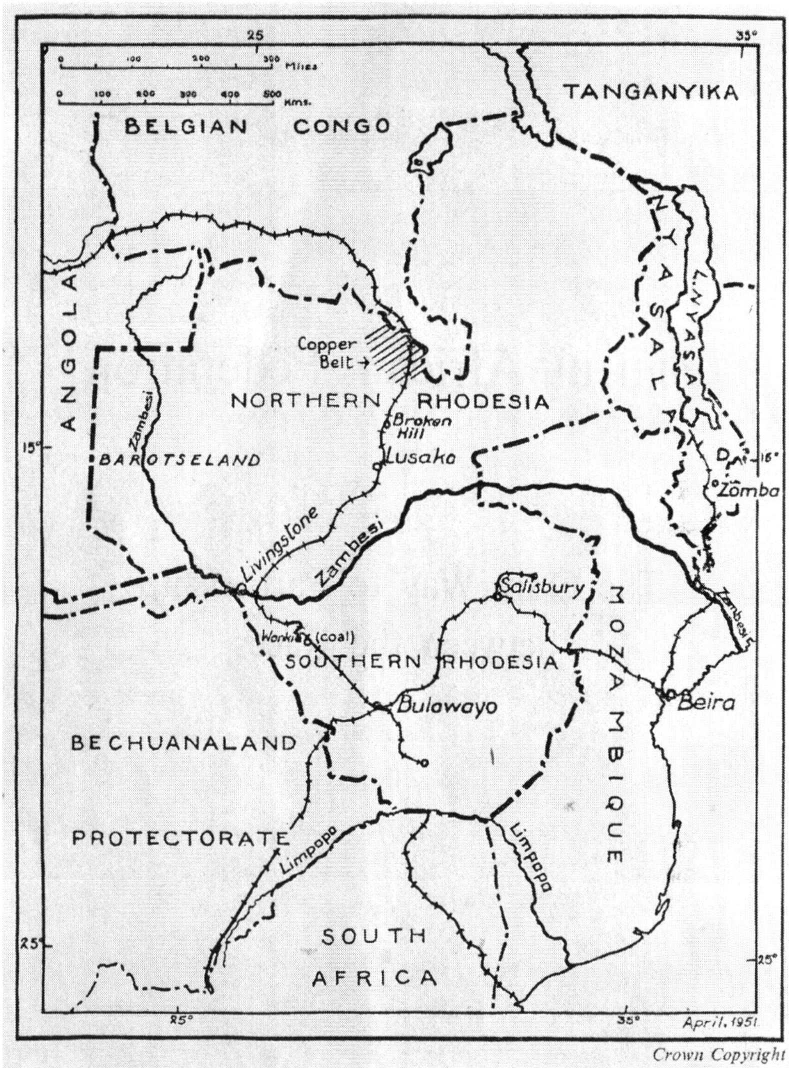

Fig. 1. "The Central African Territories," from *Central African Federation: The Only Way to Partnership between the Races* (London: London Committee of the United Central Africa Association, 1951), 2.

Nevertheless, few Malawian writers have had their work internationally recognized, as I explore in chapter 3.

Given the global visibility of the anti-apartheid struggle and the important role writers in exile played in it, it is not surprising that South African literature has dominated discussions of the region—particularly when one considers South Africa's formidable economic and publishing power. After the transition to multiparty democracy in 1994, South Africa retained its sense of exceptionalism in a different form, positioning itself as a beacon of hope for African postcolonial nations that were still mired in single-party rule, such as Zimbabwe. Both Zambia and Malawi became multiparty democracies in the early 1990s, but their economic struggles, which can be traced to the colonial period, have resulted in the intervention of neocolonial bodies like the World Bank and the International Monetary Fund in their governments since the mid-twentieth century. As Neil Lazarus argues, the past several decades since the end of apartheid have challenged this notion of South Africa as the "rainbow nation."[62] The African National Congress, the liberation party in power since the end of apartheid, has faced allegations of corruption and struggled to lift millions of South Africans out of poverty. The nation has also been beset by recurrent violence against foreign nationals, especially from other parts of Africa, as I discuss in chapter 4. Nevertheless, South Africa remains an influential cultural and literary powerhouse, with its writers continuing to win a hefty share of international prizes, including most recently Damon Galgut's winning of the Booker Prize. South African media is also prominent across the continent and especially in southern Africa. South African DStv is available throughout the region, and South African newspapers, tabloids, and magazines like *Drum* line grocery-store shelves in Zambia and Malawi, a trend that goes back to the colonial period.[63]

By foregrounding Malawian, Zimbabwean, and Zambian writers in this study, I aim to show how these writers have engaged with a variety of transnational influences that include, but are not limited to, those from their powerful neighbor to the south. This book does not provide comprehensive histories of each of these literary traditions, but rather looks to some of their points of interconnection, many of which were forged through periodical networks. To this end, I build on other recent work that has taken a transnational approach to various parts of this region, from Mphande's work on the Nguni diaspora to Stefan Helgesson's study of Anglophone and Lusophone print networks in South Africa, Mozambique, and Angola.[64] Similarly, Ranka Primorac and Stephen Chan explore Cold War politics in Anglophone novels by Black writers from southern Africa, including Bessie Head and William Saidi, whose magazine writing I consider here. Elsewhere, and in contrast to the many readings of Zambian literature as insular and provincial, Primorac locates what she calls a "frontline" orientation and cosmopolitanism in Zambian literature resulting from writers' keen awareness of the ongoing struggles against white supremacy just across its borders in Southern Rhodesia, South Africa, and Namibia.[65] It is not surprising that this sense of regionalism emerged out of a periodical publication, *New Writing from Zambia* (*NWZ*), launched by the New Writers' Group in 1964. By turning to the literary forms in newspapers and magazines from previous periods, we can observe such regional affiliations and alternative literary geographies at an even earlier moment.

After an initial period of mostly missionary-sponsored publications like *Vyaro na Vyaro*, in the 1930s, African newspapers across the region became increasingly interconnected through the monopolistic tendencies of white "liberal" entrepreneurs like Bertram F. G. Paver, who founded Bantu Press (Pty) Ltd in South Africa in 1932.[66] The Bantu Press's national weekly newspaper the *Bantu World*, which began publication the same year, marked the shift in South Africa from an independent African press to what Les Switzer calls a "captive one" that was owned and influenced by white capital. Paver purchased numerous newspapers throughout the region, including South Africa's first Black-run newspaper *Imvo Zabantsundu* and Southern Rhodesia's *Native Mirror*, which then became the *Bantu Mirror*.[67] As Sylvester Dombo documents in his comprehensive history of Zimbabwe's private print media, Paver lost South African government funding in 1950 for refusing to support apartheid.[68] Paver's liberalism, however, did not prevent him from aligning himself with Godfrey Huggins, the architect and first prime minister of the Central African Federation.[69] This troubling consolidation of British colonial interests and private media networks nevertheless resulted in an increased regional circulation of information. The *Bantu Mirror* was now published in three regional languages (Nyanja, Bemba, and Shona) and reached other parts of the federation about a week after its publication in Southern Rhodesia.[70]

This book's literary history begins with one of Paver's publications, *African Parade*, southern Africa's first "modern" lifestyle magazine published outside South Africa. *African Parade* was a product of, and played an essential role in imagining, the Central African Federation (1953–1963). While colonial geographies like this one aimed to control the movement of bodies, material goods, languages, and texts, as well as less tangible ideas and ideologies, they also created the opportunity for African intellectuals, writers, and politicians to seize on these same spaces for their own ends. In the case of the federation, many members of the educated African elite were swayed by the promise of multiracial partnership and transnational mobility that the federation seemed to afford, anticipating that it would eventually form the basis for an African-run superstate. The editors of *African Parade* saw the publication as contributing to a Central African literature with both national and transnational dimensions, and many of the most notable authors from the region, including Steve Chimombo, William Saidi, Fwanyanga M. Mulikita, and Charles Mungoshi, began their careers on its pages. *Parade* also serialized the first novel by a Black Zimbabwean writer, Ndabaningi Sithole's *Busi*, from 1959 to 1961.[71] Despite these achievements and the enormous amount of fiction it produced—more than four hundred stories in its first decade—the form and significance of the magazine and its contributions to the literature of the region and to African and global literatures is largely unexplored.

Like many of the missionary and government-produced publications that preceded it, *African Parade* was published in English and various African languages. *Parade*'s even broader scope, however, meant that it was published in several of the most widely spoken indigenous languages in Southern Rhodesia (Shona and Ndebele), Northern Rhodesia (Bemba and Nyanja), and Nyasaland (Nyanja). In *Parade*, as well as later publications like the *Malawi News*, language served as a means of creating new geographies of affiliation, from the nation to the region to the globe, even as the language politics of these magazines reproduced certain missionary and colonial-era legacies. English was embraced by *African Parade*'s editors and readers as the "national" language of the federation, and the role of its vernacular languages was heavily debated on the magazine's pages. Throughout the region, English was a language of colonialism and imperialism as well as a language of resistance. Indeed, both Malawi and Zambia selected English as their official languages when they achieved independence in 1964. Not all Englishes were the same, however. As I discuss in chapter 2, American English was embraced by newspaper and magazine writers across the region to forge pan-African connections across the Atlantic.

The role of the region's African languages in literary production is even more complex. Given that African-language writing was encouraged by missionaries and colonial literary bureaus throughout the region, it has tended to be read as particularly didactic, and, as Michael Chapman points out, as contributing to separate (usually lesser) "ethnic literatures" rather than national literatures.[72] In South Africa, this practice was sometimes seen to directly support the apartheid government's insistence on separate homelands for the nation's various ethnic groups.

In contrast, Chichewa/Nyanja, the other primary language considered here, is often studied in relation to Malawian nationalism. While missionaries and British colonists had selected Nyanja as the language of colonial Malawi, favoring it over other languages like Tumbuka or "dialectical variations" of Nyanja such as Chichewa, Malawi's first president, Hastings Kamuzu Banda (an ethnic Chewa) gave Chichewa its national status, "arguing that it was chi-Nyanja that was a dialect of Chichewa."[73] Notwithstanding its association with Banda's autocracy, Chichewa/Nyanja (which, despite variations, share a single dictionary) is a significant "trans-regional" language.[74] Nyanja (or Cinyanja, "the Nyanja language"), as it is known outside of Malawi, is the second-most-spoken indigenous language in Zambia, following Bemba, and it is one of Zimbabwe's official languages. Nyanja is also spoken in South Africa due to the country's sizable migrant population from areas to the north. All of this leads Steven Paas to estimate that the language has more than fifteen million speakers and "probably is the most widely spoken language in the entire region of Southern and South-Central Africa."[75] Like English, then, Chichewa/Nyanja is a language of both connection and contestation, one that opens new insights into literary transnationalism across the region.

Although I have thus far highlighted the connections and affiliations that the forms in periodical media enable us to see, these forms also reveal power dynamics and inequalities. South Africa has wielded a significant influence on writers in Malawi, Zimbabwe, and Zambia, who have reworked South African literary styles and genres for their own ends. South Africa also serves as a key node in the dissemination of global culture to the rest of the region through popular periodicals like *Drum*. By comparing, for example, how the work of African American writers like Langston Hughes was variously appropriated by writers in southern Africa, this book illuminates the kind of "lateral networks" between global minoritized cultures that have been studied under the rubric of "minor transnationalism."[76] Minor transnationalism has been an important corrective to global literary studies in its emphasis on literary networks that do not necessarily pass through major publishing centers and institutions.[77] By attending to the regional imaginaries that are evident in periodical forms, we can see the subtle power dynamics and hierarchies within these lateral exchanges. As I discuss in chapter 1, writers in the former Central African Federation and South Africa responded differently to African American writing and culture based on their own colonial and postcolonial experiences, underscoring Brent

Hayes Edwards's claim that writers' engagement with internationalism is rooted in their "historical relations to the nation."[78]

Such regional relationships and circulations are usually elided from world literary models that focus on textual travel at a global scale. Franco Moretti, for example, asserts that novels belong to the world literary system's "most mobile strata, and by concentrating only on them we would probably overstate the mobility of world literature."[79] In the case of Malawian, Zambian, and Zimbabwean literatures, however, this is simply not true. The many literary forms published in *African Parade* reached audiences across the African continent and the globe before the first novels in English from most of Central Africa were even published.[80] More importantly, it is necessary to rethink our concept of literary mobility. In an essay on new ways of reading world literature, Wai Chee Dimock identifies a provocative image of what happens when one moves to a different scale of literary analysis in Mandelbrot's essay "How Long Is the Coast of Britain?": "As the scale 'is made smaller and smaller, every one of the approximate lengths tends to become larger and larger without bound. Insofar as one can tell, each seems to tend toward infinity.'"[81] Taking Mandelbrot's image, we can see that space is altered when we zoom in on a particular region, and if we can actually see the jaggedness of the terrain, we can appreciate the great deal of movement that takes place as a form travels over each rocky mile—whereas from farther away, it might appear that a form has not moved or changed at all. When I argue that the forms considered here tend to travel faster and farther than printed books, I have this picture in mind. To give a more concrete example, also evoked above: a single copy of a newspaper in southern Africa is read by a dozen or more people, often as they travel local distances by minibus. This amount of circulation is remarkable, but it is often invisible to theorists like Moretti. Reading the forms in periodical media, however, requires that we take into account the "infinitely" long distances produced by reading simultaneously at the scales of the local, national, regional, and global. It is through this kind of reading in motion that new literary geographies and ideas of community begin to emerge.

FORMS OF MOBILITY

In a recent issue of the *Chimurenga Chronic* on alternative cartographies, Yvonne A. Owuor describes the boatmen on the Congo River who "sing vessels from the river into the Atlantic unmolested."[82] Their songs, she argues, are "poem-maps," or "navigational literary artefacts."[83] Owuor's "poem-maps" are an example of what I call *forms of mobility*: literary forms that are born of motion and that serve as a means to navigate changing terrains. The literary forms I consider in this book not only are "portable," in that they "can be picked up and moved to new contexts"—which Caroline Levine suggests is an "affordance" of all forms—but also are shaped by their routes, means, and imaginations of travel.[84] In the chapters that follow, I trace the ways writers' and editors' visions of these forms' real and imagined travels shaped their ideas of the readers and publics they might be writing to and for, which in turn influenced their literary styles, languages, and registers. In other words, forms of mobility display what Michael Warner calls a "reflexivity about their circulation": these forms are in motion and also envisage this mobility in particular ways.[85]

There has been growing engagement with mobility, and to a lesser extent the interdisciplinary field of mobility studies, in African literary and cultural studies. This work, which generally focuses on contemporary mobilities, builds on decades of robust scholarship on migration and the African diaspora but turns its focus toward "hidden or less obvious dimensions of mobility and other forms of physical movement" beyond migration[86] as well as to representations of "concrete forms of mobility"—from automobility to new communications technologies like Skype—that enable a rethinking of the "taken-for-granted" relationship between mobility and cosmopolitanism (or Afropolitanism).[87] What this book shares with these studies is an interest in nuancing our understanding of African mobilities—particularly intra-African travel—through close attention to the ways movement is experienced, represented, and imagined by African writers and cultural producers. My emphasis, however, is on tracing various literary forms across time and space to discover the ways they have both shaped and been shaped by ideas of mobility, rather than on what Anna-Leena Toivanen calls "literary portrayals of concrete, tangible forms of mobility."[88] Each of the forms treated here—migrant forms, township tales, weekend stories, pan African time machines, and digital diaries—has a different relationship to mobility. Mobility is variously understood in terms of regional migration, fantastical leaps to outer space, circulation within the domestic or national sphere, time travel, and the friction between virtual and material networks.

These forms are not only useful for studying diverse kinds of movement and travel in themselves but for making visible the workings of power in the production of space and the imagination of new collectivities.[89] Space making has long been understood by postcolonial critics and geographers as a key facet of colonial and imperial domination; consequently, the mapping of alternate geographies can serve as a means to "indict," "(re)define," "control," and reimagine "social worlds."[90] Africanist scholars have increasingly turned to the ways writers and texts map alternate spaces in order to conceive of new literary geographies.[91] A focus on mobility can provide insight into how such spaces are produced and made meaningful. Tim Cresswell defines mobility as "socially produced motion" that contributes to the "production of time and space."[92] The work of mobilities studies scholars like Cresswell on "geographies of mobilities" dovetails with insights into the relationship between mobility and geography in African studies. In another recent issue of the *Chimurenga Chronic*, for example, Achille Mbembe presents an African model of spatial organization based on mobility, finding that in precolonial Africa, mobility drove "the delimitation and organization of space and territories."[93] Fittingly, this issue of the *Chronic* is filled with maps on the move that highlight paths and itineraries rather than fixed territories.[94]

Publications such as the *Chronic* point to the potential synergies between mobility studies' focus on the social production of space and literary studies that are attentive to the role of material circulation in shaping texts and publics. Following the publication of her groundbreaking study on the circuitous global travels of Bunyan's *The Pilgrim's Progress* and its translation into eighty African languages in *The Portable Bunyan*, Isabel Hofmeyr concluded: "To alert ourselves to the outlines of such collectivities whose contours we do not automatically see, it is to the material questions of circulation that we must turn."[95] Since then, literary scholars—and not only those in the fields of book history or periodical studies—have increasingly taken up this question and read such forms as fundamentally shaped by their mobility. Nathan Suhr-Sytsma, in his influential *Poetry, Print, and the Making of Postcolonial Literature*, foregrounds the "dynamic interactions" between poetry from across the nonmetropolitan, English-speaking world and the material conditions and institutions that impacted its publication, seeking "to discover in what ways the difficult, mediated process of circulation may be integral to difficult, rewarding texts."[96] Ouma and Krishnan's special issue on African small magazines is also notable for "read[ing] outwards" from the "material foundations" and circulations of these magazines to see the ways "alternative, lateral and multiple publics were forged."[97] Scholars have also begun to attend to the ways circulation is essential to African digital forms.[98]

Drawing on insights from both of these fields, I aim to keep in view the idea that southern African writers—much like Ouwor's boatmen—use self-reflexively mobile, media-based literary forms to navigate entangled spaces and communities, including the township, nation, region, continent, globe, and interplanetary space. These spaces constitute what Karima Laachir, Sara Marzagora, and Francesca Orsini aptly describe as "significant geographies," or the "*conceptual*, *imaginative*, and *real* geographies that texts, authors, and language communities inhabit, produce, and reach."[99] These spaces do not fit into one another like "Russian dolls," with each smaller geography contained within the next.[100] Rather, each of these meaningful geographies relates to others, producing a network of affiliations that takes a somewhat different configuration in each form. For example, while the township tales discussed in chapter 2 focus on the space of the township—peri-urban, segregated areas located just outside larger cities—the township exists in a wider geographic nexus as a kind of micronational space, a locus of cosmopolitanism, and even an interplanetary space.

Forms of mobility express spatial affiliations and communities in motion—as they were constructed, imagined, negotiated, and contested—often in situations of colonial or state oppression and censorship. However, the spaces these forms of mobility map were not necessarily liberatory. Writers' utopian visions of Central Africa as a great African state essentially supported settler colonial ambitions for a federation that delayed Black majority rule in the region. And in Malawi, Banda's mapping of the new nation onto domestic space through his reinvention of Malawian kinship networks was touted as freeing women from the constraints of the home, even as it contained them more securely within it by making it the source of their, and his, political power. The maps that emerge when we look at new literary forms on Facebook also in many ways re-create "neoimperialist cartographies."[101] Nevertheless, these mobile forms still differ from colonial and imperial mapmaking practices in that they do not "coloniz[e] space" by erasing "the practices that produce it"—as in the UCAA pamphlet's map of the federation described above.[102] Rather, by highlighting their own means of travel and visions of mobility, such forms illuminate "the itineraries that were the conditions of its [the map's] possibility."[103] The *Chimurenga Chronic*'s inaugural issue, which uses the newspaper as a time machine, is a particularly good example of this work. By traveling back in time, the

Chronic reveals the various trajectories and itineraries of an as yet unrealized pan Africanism.

These forms of mobility also traveled across languages, illuminating the complex, fluid, and often uneven ways writers, readers, and editors engage with language in environments where multilingualism is the norm, suggesting new ways of approaching comparative and world literatures. As demonstrated by many of the contributions to the recent volume *Dynamism in African Languages and Literature*, African multilingualism is marked by the flexibility with which speakers "deplo[y] rich language repertoires, including his/her own 'ethnic' vernacular(s) and languages of wider communication."[104] This has resulted in a "convivial multilingualism" that embraces border crossing, "incompleteness," and "multiple, layered and shifting identities."[105] In contrast to this emphasis on "conviviality," other theorists of African language translation have read linguistic fluidity through the lens of conflict—although conflict too is understood to be ultimately productive. Unlike theorists of world literature like David Damrosch—whose suggestion that world literature "gains in translation" privileges the target language and literature into which one is translating over the source—Simon Gikandi argues that a non-Eurocentric model for a "new comparative literature" will afford more attention to the frequent "instability" of source languages from the Global South.[106] Indeed, in the southern African periodicals treated here, there are ample examples of what Gikandi refers to as "the grammars and locality that over-determined its [the original text's] production and circulation."[107] Whether authors were writing in a print magazine or on a blog, the matter was not as straightforward as choosing one or more languages over others; it also involved the use of a particular orthography (Nyanja being somewhat different from Chichewa), the choice of a place-based language variant (the Zulu of Mooi River versus that of Johannesburg in Maphoto's blog), wrestling with the political implications of these choices, or deciding when and how to switch between languages within a single text—a practice that has become more and more feasible on digital platforms like blogs and Facebook that are not subject to editorial intermediaries. Other writers and translators of African languages, such as Ngũgĩ wa Thiong'o, have drawn attention to the ripple effects that the instability of a language's orthography and grammar can have on the composition or translation of an entire text.[108]

Taking cues from these and other theorists, I focus here on the ways fluid, "unstable," and ultimately "*mobile*" translations produce changing forms of affiliation and disaffiliation between languages, texts, and reading and writing communities.[109] In most of the publications I consider, translation appears very differently from the way it is usually presented in academic contexts (including anthologies of world literature and monographs such as this book), where source and translated texts are placed side by side or immediately following one another. Instead, in the periodical forms in my corpus, translation is always in motion—spatially and temporally—and often across more than one language. Authors writing on blogs or Facebook pages sometimes provide translations in the comments section when prompted by readers, or even rely on readers to provide translations for one another, resulting in translations that are dispersed throughout these digital forms. Similarly, in *African Parade*, translations were scattered throughout the magazine's pages, and sometimes across more than a single issue. In fact, it was often unclear which text was the "original" since translations were unmarked. Stefan Helgesson and Christina Kullberg suggest that even in publications that present translation in a linear (and usually hierarchical) way, languages are "entangled" or "made to fold" with one another in "a translingual event with multiple implied audiences."[110] In the multilingual publications in this book, texts in different languages are indeed folded with one another, but more than this, translation is an ongoing event, unfolding across time, space, and multiple languages simultaneously.

Translation-in-motion registers the subtle overlaps, gradations, and flux between literary languages and forms in regional and diasporic contexts where languages, literatures, and cultures are often closely connected, but nevertheless distinct, as was the case in southern Africa. There is a particularly telling example of this phenomenon in the January 1954 edition of *Parade*, an issue in which the question of the magazine's languages of publication was at the forefront. While some readers argued against including material in vernacular languages, *Parade*'s editor defended their inclusion, as did a reader letter in Shona and its translation on the Nyanja page. The anonymously authored letter on the Shona page requests that more material be published in Cizezuru, the dialect of Shona spoken in Harare, as well as other "black languages."[111] The Nyanja translation is not immediately apparent as such since its title reads, "Mapeji Acinyanja Acuruke," or "The Pages in Nyanja Should Increase." Nevertheless, in both the original letter and its Nyanja translation, the argument is the same: the magazine should increase the number of pages in Black languages ("zinenero za anthu akuda")—which at the time were limited to two pages for each of the four vernacular languages. In Nyanja, the writer argues, "Mapeji a Cishona, Cinyanja, Cibemba ndi Cindebele ndi ocepa. Ine ndine M'shona ndipo ndimadziwa Cishona cokha. Sindinathe kuwerenga Cizungu, koma ndimatha kulemba ndi kuwerenga cinenero canga" ("The pages in Shona, Nyanja, Bemba, and Ndebele are few. I am Shona and I only know Shona. I cannot read English, but I can write and read in my language").[112] There is a strange kind of ventriloquism that occurs when the writer says in Nyanja that they "only know Shona." This disconnect is heightened by the fact that the original language changes in translation from "Cizezuru" to "Cishona," presumably because the more specific Harare-based dialect Cizezuru might not have been recognizable to Nyanja speakers outside Zambia. And yet, while the Nyanja translation registers this linguistic distance, its ventriloquism is also a form of "speaking" both languages simultaneously. Writing "I only know Shona" in Nyanja thus becomes part of the letter's argument for more pages in *all* the magazine's Black languages. While translation between African languages in the magazine overall appears to be rare—reflecting a larger historical trend—these letters demonstrate the possibilities of a mobile translation to express linguistic proximity and solidarity while also capturing meaningful linguistic differences.

In highlighting this example, I wish to draw attention to the way understanding translation as mobile points us to a particular way of reading literary forms in motion. Like language, literary forms change as they move, even when they move between closely related literary and cultural traditions. Rarely, however, is this a process of simply transferring meaning from one language to another or "picking up" a form and setting it down elsewhere.[113] By reading formal adaptation, like mobile translation, as a "process of affining and deciphering across plurilingual entities," we can observe subtle, granular shifts in literary form as texts travel across spaces such as southern Africa.[114] My argument here is that the editors, writers, critics, and readers of southern African media-based forms have long been actively engaged in this process of reading in motion. In reworking forms from various other parts of the region and the wider Black diaspora for their own contexts, cultural producers have often found themselves "speaking" more than one literary language simultaneously, much like the Nyanja writer above, and thus registering both affinities and solidarities as well as the distinctions and distance between them.

In this book, I aim to read in motion as these readers and critics did and do. Like the reader of Maphoto's blog, who described the experience of reading as a form of travel (first by jet and then by public plane), literary critics have presented African literatures as "loaded vehicles" and compared themselves to "outraged touts for the passenger lories of African literature."[115] In reading African literatures as communal vehicles on the move, these critics extend the work of scholars of oral forms, such as that of Lupenga Mphande on *izibongo*, mentioned above. As forms created from, structured by, and designed to record a common history of migration and diaspora, *izibongo* are nothing if not forms of mobility.[116] Mphande's study points to closely related yet distinct forms of *izibongo* across the Nguni diaspora in southern Africa, which become visible when we read these forms in motion. In contrast, as *izibongo* have been read elsewhere—from studies that compare praise poetry to Western literary forms to world literature courses in North America—they are almost always located as specifically South African forms.[117] Reading in motion, as Mphande does, reveals a large dispersal of *izibongo*. Similarly, by tracing various forms of mobility as they travel through periodical print and digital networks, this study limns multiple centers of literary influence and relation across the southern African and Black diasporas. These multiple centers only become visible when we read at this more granular level, observing subtle shifts in form and language over months and years and in publications that have traveled extensively within a regional network and beyond.

Each chapter of this book moves between the forms described above and the publications in which they appeared. Individual chapters center on at least one and as many as four publications, and though I attend to some of the other materials in these periodicals (news, opinion pieces, leisure materials, etc.), the focus remains on the new categories of fiction that I identify within and across these publications. Beyond the periodicals, I also draw attention to the wider networks through which such forms circulate, including short story collections, national literary anthologies, other newspapers and magazines, websites, and social media platforms like Facebook and WhatsApp. Each chapter of this book is thus based on a large archive of material that spans as few as several years, in the case of newer publications like the *Chimurenga Chronic* and *Jungle Jim*, and as many as four decades in the chapter that deals primarily with the *Malawi News*.

Reading across forms and networks in this way exacerbates the issues of scale that have troubled various approaches to world literature. How can world literature claim to account for the world when it neglects "99% of the archive"?[118] In terms of the archive considered here, the *Malawi News* alone has published approximately four thousand fictional stories since Malawi's independence in 1964, as compared to fewer than a hundred novels published by Malawians during this time. The sheer number of African short stories has contributed to what F. Odun Balogun describes as the form's "near-complete critical neglect."[119] The volume of short fictional forms in my study is compounded by the fact that they appeared in capacious publications: some issues of *African Parade* were nearly 100 pages long, and the first edition of the *Chronic* had more than 250 pages. To work with so much material, some literary critics have begun to employ a variety of big data, or "distant reading," methods. This book, which is much more traditional in its close attention to individual stories, nevertheless seeks to account for the ways sizable bodies of texts change over time and space by tracking particular forms as they travel through publications and networks. Reading in motion thus moves between close and distant reading, much as it moves between work and network.[120] To accommodate this vast amount of material, this book's chapters are relatively lengthy. Many of the texts that could not be directly included in my analysis can be found in the book's notes—pointing to a wider network of stories and publications beyond those treated here.

This book is organized chronologically, and chapter 1 compares changing imaginations of nationalism, regionalism, and the Black diaspora through the lens of literary form in two popular magazines, South Africa's *Drum* (1951) and its lesser-known contemporary from the Central African Federation, *African Parade* (1953). While most novelists from the former federation—Malawi, Zimbabwe, and Zambia—gained international attention only decades later, *Parade* was read by Anglophone readers around the world, from Sydney to Harlem. By publishing local writers in five regional languages alongside well-known global authors, *Parade* situated Central Africa as a unique literary geography and as a potentially powerful political space, which it likened to the United States. I argue that *Parade*, inspired by South Africa's iconic *Drum* magazine but dissatisfied with its elision of African life outside South Africa's cities and its inattention to the migrant labor system that funneled workers from across the region into South African industries, engaged in a mobile adaptation of *Drum* and its idea of "being-black-in-the world."[121] *Parade*'s migrant forms in English and Nyanja feature a process of continuous regional migration, generating new textual forms and a more expansive conception of African modernity, one rooted in the reality of unremitting migration across borders—both within Central Africa and beyond. The chapter points to the lasting impact of these migrant forms on the region's literature and shows that by collapsing the distinction between the mobility of migrant workers and more cosmopolitan travelers, *Parade* provides insight into African mobilities that have been overlooked in African literary criticism.

Chapter 2 follows these stories of migration to their frequent destination: the marginalized urban townships located on the peripheries of major cities throughout southern Africa. As the dreams of some Southern Rhodesians of turning the federation into a large African state waned and white supremacists solidified their control of Southern Rhodesia (Zimbabwe) in the late 1950s and early 1960s, these townships became the location for growing nationalist movements as well as a nascent African futurism, which envisioned travel to outer space as a way to transcend Earth's racial boundaries. This chapter considers a little-studied but global form that I call the "township tale": serialized, character-driven narratives published in magazines and newspapers around the world. While these tales have primarily been read as a means for writers to critique their immediate social and political environments, I argue that they have also mapped broader affiliations. The chapter follows various adaptations of Langston Hughes's Here to Yonder column (republished in South Africa in *Africa!* magazine) from across southern Africa, including Casey Motsisi's Johannesburg-focused On the Beat, Bill Saidi's Bits and Pieces from Harare and Lusaka after Dark, and Daniel Dlamanzi's Makokoba Park Talk, set in Bulawayo. In chronicling their travels in and around the colonial township, each of these writers created alternative maps of Black urban life in relation to various impediments to local mobility—from poor bus service to pass laws that restricted Africans' movement—as well as their imaginations of more cosmopolitan spaces and means of travel, such as American cars. Nevertheless, all these writers sensed the limits of this cosmopolitanism to transcend the global color line, and for this reason, resigned themselves to rocketing into outer space, a location that some writers compared to a heavenly respite and that others presented as even more peripheral than the township. Ultimately, the township in these tales serves as a key vantage point from which writers could navigate between complex ideas of belonging (and failing to belong) to local, national, and global spaces, with the interplanetary signifying the insufficiency of a single-world framework for understanding Black spatial imaginaries.

Departing from the regional scope of the first two chapters, chapter 3 focuses on a newly independent Malawi. Following independence in 1964, President Banda cut Malawi off from its neighbors, discouraging migration and censoring local and foreign publications. In this environment, the state-controlled *Malawi News* was one of the few outlets for Malawian writers, who adapted various literary genres and styles—from the proverb and the fable to the serial stories in international women's magazines—to "Kamuzu's paper."[122] Although these stories were referred to somewhat dismissively as "weekend stories," in reference to their ephemerality, they have demonstrated a surprising mobility and longevity via their reproduction in countless national anthologies. These stories were also "weekend stories" in the sense that they were read at home on "boring weekends" and as such provide insight into the way the public and private spheres were constructed. Attentive to Banda's reinvention of Malawian kinship networks and his harnessing of women's social and political mobility for his own ends, I argue that the *Malawi News* shaped a domestic form of short fiction that thematizes spaces like the nation, home, school, and initiation camp and that this fiction has been used to imagine the Malawian nation in relation to the region and the world through the lens of gender and sexual norms. Drawing on the work of writers and critics published in the *Malawi News* from the 1960s to the present in both English and Chichewa, I trace the emergence of this form and its particular kind of domestic realism that naturalized the social world of Banda's paper as "the world." While this form of the short story has been highly mobile domestically, it has been misinterpreted on the few occasions it has traveled beyond Malawi and into international circuits. Rather than tell a familiar story about literature from the "periphery" failing to be appreciated by global (read Western) audiences, I argue that this incident highlights the degree to which Malawian literature has been shaped by the newspaper and its vision of national and literary sovereignty based on the ability to define one's own gender and sexual norms. We can trace this legacy to Banda's expansion of the domestic sphere to encompass the nation, a conception that young women in Malawi today are contesting in their own fiction.

Chapter 4 returns to where the book began, with a consideration of the relationship between South Africa and the broader region and continent through two South Africa–based publications, the *Chimurenga Chronic* and *Jungle Jim*. Specifically, I explore how these digital-age literary projects have self-consciously modeled themselves on some of the iconic print media forms that I consider earlier in the book. Featuring both print and digital components, these publications style themselves as a print newspaper and pulp magazine, respectively, and engage with many of the genres one would expect in those platforms, from letters to the editor and news reports to science fiction and detective stories. By using these print forms as "low-tech time machines" that not only travel in time but also produce what I call a "pan African spacetime," the writers in these magazines remobilize twentieth-century pan-African aspirations for twenty-first-century ends. Both the *Chronic* and *Jungle Jim* are self-reflexive about being published in Cape Town, South Africa, and thus their pan-Africanism takes on a dual form: reexamining South Africa's place in Africa as well as the African continent's place in the diaspora and the world. Through stories that deal with the issue of alienation—not only from time and history but also from space and the right to mobility—these stories produce a pan African spacetime that centers Africa in global space and history while also drawing attention to questions of belonging, migration, and xenophobia past and present.

Finally, chapter 5 addresses the rapid development of new literary forms on social media platforms like Facebook. While recent approaches to digital literature cast the web as a singular, global space and treat Western online practices as normative, I argue that these approaches have obscured the various kinds of digital worlding that are practiced around the globe. Following the success of Maphoto's *Diary of a Zulu Girl*, other "digital diaries" appeared across the region. I use the "Chichewa Stories" Facebook pages as well as diaries by young women writers from South Africa and Malawi as examples of the intimate connection between contemporary digital forms and their print predecessors. Though seemingly accessible "everywhere," these digital forms and their routes of circulation are still embedded in material networks and structured by inequalities in digital infrastructures. While Facebook as a platform envisions itself as "building the world we all want" online, I ask what kinds of worlds these Facebook pages are producing. In particular, I point to the way Facebook forms by young women writers eschew a sense of placelessness or a singular vision of worldedness in favor of creating mobile reading communities that play between different scales of affiliation.

Forms of mobility suggest new modes of reading world literatures that are attentive to the ways writers and readers actually engage with texts in time and space. It is often thought that close reading has an advantage over distant reading because of the proximity it offers to the lived reading experience, but reading in motion—especially when it comes to the materials in my corpus—re-creates this experience even more closely, since it is better attuned to the gaps in space and time that punctuate reading.[123] The forms in periodical print and digital media are well known for their temporal aspects (the disruptions of serialized fictions or the brevity of flash fiction, for example), but they are also experienced across space, as readers engage with portable forms while on the move. In describing the Congo River boatmen's songs as "navigational literary artefacts," Owuor highlights these songs' simultaneously creative and critical attributes and also points us away from abstract geographies to the people who created them; these poem-maps are "life stories" and "embodied geograph[ies]."[124] Like these songs, forms of mobility direct us to the writing, reading, and editing communities that created them, used them, and made them meaningful.

CHAPTER 1

Migrant Forms

African Parade's *Transnational Central Africa*

African Parade magazine, published out of the former Central African Federation, is full of stories of travel and migration by every conceivable means: foot, car, bus, boat, train, plane, and even rocket ship.[1] *Parade* began publication in 1953, the same year the colonial federation was formed out of the British protectorates of Nyasaland and Northern Rhodesia and the self-governing colony of Southern Rhodesia (today's Malawi, Zambia, and Zimbabwe). This chapter considers the role that *Parade*—particularly through its many narratives of mobility—played in imagining this contested political space in relation to the surrounding region, the African continent, and the wider Black diaspora. Frequent movement was a way of life for many Central Africans, who traveled in search of work to white-owned farms and mines in Southern Rhodesia and the Northern Rhodesian Copperbelt, as well as to South Africa's cities and diamond and gold mines. Others sought out educational opportunities in East and South African universities such as Makerere and Fort Hare. A smaller number, including some of *Parade*'s editors and writers, journeyed overseas to the United Kingdom and United States. The magazine itself circulated via many of these same routes, traveling from *Parade*'s headquarters in Salisbury (now Harare) to cities throughout the federation and hubs in East and South Africa, as well as to various locations in Europe, North America, and Australia. While most novelists from the region gained international recognition only decades later, *Parade* forged early, if less celebrated, connections between Central African writers and the wider world.

Publishing eclectic forms in five regional languages—English, Nyanja, Shona, Ndebele, and Bemba—*Parade* depicted the migrant experience as a foundational, constant, and yet deeply varied aspect of African life. Within the covers of a single issue from June 1956, for example, we find the serialized story of a prostitute in Bulawayo who has left her rural home, a soldier's narrative of intra-African regional travel during World War II, a Nyanja story about a man who suffers after leaving home for his wife's village, and Ndabaningi Sithole's "Rhodesian American Diary," as well as stories of the joys and perils of modern transportation, from "My Journey through Space," about a plane trip from Nyasaland to Southern Rhodesia, to "Motor Cycle Adventure" by K. E. Maulu. These narratives presented a capacious vision of mobility that included local, regional, and international travel, both by necessity and for pleasure. Taken together, they point to what I identify as *Parade*'s particular conception of African modernity, one rooted in the reality of unremitting migration across borders—both within Central Africa and beyond.

The June 1956 issue also underscores that *Parade*'s migrant narratives were generically and linguistically mobile, taking the form of fables, local histories, short stories, genre fiction like crime and romance, and hybrid genres that defied ready-made categories. Similarly, the magazine's stories moved somewhat haphazardly across languages. In its first seven years of publication, every issue of *Parade* dedicated two pages to material (fiction and nonfiction) in each of the vernacular languages. English stories and articles were sometimes translated into the magazine's African languages, but not necessarily all four, and these translations did not always appear in the same issue as the original story. The inclusion of this material was a source of constant debate in the magazine, with some readers requesting more pages in local languages and others suggesting that they had no place in "a national magazine" read "not only in Central Africa, but all over Africa."[2] With its readership divided on the issue, *Parade* continued to include material in indigenous languages until 1961, citing "the dire need for literacy and healthy literature for thousands of Central Africans" who were not "privileged" enough to know English.[3]

Through its changing matrix of forms and languages, *Parade* reflected—and sought to express—a political space that was in flux. The magazine was instrumental in charting the changing cultural, political, and literary geography of the newly formed Central African Federation, which it identified as a national as well as transnational undertaking, despite the federation's reality as a colonial project that was imposed against the will of the African majority. A "typical African middle-class publication," *Parade* espoused the ideology of the mission-educated African elite in Southern Rhodesia, who embraced the federal rhetoric and policy of "partnership."[4] Although partnership suggested "racial-co-operation," Africans were commonly depicted as "junior partners" in the enterprise, and the term was so ill defined in concept and practice as to render it "a meaningless platitude."[5] Nevertheless, to this small group of African journalists, writers, and politicians, all of whom were men and many of whom had been educated in South Africa, the formation of a Central African multiracial state seemed preferable to the increasingly repressive situation in South Africa, where the National Party had formally implemented apartheid in 1948. And while African nationalists, especially in Northern Rhodesia and Nyasaland, had fiercely opposed federation—rightly perceiving it as a means to delay Black majority rule—*Parade*'s first editor, Lawrence Vambe, along with other politically moderate Africans in Southern Rhodesia, had hoped that the incorporation of more Africans into the state would mitigate the forces of white domination in their country and pave the way for an African-run superstate. Particularly in its first several years, *Parade* purveyed this utopian vision of the federation's transformation into a large African nation while also celebrating the distinctive cultures and languages of its territories—two of which, Malawi and Zambia, gained their independence within the magazine's first decade.

Parade's efforts to work within this colonial structure may explain why it has been generally overlooked by scholars.[6] *Parade* certainly does not align with anti-colonial sentiment, nor does it fit within the "necessarily collective, political, and oppositional" framework ascribed to "minor" literature.[7] While I acknowledge the problematic role *Parade* played in making the federal project attractive to Central Africans, the magazine deserves consideration. In addition to its significant contributions to Central African literature, which include the publication of the first novel by a Black Zimbabwean, *Parade* points to a particular configuration of modern African subjectivity based on Central Africans' experiences of continuous migration. In particular, I look at the ways the magazine's many mobile forms mapped Central Africa as a national space and connected it to broader geographies, from the wider African continent to the diaspora. Analyzing material in English and Nyanja, the language spoken by one of the region's largest groups of transnational migrants, I argue that *Parade*'s narratives feature migration as a continuous, complex, and multiscalar phenomenon, generating new textual forms and affiliations.

Parade's "migrant forms," as I call them, not only depicted mobility but also traveled across languages, genres, and publications, creating connections across multiple textual fields and geographies. The linguistic mobility of these forms signaled the efforts of *Parade*'s editors and writers to forge a multilingual national literature out of the many languages and cultures of Central Africa. Because the magazine was written primarily (but not exclusively) in English, the magazine's writers and editors hoped this literature would reach readers across the African continent and the globe. In terms of genre, *Parade*'s migrant forms were inspired by a variety of literary sources, from local oral traditions and histories to the popular genres in international periodicals. In particular, many of *Parade*'s writers adapted aspects of Black South African writing and culture, which reached Central Africa through popular magazines like *Zonk!* and *Drum*. These South African publications also served as key vehicles for the dissemination of African American literature and culture, with which *Parade*'s writers engaged through the prism of the federation's racial politics.

Although *Parade* republished and adapted material from a host of international sources, in this chapter I focus on *Parade*'s relationship to its well-known contemporary, South Africa's *Drum* magazine.[8] A reader who picked up a copy of *Parade* on a street corner in Salisbury would be forgiven for mistaking it for a copy of *Drum*. *Drum* pioneered the form of the modern magazine in Africa, and *Parade* in turn set out "to do a *Drum*" for Central Africa, adopting *Drum*'s template of cover girls, investigative reports by "Mr. Parade" (a name patterned after that of the iconic "Mr. Drum"), world news roundups, picture parades, serialized and short fiction, American slang, and plenty of advertisements for modern amenities.[9] And yet, while it clearly imitated some of *Drum*'s most distinctive styles, forms, and language, *Parade* also aimed to vernacularize and reterritorialize *Drum*, which was published only in English and remained largely South Africa focused. Whereas *Drum* elided African life outside South Africa's cities, especially in its fiction, *Parade* presented a vision of modern African life founded on the continuous travel across borders—and the connections between rural and urban areas—that was a central part of life for Africans in the federation.

My aim in this chapter is not to idealize the condition of migrancy but to point to the new insights *Parade* provides into African mobilities that have been overlooked in literary criticism. Discourses on Afropolitanism, for example, have been critiqued for privileging the migrant experiences of a small subset of diasporic elites as well as certain genres, languages, and geographies, namely the global novel in English written in and about Euro-American metropoles. As a multilingual, Africa-based magazine, *Parade* is a vast and understudied archive in which to investigate conceptions of movement, many of which blur the boundaries between traditional notions of labor migrancy—often presented as one of the most abject forms of mobility—and the cosmopolitan idea of unfettered travel across borders. Furthermore, *Parade*'s migrant forms deal with both extra- and intracontinental travel, the latter of which is vastly underrepresented in African literary criticism and in diaspora studies more broadly.

To this end, I explore how *Parade* and its writers, through a mobile adaptation of *Drum* and its representations of Black life in the region and beyond, presented movement as a constitutive way of being and belonging in the world. *Parade*'s regional and international travel narratives and letters enabled a shifting comparison of Central Africa to both apartheid South Africa and the United States. This comparison served to showcase the perceived benefits of federal multiracialism while also providing a limited means of criticizing its shortcomings. Turning next to the magazine's fiction, I demonstrate how *Parade*'s migrant forms altered some of the formal elements of *Drum*'s most popular genres of fiction, including Jim Comes to Joburg stories and crime fiction, with a particular focus on the changing functions of two traveling archetypes: the migrant and the gangster, or *tsotsi*.[10] While these figures travel in the sense of migrating from one publication to another, they also signify particular conceptions of movement—or of the capacity for movement. Migration is a thematic and formal feature of many of *Parade*'s narratives, and the migrant, associated in *Drum* with the rural and the traditional, is refashioned as a figure that can move across spatiotemporal categories (rural and urban, past and present, traditional and modern) and whose iterations appear in a variety of genres. Through its migrant forms, then, *Parade* envisioned and produced a new political and literary geography based on perpetual movement between national, regional, and diasporic spaces—an endeavor that speaks to the challenges facing African writers on the continent and in the diaspora today.

A MOBILE ADAPTATION

Periodicals are often described through various metaphors of mobility, as "spindles and joints," "wings," and "vehicles."[11] Whether real or imagined, travel is integral to the magazine as a form. This was particularly true of commercial publications like *Drum* and *Parade*, whose popularity and perceived reach were a key part of their identity and cachet. *Drum* proclaimed on its cover that it was "A Magazine of Africa for Africa," and later, "Africa's Leading Magazine." This claim was not mere bluster: *Drum* opened offices in West and then East Africa and eventually published as many as ten different editions of the magazine. These included an "International Edition," as well as editions for Ghana, Nigeria, the Federation of Rhodesia and Nyasaland, Central Africa, and East Africa. As recent critics have argued, the magazine's pan-African scope facilitated its dissemination of a new vision of Africa and Africans in the era of decolonization,[12] as well as an expanded "imaginary of being-black-in-the-world."[13] And yet *Drum* did not cross borders seamlessly or without competition as it spread across Anglophone Africa. Audiences in Ghana and Nigeria demanded that *Drum* include more local content,[14] while others created their own versions of the magazine, as the writers and editors of *Parade* did in Central Africa. When we read both *Drum* and *Parade*, as readers at the time were doing, it becomes apparent that *Drum*'s vision of "being-black-in-the-world" required some translation for Black audiences outside South Africa's borders.

My argument here is that *Parade* engaged in a particular kind of "translation" of *Drum*—a mobile adaptation of the magazine's language, forms, and ideas of Africanness and Blackness.[15] In other words, the magazine's editors and writers were involved in their own form of reading and writing in motion. This fluid mode of literary adaptation reveals the magazine's shifting appropriations and affiliations across the southern African and wider Black diasporas, many of which were routed through *Drum* or South Africa. It also captures the way travel itself—through forms like the letter and the travel diary—was presented in the magazine as an essential means of engaging, interpreting, and producing the world.

Parade's mobile adaptation of *Drum* involved marking its simultaneous proximity to and distance from it—and, by extension, its proximity to and distance from apartheid South Africa. *Parade* presented itself as an iteration of magazines like *Drum*, "one that belonged to Central Africa," but also as something unique: an effort "to put on record that aspect of African life which is as yet little known and inadequately portrayed in word and picture."[16] Similarly, *Parade*'s selling line on its cover, "Central Africa's Most Widely Read Magazine," echoed *Drum*'s claim to be "Africa's Leading Magazine," while a smaller line below it highlighted *Parade*'s status as "The ONLY Magazine in Southern Africa Edited and Printed by Africans for Africans" (fig. 2). *Parade*'s emphasis on its African editorship and production was reiterated on the Nyanja page in the magazine's first issue: "IYI NDIYO MAGAZINE YOYAMBA NDIPO IRI YOKHA KUNO KUMWERA KWA AFIRIKA IMENE IMASINDIKIZIDWA NDI ANTHU AKUDA KUTI IZIWERENGEKA NDI ANTHU AKUDA" ("This is the first and only magazine here in southern Africa printed by black people so as to be read by black people").[17] Claiming not only Central Africa but

Fig. 2. *African Parade*, December 1957. Courtesy of Padare reNhau.

"Southern Africa" as its purview, *Parade* drew a direct contrast between itself and *Drum*, which boasted numerous Black writers and journalists but was edited by white men. While *Parade*'s claim to be a magazine "by Africans for Africans" can be read as a gesture that essentialized African culture, it was a key part of the way the magazine positioned itself as the only outlet capable of accurately representing modern African life to a multiracial audience.

Parade's selling line might seem to suggest that it was a more radical magazine than *Drum*, which it was not. In fact, neither magazine was primarily political. Both *Drum* and *Parade* had white owners—Jim Bailey and Bertram F. G. Paver, respectively—whose liberal leanings usually stopped short of interfering with their commercial interests. While *Drum* published numerous exposés on the poor conditions of prisoners and farmworkers in the Union, David Rabkin speculates that Bailey's connections to the mining industry prevented the magazine from addressing the abuses on the mines and of the migrant labor system more broadly.[18] In general, critics of *Drum* have pointed to its failure to take a "more militant stand against the apartheid state," emphasizing that its main contribution to the struggle against apartheid was its promotion of a particular Black urban subjectivity.[19] In comparison, *Parade* was a more paternalistic endeavor. Cedric Paver, who served as manager of African Newspapers Limited, the company founded by his brother Bertram and that published *Parade*, argued that the role of the African press was "to make reasonable citizens of the thousands of Africans who were taught to read, to provide a fair and unbiased news service, [and] to equip Africans for the responsibilities of freedom and democracy."[20] In reality, African Newspapers served as a popular, and therefore highly effective, platform for marketing the multiracial federation, which white liberals such as the Pavers preferred to either Black majority rule or the formation of another racialized state like South Africa.[21] To this end, *Parade* emphasized African advancement through Westernization and held up its own newsroom as proof "that partnership has been possible between white and black."[22] Although they would be disappointed by the federation's false promises, journalists like Vambe and William Saidi were initial believers in the project and saw African Newspapers as playing an essential role in countering the misrepresentation of African nationalist leaders in the European press.[23]

In distinguishing itself from *Drum*, *Parade*'s selling line also demonstrates how the magazine frequently positioned South Africa as a foil for the federation. The proximate specter of apartheid was used by federal authorities to draw concessions from Black Southern Rhodesians, and this gesture is reflected in *Parade*'s general approach to South Africa as a cautionary tale, the "land of apartheid and Bantustans."[24] This comparison served the magazine's aim of advocating for the federation, but also provided some limited opportunities to point out the federation's shortcomings. An editorial in the magazine from 1955, for example, argued that white residents blocking the building of new townships near their homes would need to "give up some of [their] cherished privileges in order that the Africans might gain," suggesting that otherwise, "we will soon be like South Africa at which we are so fond of throwing stones."[25] Indeed, despite some modest political, social, and educational improvements for Africans in Southern Rhodesia following federation,[26] multiracial partnership was best likened to the relationship between "the 'horse' (the African) and its 'rider' (the European)," as Godfrey Huggins, the first prime minister of the federation, so infamously described it.[27] Still, the image of stark racial segregation in South Africa loomed large in the magazine's imaginary. Later, *Parade*'s editor expressed his shock after the South Africa Jazz Revue's visit to the federation. How was it possible for this group of multiracial artists to have come out of South Africa, "a country where apartheid is supposed to be preached and put into practice in every form of activity?"[28] He went on to suggest that such a group would never have been formed in the federation, "[w]hich goes to show that in some respects racial prejudice and apartheid is more in evidence in practice in this country than in Nationalist SA." Through such comparisons, *Parade* engaged in a shifting negotiation of its political environment, a mobile adaptation made possible by the distinct but overlapping political and racial dynamics in the federation and apartheid South Africa.

While *Parade* lacked *Drum*'s vast distribution networks and hubs across the continent, it signaled its mobility and reach through articles about its new markets as well as letters from readers of various kinds. *Parade* was not forthcoming about its circulation numbers, but it appears to have had a less than ideal number of subscribers in its first several years of publication, as evidenced by a November 1955 reminder to readers not to default on their subscriptions, and later, a pointed salute to the "thousands of loyal and cultured subscribers, who, in this modern age, realize that not to read at all is to be very much dead-alive."[29] Similarly, an article from January 1955 celebrated that *Parade* had "blazed its trail into East Africa, where a steady flow of subscribers is reaching its circulation department," with a follow-up piece from 1957 asserting that *Parade* was "becoming as popular there as it is in the Federation and the Union of South Africa" and boasting that "DRUM's Kenya representative was an early visitor to [*Parade*'s] stand."[30] The most consistent way *Parade* signified its readership and travels, however, was through readers' letters to the editor and pen pal requests. Many of *Parade*'s readers imagined its reach to be quite far, as evidenced by a June 1956 reader's letter from Lilongwe, Nyasaland, requesting pen pals from "South Africa, Gold Coast, U.S.A., Nigeria, India, U.K., Denmark and Jamaica." Although readers from southern Africa authored most of the magazine's letters, *Parade* drew special attention to letters that came from farther afield, such as those from "Australia!" and "Canada!" on its "Pen-Pal Shrine" page in December 1957. While it is tempting to read these letters as proof of the magazine's reach, some of the magazine's letters were likely fictionalized; Bill Saidi, one of the magazine's writers, admits to having been tasked with writing them on occasion.[31] In this regard, the letters in these sections of the magazine are closely related to many of its more overtly fictional forms, which, as I argue below, used the letter as a primary way to map migrant journeys and routes—both real and imagined.

Through the letter as a mobile form, *Parade* limned its most "significant geographies" and affiliations, which included its immediate region of southern Africa as well as the African diaspora in the United States.[32] *Parade*'s editor described a letter it received from the Harlem Writers Club as "one of the best tributes we have had." The November 1955 letter by V. H. De Jones reads, "Some of my colleagues in South Africa have been sending me The African Parade. As an American Negro, I am deeply impressed with it." De Jones goes on to say that the magazine must now "be developed" and requests that copies of *Parade* be sent monthly to the club at Harlem's main library. Perhaps because of this exchange, the Harlem library, today the Schomburg Center, maintains more than a decade of *Parade* on microfilm from 1955 onward. This letter also points to the key role South Africa played as a conduit for Black transnational exchanges to and from the wider region of southern Africa. *Drum* published a good amount of material on African American culture and life, beginning with the regular feature "Negro Notes from the USA" in its first iteration, *African Drum*. In addition to articles and feature pieces, the magazine included stories and poems by the African American writers Countee Cullen, Gene Davis, and Langston Hughes, the last of whom served as a judge for *Drum*'s short story competition in 1953 and 1954. As numerous scholars have demonstrated, *Drum*'s vision of the "New African" owed much to the Harlem Renaissance's figuration of the New Negro.[33] It is less well known, however, that *Drum* played an important role in spreading African American literature and culture to the federation. D. D. Phiri, a prominent historian and one of Malawi's veteran creative writers, maintains that he and other Malawians "learned a lot about African Americans through *Drum*."[34]

While both magazines highlighted African American achievements, *Parade*'s identification with African American culture was grounded in its comparison of the federation to the United States, which it held up as a model multicultural and multiracial nation and as a template for a future African-run federation. Though Vambe's dream soured as the real-world implications of federation became apparent, he initially held a simultaneously idealistic and pragmatic vision of its potential:

> I was convinced that, given the opportunity, the African people could govern both themselves and the white settlers justly and without discriminating against any minority. On the other hand, I was realistic enough to see that once in power and independent, the Africans in each respective state in Central Africa would be unlikely to sacrifice their parochial interests for those of greater unity and economic viability in a Federation of their own making. How much better, I told myself, for us black people, eight million of us, in the two Rhodesias and Nyasaland to accept the existing structure of the Federation and concentrate on the elimination of all its injustices. Win we must in the near future. In the end we would be in control of a huge African state with vast resources, copper in Northern Rhodesia, agricultural wealth, tobacco and secondary industries in Southern Rhodesia and the tourist attractions of Nyasaland.[35]

Out of an "existing structure," Vambe conceives of a new geography with both national ("a huge African state") and transnational characteristics, in some ways prefiguring the short-lived Pan-African Freedom Movement for East and Central Africa (PAFMECA) that was launched in 1958.[36] At the same time, Vambe's call for victory over oppression ("Win we must in the near future") is framed not in terms of independence from colonial rule but rather as the elimination of the injustices of an already independent entity. In this way, Vambe's vision of Africans in the federation presents their plight and possibilities as more similar to those of African Americans in the United States than of other colonialized populations in Africa or elsewhere.

However flawed and naive, Vambe's comparison of the federation to the United States was meant to stake a claim to African citizenship.[37] Vambe's visit to the United States over several months in 1957, during which he "looked for the positive in the American system," was crucial to many of his political conceptions.[38] Commenting on deputy prime minister Sir Roy Welensky's trip to the United States in May 1956, the editor wrote, "America, I feel, has a lot to offer young countries such as the Federation. . . . By some magic trick she has been able to wield races from all parts of the globe into one single nation."[39] The global frame of this assertion is significant; *Parade*'s editor saw the United States as a nation forged out of international migration long before discourses of globalization were commonplace. Similarly, in a later installment of the regularly occurring column As Man to Man, the author, identified only as "F," discusses the importance of fostering a strong national consciousness such that "each individual thinks of himself as being a member of that nation," just as in the United States, "each individual, if asked what he is, will proudly answer, 'I am American.'"[40] If the federation, which was "inhabited by people of various races and colors," were to achieve "greatness," everyone had to think—and had to be permitted to think—in this way.

Parade, however, was not entirely uncritical of American race relations. Indeed, its comparison of the federation to the United States became a way to talk about both the possibilities of multiracial nationalism and some of its failures. Like the Mozambican literary journal *Itinerário*, which Stefan Helgesson suggests "sees suffering as integral to black American culture," *Parade* drew attention to instances of persistent racial inequality.[41] This set both magazines apart from *Drum*, which, Helgesson finds, "pays virtually no attention at all to American racism. It idealizes the USA as a land of opportunity for 'blacks.'" Through various travel diaries, *Parade* engaged with Black internationalism differently than *Drum* did, illuminating the "*décalage*"—the gaps and discrepancies—that Brent Hayes Edwards identifies in articulations of the African diaspora based in part on varying conceptions of the nation.[42] Reporting on a press conference he attended at the White House with President Eisenhower for *Parade* in 1957, Vambe notes that he was "the only black man in the assembly," and in his observations of Washington, DC, he writes, "Negroes are fully integrated. . . . But it is clear to me they are the poorest section of the community."[43] Similarly,

Angeline Dube, in her *Parade* piece "America as I Saw It," spends a significant amount of time addressing the color bar in the United States, and particularly in the South.[44] In addition to these depictions of systemic racism, another short article titled "Shot for Being Smart Nigger," which reports on the murder trial of Elmer Kimble, a "white American Negro-hater," showed the United States to be a country that was not immune to shocking racial violence.[45]

Beyond these nonfiction articles and travel diaries, one of the earliest ways images of African American suffering entered *Parade*'s discourse was through the serialization of *Uncle Tom's Cabin* from September 1954 until early 1956. This was likely the first time the text had been made widely available to Central African audiences. Whereas *Drum* had serialized Alan Paton's *Cry, the Beloved Country* (1948), *Parade* selected Harriet Beecher Stowe's "famous book" on American slavery. Although the two texts are similar—both were written by white authors and have been heavily criticized for presenting patronizing models of racial harmony—the magazines' respective choices reveal an important distinction. While *Drum* presented a story steeped in South Africa's unique racial situation, *Parade* aligned itself with US racial history, including its relationship to the African diaspora through the slave trade and recolonization movements. In presenting the text to its readers, *Parade* emphasized the power of literature to transform society, arguing that *Uncle Tom's Cabin*, "more than any other single factor, stirred the conscience of the American nation against that evil institution, slavery. Had this book not been written, perhaps the black man's soul, which was cashed for gold, would have continued not to be his own for a much longer time than was the case."[46] In this respect, *Parade* may well have been describing its own efforts to forge a multiracial nation in the federation through nonviolent means.

Given *Parade*'s frequent use of the United States as a national model for the federation, it is not surprising that many of its writers performed a gesture similar to that of "American ethnic writers" in the first half of the twentieth century, who, Werner Sollors argues, worked to "[recast] the United States as a multiethnic country."[47] In other words, the "magic trick" of which *Parade*'s editor wrote—which made the United States appear to be a beacon of modern multiculturalism—was not a trick at all, but rather the result of painstaking interventions by America's ethnic writers. Sollors suggests that these writers often embraced themes and images of modernity because "[i]n a social setting in which incongruity resulting from the incompatibility of various pasts may have been the most widely shared cultural feature, there was perhaps no alternative."[48] Writers in the Central African Federation faced similar challenges, and they often responded by promoting the shared modernity of the federation's diverse populations.

To this end, *Parade* published numerous travel stories and photo spreads on the various territories of the federation, such as "My First Impression of a Northern Rhodesian Town," "A Glimpse into the Protectorate of Nyasaland," and "Meet the Rural African of S. Rhodesia." The last article, in particular, demonstrates the magazine's commitment to addressing the growing urban-rural divide. Beyond calling attention to the critical role of the rural population, which the author calls "the vital backbone of the country inasmuch as it grows the food that is vital to the wellbeing of everyone else in the Colony," the article also insists on the cosmopolitan character of rural people, who are described as being "well dressed as well as well fed" and making "'hot' money."[49] The "Picture Parades," a staple of the magazine, accomplished a similar task by featuring personalities and socialites from the three territories dressed in the style of the day, which was epitomized by American zoot suits, trench coats, and fedora hats. Although this style was associated with America, it was also immediately linked to the more cosmopolitan South Africa. As Saidi notes, "We knew that someone had just returned from South Africa if he was dressed in that way."[50] Through articles and photos such as these, *Parade* emphasized a shared regional cosmopolitanism based on travel.

While these travelogues were sometimes reminiscent of *African Drum*'s original serial, "Know Yourselves," which profiled various southern African ethnic groups, *Parade* described the aim of such pieces in distinctly nationalist terms. In "A Glimpse into the Protectorate of Nyasaland," the author, named only as "A Traveller," argues that travel between the territories has improved and that "[b]y the very nature of our present political and economic set-up it is unpatriotic for any intelligent African to profess ignorance of any of the territories forming what we call the Federation of Rhodesia and Nyasaland."[51] Whereas *Drum*'s urban audiences rejected the "tribal" emphasis of the "Know Yourselves" feature, *Parade*'s editors suggested that familiarity with all the people in the federal territories was essential for transforming a "geographical expression" into a "budding Central African State."[52] The same article, however, also points to disparities in movement across the federation based on its "economic set-up," in particular Nyasaland's lack of industry that forced Nyasa men to find work in other territories. In this way, *Parade* presented travel and migration through the three territories as a way to forge a broader Central African identity while acknowledging, to some degree, the inequities of this system. By collapsing the distinction between migrant workers and cosmopolitan travelers and insisting on the stylishness of both the urban and rural populations, the magazine implied that mobility was a way of being modern in the world—a way of living that took into account a broader swath of subjectivities and class positions than do current models of Afropolitanism.

By the late 1950s, it had become apparent to many that federation would not lead to the African-led state that Vambe and his colleagues had envisioned, but rather threatened to inaugurate an independent, white-ruled dominion. Vambe left Southern Rhodesia for London in 1959 to serve as information attaché of the Federal government,[53] and under later editors such as Davies M'gabe and Tinos Guvi, *Parade* became more vocal about ongoing racial oppression in both the federation and the United States, publishing articles that compare the color bar in Southern Rhodesia and America's Deep South to Nazism, a profile on Malcolm X asserting his centrality to American history, and exposés on America's racial "crisis."[54] In line with trends on the continent following Ghanaian independence in 1957 and the 1958 All Africa People's Conference, *Parade* began identifying the federation in increasingly Pan-African terms. An article titled "The Year 1960 and the Changing Face of Africa" describes the "international battle" in which "the African himself is wrestling for power so that he can call Africa his own land and rule it."[55] By 1964, *Parade* had stopped pulling its punches: in an issue celebrating Malawian independence, it accused various Cold War powers of hypocrisy and self-interest in refusing to acknowledge that African majority rule was on the horizon: "That is why Communists accuse the western powers of their racialism, and yet close their eyes about Hungary; why America doesn't vote against apartheid in South Africa because she knows her Deep South is a stink; why Britain is in the same trait, when she knows that by an Act in Council of the 18th century, she could INTERVENE in Southern Rhodesia."[56] The editor went on to demand that the Southern Rhodesian government "recognize the rights of the four million blacks whose rightful home is Southern Rhodesia." *Parade*'s growing engagement with Pan-Africanism in the early 1960s, though rarely a full-throated endorsement, signaled its disillusionment with the promises of multiracial democracy and "partnership," both in the federation and in the United States.

Throughout the life span of the federation, *Parade* was instrumental in mapping Central Africa in terms that were both rural and urban, national and international. By engaging in a mobile adaptation of *Drum*'s representations of Black experiences in South Africa and the United States, *Parade* explored the potential and ultimately the impossibility of establishing a multiracial democracy in Central Africa. A similar need to translate Central African experiences emerges in a comparison of *Drum*'s and *Parade*'s fictional forms. As I show below, *Drum*'s fiction stopped presenting migrancy as a way of being Black in the world and thus left few roles for Africans from outside South Africa in the magazine.

"JIM COMES TO JOBURG," BUT THE *TSOTSI* STAYS: *DRUM*'S EARLY FICTION

When *Drum* magazine began, it was aimed not only at South Africans but also at the entire African continent and even the diaspora. Advertised as "A Magazine of Africa for Africa," it was meant to "provid[e] a means of expression and encouragement for all Africans," including the "more than 150,000,000 Bantu and Negro inhabitants of this continent" and the "millions of other Africans in the new lands of the Western hemisphere to whom 'The African Drum' will bring a message from the motherland."[57] In its effort to appeal to what it envisioned as a broad continental and even diasporic audience, the *African Drum*, as it was first called, published a number of stories on the theme of African migration to the city, which the editors described as "an experience common to all Africans."[58]

African Drum's very first story, Albert Mbeba's "Rhodesia Road," features migrants from outside South Africa as its protagonists, but it also foretells the erasure of the migrant, and the foreign migrant in particular, from the magazine's pages. It is also the magazine's only translated story—a fact that has been overlooked in most critical treatments of it.[59] This oversight is not surprising considering the editor's presentation of the text to the reader, which elides the process of translation almost entirely. In a box offset from the rest of the text, we are told that "'Rhodesia Road,' such as we present it here is a condensation from the original MS written in one of the Nyasaland languages," but neither the short book's original title, *Ku Harare*, nor its original language, Tumbuka, is specified.[60] Further, the story is depicted as "condensed" rather than translated from a manuscript, not a book, and the translator—for presumably one must have existed, even if it was the author himself—is not acknowledged. Glossing over the text's translation, the editor highlights aspects of its content and form that make it a "good," broadly relatable story and emphasizes its unmediated clarity, arguing, "There is in 'Rhodesia Road' a freshness, simplicity and immediate rendering of emotions and experiences." Together, these paratextual elements underscore the story's legibility and transparency, eliding its many layers of translation—of language, content, and form. Nevertheless, the fact of the story's translation asserts itself subtly in the text through words that either remain in Tumbuka or are influenced by its grammar.

Like "Rhodesia Road," many of the earliest stories in *African Drum* feature the migrant as their protagonist—a figure that Deleuze and Guattari suggest is defined by "reterritorialization"—or depict the migrant's inevitable return.[61] In these stories, migrants seeking to earn money to bring back to their rural areas journey to the city, where they are persecuted by *tsotsis*, or gangsters, as well as the police after falling prey to vices such as gambling, drinking, and prostitution.[62] This genre of fiction, nicknamed Jim Comes to Joburg, has a long history in South African writing and has generally been seen to promote a "back to the land" message consistent with the South African government's desire to prevent the formation of a Black urban proletariat.[63] Initially patronized mostly by white authors (with a few notable exceptions, such as R. R. R. Dhlomo and Peter Abrahams), the genre highlighted the detrimental effects of white civilization, symbolized by the city, on Africans. In these narratives, the city is presented as a place that the migrant must endure while accumulating enough wealth to return home, and there is a strong association of "urbanization with victimization."[64] The migrant's eventual and necessary return to the village is one of the genre's most enduring themes.[65]

The first version of *Drum*, in which this kind of story appeared, sold miserably. In response, the magazine altered its content and style to better appeal to Black urban South Africans, who, in the words of Anthony Sampson, the magazine's new editor, requested jazz, "hot dames," and "anything American."[66] One of the effects of this shift was that the rest of southern Africa was effectively written out of the magazine's geography. *Drum* dropped its "Know Yourselves" feature, which had profiled cultures from across the region, and from this point forward included fewer articles on current events from the Central African Federation (roughly one article per year from 1952 to 1956).[67] Equally, in terms of the magazine's fiction, the *Drum* writers moved away from the Jim Comes to Joburg genre and increasingly preferred to set their work firmly in South Africa's major cities. While many of these stories did feature crime, among other degradations of city life, the intention was no longer to deter migrants from staying.

In these new stories, the figure of the migrant was steadily replaced by the gangster, who was envisioned as a product of the urban environment.[68] In his 1951 essay "The Birth of a Tsotsi," Henry Nxumalo locates the sources of tsotsism in the "grinding poverty and the sea of squalor that surrounds the 'Golden City,'" but unlike the authors of earlier articles in the magazine, he says little about how South Africa's exploitative migrant labor system contributed to this situation.[69] In imagining the *tsotsi* as born of the township ("Of course, tsotsis are made as well as born: they are made every day on the Reef"), the *Drum* writers disavowed the tribal connections and "endemic predicament of migrancy" that the apartheid government was increasingly foisting on the growing Black urban population through the promotion of independent rural homelands, or *bantustans*, to which Black South Africans were expected to return when they were too old or infirm to work in white-run industries.[70] Nxumalo's emphasis on the "birth" of the *tsotsi* in the city takes on additional meaning in the context of the 1952 amendment to the Urban Areas Act, which prohibited "natives" from remaining in urban areas for longer than seventy-two hours unless they were either born there or had worked for a single employer in the area for at least ten years.[71] By erasing the migrant origins of the *tsotsi*, the *Drum* writers promoted a figure that denied the gesture of return in favor of permanent relocation to South Africa's cities. Many stories reference particular townships or urban locations within these cities, such as Newclare, Sophiatown, and Alexandra in Johannesburg, and even particular roads, making it clear that *Drum* was now addressing a primarily urban audience that would know and identify with these locations without too much elaboration or description.

The *tsotsi* has frequently been interpreted as a figure of Black urban resistance to white oppression.[72] While the political efficacy of this figure has been debated, here I am concerned with how, in order to use the *tsotsi* as such a symbol, the *Drum* writers cast him as the antithesis of the migrant, who stood for the foreign, the past, the tribal, and the traditional. While the migrant's illegality was portrayed as a deficit and a weakness, the *tsotsi*'s criminality was glamorized as subversive of the apartheid order (which sought to control the movement, consumer habits, desires, etc. of Black South Africans). Such depictions had much to do with varying conceptions of these archetypes' capacities for movement, across both space and literary genre, which in turn reflected the different ways migration was experienced in South Africa versus in the federation. Rosalind Morris describes how, out of a climate in which the movement of Black South Africans was increasingly restricted by oppressive legislation such as that described above, the *tsotsi* emerged as a sign of "unfettered mobility."[73]

In Morris's reading, this mobility extended to an ability to cross boundaries, whether generic (the *tsotsi* "migrated" into South Africa via the jazz musical, gangster film, and noir cinema), linguistic (the hybrid language of tsotsitaal), or aesthetic.[74] The *tsotsi* was also a cosmopolitan figure, linked by his style—especially his fashionable American zoot suits—to urban cultures throughout the Black Atlantic. The *tsotsi* was "the figure through whom style lays claim to the political,"[75] and it was precisely this politicized style that many *Drum* writers sought to exploit by fashioning themselves as "intellectual tsotsis."[76] *Drum*'s new hero was epitomized by the protagonist of Arthur Maimane's serials "Crime for Sale" and "Hot Diamonds," a former criminal turned police officer who ultimately leaves the force to become a private detective, specializing in blackmailing criminals. O. Chester Morena's fluidity and liminality as a character flew in the face of the apartheid government's efforts to control movement and assign stable, clear roles to Black South Africans. Moreover, Morena (a.k.a. "The Chief") was nothing if not stylish, a true picture of the intellectual *tsotsi* who ruthlessly and ingeniously took what he saw as his due—in "Hot Diamonds," for example, he procures a new leather bag and "nice suits" with taxpayer money.[77]

By contrast, the migrant in *Drum* was a figure whose movement was fundamentally circumscribed by the patterns and circuitry of migrant routes and the structures of capitalist modernity (the white-owned farm, the mine, etc.). The migrant's criminal activities were associated with desperation and deviance rather than resistance to the white-run state. Mac Fenwick observes that the foreign gangs that appeared in *Drum*, such as the infamous "Russians" composed of Basotho migrant workers, were devoid of both stylishness and subversive potential: "With the Sotho blankets that they wore as a kind of uniform, and their explicitly rural orientation, the Russians did not hold much appeal for the cosmopolitan and wholly urban Sophiatown writers."[78] The migrant was also necessarily apolitical: unable to protest the unjust system for fear of being discovered without a pass and deported, the migrant labored to remain invisible and, not surprisingly, was almost entirely absent from most *Drum* stories post-1952.

The migrant's invisibility and sublimation in *Drum* was a result of his being restricted almost entirely to the Jim Comes to Joburg genre. Thus, while a figure like Morena could be both a hero and a criminal, the migrant—particularly the foreign migrant—could not occupy these positions simultaneously in *Drum*'s fiction. We see this separation of roles, for example, in "Ntombo Gets a Job" by Douglas Sidayiya. Published in March 1952, three months before the passage of the more stringent amendments to the Urban Areas Act, this story captures the magazine's transition from featuring migrant narratives to publishing crime stories set almost entirely in urban areas. It is also one of the only stories aside from "Rhodesia Road" that casts a foreign migrant, in this case from Southern Rhodesia, as its protagonist. Varying the typical structure of the Jim Comes to Joburg genre, which begins with the journey to the city, Sidayiya's story opens in the city and hinges on its hero's inability to return to his rural home. Because of his lack of money and mobility, the foreign migrant must either disappear into Johannesburg's criminal underworld or become visible and legible in the urban space by gaining legal employment. Ntombo chooses the latter and manages, with much difficulty, to find a position working as a waiter in a hotel. It is fitting that Ntombo's new role also entails a change in his visual appearance, marked by his uniform: Ntombo "smile[s], don[s] his white jacket, and start[s] his duties and a new life."[79] This aspiration—to become visible within the city as a legal worker—rendered the migrant unfit to play the hero in later stories. In contrast, *Drum*'s "new hero,"[80] the *tsotsi*, stood resolutely outside apartheid's sociopolitical order and gained legitimacy as a figure of resistance through his "unintelligibility."[81]

As *Drum* turned its focus to South Africa's urban areas, it ceased almost entirely to represent foreigners, focusing instead on the tensions between various sectors (racial, ethnic, class, and rural and urban) of South African society. When we do catch brief glimpses of them, these migrant figures are hopelessly rural and unsophisticated. For example, Shigumbu, "the soft-hearted but dried-up bachelor from Nyasaland," a minor character in Es'kia Mphahlele's "Lesane" stories, is a small-time criminal, selling marijuana and "trying desperately hard not to annoy the authorities lest he be sent back to his homeland."[82] Shigumbu's criminality is in no way glamorous, and both his appearance and speech lack the *tsotsi's* essential style. Shigumbu's overall appearance is epitomized by his false teeth, which "gave him an evil, snarling appearance when they touched the empty gums of the lower jaw."[83] While the *tsotsi* in *Drum* drew his power from the politicization of style, Shigumbu appears at once malevolent and impotent.

Notably, Shigumbu's speech is affected not only by his false teeth but also by his mother tongue Nyanja—he does not distinguish his *l*'s from his *r*'s—which becomes yet another mark of his foreignness and incapacity. While the *tsotsis'* language, tsotsitaal, was also a language with "migrant" origins—composed out of Afrikaans, isiZulu, isiXhosa, Sesotho, Xitsonga, and English[84]—it was presented in *Drum* as a product of the urban space: the fashionable "new lingo in the town-ships, bright as the bright-boys."[85] Shigumbu's speech, however, is linked to mental deficiency rather than stylishness or wit: "After three years of city life he had decided that Johannesburg was 'rittel bit better than Nyasaland, bludder,' quite aware that he was comparing a city with a country."[86] In stories such as this one, we see how criminality was bifurcated in *Drum*: crime as resistance was associated with the South African *tsotsi* and petty, insidious crime with the foreign migrant. However, in *Parade*'s migrant forms, discussed below, mobility, style, and even glamourous criminality were no longer reserved for the *tsotsi* alone; the migrant, too, was a figure characterized by continual movement across space, language, and genre.

AFRICAN PARADE'S MIGRANT FORMS

While *Drum* was available in the federation's urban centers, readers could not always obtain the magazine's most current issue.[87] This made it difficult for readers and writers from Central Africa to engage with *Drum* as fully as they might otherwise have done. The news in past issues was no longer as relevant, and other parts of the magazine "expired," such as product-sponsored offers and letter of the month competitions. Neither could readers from outside the Union compete in the "Spot Mr. Drum!" contests, which took place in South Africa's major cities. Central African creative writers also found it difficult to publish their work in *Drum*. Aside from Mbeba's "Rhodesia Road," *Drum* published no fiction by authors from Central Africa in its first two decades, although it did include work by several writers from America and West Africa, including Langston Hughes and C. O. D. Ekwensi. Somewhat paradoxically, then, it was more difficult for writers and readers from countries that were geographically close to South Africa to participate in *Drum*'s literary sphere than it was for those who were half a world away.

The spatial and temporal *décalage* between *Drum* and readers and writers in the federation was exacerbated by the magazine's rapid alteration of its editorial style when it transitioned from *African Drum*'s early Jim Comes to Joburg stories to narratives depicting wholly urbanized Africans. This change may have been particularly jarring for writers who were several months behind and still reading the fiction of the old *African Drum*. The Malawian writer and critic D. D. Phiri recalls having his work rejected by *Drum*. Instead, he found a home for his story "It Happened Eighty Years Ago" in *Parade*, which he calls "an imitation of *Drum*."[88] Phiri's story of a Nyasa girl who is captured by slave raiders and brought to Tanzania—where Phiri was living at the time—was published in March 1954 and was one of *Parade*'s first pieces of fiction. Although it recounts one of the most extreme forms of forced and violent regional migration, Phiri's tale, which ends in the girl's return home and the rejuvenation of her village, follows the basic template of the Jim Comes to Joburg genre, as did many of *Parade*'s early stories. The Shona story "Murume Waitengesa Huku Mu Harare," or "The Man Who Sold Chickens in Harare," which appeared in the same January 1954 issue in English as "The Man with a Beard," was also typical of the genre. It opens with the protagonist's momentous arrival in the city, which "burst upon his vision like a mirage in a desert," and ends with the man in jail and vowing never to return to Salisbury again.[89]

Although many of *Parade*'s early stories adhered to the Jim Comes to Joburg formula, others used themes of travel and migration not to warn migrants of the dangers of leaving home but rather to show migrancy as a way of being and belonging in the world. These migrant forms were distinct from the Jim stories in that they featured, were structured by, and textualized continuous regional migration. Unlike *Drum*'s stories, which focused on the figure of the urban gangster, many of *Parade*'s narratives recast the migrant as a central character who could move across spatial, linguistic, and generic boundaries. These narratives connected cities to rural areas, which were still considered viable and vital to the federation, and portrayed the complexities of migrant life in the region—albeit from a largely male perspective. Female migrants, in the few stories in which they appeared, remained stuck in the "Jane Comes to Joburg" genre, which warned them of city dangers.[90] For male migrants, however, these narratives pointed to permanent mobility as a way of inhabiting the modern world. In this way, *Parade*'s migrant forms contributed to the magazine's imagination of Central Africa as a national space knit together by various kinds of movement throughout its three territories, much like the travel narratives discussed above. In some cases, these forms also mapped travel routes beyond the federation, demonstrating Central Africa's fundamental connection to the rest of the region.

This vision of unfettered regional mobility both supported and undercut colonial interests. As an economic project, the federation was designed in part to facilitate the capture of African migrant labor for Southern Rhodesia, its growing "industrial hub."[91] While a quarter of Nyasaland's adult male population and one-sixth of Northern Rhodesia's were working in Southern Rhodesia in 1954, Peter Scott suggests that "interterritorial migration [was] waning" due to increased African farming and other forms of local employment.[92] Southern Rhodesia competed for these workers with the Northern Rhodesian Copperbelt and especially with South Africa, where many migrants perceived the working conditions to be better and the wages higher. However, the 1950s was a period of shifting federal labor policies, which briefly encouraged labor stabilization and then, due to slowing growth and overcrowding in urban areas, stopped encouraging "alien" migration from Nyasaland and Northern Rhodesia to Salisbury in the late 1950s.[93] While federation had promised freer movement throughout the three territories, migrants found their mobility increasingly regulated and restricted.[94] For Nyasa migrants in particular, refusing prescribed migrant itineraries and "settling in motion" had long been a form of self-determination.[95] It is therefore not surprising that *Parade*'s narratives in Nyanja, which I focus on here, indicate a strong desire for less restricted forms of mobility.

Migration was not only a thematic feature of *Parade*'s migrant forms but also a formal one. In this respect, *Parade*'s migrant forms resemble many migrant oral traditions from the region, such as *sefela* (plural *lifela*), a genre of poetry that was sung or chanted by Basotho migrants who worked in South Africa's mines as early as the second half of the nineteenth century. David Coplan argues that in *lifela*, "form follows character . . . traveling is the only theme that holds them together."[96] The migrant's journey was often the occasion for the telling of such poems, in addition to being the subject of many *lifela* and a formal feature that structured them. Many of *Parade*'s stories are difficult to categorize according to familiar literary genres, given their loose, fragmented plots and diverse concerns. Instead, like *lifela*, these stories are given shape or "sustained" by the journey itself.[97]

Gammon Mala's Nyanja story "Kwelani Galimoto Wa Ulere," or "Ride a Free Car," is one such story whose form reflects the continuous migration that it describes. Published in *Parade* in 1955, Mala's narrative depicts a trip across Northern Rhodesia in an Ulere ("free") car, the local name for the colonial "Free Migrant Transport Service," which provided transportation from the federal territories to Southern Rhodesia. In contrast to the Jim Comes to Joburg narrative structure of departure, arrival, and return, Mala's story takes place entirely during the journey itself, which becomes the occasion for a number of loosely related (and ultimately unresolved) events: one of the drivers tells jokes to the women; a woman cries thinking of her home in the village; the car picks up a group of women on the side of the road; and the jokester driver tries to charm the youngest and prettiest of them. Much as it does in *lifela*, traveling "holds together" all these different incidents. As if to acknowledge this indebtedness to earlier migrant genres, the story references the singing of songs during the journey: "Nthawi zina ngati nthanthi zace zatha tinkaimba nyimbo zokumbutsa kumudzi komwe tinacokera" ("Sometimes, if his [the driver's] jokes stopped we were singing songs that reminded us of the village where we had come from").[98] The songs not only were sung on the road but also express a longing for the village that likens them to oral migrant tales, as does the depiction of this singing as ongoing through the use of the past continuous tense (-nka-). Much of the story is told in a way that emphasizes the continuousness of the journey's events: "Ndithudi, kawiri kawiri umangomva akazi akuseka, 'Hahade'" ("Indeed, again and again you were just hearing the women laughing, 'Hahade'").[99] This has the effect of temporally situating the migrants' travels as a mode of narrative as well as what Paul Carter describes as a perpetual "mode of being in the world."[100]

In Mala's narrative, this particular journey is likened to other Ulere journeys of its kind. Describing the way this group of strangers have become like family during the trip, the unnamed narrator suggests, "Kawiri kawiri zikucitika pa maulendo onse a Magalimoto amene apita kutali" ("Again and again this happens on all Car journeys that go far").[101] The Ulere system, which gained popularity after World War II, was designed to encourage migration to Southern Rhodesia and "increase labor efficiency" by cutting down the time and risk associated with migrant travel.[102] However, Scott notes that since the Ulere service was free and did not require its users to commit to working for a particular employer, some migrants "abused" it for illegal migration to South Africa.[103] At first glance, "Kwelani Galimoto Wa Ulere" appears to be an advertisement for the Ulere system, especially since its title uses the imperative tense. The story's structure and narrative mode, however, invite a more subversive reading. Mala's narrator recounts that he and others began their journey in Fort Jameson, Northern Rhodesia—one of Southern Rhodesia's few remaining sources of migrant labor in Northern Rhodesia—and were heading to Lusaka, where they would then catch a train to Harare (Salisbury).[104] The migrants' eventual arrival in Harare is planned, but by no means assured, and the narrative ends in medias res, with the journey ongoing. In this way, "Kwelani Galimoto Wa Ulere" evokes what Anusa Daimon describes as Nyasa migrants' practice of "settling in motion," a form of resistance to the routes and destinations prescribed by colonial authorities that involved entering Southern Rhodesia from the north or east and making their way south, where they entered South Africa illegally.[105] To assert their right to mobility, Nyasa migrants employed "social networks, bribes, theft, forgery, and manipulation of the Rhodesian labour recruitment infrastructure."[106] Mala's narrative does not directly refer to such practices, but by remaining focused on the journey and deferring the migrants' arrival, the narrative itself settles in motion. Read in this way, the narrative is far more than mere propaganda for Ulere: it points to the possibility that migrancy can be a resistant state of being.

Serialized stories—a perennial favorite in *Parade*, as opposed to the *Drum* editorial team's general preference for contained short fiction—served as another means of capturing long journeys and the ongoing quality of Central African experiences of migration. Frequently structured by border crossing—within the federation and beyond—these narratives mapped Central Africa in relation to the broader region and the African continent. In particular, many of these serialized adventure stories captured the allure and danger of international journeys outside the federation, which many migrants pursued against the wishes of federal authorities.[107] Migrants—or figures linked to migrancy—were often the protagonists of such narratives. In "A Race with Chance" by Mtandi Pambana, which began serialization in November 1954, two men from Southern Rhodesia smuggle wholesale liquor over the border from Portuguese East Africa (PEA), today's Mozambique, into Southern Rhodesia. Although George and Tasiya, whose name means "we have left," are not migrants, the story situates their escapades along regional migrant routes, both sanctioned and unsanctioned.

Arriving at the train station in Umtali, Southern Rhodesia, George and Tasiya find themselves in a crowd of people awaiting the train to Salisbury, where most Central African migrants would be heading. Avoiding eye contact with the African police officer who is watching them, George and Tasiya instead board a train to Beira in PEA in the company of Nyasa migrant workers returning home. Migrant workers from Nyasaland often crossed the border into Mozambique in order to enter South Africa illegally.[108] Although George and Tasiya are engaged in a different type of journey, theirs also involves skirting border authorities. They jump off the train to cries of "Hey, *wena*"—"Hey, you" in Ndebele—from the stationmaster and walk to their destination to avoid needing a pass to enter PEA.[109] The rest of the narrative recounts their harrowing journey to evade the border watchmen and bring their illegal goods back into Southern Rhodesia. In the end, George vows to find another way to make money in the future: "After all a diesel engine driver is not yet a surplus on the labor market."[110] Though the story suggests a return to legal modes of employment, the bulk of the story's excitement derives from the prospect of earning a large sum of money through illegal border crossing via routes that overlap directly with clandestine migrant routes. In stories such as this one, the migrant emerges as a dangerous and subversive figure, much like the *tsotsi* in *Drum*. This trend of conflating the migrant and the more cosmopolitan *tsotsi* is particularly evident in *Parade*'s crime fiction, which I address in the next section.

Parade's migrant forms are also remarkable for the way they textualized this constant regional travel: in these pieces, writing itself is envisioned as both a product of motion and a means of "making the journey known." In many stories, this textualization was achieved through actual or symbolic use of the letter as a form, echoing the magazine's display of its own travels—real and imagined—through its many letters from readers. The letter was a quintessential migrant genre in that it was often the only means by which migrants could communicate with family at home in rural areas and with other migrants who had traveled ahead of them. Letters were a key part of Nyasa migrants' "strong transnational social networks," providing them with instructions on how to navigate the journey south (including how and where to cross borders), the location of police stations, and the wages to expect in particular locations.[111] However, letters could also be incriminating, serving as proof of the migrant's intention to find work in South Africa. In a number of narratives in *Parade*, letters are presented as evidence that someone is watching and recording what happens on a journey, providing both a warning and a subtle clue to those who would travel. These letters also tapped into the magazine's diasporic imaginary in their resemblance to the "Talking Book," which Henry Louis Gates identifies as the "ur-trope" in African American fiction.[112] Like the talking book, the talking letter is presented as magical and inaccessible to the illiterate and is repeated and "signified upon" in various ways throughout the magazine. In *Parade*, however, the letter is most immediately associated with telling what has happened on a particular journey. The letter as a migrant form is thus another example of *Parade*'s mobile adaptation of a trope that appears in various iterations across the African diaspora.[113]

One story that uses the letter in this way appeared in *Parade* several times in different guises, suggesting its relevance and appeal to readers. "Kasumbalala and the Letter" by M. N. Manduli of Lusaka was published in *Parade*'s first issue in November 1953 in both English and Nyanja, the former in Is It Fact or Fiction? and the latter on the Nyanja page.[114] Readers familiar with Zambian folktales have the advantage of knowing that the protagonist's name, Kasumbalala, likely refers to the "mischievous moth," a small creature whose "wickedness" brings misfortune to those around him.[115] The story begins by explaining that "[w]hen whitemen [*sic*] first came to Kasumbalala's area nobody knew anything about writing or reading" ("Pamene Azungu anafika ku Kasumbalala kunalibe munthu amene anadziwa kulemba kapena kuwerenga").[116] Therefore, when Kasumbalala is sent by one white man to deliver some loaves of bread and a letter to another white man, he is shocked to be caught having eaten one loaf on the journey and wonders how the letter was able to tell on him. The next time, Kasumbalala hides the letter under a rock so that it will not see him eating some of the oranges he is delivering, but still the white man knows after reading the letter that two are missing. In each instance, the written word or text, represented by the letter, is personified; it is imagined as observing and recording the journey's events along the way to relate them later. Finally, Kasumbalala beats the letter to try to prevent it from reporting his actions, to no avail. In the end, he still does not understand how the letter works but decides that he must try to "be like the letter so that his words would also always be true and trusted."[117] The Nyanja version specifies that to be "monga kalata," or "like the letter," means to "akhale wokhulupirika": to "remain trustworthy."[118] In these first iterations of the story, Kasumbalala does not conceive that he too might learn to read and write. He also does not understand that the letter is fixed before he sets out on his journey; instead, he imagines that it is constructing a tale about the journey during the journey itself—in other words, that the writing takes place in motion.

These first versions of the story in both English and Nyanja appear to be purely didactic, meant to teach new readers that writing carries a stable, unchanging truth. This story changed, however, as it traveled through its subsequent translation, giving credence to Kasumbalala's perception that writing is a product of motion. A Nyanja iteration of this story by I. J. Bwelezani appeared in *Parade* in April 1955 with the title "Kanthu Konama," or "A Small Thing That Lies." Like many Nyanja fables, "Kanthu Konama" plays with language, and both the author's name and the story's title are particularly suggestive. Bwelezani, a command, means "repeat," which hints that the writer is using a pen name to draw attention to the fact that the story is a familiar tale being retold. The story's title is equally ambiguous, for the "small thing that lies," or "little liar," could refer to either the protagonist—a young boy who remains unnamed—or to the letter and likely is meant to refer to both. Whereas the mischief of "saying lies" is associated only with the boy in the story's earlier version, in this one the letter is also capable of inventing what happens on the journey. By self-consciously repeating this narrative with a small difference, Bwelezani's story engages in a mobile adaptation of the tale's previous versions, presenting the letter as a form of reading and writing in motion with subversive possibilities.

Bwelezani's lengthier retelling also gives the boy some interiority and motivation. He eats the oranges because "[u]lendo woyamba mtumikiyo anayamba kufa ndi njara pa njira" ("on the first journey this messenger started to die of hunger on the way").[119] After the story's protagonist realizes that it is the letter that is telling the white man "zimene ankacita pa njira" ("what he was doing on the way"), he hides it under a rock and begins to "kunyoza," or "insult" it, saying, "Lero ndakagwira maso sikakanena bodza kanthu kaja" ("Today I went and held its eyes, it won't go and say lies that little thing").[120] As the story's title suggests, the letter is thought to be capable of this kind of deception, or, in other words, of manipulating and constructing what has happened on the journey. Unlike in the previous version of the fable, the protagonist of this story does not reform in the end. Instead, he suffers real consequences for his actions; his boss gives him ten lashes for the ten missing oranges. This story points to the letter's power to recount what has happened on a journey. Further, the conflation of the boy and the letter, both small things that lie, suggests that the boy too might learn to harness the power of the written word to tell stories about what happened "on the way." Indeed, this is what many migrants did as they wrote and received letters revealing valuable information about the journey south.

It is fitting that on the same page as this story, a narrative by K. Billiard Mtima emphasizes the importance of using writing to convey what one has experienced on a journey. In the text "Kuceza Kwanga Ku Rhodesia," or "My Visit to Rhodesia," which is not titled to indicate whether it is a fictional story, a man describes his trip to Rhodesia to see his son, who is the head teacher at a mine in Southern Rhodesia. Mtima begins his story with the precise details of his journey: "Ndinanyamuka pa 6 December 1954 ndipo ndinafika pa malo ace a nchito 10 December 1954. Ulendo wanga unayenda bwino kwambiri. Malo onse obvuta kwambiri monga Dondo onsewo ndinapyola bwino" ("I left on 6 December 1954 and I arrived at his place of employment on 10 December 1954. My journey went very well. All of the very difficult places like Dondo I passed through well").[121] Dondo Junction in Portuguese East Africa was known for its police presence and rigorous checking of passes for migrants.[122] These detailed instructions, which include an estimate of how long the journey might take, served as a potential guide for other migrants. Indeed, the fact that he is writing for people at home in Nyasaland, who have not yet traveled outside the territory, is underscored at the story's end:

> Cacikulu cimene cinandikondweletsa ndi nzeru imene mwana wanga anandipatsa yakuti ndizilembela makalata ku anthu a nyuzi. Mwa ici candikondweletsa ine kuti ndikudziwitseni anzanganu amene mukhala osaonako ku maiko ena akutali.
>
> The main thing that made me happy was the wisdom that my son gave me to write these things in letters to the newspaper people. It has pleased me to inform you my friends, who stay without seeing other far away countries.[123]

The narrative ends self-reflexively by using the structure of a traditional fable, which usually concludes with a moral or lesson. What the writer gains from his journey is the knowledge that he should write about his travels to educate others—knowledge of which the text in front of us is a product. Unlike the stories discussed above, in which the literate reader understands how writing works while the characters do not, here the protagonist has transformed from a reader who once read the newspaper into someone who now writes for it. That *Parade*'s readers should also aspire to be writers is another moral of this story. In fact, *Parade*'s readers contributed in increasing numbers to the magazine and, by 1956, the subtitle of the feature Is It Fact or Fiction?: Short Stories by African Writers was amended to Short Stories by Our Readers.

In this and other stories in the magazine, travel between urban and rural areas was encouraged to maintain the bonds between families in rural areas (often parents and grandparents) and their children who had left Nyasaland to work.[124] Mtima's story points to the fact that many Nyasa migrants, who were often better educated than their Rhodesian counterparts, aimed to settle in Southern Rhodesia permanently, despite increasingly stringent labor policies, such as the 1958 Foreign Migratory Labor Act (FMLA), that made interterritorial migration relatively difficult.[125] "Kuceza Kwanga Ku Rhodesia" also highlights the diversity of the workers on the mines, who hailed from various regions and tribes but were united in their Christian faith. While Southern Rhodesian labor policies were intended to separate migrants along the lines of education, ethnicity, home territory, and length of stay, this story reflects the sometimes-subtle ways *Parade*'s migrant forms advocated for a shared Central African identity within the federation.[126] It also shows how labor migration can produce worldly subjectivities that are usually attributed to more cosmopolitan forms of travel.

The letter as a migrant form reappears in various guises in *Parade* and beyond, demonstrating the lasting impact of the magazine on the region's literature. In addition to the fables and readers' narratives discussed above, the letter features centrally in serialized fictions such as Fwanyanga M. Mulikita's "Human Caterpillars Were Eating Away the Leaves of His Family," published in *Parade* from May to December 1954, and in recent novels like Malawian Joyce Jaffu's 2007 *Kalata Yochokera Ku Joni*, or *A Letter from Joburg*.[127] Set in a village in Barotseland in Western Zambia, Mulikita's story portrays a family's grief and confusion about the death of their son on the Copperbelt, which is conveyed to them in a much-debated letter from European authorities. Mulikita went on to become one of Zambia's most prominent short-story writers, and "Human Caterpillars" was republished in his seminal 1968 collection *A Point of No Return*. Similarly, in Jaffu's narrative, which might be described as a short, didactic novel or novella, a letter is the means by which a woman learns that her husband, who has gone to work in the mines in Johannesburg, has married a South African woman and will not be returning to Malawi. While these narratives were published more than fifty years apart, they both feature the letter as a form that signifies the migrant's journey and in particular the ongoing impact of regional migration on Central Africans. These texts are emblematic of the ways such migrant forms continue to cross generic, linguistic, and spatial borders and to present migration as a fundamentally modern condition.

REFIGURING THE *TSOTSI: AFRICAN PARADE*'S MIGRATORY CRIME FICTION

Migration was also a key thematic and formal feature of *Parade*'s crime fiction. In particular, the issue of migration entered the genre through the figure of the South African gangster. When the *tsotsi* appeared in Central African crime fiction, he no longer symbolized a politicized style or form of resistance as he did in *Drum*, but was refigured as a foreigner, as the continued use of the original South African term *tsotsi* emphasized. Relocating the South African gangster in Central Africa was thus another form of mobile adaptation: a translation and reversal of the dynamics between the two central archetypes in *Drum*'s fiction. Whereas *Drum* sublimated the migrant figure to affirm the fundamentally urban character of modern Africans, *Parade*'s crime fiction engaged in a similar "rerouting" of the *tsotsi*. No longer glamorous, the *tsotsi* was inscribed as a hopeless criminal without style or mobility, opening the possibility for the modern Central African man to gain social mobility and stylishness in his place.

The generic convention of the foreign villain is not uncommon in crime fiction from around the globe.[128] In fact, it was one of the genre's earliest features. However, while there is often some correlation between the predominance of certain "Others" as fictional villains and an actual increase in immigration or crime[129]—leading, for example, to fears of "reverse colonization" in late nineteenth-century British gothic and mystery novels[130]—in southern Africa, there is little evidence of the mass migration of Black South Africans to the territories farther north.[131] Rather, the *tsotsi* in *Parade*'s crime fiction indexes the general perception—echoed elsewhere in the magazine—of urban South Africa as at once more "advanced" and more violent and morally degraded than the federation.[132] As an archetype, the *tsotsi* was uniquely able to capture this paradoxical vision of South African culture: his enviable style and urban sophistication represented the allure of modern cities like Johannesburg, while his ruthlessness and violence, often exercised against other Africans and against migrants in particular, pointed to its dangers. Many of *Parade*'s stories, particularly those of the Jim Comes to Joburg genre, expressed the fear that migrants who spent time in South Africa's cities would bring urban vices and criminal tendencies home with them and can be read as an effort to dissuade Central African migrants from seeking work in South Africa—thus keeping their labor in the federation. In Central African crime fiction, anxiety over social and cultural disintegration as a result of the migrant labor system ultimately manifests as the fear of a *tsotsi* "reverse migration," against which Central Africa, as a national space, must defend itself.

In its efforts to teach readers that "crime does not pay" while also entertaining them, *Parade*'s early crime fiction adopted aspects of the hard-boiled detective fiction that was ubiquitous in *Drum*, combining it with elements from the Jim Comes to Joburg stories.[133] Formally, many of *Parade*'s crime stories inverted the basic template of the Jim tale in order to valorize the local hero and punish the South African gangsters who had come to the federation to prey on its citizens. In *Parade*'s first crime serial, "The Man with Missing Fingers" by K. A. Zizi (November 1953–March 1954), the story's average but hardworking hero Joe is duped into gambling away his new leather jacket to a *tsotsi* named "Benoni Billy," whose name links him to a notoriously rough area outside Johannesburg. In this way, the story evokes the familiar scenario in which the unassuming migrant is victimized by *tsotsis*, "who always spoke and boasted so loudly, [and] were mostly the people who gambled."[134] The story, however, gives Joe the opportunity to avenge himself. When Joe returns with his friend Samuel to demand that Benoni Billy return his jacket, they find the latter dead with a knife in his back and see a man with three missing fingers driving away from the Wellfit clothing factory where Billy worked. While tracking the gangsters, Joe and Samuel find themselves in a nearby village where everyone is drinking skokiaan, or home-brewed liquor. The police arrive, and Joe and Samuel are arrested along with the others since "the law says that anyone found near a skokiaan drink is guilty of a crime."[135] Through this element of the plot, "Missing Fingers" points to another classic city vice in the Jim stories: illegal drinking. It was through such minor offences that most Africans encountered the police in southern Africa.[136]

Zizi's story, however, reconfigures the Jim narrative to turn its protagonists from helpless, accidental criminals—as migrants were so often portrayed in *Drum*—into upstanding citizens who assist the police in fighting crime. On their way to the jail, the police van collides with the gang's lorry, spilling the prisoners onto the road. Joe takes this opportunity to explain the situation to one of the European policemen, who "listened carefully, and said 'I think this man is telling the truth.'"[137] Like many stories in *Parade*'s early years, this story gestures toward the importance of interracial cooperation, clearly modeling federal propaganda for partnership. However, from this point forward, Joe asserts his authority and commands the police investigation, sitting in the front seat of the van and giving directions to the European policeman who is driving—a subtle reversal of the frequent depiction of partnership as European led. The police follow the tracks of the gang's van to a river but are stumped when the tire marks do not continue out onto the opposite bank. Joe, seeing "a dull reflection from the downstream direction," realizes that the lorry is parked in the river and, in the chase that ensues, eventually nabs "Missing Fingers" with Samuel's help.[138] In the end, all the members of the gang are found guilty—thanks to their fingerprints, no less—and are sentenced to death. The police inform the owner of the factory of Joe's role in capturing the thieves and, as "a mark of esteem," Joe is rewarded with "a brand new suit of clothes."[139] Joe is no longer the victimized migrant of the Jim genre; his brand-new clothes signify his new status as a valued member of the community.

In this and other stories published in the early years of *Parade*, social status—and style—are gained by assisting law enforcement rather than by becoming a tsotsi, as in *Drum*. In contrast to Maimane's Detective Morena, who exemplified the vigilante figure of the hard-boiled genre, Joe is a model of partnership and good citizenship. Though paternalistic, stories like "Missing Fingers" signal *Parade*'s efforts to use the colonial federation to stake a claim to African belonging in a multiracial society by becoming part of the state apparatus. It seems no accident that the issue containing the conclusion of "Missing Fingers" also features an article encouraging Africans to join the Southern Rhodesia Police Force, which includes statements from decorated African police sergeants testifying to the "good pay, good conditions and the varied experiences" police work offers and emphasizing that the police are "always smart in their appearance."[140] In general, style in *Parade* was associated with law-abiding consumerism, whereas in *Drum* the *tsotsi*'s style supposedly circumvented the capitalist system that underwrote and sustained South African inequality.[141] Another *Parade* article, "The Man about Town," describes the "true representative of the African race in Southern Africa" as "a man who makes no bones about the fact that money is to spend on the good things of life—a man who believes that life must be lived and enjoyed."[142] Money was to be earned and spent, not stolen or extorted. Similarly, reading about crime—rather than engaging in it—was presented in *Parade* as the ideal pastime of the modern gentleman.[143]

Beginning in the 1960s, however, when the ruse of partnership was no longer tenable, *Parade*'s crime fiction began to look much more like *Drum*'s, with an emphasis on the "intelligent gangster," a vigilante who worked alone rather than with the police. Spink, the protagonist of *Parade*'s serialized crime story "Death of the Stranger" by Rudolph P. Chanda, published from February through May 1961, is described alternately as an "intelligent gangster" and a "gentleman gangster." The story thus retains aspects of *Parade*'s earlier crime stories in that Spink, like Joe, is shown to be an upstanding citizen. Spink nevertheless resembles the *tsotsi* of *Drum*'s fiction in his ability to move across categories: although he is part of a gang of ex-convicts, he has a degree in science, speaks English "like a University professor," refuses to smoke dagga (marijuana), and is a dedicated family man with "a beautiful South African–born wife."[144] As a native South African "brought up in the notorious back allays [*sic*] of Orlando," Stella lends her husband gangster credibility and a cosmopolitan aura: "She did not squirm at the profession of her husband. If anything, she rather admired him as she would admire a film actor."[145] In other articles in the magazine, it was suggested that South African women were desirable mates for Central African men because they were often more educated than their Central African counterparts.[146] In fact, Spink and his wife Stella met as "pen friends"—members of a letter-writing forum that was popular among *Parade*'s male readers, particularly those who wanted to contact women from South Africa. This detail encouraged readers to identify with the educated and handsome Spink and shows the fluidity and mutability of the migrant forms in the magazine.

While Spink assumes the glamour associated with the gangster figure in *Drum*, the South African *tsotsis* in the story are depicted as brutal and thuggish. "Snatchy," Stella's "homeboy" who also hails from Orlando, wears the evidence of his South African upbringing and experience on his body: a large scar on his neck marks the time someone "tried to lynch him, so the story went . . . when he had double-crossed them in a Jo'burg stick-up job."[147] This detail is reminiscent of *Drum*'s portrayal of foreign migrants like Shigumbu, who bear the marks of their foreignness and insidious criminality on their bodies. Further, as its title suggests, the story's events are set in motion by the death of a "stranger," the leader of a rival gang, at the hands of one of Spink's men. Although we are never certain of the stranger's origins, his foreignness is implied. In this way, a complex picture emerges of the relationship between local gangsters and foreign *tsotsis*, who vie for control of the territory as well as for women. Stella, for example, is kidnapped by Snatchy, who tries to take her back home—a symbolic reappropriation of a woman who was "stolen" from the Union of South Africa by Spink. However, it is Spink who, using his "gangster instincts," is victorious in the end. Ultimately, "Death of the Stranger" restages the death of the migrant in *Drum*, but instead of making way for the *tsotsi*, it replaces the migrant with another figure: the Central African "gentleman gangster." While the *tsotsis* in *Parade* were restricted to the same kinds of reductive portrayals and well-worn routes that confined the migrant in *Drum*, *Parade*'s new gangster was modern, stylish, and worldly.

The influence of *Parade*'s crime stories on later crime fiction from the region is evident in G. H. Shonga and J. N. Zulu's *Matsotsi*, or *Gangsters*, published by the Zambian Publications Bureau in 1963. Told in three separate parts from different points of view, this difficult-to-categorize text chronicles the adventures of an Angolan detective working for the South African police force in Johannesburg, where he helps to contain the *tsotsi* menace and prevent it from spreading farther north. Like many of the crime stories in *Parade, Matsotsi* depicts the gangster as a social pariah linked specifically to South Africa:

> Matsotsi asiyana ndi ngwazi zimene zimenya nkhondo yofuna kutenga ufulu wa dziko lao m'manja mwa atsamunda. Kwao ndi kufuna kusakaza miyoyo ya anthu anzao pakufuna kutolapo phindu la iwo okha panthawi yocepa. Kwathu kuno matsotsi kulibe, komatu tikapusa, mtsogolomu adzawanda cifukwa dziko likutukuka. Motero tiyeni tikhale maso! Angatilowere.

> Tsotsis are different from the heroes who are fighting the war to free their nation from the hands of the colonialists. There they want to destroy the lives of their fellows to make quick money. Here at home there are no tsotsis, but if we are not watchful they may soon become plentiful because the country is developing. So let us keep our eyes open! They may invade us.[148]

Matsotsi turns the *tsotsi* from a cosmopolitan figure of aesthetic and political resistance, as he has often been read by critics of *Drum*, into a petty thief who preys on other Africans and on migrants in particular. Further, the fear of a *tsotsi* invasion is directly linked to the migrant labor system through the phrase "let us keep our eyes open," which is repeated at the moment of Detective Balala's arrival at Johannesburg's crowded train station, a place called "Keep Your Eyes Open" by Zambians and Malawians as a warning to fellow migrants to stay vigilant against *tsotsi* thieves. *Matsotsi* demonstrates that Central African crime fiction continued to be marked by a concern with regional dynamics, and the issue of migration specifically, even as the federation was dissolving in 1963. This feature of the genre can be traced to *Parade*.[149]

I have argued here that *Parade*'s migrant forms engaged in a particular kind of literary, cultural, and linguistic translation through its constantly evolving, mobile adaptation of various fiction and nonfiction genres that were popular in *Drum*. This reading reveals subtle overlaps and distinctions between the literary traditions of South Africa and the former Central African Federation; those of the latter are too often ignored in critical treatments of the region or treated as appendages of South African literature. By reading these forms in motion, with an eye to both their proximity and distance, we can see that while the South African genres described above remained more narrowly focused on life within South Africa, and particularly its major cities, similar genres in *Parade* depicted an image of African modernity based on mobility. *Parade*'s migrant forms appeared in various guises and moved across generic boundaries, incorporating elements from a plethora of genres, including oral migrant tales, letters, Jim Comes to Joburg stories, and crime fiction. While each iteration discussed here deals with migration and transnationalism thematically, these issues were also embedded as formal features of the texts, particularly through various manipulations of the migrant and the *tsotsi* as archetypes and in the use of processes of continuous migration to structure a variety of narratives. These texts were products of movement: of both the enduring reality of migrant labor in Central Africa and the movement of literary forms across space, genre, and language. They also produced a particular idea of unfettered regional mobility that continues to inflect contemporary literature.

This is an auspicious moment to consider *Parade*, for now, as in the 1950s and early 1960s, "the continent and its regions, rather than singular nations, are the theatres of problem-identification, reaction, and aspirations."[150] These continental and regional affiliations have not always been visible in recent literary criticism. By excavating older genres, such as those in *Parade*, we can recognize the many forms and geographies of African literary migration. These are forms that are being recuperated and remobilized today by South African literary projects like the *Chimurenga Chronic*, discussed in chapter 4. A self-described "time travelling-machine," the *Chronic* archives, performs, and otherwise engages with older print forms like those discussed here in order to redeploy the complex geographies they imagined. While *Drum* elided much of the region of southern Africa in its pursuit of a modern African identity, the *Chronic* and similar publications have reimagined the relationship between South Africa and the African continent through renewed attention to regional and global migration.

CHAPTER 2

Township Tales

From Here to Yonder to Lusaka after Dark

Since 1991, Malawian writer Lawrence Kadzitche has published a column featuring a character named Katakwe, which in Chichewa means a "clever" or "wise person."[1] As is often the case for the classic trickster figure, Katakwe's cleverness frequently gets the better of him, leading him into a variety of compromising situations with women, witch doctors, and preachers, among many others.[2] In one such story, "Mgodi Uvuta" ("Mine of Trouble"), set in Chingwirizano, a township or urban location on the outskirts of Malawi's capital, Katakwe's wife catches him doling out drinks and money to prostitutes at a local bar. On the surface, a column so firmly rooted in the Malawian milieu would seem to have a limited ability to articulate broader communities. But when we look more closely, we can see that such local spaces often reveal their entanglement with regional and global affiliations and power dynamics. When Katakwe enters the bar in Chingwirizano, a woman named Yaliyali, "a prostitute who knew how to take advantage of men" ("hule lodziwa kudyera amuna"), approaches him and says, "A Walodi Banki, lero mukuti bwanji?" ("World Bank, what are you saying today?").[3] "Walodi Banki" is a transliteration of "World Bank," and we learn that Katakwe has been given this nickname because he grants generous "loans" in the form of alcohol and money to the prostitutes who work the bar. "Zakumwa ndi *your choice*. Tafika ife a mponda matambala" ("Drinks are *your choice*. We have arrived, we who walk on money"),

Katakwe tells her. In other words, the rich man is here. The woman rolls her eyes at Katakwe, but he persists: "Ifetu timapereka *ten times the usual charge*" ("We are granting *ten times the usual charge*"). Even though he has a wife and five hungry children at home, Katakwe offers the woman many times what she usually charges for her services. When Katakwe's wife finally arrives, Yaliyali mistakes her for the competition, telling her, this mine is *mine*.

The story's language illuminates the local township's embeddedness in regional and global political economies and imaginaries. Since the late 1800s, Malawi has served as a labor reserve for the mines and other industries in South Africa, where men who were away from their families for long periods sometimes engaged in extramarital relationships. This history is reflected in the Chichewa word for prostitute, *hule*, which is derived from the South African Afrikaans word *hoer*.[4] Katakwe's speech is also full of English phrases that evoke capitalist consumerism and Western donorspeak—an effort to signal his worldliness and power to the women. The story's extended play on Katakwe as the World Bank refers to the fact that Malawi, which is ranked as one of the world's poorest countries, has accepted a great deal of funding from the international organization. The World Bank, which emerged as part of the new global financial system following the Second World War, was the Central African Federation's largest foreign investor in the 1950s, providing loans for (highly contentious) projects and the implementation of legislation such as the Native Land Husbandry Act, which extended Western ownership practices to land in the African reserves.[5] Projects like these were pursued under the guise of "development," but they ultimately served to make the federation more profitable—providing white settlers with a means of justifying its continued utility to Britain, which was under increasing pressure to decolonize.[6] Today, the World Bank continues to be viewed very unfavorably by many Malawians, who blame the IMF and the World Bank for turning the country's 2001–2002 food shortage into a full-on famine by requiring Malawi to sell off its grain reserves. Through the character of Katakwe, Kadzitche cleverly critiques the Malawian government's policy of accepting aid that often lined the pockets of politicians and their supporters and left average Malawians in poverty, just like Katakwe's neglected family.

Serialized, character-driven narratives like Katakwe have been published in magazines and newspapers around the globe, from "The Owl" in the Gold Coast's *Western Echo* in the late 1800s to Langston Hughes's Here to Yonder column in the *Chicago Defender*.[7] In southern

Africa, early iterations include R. R. R. Dhlomo's "R. Roamer Esq.," published in the *Bantu World* in the 1930s,[8] and Lawrence Vambe's "Magaisa IBenzi," or "The Eccentric Magaisa," which appeared in the 1950s in Cizezuru in the *African Weekly*.[9] These humorous columns and cartoons revolved around the escapades of an "average" man—these characters were distinctly male—who represented the foibles, plights, and small victories of the larger population. Reflecting on "The Eccentric Magaisa," Vambe suggests that Magaisa was "a character through whom I was able to tell my people some unpleasant truths about themselves, which they would not otherwise have stomached."[10] Such columns were often rooted in particular urban locations and have been read as a way for writers to critique their immediate social and political environments.

While these narratives have played an important role in expressing local realities, my argument here is that they also articulate national, regional, global, and even interplanetary identifications. I refer to these columns as "township tales" because they are set in townships: peri-urban areas on the edges of white metropolises. In southern Africa, townships were designed to regulate Africans' physical and social mobility, but their proximity to colonial cities, which relied on the controlled influx of African labor, meant that these were spaces defined by movement, permeability, and the constant negotiation between "here" and "yonder," as Hughes put it. The township tale is equally liminal in terms of its language and form, combining fictional elements with reportage and making use of the resources of print as well as the oral tradition. The "tale," a form that straddles print and orality, is thus a fitting name for this type of column.[11] One of the central formal features of the township tale is the humorous speech of the protagonist, who mixes colloquial language, foreign slang, and his own neologisms to comment iteratively on local, national, and global events, in this way continually imagining and reimagining the relationship between his location and various elsewheres. These flawed heroes do not have a clear or predicable character arc; instead, they thrive in the medium of the periodical because of its cyclicality and repetition. Month after month and year after year, these township tales presented rich, sometimes contradictory identities and affiliations, from a localized nationalism to an emergent futurism that imagined transcending the earth's color line by traveling into outer space.

There are many examples of the township tale from southern Africa. In this chapter, I examine a particular chain of adaptations by writers in the Cold War period who made no secret of being influenced by one another's work and whose columns address interlinked aspects of the post–World War II world order, including colonialism and neocolonialism, white supremacy, and global capitalism. Beginning with Langston Hughes's Here to Yonder column, first published during World War II in 1942, I track the form of the township tale as it circumnavigated the globe in the 1950s and early 1960s. Hughes's protagonist, Simple, is an average working-class Harlemite who, like Katakwe, enjoys boozing and womanizing. Simple voices—in slangy, commonsense language—a Black nationalist perspective that stands in contrast to the more cosmopolitan Hughes. The Simple stories pointed to the hypocrisy of fighting Nazism abroad while continuing to support segregation at home,[12] and their blend of localism, nationalism, cosmopolitanism, and futurism—displayed in Simple's flights of fancy into outer space—was highly suggestive to many southern African writers and readers, so much so that sixteen of Hughes's Simple stories were published in South Africa's *Africa!* magazine in the mid-1950s. Casey Motsisi, the subeditor of *Africa!*, was inspired by the Simple stories to write a similar column for *Drum* magazine called On the Beat, set in Black urban Johannesburg. Although Motsisi's column has received a good deal of critical attention, I include it here as an important link between Hughes and other writers from the region, who have been omitted from critical considerations of Hughes's "Afro-planetary vision."[13] Motsisi exposed the contradictions of apartheid and the global order that sustained it through references to impeded forms of local mobility as well as to the space race between the United States and Russia. Inspired by both Hughes and Motsisi, columns by two Southern Rhodesian writers in the late 1950s, Bill Saidi's Bits and Pieces from Harare and Daniel Dlamanzi's Makokoba Park Talk, depict travel by bus, car, and rocket ship. Against the backdrop of an intensifying Cold War, these columns, both of which were published in *African Parade*, express a clear allegiance to capitalism and a relatively positive view of the United States in line with *Parade*'s general perspective. (There is no evidence, however, that the magazine was funded by the CIA-backed Congress for Cultural Freedom [CCF], as many "small magazines" on the continent were.[14]) The final related column I consider is Saidi's Lusaka after Dark, which he wrote after moving to Zambia in the early 1960s. In this column, Saidi captured racial, class, and gender divisions on the eve of independence, turning toward internal rather than external impediments to the new state.

Mapping the township tale as it traveled from Harlem to Lusaka affords the rare opportunity to observe a microcosm of generic development as it unfolded from one urban periphery to the next. By reading in motion, we can see how these columns traveled across time and space and between publications, revealing striking similarities and important differences in the ways writers adapted this form to various political and social contexts. Such a reading illuminates the layered, overlapping affiliations that are often elided by approaches to literary travel and adaptation that rely on a clear distinction between "foreign"—read "global"—literature on the one hand, and local or national literatures on the other. This distinction underpins Franco Moretti's hypothesis that literary evolution results from a "compromise" between "foreign form" and "local materials" and David Damrosch's assertion that world literature must travel outside its culture of origin.[15] But how far does literature need to travel to be considered worldly? While textual circulation between neighboring European countries with distinct languages and literary traditions certainly grants a text the status of world literature in models such as Damrosch's, why does the same type of travel usually fail to qualify in African contexts? Nontraditional periodical forms like the township tale that traveled widely via periodical publications complicate approaches to textual travel like Moretti's and Damrosch's and demonstrate how difficult it is to differentiate "here" from "yonder" in closely related but distinct regional environments. In Lusaka after Dark, for example, Saidi reads the Zambian capital through the lens of Harare township, whose image is filtered through a fictionalized Johannesburg, itself based on an imagined Harlem, revealing a palimpsestic spatial imaginary.

While these columns traveled swiftly across the region and globe, they also explored mobility, or a lack thereof, in the townships themselves. Through various representations of travel—by foot, bus, car, and rocket ship—writers negotiated the township's relationship to broader geographies and critiqued colonialism and racism. In the colonial period, African townships were designed to optimize white control of a Black, largely male underclass through a complex system of restrictions on Africans' physical and social movement.[16] This system included pass laws that regulated travel to and within urban areas as well as laws that dictated everything from the types of houses available to residents to the beer they could drink. With increased demands for African labor after World War II, townships in southern Africa grew until they were bursting at the seams, straining their already inadequate infrastructure. In many of the township tales considered here, writers articulate their frustrations with various impediments to local mobility, from the requirement to carry a pass to the lack of adequate bus services. This absence of basic services, from lights to buses to pubs, was also understood, particularly by a growing African middle class, as a barrier to social mobility, and even to modernity itself. In turn, Vambe, editor in chief of African Newspapers, which published *Parade*, suggests this predicament led to the growth of African nationalism in Southern Rhodesia's townships: "One soon realized how cosmopolitan the African residents of Harare were and what, in the long run, the economic, political and racial consequences of this imposed human order would likely be. . . . In other words, by creating a place like Harare for his immediate advantage, the white Rhodesian was inadvertently making a contribution to black unity and finally and conversely to the annihilation of this very wildly unbalanced way of life."[17] Given such conditions, it is no wonder that in many of these tales, the township is presented as the location of a micro- or localized nationalism, especially in places like South Africa and Southern Rhodesia, where intensifying state oppression was intended to quell broader nationalist movements.

This is not to say, however, that the townships in these columns are depicted only as "sites of struggle."[18] Motsisi, Saidi, and Dlamanzi declared their cosmopolitanism by filling their columns with references to global, and especially American, popular culture and imagining alternate forms of travel within and beyond the township, from driving Chevy cars to taking rocket ships to outer space. These writers embraced what Stephanie Newell describes as a "local cosmopolitanism," asserting their "entitlement—to imported fashions, to the English language, to an audience" at a moment when this gesture was seen as "illegitimate" and "out of place."[19] Through the work of these writers, the townships were figured not simply as abject spaces or romantic sites of resistance but as richly lived "places"—full of music, art, fashion, and literature—that exceeded the restrictions of the colonial state and where the line between collaborators and resisters was often blurred.[20]

Nevertheless, there is evidence in these columns of what Ian Baucom describes as "a weariness tinged with melancholy, a cosmopolitanism blasé by policy and for survival" that results from the township's simultaneous proximity and distance from the white metropolis next door.[21] In "the view from the township," Baucom locates global modernity itself: "the experience, the dialectic, of engaging such a capricious, illusory spectacle of desire from a weary/angry/hungry space of experience actively distanced *and* no longer distant from [it]."[22] In the Sophiatown writings of South African writer Can Themba, Baucom identifies not only "borrowed" depictions of global popular culture but a "township modernism" that steps behind the "curtain" of the modern spectacle.[23] While the township tales that I consider here might also be understood as modernist in their formal and linguistic experimentation and their depictions of a similar weariness and resignation, there are several key distinctions between township tales and township modernism. Not only was there a greater earnestness in the township tales' cosmopolitan representations, as described above, but the view from Hughes's, Motsisi's, Saidi's and Dlamanzi's townships extended much farther than "the gleam" of the neighboring white city.[24] Instead, by locating modernity itself in the cosmos, these writers pointed to the insufficiency of a single-world framework for capturing Black modern experiences, exhibiting what we might call a "township futurism."

Through this township futurism, the writers considered here signaled the limitations of "planetary humanism" for addressing race and racism.[25] The protagonists of each of these columns eventually decide that to find true equality they must leave the planet, setting out instead for the moon or even Mars. The township's peripherality therefore relates to another paradigmatically modern "distant" space: outer space. In most of these columns, outer space is evoked not as an "alternate destiny," as it would later be by Sun Ra,[26] but as a last resort, the leap to an extreme resignation and frustration resulting from the realization that "Black life is not lived in the world that the world lives in, but it is lived underground, in outer space."[27] These flights to space signify somewhat differently in each of these columns, ranging from Dlamanzi's vision of space as a heavenly retreat from Earth's low morals to Casey Motsisi's desire to be knocked unconscious and sent to the moon, which resembles what Ramzi Fawaz calls "an abandonment of the very idea of 'uplift' as such."[28] In several of these columns, references to rockets and the space race also serve as a means to critique neocolonialism or the limited role afforded to Africa in the Cold War.

Much like futurist literature in other contexts, these columns were characterized by their many contradictions, including their gender politics.[29] During the colonial period, the legislation that governed townships in South Africa and the Central African Federation was not only racially defined but gendered as well. Colonial officials viewed female migrants as corrupting and dangerous to the male migrant workers, who were expected to eventually return to their wives and children in rural areas. With the continued influx of women to the cities, however, the creation of a class of urban Africans was inevitable. Because women were so essential to the production of African urban and modern identities, they were variously apotheosized, stigmatized, and chastised by both colonial officials and their own menfolk, who were also concerned with managing women's social and physical mobility.[30] The male protagonists of these township tales closely monitor the changing identities of women, who come to signify the possibilities and perils of African nationalism, the benefits and dangers of modernization, the unique local identities of the townships in question, and even the need to escape to outer space.

FROM HERE TO YONDER TO SIMPLE IN *AFRICA!*

On November 21, 1942, Langston Hughes published his first Here to Yonder column in the *Chicago Defender*. In it, he explained his intention to use the column to connect global events—World War II, in particular—to the daily lives of the paper's working-class African American readership: "Things that happen away off yonder affect us here. The bombs that fall on some far-off Second Front in Asia rattle the dishes on your table in Chicago or New Orleans, cut down on your sugar, coffee, meat ration, and take the tires off your car. Right now Hitler is about to freeze your salary or your work, although his activities at the moment are centered around Stalingrad. But it is not so far from here to yonder."[31] Readers of the later Simple stories, collected in volumes such as *Simple Speaks His Mind* (1950), *Simple Takes a Wife* (1953), and *Simple Stakes a Claim* (1957), may be unaware of the global ambitions of the Here to Yonder column in which Simple made his debut, since these later volumes are more consistently set in Harlem. Travel and globality, however, were among the column's most essential features, and, as Donna Sullivan Harper points out, Hughes touted his ability to write it based on the fact that "for the last twenty years, half writer and half vagabond, I have travelled from here to yonder around the world and back again."[32] The setting of Hughes's *Defender* column reflected these wanderings: it ranged from New York, his home at the time, to the many places Hughes traveled and where news was being made: Chicago's clubs, riot-scarred California, Communist Russia, Mexico, and Japan. From these journeys, Hughes drew the conclusion that "Alabama and Africa have the same problems," or "Here is yonder, and yonder is here."[33] In other words, Hughes's aim was not just to bring global events to local readers but to collapse the distance between "here" and "over there"—to show the fundamental similarities and interconnections of global and local concerns.

As his column evolved, Hughes took this project one step further. More than simply encouraging a cosmopolitan awareness in his readers, Hughes troubled and reconceptualized this awareness, demonstrating the ways it failed to address issues of racism and racial inequality. Hughes accomplished this task by adding another voice to the column that could speak for "here," or the local reality of his readership. Three months into the column, Hughes introduced readers to his "Simple Minded Friend," an average, working-class man whom Hughes used initially as his counterpoint.[34] In informal, slang-infused speech, the Friend voiced what Hughes imagined to be the commonsense opinions of the "black masses," including potential objections to Hughes's more "educated" positions.[35] The Friend was immediately popular with readers and began to appear more and more frequently, gradually transforming into a fully rounded character known as Jesse B. Semple, or just Simple. Through the interplay between the narrator (initially Hughes and then an unnamed character sometimes called Boyd) and Simple, whom the former sometimes refers to as a "race man" and a "Negro nationalist," the Simple stories staged a dialectic between Black nationalist and cosmopolitan identities.

Throughout the early *Defender* columns, Simple resists any conflation of "here" and "yonder" that fails to account for race. In the first columns in which the Simple Minded Friend appears, he and Hughes debate African American participation in and support for World War II. Whereas Simple says, "I want to beat Jim Crow first. . . . Hitler's over yonder, and Jim Crow is here,"[36] Hughes argues that defeating fascism abroad is a means of fighting racism and segregation at home: "Even if [the army's] guns aren't aimed at the Klan. We can aim half way across the world and shoot the under-pinning out from under the Ku Kluxers right on."[37] In these conversations, Hughes expressed his belief—voiced in earlier propagandistic poetry—that Hitlerism both posed a genuine threat to the world and set the stage for a racial reckoning in America.[38] But despite efforts like the "Double V" campaign, or "victory over racism at home and abroad," racial progress stalled during the war.[39] The wartime boom, moreover, failed to bring Black Americans the same economic benefits enjoyed by whites.[40] Hughes used Simple to articulate the resulting frustration and disillusionment, which manifested in riots like the one in Harlem in 1943. In "Simple Looks for Justice," Simple powerfully demonstrates the hypocrisy of the "yonder is here" logic when he reverses its direction. Regarding his participation in the riots, which began after a white police officer shot a Black soldier in Harlem, Simple defends himself against the narrator's accusation that breaking store windows with bricks is no way to get justice, arguing, "That is the way the Allies are trying to get it, bombing the insides of Hamburg and breaking up everything in sight Over There!"[41] More than this, Simple argues that the windows are in fact *his* to break, given that Black labor and patronage has subsidized white property and prosperity since the time of slavery. In this and many other instances, Hughes employs Simple to demonstrate the limits of a global outlook that is not also antiracist. As Simple puts it succinctly: "These white folks are more scared of Negroes than they are of Hitler."[42]

As the latter story makes clear, Harlem was not just the setting for the Here to Yonder columns and the later Simple stories but a terrain for negotiating competing worldviews. Though not a township per se, Harlem shares the township's peripherality, as a space that is both part of and separate from New York City.[43] In this sense, Harlem gave spatial form to the larger Black experience in America: as Duke Ellington, Hughes's contemporary, put it, "We are something apart, yet an integral part."[44] Although Harlem was the center of Black cultural, literary, and political renaissance in the 1920s, by the 1940s, the effects of the Depression and ongoing segregation were clearly visible.[45] Simple's relationship to Harlem reflects this: it is a place of racial pride, protection, and resistance for Simple, but it is depicted without romanticization, particularly in the Here to Yonder columns.[46] In "Simple and Harlem," which was later anthologized as "A Toast to Harlem" in *Simple Speaks His Mind*, Simple emphasizes the sense of safety and belonging he feels in Harlem, which because "[i]t is full of Negroes" provides a measure of "protection" from "folks that don't like [him]."[47] While Simple celebrates the benefits of Harlem's "apartness" as a Black space, the foil reminds him of the negative implications of racial segregation, such as the fact that Simple, like most Black people in Harlem, does not own his home. Nevertheless, Simple feels a sense of ownership over Harlem's public spaces, which facilitated both social and physical mobility: the sidewalk, where one might strike up a conversation with the likes of Duke Ellington or Lena Horne, and the subway trains, which "Negroes is even running." Ending discrimination in subway and bus driver jobs was among the few gains made by Black political organizations in Harlem in the 1940s,[48] and Simple connects the freedom and mobility that the subway affords him—"it does not take all day to get downtown, neither are you Jim Crowed on the way"—with the way Black drivers fly through stations at ninety miles an hour as if saying, "White folks, look at me! This train is mine."

Simple's Harlem is connected to New York City, but it remains a distinct space, almost a "nation within a nation."[49] The cosmopolitan narrator takes issue with Simple's emphasis on Harlem as a space exclusively for Black people—specifically, his admission that he is glad white people are afraid to come to Harlem at night—telling him that he is talking "like a Negro nationalist" and espousing the kind of racial thinking that "causes wars." Undaunted, Simple says he "would not mind a war if [he] could win it," and that in such a case he would need Harlem, and his own window, from which to shoot. In a last plea for cosmopolitan neighborliness, the narrator insists that "[w]hat Harlem ought to hold out to the world is a friendly hand not a belligerent attitude." As he often does, Simple has the last word. He replies with characteristic irreverence: "It will not be my attitude I will have out that window."

This story seems to depict two radically different imaginations of Harlem, as a site of armed resistance on the one hand and as a place that opens its arms to the rest of the world on the other. The idea that these visions might not be incompatible is implied in the original column's version of the story, which subtly suggests a more complicated relationship between Simple and Harlem. In the later book version, Simple declares his "love" for Harlem and compares it to heaven. The narrator retorts, "Heaven is a state of mind," to which Simple replies, "It sure is *mine*," showing an unequivocal love for Harlem and a sense of ownership.[50] In contrast, in the column, Simple neither toasts Harlem nor compares it to heaven. Instead, he says he "likes" (not loves) Harlem because it "is the only place I ever been where I feel like I got the world in a jug and the stopper in my hand!"—a statement that the interlocutor interprets as equating Harlem with heaven.[51] Simple carefully corrects him: "'I DID not say Harlem was heaven,' said Simple, 'but it is mine!'" This powerful image of the world contained in a jug, with Harlem as a stopper, was left out of the book version. As the image suggests, the Simple of the Here to Yonder columns sees Harlem not as an earthly paradise, but as a stopgap—a place to temporarily seek protection until the rest of the world becomes a fairer and freer place to live. This complex, ambivalent relationship between character and place also appears in the township tales from southern Africa, likely as a result of their publication in magazines and newspapers filled with local and global news stories that made it difficult to separate these columns from contemporary events and thus to romanticize the township as a heavenly respite.

Sometimes, however, even having Harlem as a stopgap was not enough. In "Simple Rocks a Rocket," published in the *Defender* in 1948, Simple imagines that "when rocket planes get to be common" men "will have girl friends [*sic*] all over the world."[52] Simple describes at length how he will fly from Hong Kong to Greece and drink palm wine in Africa and saki in Nagasaki. The narrator accuses him of having a "far-fetched" imagination, but Simple insists, "No place will be far-fetched when them rocket planes gets perfected."[53] Simple seems finally to have embraced the narrator's cosmopolitan outlook and the idea that here is yonder and yonder is here—albeit for the inglorious purposes of womanizing and drinking his way around the world. However, a closer reading of the Simple stories suggests that Simple equates drinking with freedom and dignity. In the book version of "Feet Live Their Own Life," Simple says, "It's a man's prerogative to just set and drink sometimes."[54] Simple cites the crowded conditions in which he grew up in a four-room house filled with sisters, cousins, aunts, and neighbors: "I never had no place just to set and think. Neither to set and drink—not even much my milk before some hongry child snatched it out of my hand." Sitting and drinking for Simple is not only a way to escape or to chase women but a chance to have a bit of time and space to rest and think. Through its hyperbole, Simple's globe-trotting in "Simple Rocks a Rocket" demonstrates the very different relationship to travel and mobility that he would need to achieve just to be able to sit, drink, and think when and where he wants.

In the book version of this column, "High Bed," published in 1950 in *Simple Speaks His Mind*, Hughes extends the column's spatial imagination all the way to outer space, making it clear that Simple's escape into the air is much more than easy jet-setting: "Why, man, I would rock so far away from this color line in the U.S.A., till it wouldn't be funny. I might even build me a garage on Mars and a mansion on Venus. On summer nights I would scoot down the Milky Way just to cool myself off. I would not have no old-time jet-propelled plane either. My plane would run on atom power. This earth I would not bother with no more."[55] While Harlem serves as a stopper—a protective barrier—that sometimes allows Simple to feel he can hold the world in his hands, he imagines a future where finding true freedom will require transcending the color line that belts the United States and the world. Only by traveling into outer space can Simple envision himself as able to do more than stop for a brief drink. Indeed, space travel will grant him the space to build a home: "a garage on Mars and a mansion on Venus." Beyond the cosmopolitan fantasy of the original column (what an age when a man can have a woman and a drink on every continent!), the book version, published just two years later, sees Simple realizing that only a more radical vision of "yonder" in outer space can expose racial injustice on Earth—an idea that appealed strongly to writers in southern Africa. Although *Simple Speaks His Mind* was published before the space race between the United States and the Soviet Union took off in the late 1950s, its many references to atomic power resonate with Hughes's later critiques of the space race and the white supremacy it signified. In particular, Hughes questioned how space travel could benefit the entire human race when its underlying nuclear technology epitomized white violence against non-white peoples the world over, as had been horrifically demonstrated in Hiroshima and Nagasaki.[56]

Simple Speaks His Mind and Hughes's subsequent collection, *Simple Takes a Wife*, were circulating among the South African *Drum* writers in the early 1950s. Indeed, Simple appealed so much to writers like Can Themba and Casey Motsisi that nine stories from *Simple Speaks His Mind* and seven from *Simple Takes a Wife* were published between 1954 and 1955 in the magazine they edited, *Drum*'s "younger sister" *Africa!* While the personal relationship between Hughes and the *Drum* writers has been explored,[57] we can gain direct insight into how Hughes's work was read and interpreted by members of the *Drum* cadre by examining its republication in *Africa!* Notably, none of the most radical stories from *Simple Speaks His Mind*, such as the pro-communist "When a Man Sees Red," were selected. The reason is likely that South Africa's 1950 Suppression of Communism Act gave the apartheid government broad powers to persecute any person, group, or publication that promoted not only communism but essentially any form of political opposition.[58] However, just as Hughes was able to continue to use Simple to comment on various social and political issues, even after he was brought before McCarthy's Un-American Committee in 1953,[59] writers in southern Africa used similar characters to critique the inequities in their own societies and to place these struggles in a global frame.

Africa! presented the Simple stories to readers in a way that showcased their simultaneous localism, nationalism, and cosmopolitanism.

In April 1954, the editors described Simple as "an ordinary American Negro from Harlem, with very interesting opinions"[60] and introduced Hughes as follows: "You've enjoyed reading Jessie "Simple" Semple's comments on America this month haven't you? And last month too? Very few brains in the world can make up such a personality and make him say such serious things humorously. Only a man of many and different experiences like Langston Hughes can do it."[61] While Simple is identified here and throughout *Africa!* according to his race and locality—as an "American Negro from Harlem" or, in another instance, "that Harlem character that all Africa is shouting about"[62]—his "interesting opinions" are understood to be far-reaching, as "comments on America" writ large.[63] To emphasize this view, a photo of the Statue of Liberty framed by the New York skyline appeared alongside the column throughout 1954. Further, much as Hughes first presented himself in his very first Here to Yonder column, *Africa!* highlights Hughes's cosmopolitanism and effectively bridges the distance between here and yonder, in this case South Africa and America, by describing him as both "*our* Langston" and "one of America's top poets."[64]

Many of the Simple stories that were selected for publication in *Africa!* focus on the day-to-day problems of urban life through the lens of Simple's never-ending "woman trouble."[65] Critics have remarked on the Simple stories' overwhelming focus on women, despite their male protagonists, and Harper suggests that *Simple Takes a Wife*, published in 1953, focused more on women and less on politics due to the repressions of the McCarthy era.[66] Similarly, the *Drum* writer Henry Nxumalo, in a letter to Hughes, describes a party he attended with several other journalists where the conversation centered on "books and stories, art, poetry, music and that great old one and only subject, W-O-M-E-N. (What bunch of men getting together informally don't talk about women?)."[67] As in post–World War II Harlem, female independence and mobility were growing realities in 1940s and 1950s South Africa, where women were moving in increasing numbers to the city and seeking positions in factories or as domestic workers.[68] Dorothy Driver observes that in response, "patriarchy manfully reasserted itself in the face of the destabilization of its traditional rural form, but it also necessarily acknowledged women's increasing power, even as it tried to exploit and contain this power."[69] This dynamic is evident in Hughes's "Landladies," republished in *Africa!* in April 1954, in which the overbearing landlady, who papers the walls with directives to roomers like "TURN OUT LIGHT—COSTS MONEY," is an example of this growing cadre of financially independent women who "don't know their place."[70] Responding to the trouble Simple is having with her, the narrator prods, "A landlady is a woman, isn't she? And, according to your declarations, you know how to handle women."[71] Simple counters, "I know how to handle women who act like ladies, but my landlady ain't no lady." An article published several months later in *Africa!* by "Nosy" on the plight of roomers in Johannesburg confirms the relevance of Hughes's story to the magazine's readers and implies that the Simple stories served as a catalyst for critiquing local issues, often through the prism of changing gender dynamics.[72]

Though *Africa!*'s editors published stories like "Landladies" that cut independent women down to size, they also edited out details about Simple's girlfriend Mabel's work as a maid for a white family in "Explain That to Me!"—the only significant omission of material in the two years the Simple stories were published in the magazine.[73] This omission suggests that continuing racial inequality in America did not fit with the image of African American advancement that both *Drum* and *Africa!* sought to portray. Instead, a number of the Simple stories chosen for *Africa!* represent women as important, if flawed, cultural brokers. As Simple puts it: "Facts, some womens—including Joyce—are about culture like I'm about beer—they love it."[74] Critiquing what he sees as women's love of culture for culture's sake and their tendency to support the work of Black writers only when it has been validated by white patrons, Simple humorously suggests that books should be filled with more "satisfying" things that will literally feed working-class Harlemites: "beefsteaks, pork chops, spare ribs, pigs' feet, and ham."[75] The fact that *Africa!* featured these stories suggests that their South African audience was interested in the role of the arts in relation to race, gender, and class. The issue of culture in relation to gender and nationalism was also taken up by Saidi and Dlamanzi in their columns from Southern Rhodesia, though from a decidedly middle-class perspective.

With their rootedness in Harlem and their far-reaching commentary on national and global issues, the Simple stories proved an enticing model for many southern African writers. Hughes crafted Simple as a character who not only bridged but problematized the relationship between "here" and "yonder." For Simple, "yonder" extended as far as outer space, an idea that captured the imagination of writers across the region. One writer who found this idea particularly compelling was Casey Motsisi in South Africa, where deepening white rule made more hopeful visions of the future appear farther and farther away.

"AROUND THE TOWNSHIPS" WITH KID BOOZE

Casey Motsisi was one of the few writers who remained in South Africa after many members of the *Drum* cadre went into exile in America, the UK, and other parts of Africa, and by mid-1958, Motsisi's regular column, On the Beat, was the only piece of fiction left in the magazine.[76] By this point, the South African political situation had become increasingly repressive, as exemplified by the assumption of the office of prime minister by H. F. Verwoerd—known as the architect of apartheid—in September of 1958. In a letter to Hughes in 1961, Motsisi discussed Hughes's influence on him (he was reading Hughes's *Simple Stakes a Claim* at the time), his own writerly ambitions, and the impossibility of publishing his manuscript, tentatively titled "Around the Townships" or "Township," in South Africa.[77]

Critics have often interpreted Motsisi's On the Beat as they have Damon Runyon's stories—another inspiration for Motsisi—as apolitical and even "amoral."[78] However, the fact that Motsisi saw himself as emulating Hughes—especially the more political stories of *Simple Stakes a Claim*[79]—and envisioned his own work as exploring life "around the townships" of Johannesburg suggests that Motsisi was interested in more than "boodle-and-booze humor" that lacked "social analysis."[80] Following Hughes's example, Motsisi used his character, Kid Booze, to expose the many social injustices of apartheid South Africa, from the infamous pass laws that restricted where he could live and his freedom of movement to the anti-liquor laws that prohibited Africans from buying alcohol outside municipal beer halls and that ultimately encouraged illegal brewing and crime.[81] Motsisi's protagonist is a writer with his own degree of cosmopolitan style and savvy, thus collapsing aspects of both Simple and his more educated foil into the single figure of Kid Booze. Because Motsisi had encountered Simple in his book iteration, which features the voice of Simple more prominently than the Here to Yonder column does, it is not surprising that Motsisi appropriated the conversational tone of the Simple stories but did not turn On the Beat into a full-fledged dialogue.[82]

In addition to its copious references to American popular culture, from Marilyn Monroe to Joe Louis, one of the primary indexes of the column's simultaneously local and cosmopolitan ambitions is its language. Like many of the *Drum* writers, Motsisi writes in what Bernth Lindfors calls "an American accent."[83] He uses American slang liberally, including words like "hooch," "pow-wow," "shindig," "janes," "dolls," and "nix." Some of Motsisi's language can be traced directly to Hughes, such as "worriation" to mean "consternation" and, more pointedly, references to Nagasaki to evoke nuclear weapons. Specifically, Motsisi uses the phrase "make you Nagasaky" to describe the atomic effects of illegal liquor on a man. Motsisi often modified these terms slightly: from "Nagasaki" to "Nagasaky" and "cherie" to "cherrie" to describe a female love interest. There are also a number of words that seem to be purely of Motsisi's own creation, such as "brainpan" (head) and "swellegant" (a combination of swell and elegant). Vicki Manus draws attention to the amount of locally specific language that Motsisi uses, including South African English slang and tsotsitaal, resulting in a "township ethos that bubbles constantly under the surface of everything he writes."[84] Through Motsisi's playful use of language, the fabric of his column was woven of here, yonder, and an invented in-between.

While ostensibly about the adventures Kid Booze has with various other "Kids," a formula he borrows from Runyon, On the Beat is ultimately structured by apartheid's limitations on his mobility and his continual efforts to subvert them. In addition to his newspaper beat, Kid Booze's never-ending quest for liquor sends him on frequent journeys across the city, effectively creating a map of Black, urban Johannesburg—from Aunt Peggy's shebeen, or unlicensed bar, in Malay Camp, located just northwest of the Johannesburg Central Business District (CBD), to the various places the Kids invite him for "midnight parties," wakes, or other drinking business. Each time the narrator is out after 9:00 P.M. he risks being arrested on "Night Special" (i.e., failure to carry a "Night Special" pass). Nevertheless, he travels frequently, visiting a different area in each column: Western Native Township in "Kid Hangover," Dube in "Kid Playboy," and Mapetla Township in "Kid Fan," among many others.[85] Sometimes overt comments are made about these areas of Johannesburg, as in "Kid Playboy," when the narrator tells us he avoids Alexandra Township because "I'm somewhat scared of hopping off to Alex, especially on the weekends on account the bright boys over there have turned the place into a gunsmoke and knife-happy township."[86] Other times, places are characterized indirectly by the stories that occur there. In Chinatown, for example, the "wake" that the narrator and Kid Mattress attend turns out to be a "stokvel" party to raise money for the host, with alcohol hidden in the empty coffin.[87] In this way, Motsisi created a detailed map of the peripheral spaces where Black South Africans in Johannesburg lived and the ways they managed, despite the many restrictions, to move throughout the city and to find space, like Simple, to "just set and drink" where they liked.

Much like Hughes's column, Motsisi's On the Beat was full of women who were finding a way to get by in the city, sometimes by duping various Kids out of their money or booze and other times by making them pay for their indiscretions—as when a woman gives Kid Playboy his illegitimate child as a wedding present. Kid Booze himself is rarely involved with women except for Aunt Peggy, who supplies him with hooch and is a frequent accomplice in his escapades. Aunt Peggy reflects the reality that many women who moved to the city resorted to illegal means, such as prostitution and illegal brewing, to make ends meet. She is also one of the most complex and contradictory characters in On the Beat in that she has learned to navigate the apartheid system to her advantage and yet is also the column's most overtly nationalist figure.

In his column from September 1959, Kid Booze investigates whether the avaricious shebeen queen—"who has apparently sworn on a mountain of Bibles that nothing will come between her and the blackest penny"—has "sold out" by continuing to brew beer using potato skins despite the African National Congress's potato boycott, which was called in May of that year to protest the poor treatment of African farm laborers.[88] For a moment, Booze wonders whether Aunt Peggy simply hasn't heard about the boycott. He then thinks better of it, since "what Aunt Peggy doesn't know about this man's burg is not worth knowing."[89] He eventually discovers that Aunt Peggy is able to continue brewing her Joe Louis beer by substituting banana peels for potatoes, for she is "a true daughter of Africa and wouldn't touch a potato even to throw it at a cop batoning her." Notably, Aunt Peggy is the only female character who is not sexualized in a column otherwise full of references to women as sex objects, from Jayne Mansfield to the description of Miss Fur Coat as "a cherrie" with lips like two bananas. Although Kid Booze and the shebeen queen are not romantically involved, their relationship in some ways resembles the one between Simple and Joyce. Just as Joyce is a figure associated with cultural nationalism in the Simple stories published in *Africa!*, Aunt Peggy is the character who most closely represents African nationalism in Motsisi's. At the very least, Aunt Peggy helps Johannesburg's Black working class survive apartheid's daily assaults by "getting the population a little giddy," a "social service, even if she gets something in the process."[90]

Unlike Hughes, Motsisi could not risk direct commentary on the political situation in South Africa.[91] Instead, taking a different cue from Hughes, he used outer space as a means of critiquing apartheid regulations, particularly the restrictions on local mobility. In Motsisi's very first column from April 1958, a Black cop bangs on Kid Booze's door in Sophiatown—a multiracial neighborhood adjacent to central Johannesburg—and asks to see his pass. Sophiatown had been designated a "black spot" in the early 1950s and was being slowly dismantled through the forced removals of its African residents to Soweto and other areas farther from the city. In the middle of the night, Kid Booze is arrested for being "in the proclaimed area of Sophiatown for more than 72 hours without a permit" and thrown into the back of the cop's pickup van.[92] Fed up with Kid Booze's refusal to "hou jou bek," or "shut your mouth" in Afrikaans, the cop punches him. Kid Booze recounts, "In a moment I'm enveloped in dark, star spangled space, and I'm beginning to wonder whether I'm the first man to be launched into outer space." At a moment when he is restricted by the pass laws and literally confined to a police van, Kid Booze's fantasy of being sent to outer space captures the absurdity of apartheid's regulations. These restrictions were so farcical, in fact, that after being released from jail, Kid Booze encounters the same cop at a shebeen. They drink together and the cop eventually helps Kid Booze home, to the spot where he arrested him scarcely twenty-four hours before.

This story must also be read through the lens of Motsisi's fascination with the space race and the increasingly heated competition between the United States and Russia for domination in this new frontier. Kid Booze evokes the United States with the image of "star spangled space" and suggests that he might deny both the Americans and the Russians the chance to win the space race by becoming the first man in outer space himself. In its characteristically irreverent fashion, Motsisi's column thus imagines Africans impacting international affairs on the broadest possible stage. Perhaps more important, however, is the way Motsisi inserts the issue of race into the space race. The story draws attention to Blackness in its description of the cop's skin color as "two shades darker than midnight" and also of space itself as "dark." As Fawaz argues, "articulating the 'blackness' of space" has served as a means for Black artists to reclaim outer space from "the colonial vision of national expansion into space promulgated by American astrofuturism."[93] Earlier *Drum* stories made similar interventions, such as "Drum on the Moon!," which envisioned the first woman on the moon as a Black woman.[94] It may not be a coincidence that like Simple's girlfriend, she is named Joyce.

In Motsisi's column, much as in Hughes's, the space race becomes a means of criticizing neocolonial narratives of the future and "progress" while also drawing attention, more obliquely, to the hardships of daily life in apartheid South Africa. This project often takes the form of mocking America's failure to surpass Russia in outer space. Kid Fan, for example, tells the narrator and Aunt Peggy that "he is broker than all the American sputniks put together."[95] Several months later, Kid Booze laments that his landlord is trying to evict him, and his Editor wants him sober. In another jab at America's supposed preeminence, he admits that things are "so gooey that [he] wouldn't mind being used as a guinea pig for the first trip to the moon—even by the Americans."[96] Although Motsisi's column is steeped in American culture, moments like these point to the fact that during the Cold War, America's image abroad was damaged by its racial inequalities at home.[97] In the aftermath of the Sharpeville massacre, when the South African police killed sixty-nine people and injured hundreds more who were protesting the pass laws, and without the United States to look to as a model of racial equality, Kid Booze's fantasy of space travel is tinged with a weariness and sense of resignation resulting from impossible race relations on Earth.

Thus, while outer space served as a much-needed escape in On the Beat, it also served as a lens through which to critique the Cold War from an African perspective. In this way, Motsisi's column echoed other *Drum* articles like "Will There Be a US of Africa?," which suggested that pan-Africanism might serve "as a force poised between Western capitalism and Communism."[98] Engaging in a kind of playful Cold War realpolitik, On the Beat depicted Soviet leader Nikita Khrushchev as a masculine figure who could drink midnight party hooch and might even be convinced by the sweet-talking Kid Malalapipe to send a love letter to Jackie Kennedy.[99] While Hughes, via Simple, proposed space travel to demonstrate the reaches of white supremacy and the inadequacy of conflating here and yonder without careful attention to race, Motsisi used it to reframe the space race from the perspective of southern Africa, outside the Cold War binary of the United States and Russia. Ultimately, Kid Booze's "beat" extended from Black urban Johannesburg to the biggest possible arena: space itself. In this way, Motsisi managed to critique not only South African apartheid but imperialism in its various guises and, despite his column's fatalism, to imagine a central role for

Africans in the making of the world's future through the figure of the space-traveling, politicking Kid Booze.

MORALS, MODERNITY, AND MARS IN HARARE AND BULAWAYO

Shortly after Motsisi's column made its appearance in *Drum*, *African Parade* began publishing two similar columns: Bits and Pieces from Harare by the "Orator" (the pen name of Bill Saidi) and Daniel Dlamanzi's Makokoba Park Talk.[100] Their protagonists—also journalists prone to boozing—flirted with Motsisi's Americanized language and cosmopolitan style but ultimately promoted an overt moralism that Motsisi's Kid Booze did not. As Dlamanzi put it in his column from July 1959, "When it comes to morals, I am just old fashioned, I guess."[101] In both columns, there is a strong connection between cultural and moral development and national development. For this reason, Saidi's and Dlamanzi's columns more closely resemble cosmographs—which imagine progress on a vertical axis extending from heaven to hell—than they do Motsisi's lateral map of Johannesburg's townships.[102] As in Hughes's and Motsisi's columns, women feature centrally and, especially in Dlamanzi's case, play an essential role in developing national cultures. But whereas Simple's "old-fashioned" views on gender are frequently balanced by interjections from Hughes's narrator, Dlamanzi presents women's moral failings as the greatest single threat to African national development.

While earlier literary forms in *Parade*, such as the migrant forms discussed in chapter 1, imagined the possibility of forging the federation's three territories into a large African-run state, Saidi's and Dlamanzi's columns did not appear in the magazine until the end of 1958 and the beginning of 1959, respectively, when the federation's ideology of partnership "was dead in all but name."[103] Constitutional changes in 1957 had diluted African representation in the federal assembly, fueling the growth of African nationalism.[104] Soon afterward, the more liberal Garfield Todd—whose modest reforms had earned him "significant black support," including in *Parade*—was forced to resign as prime minister of Southern Rhodesia by his own party.[105] In this context, Saidi's and Dlamanzi's township tales reflect the Black middle class's gradual turn away from the empty promises of multiracialism and toward the nationalist movement. In the late 1950s and early 1960s, the Black townships in Salisbury and Bulawayo became bastions of nationalist support and activity, in large part because of their poor conditions and lack of housing and other services. In reporting on these areas, Saidi and Dlamanzi benefited from the greater press freedom in Southern Rhodesia as compared to South Africa. As Lawrence Vambe, editor in chief of African Newspapers from 1956 to 1959,[106] put it, "Provided you did not deliberately and openly incite people to rebel or break the laws of the country, you could dig up any unsavory facts about their social environment or express any unacceptable political point of view."[107] Saidi and Dlamanzi certainly did their best to expose the worst of the townships' conditions, but they balanced this effort with attention to their inhabitants' cosmopolitanism, including their fashion sense, cars, music, and liquor preferences. These tales conveyed the townships' simultaneous worldliness and out-of-this-worldness, with multiple references to outer space meant to elicit shock at the state of their basic provisions, or the lack thereof.

Harare location was the first area where Africans could live in Salisbury, the capital of Southern Rhodesia and the legislative center of the federation. Like most other "native locations" in Southern Rhodesia, Harare was modeled on its South African predecessors with the aim of achieving both racial segregation and tight economic and political control of the Black population.[108] Due in part to the Land Apportionment Act of 1930, which among other things gave white Rhodesians the ability to protest the building of housing or amenities for Black people near white neighborhoods, Southern Rhodesia's townships were vastly overpopulated and underserviced.[109] Harare was governed by an all-white Salisbury town council, which raised funds for public services in the township through beer hall profits. The effect of this arrangement, Vambe explains, was that "[his] people simply had to drink in order to have houses, roads, lights, clinics or any other services."[110] Black Southern Rhodesians, who comprised most of the workforce in Harare by the mid-1950s, were increasingly frustrated by the lack of real upward mobility.[111] Africans were prevented from exercising any kind of ownership in the township; they could not buy houses, own pubs, or run transport companies.[112] Vambe attributes the fact that Harare had become "the breeding ground of the Zimbabwe black nationalism as well as of its foremost thinkers and planners" to its dire living conditions, its "painfully slow" development, and the "hostile" relationship between the governing town council and the township residents.[113] Although Saidi does not address nationalist politics directly in Bits and Pieces from Harare, the failure of Harare's white "city fathers" to provide adequate infrastructure and facilities for the township's residents is a prominent theme in the column.

Saidi's first Bits and Pieces appeared a scant nine months after Motsisi's On the Beat began publication in *Drum*.[114] Its first installment in December 1958 supports Vambe's assessment that by the late 1950s, "the atmosphere in Rhodesian racial politics was becoming hotter":[115]

> Harare is like any other township in the Federation, geographically speaking, that is. The only damned difference, and it's a big one too, is that, as some outspoken commentators have said, it is possessed by some of the hottest heads this side of the solar system. The cream of Harare is like the molten larva [*sic*] of a volcano; the scum is like the particles that scatter as soon as the volcano erupts.[116]

Although his column was rooted in Harare, the Orator's description telescopes rapidly from Harare to the entire federation and then "this side of the solar system," immediately situating the township within the broadest possible geographic frame. Saidi's vivid image of Harare as a volcano spewing lava and particles also gives new meaning to the "bits and pieces" of the column's title and signals the township's reach and importance to Southern Rhodesia's growing nationalist movement. Indeed, Vambe later described Harare as "the biggest, the most vital and *explosive* black ghetto in Mashonaland, if not in all Zimbabwe."[117]

This first column's "tailpiece," or footnote, also points to the intensification of earlier nationalist movements in other parts of the federation, particularly in Nyasaland, to which Hastings Kamuzu Banda had returned to lead the movement in July 1958: "When a Nyasa man was asked what he thought about aliens not being allowed to buy houses in New Highfield [a newer township for leaseholders], he said: 'They can do anything to me just now. But not when I become Minister of the Interior in Dr. Banda's government. I'll definitely tell them where they get off.'"[118] Prime Minister Whitehead, Todd's successor, declared a state of emergency in Southern Rhodesia two months after this column was published, in February 1959, largely in response to anti-colonial violence in Nyasaland, where Banda was arrested in March.[119] Hundreds of members of the Southern Rhodesia African National Congress were also detained.[120] While earlier articles in *Parade* had emphasized a shared Central African identity, Saidi, whose father was from Nyasaland, seems to suggest a new form of solidarity across the federation based on its growing nationalist movements.

Saidi also presented Harare as a highly developed cosmopolitan center that was connected to other parts of the world through popular culture. He accomplished this in part through his performative use of language, particularly American slang. His lexicon often overlapped with Motsisi's, including words such as "hooch," "janes," "joint," "booze," and references to American movie stars, singers, and gangsters like Al Capone. As in Motsisi's column, this Americanized language was used to discuss distinctly local issues: the lack of representation in the legislative assembly, unfair drinking laws, transportation issues, and new social trends in the township. In the Bits and Pieces from Harare from March 1959, the Orator describes his "pal's" shocked reaction when he visits him in Harare, which, having recently gained streetlights, is now "lit like Broadway":

> "Say, you look like you've just married Maryln [*sic*] Monroe!" I asked him why and he said I looked so diplomatic and sophisticated that he wouldn't have been surprised if I had told him that I was from Hollywood's Beverley [*sic*] Hills. . . . Well, things have changed in Harare and it was not only my attire that impressed him but the whole works itself. When he saw Africans driving in '59 Chevs, he asked: "If you are going to tell me that that guy owns that beautiful piece of work, I am going to see a psychiatrist just now."[121]

Saidi's description is notable for its conflation—rather than simple comparison—of Harare and Hollywood. Hararians had become so stylish that they could be mistaken for Americans, another variation on Hughes's suggestion that here is yonder and yonder is here.

Nevertheless, the same column quickly disabuses the Orator's friend, and the reader, of the idea that this cosmopolitanism can be taken as evidence of real progress or improvements to mobility—social or otherwise. While the friend is particularly shocked to see Africans driving American cars, the same column complains of the township's "Transport Blues," and specifically its overcrowded bus and railway station. The Orator also admits to his friend that there is still not a single African in Southern Rhodesia's Legislative Assembly, and it is hard to miss the sarcasm in his summary of the encounter: "This simple but informative anecdote just shows you how Harare has advanced in the past

15 years." The timing of this piece was significant: the federal government had banned Southern Rhodesia's African National Congress the previous month, in February 1959. Through these juxtapositions, Saidi amplifies Harare's cosmopolitan style but also points to its limits by drawing attention to the impediments to mobility and political rights that Harare's residents—and Africans in the Central African Federation more broadly—still lacked.

More than any of the township's other restrictions, Southern Rhodesia's drinking laws for Africans are a continuing source of strife for the Orator. Like Kid Booze and Simple before him, the Orator is fond of drink, and alcohol signifies his worldliness and serves as a prism for his broader cultural and political critiques. Over time, Saidi's position evolved from a willingness to praise the city council's modest improvements to Harare's drinking facilities to a direct argument for the African ownership of pubs. While European liquor was illegal until 1962, Africans were allowed to buy locally brewed beer, and later "European-type beers and light wines," at government-run beer halls.[122] Vambe describes how illegal, homemade nightclubs called "Mahobo" parties and shebeens grew out of these restrictions and "European liquor became the very symbol of economic and cultural superiority."[123] Saidi's column from March 1959 demonstrates the social clout associated with European liquor. The Orator boasts that one "would mistake" a Mahobo party for "a birthday party organized by a film star. You will find ladies with cute faces asking you whether you would like to drink gin, brandy, whisky or champagne."[124] A short month later, however, he is more than willing to abandon the Mahobo scene for the new pub that the city council plans to build in Harare "with all the trimmings of a joint in Hollywood's Mocambo."[125] In this instance and others, Saidi praises the council for "giving an ear to the grievances of the African Advisory Board" and touts the township's cosmopolitan amenities.

By the following year, Saidi had become more critical of the township's drinking culture and especially the city fathers' encouragement of African alcoholism to fill their own coffers. Like Motsisi, Saidi expressed his frustration with the absurdity of these regulations and his resulting world-weariness through references to outer space. Responding to the city's plans to build an expensive new pub for Hararians with its beer hall profits, the Orator suggests that perhaps the council should hold a boozing competition for Africans: "They would probably get so much money out of it they would be able to build a pub in outer space for these Hararians."[126] Pointing to the ridiculous amount of money generated by the beer halls, Saidi laments that this money did not go to other direly needed services in the township. Awash in alcohol, Harare lacked basic amenities like transportation, and even the liquor that flowed freely at Mahobo parties might be put to better uses: "This business about buses has got me so sore that I am just thinking of inventing my own transport—something like a space-ship which runs on a pint of gin and a liberal dose of vermouth. It might work better than the derelict things they call buses."[127] Through this fantastical vision of fashioning his own alcohol-powered spaceship, Saidi highlights the absurdity of the township's governance and the toll of these quotidian hardships on its residents. In March 1960, in a weary voice that sounds like Motsisi's, he suggests, "When you think you're tired of living, go and see the Russian scientists about a one way-ticket to the moon."[128] As in Hughes's and Motsisi's columns, Saidi's leap from the local to the interplanetary signifies his increasing frustration and hopelessness in the face of Earth's dense web of racist rules and legislation.

In the lead-up to Britain's review of the federation in late 1960, many Africans fearfully anticipated the emergence of an independent, white-ruled dominion.[129] This fear stoked African nationalism, and as Salisbury emerged as a "stronghold" of the National Democratic Party in early 1960, Saidi expressed his allegiance to Harare in more nationalist terms.[130] In a section of the column from June 1960 titled "Damned These Pass Laws," the Orator frames his right to move around Harare unimpeded in relation to African nationalist demands, telling the cop who stops him, "I don't go around with a pass because this is free country and I've got my rights."[131] Similarly, comparing Harare to neighboring Highfield, he announces, "I must admit here that I am a patriot. In other words, I like Harare like an Eskimo loves his igloo."[132] Saidi remaps his patriotism onto the township and, much like Simple, who suggested that Harlem made him feel that he could contain the world in a jug, he compares the township to another small, contained space: the igloo. Harare, like Harlem, is a stopgap, a place for the Orator to call his own until Southern Rhodesia can be a free country.

Given this situation, it is not surprising that Saidi displays an ambivalence similar to Simple's about Harlem and Motsisi's about Johannesburg and criticizes Harare in a proprietary way. The "bits and pieces" discussed in Saidi's column are often, as he says in its first installment, the "scum" of the city. These undesirable characters include criminals, rude men in taxis, corrupt politicians, and "loose" women, all of whom contribute to Harare's moral and social decay, even aside from their tendency to dupe the Orator. In the Bits and Pieces from February 1960, the narrator chronicles several unfortunate situations that befall him, including his experience of being tricked by a man with a fake camera who convinces him to take part in the "jumpology" fad (having your picture taken while jumping in the air) and then steals the change that falls out of his pockets as well as being arrested while trying to help the police chase down another man. From incidents such as these, the Orator draws the conclusion that "Harare is a funny place. Anything can and usually will happen around this dump"—a sentiment that was expressed in a variety of ways throughout the column's life span.[133] Though weary of Harare's limitations, Saidi, like Simple, staked his claim to this small space that was his own.

Daniel Dlamanzi's Makokoba Park Talk began publication in *Parade* in January 1959, just one month after the debut of Saidi's Bits and Pieces, and was meant to appeal to readers "in the Bulawayo townships in particular."[134] Dlamanzi's first column indicates a playful rivalry between him and Saidi and emphasizes his column's focus on morals and decency, particularly in relation to women. Just as Saidi's first column drew attention to Harare's uniqueness "this side of the solar system," Dlamanzi frames Bulawayo's social scene in cosmic terms. Describing an event for Stanlake Samkange in Vashee Hall, Dlamanzi marvels at the beautiful women he encountered, calling them "a glaxy [*sic*] of earth-treading stars!"[135] He laments that these "highly sophisticated" ladies don't attend the usual township functions and challenges the young people of Bulawayo "to prove that Salisbury is not very far ahead of them. It is high time we had social clubs which can organise decent social functions to which high society women can go." Dlamanzi's first column was well received, and in the next installment he reports that "our Bulawayo wonder boys are responding so favourably to my January paroxysms that they have by now gone even as far as extending invitations to inhabitants on Mars to join their newly formed Federal Entertainment Association."[136] From the column's start, Dlamanzi demonstrated his interest in rivaling Harare's cosmopolitanism by playfully suggesting that Bulawayo, with its sophistication and decency, could have an interplanetary reach.

Founded in 1894, Makokoba is the oldest township in Zimbabwe.[137] Terence Ranger describes Makokoba as a "little place," with only twelve thousand residents in 1960, that nevertheless "contained a world."[138] It was connected to surrounding rural areas and "memories of the Ndebele state" as well as to the rest of Southern Rhodesia and southern

Africa through the many migrant laborers who lived there, boasting a plethora of languages, religions, and customs.[139] As compared to Salisbury, Bulawayo's townships had attracted more permanent Southern Rhodesian wage laborers from an earlier period, who were generally more committed to the creation of a stable civil society and social order.[140] Nevertheless, as in Harare, the 1950s was a turbulent period of demographic, social, and political change that gave rise to what Ranger calls a "fractured nationalism" in Bulawayo. The banning of the ANC in 1959, one month after Dlamanzi's first Makokoba Park Talk column, created a political "vacuum," in which "[t]here was no one to hold nationalism together."[141] Rising unemployment further fractured the African population, whose poorer sections took out their frustrations on women and migrant workers.[142]

Makokoba in particular had attracted large numbers of female migrants. Hugh Ashton, Bulawayo's young director of the African Administration, had decided not to enforce the Native Urban Areas Act and remove "unmarried" women—in many cases women whose marriages were not recognized by the colonial state—from Makokoba, as Salisbury had done.[143] Instead, he built more townships, several of which allowed for leasehold tenure.[144] As a result, "Makokoba filled up with girls in the 1950s. It was the chosen destination of young women running away from rural families in search of the exciting life of town."[145] The preponderance of young, unwed women led many, such as Charlton Ngcebetsha, founder of the *African Home News*, to see Makokoba as the locus of the "most shameful conditions . . . married people with their children and bachelors as well as unattached women sleep together in disgustingly over-crowded small houses."[146] Nevertheless, Ngcebetsha described the township as the best place for single men to live for virtually the same reasons: women and beer were plentiful. In this space of fractured nationalism, Dlamanzi's column joined the chorus of voices turning against urban women, identifying their "loose morals" as both a symptom and cause of Makokoba's decline.

Dlamanzi's column closely resembles Casey Motsisi's On the Beat in both its Americanized language and its structure. Dlamanzi appropriates Motsisi's habit of referring to various gangsters as "Kids," describing them similarly as "Pals" and organizing the column around their adventures and misadventures. Some iterations of "Makokoba" even seem to be directly based on Motsisi's column, particularly the second installment from March 1959, which follows the same basic plot as Motsisi's second On the Beat column from May 1958. In the latter, Motsisi laments his misfortune at being invited to a "midnite party" by Kid Hangover, who charges his guests for "over-doctored" liquor, particularly when he wakes up hungover and penniless the next morning.[147] Similarly, Dlamanzi finds himself made "a sad spectacle of misery" by "a bunch of bad boys" when he is invited to a "week-end party," or "what they call 'a Mahobo party' in Harare and 'stalk fella' in Bulawayo."[148] Styled as Bulawayo's "social critic," Dlamanzi insists that these parties "are what the Yankies call 'lousy'" as guests are asked to pay for their own food and alcohol once they arrive, usually in order to help the hosts pay their rent.[149] Like Motsisi, Dlamanzi enjoys playing with language, as we can see from his description of the party's address as "room number mischief thousand and twenty beer-bazaar." However, unlike Kid Booze, a bachelor who decides to engage in the revelry, Dlamanzi's narrator is careful to enjoy the booze only and to stay away from the "dolls" at the party because he doesn't want anything getting back to his wife. In this respect, Dlamanzi's character behaves quite differently from Kid Booze and Simple, the latter of whom finds himself in a similar situation in a *Defender* column from March 1954 titled "House-Rent Parties Returning; Simple Sees Depression Coming." Simple tries to convince the educated foil to attend one such party with him, and when he expresses reservations about "bootlegging and pay parties coming back," Simple argues, "Sometimes you can have more fun at a pay party than at a free one. At a free party, to which you is invited, you has to behave yourself. At a paid one, you can clown down."[150] Unlike Simple, who not only wants to enjoy himself but worries that "[i]f everybody said no, poor Mamie could not pay her rent," Dlamanzi's character sees these parties as evidence of social and moral decay. Columns like this one highlight the difference between Simple's working-class sympathies and Dlamanzi's protagonist, who aspires to middle-class status.

Like all the protagonists of the township tales considered here, Dlamanzi's makes no secret of his love for drink. In his column from June 1959, Dlamanzi describes how unfortunate it would have been for his readers if he had been murdered by the "gang of mobsters" that attacked him the previous weekend. "And that would be a very sad thing as you know," he muses, "For who would you be boozing with at this time and telling you stories of the booze world?"[151] However, in line with his overriding attention to women's morality, Dlamanzi's protagonist is particularly distressed by the new trend he observes of women drinking in the townships. In the editor's introduction to Dlamanzi's April 1959 column, he describes women as "nation-builders" with "tremendous influence over their husbands and children."[152] Thus, the "bottle-kissing mamas" that Dlamanzi describes won't "do our Society any good." Dlamanzi reports that he and his wife are "very much upset by this very distressing business." So upset, in fact, that he contemplates leaving Earth and its low morals entirely: "I shall soon book myself a place on the Jupiter Rocket for the purpose of settling permanently somewhere on the moon. And you, Mr. Parade, should be the second to follow me." Like Simple, Kid Booze, and the Orator, Dlamanzi's character references outer space as a means of transcending earthly problems. In this case, however, it is not only racial prejudice he is fleeing but women's immorality. Notably, his vehicle of choice is one of the United States Jupiter rockets, intermediate-range nuclear missiles that symbolized American military might. Unlike Hughes and Motsisi, Dlamanzi expresses a more or less uncritical affiliation with American culture.

If space represents a pseudoheavenly escape from earthly sin on Dlamanzi's map of Makokoba's moral terrain, Ma Nora's shebeen marks the lowest point. In his column from July 1959, Dlamanzi visits Ma Nora's with his friend "Pal Shellet Maningi."[153] Although Dlamanzi frequents this particular shebeen, Ma Nora does not become a semiheroic character as Aunt Peggy does in Motsisi's column. Instead, Ma Nora's is "a place which would make hell look like Paradise. The patrons are guys whose drinking proclivities equal only those of the original John Barleycorn and that's saying little for them. Me, they say I shouldn't be there, since my pa and ma were ardent members of the Association for the Preservation of Morals." Dlamanzi looks down on his pal for flirting with one of the "janes" who is wearing too much makeup: "I tell you if there are more dames like this one around these places, I wouldn't be surprised if they transferred hell from wherever it is to here." Notably, Dlamanzi describes the shebeen not only as a place of sin but as hell itself.

Dlamanzi's column did not run as long as Saidi's, possibly due to the July 1960 *zhii* riots. These riots first broke out in Harare after the arrest of several National Democratic Party leaders and then spread to Bulawayo, where the federal army and police arrested more than five hundred people and killed at least two.[154] Many businesses and beer halls in Bulawayo's townships were looted and set ablaze.[155] Ranger identifies "gender relations" as a primary underlying cause of *zhii*: "With Ashton's policy of clearing 'single' men out of Makokoba into newly-built hostels and evicting their 'illegal' wives there was great tension in the township. Mpopoma married leaseholders feared and disliked their 'single' lodgers. *Zhii* could be seen as the last throw of the 'bachelors.'"[156] In the Makokoba Park Talk installment from April 1960, Dlamanzi and Pal Maningi Esquire visit Mpopoma, a nearby township, "where cut-throats and hoodlums thrive at a let-me-alone pace as bugs breed themselves at the ad infinitum rate in Makokoba."[157] The column points to many of the social tensions that erupted in *zhii*, particularly the animosity that Mpopoma's better-off leaseholders felt toward their lodgers, whom they were forced to house in order to afford their own home payments, and whom they saw as a source of crime and a threat to their women.[158] Dlamanzi and his pal visit Ma Msindo's shebeen for a "really good booze assault" but end up listening to an angry "sermon" by Pa Msindo after he catches his wife blowing kisses to all her customers. "And any of you with any guts left in you, must see that they do not allow their houses to turn into 'shebeen' dens. You'll lose all you've worked and paid for," Pa Msindo warns, in a sermon that might even inspire Billy Graham "to have his programme broadcast on the moon just in case the guys there are thinking of coming to earth and enjoy what guys do"—a comment that once again points to Dlamanzi's favorable assessment of America's cultural reach. On its face, Dlamanzi's column suggests that immorality is the cause of ruin, from Makokoba to Mpopoma to the moon. However, it also exposed the social conditions and tensions that led to *zhii* and, given that Makokoba had become a flash point for Southern Rhodesia's political tensions, it is understandable that *Parade* discontinued Dlamanzi's column. In his final column from October 1960, Dlamanzi reports that his editor "has taken me away from my page and after threatening a sack, a transfer to the Congo," but will keep him on to do a different story fittingly titled "Wages of Sin."[159]

Following Dlamanzi's lead, Saidi adopted a tougher stance on moral issues in some of his Bits and Pieces columns and was also adamant about the relationship between culture and nation-building. In his column from July 1959, in which he denounces men who have affairs with other people's wives, the Orator concludes, "Fellows, culture is one business that can or cannot build a nation. . . . My pal, Daniel Dhlamanzi [*sic*], is always hollering about social weaknesses being rife in his section of the country. Well, I've got the same complaint. . . . We don't want to fall like the Romans do we?"[160] Saidi similarly uses the imagery of heaven and hell in his descriptions of Harare and its social and political environment, but he is careful to train his eye on what he saw as the real source of this immorality: the unfair laws and restrictions placed on Africans by the colony's white government. In his column from September 1959, the Orator addresses the problem of corrupt African clerks selling "town passes" on the black market. These passes, which Africans were required to have to work in Salisbury, could take an inordinate amount of time to obtain legally. Saidi's column concludes that regulations like this, and the corruption they encouraged, were endangering Africans' moral health: "I guess the only thing to do is to tell the authorities to change these damned pass laws and give the poor clerks a chance to sniff the scent of flowers in heaven. As it is, how the hell are they going to appear before the Archangel?"[161] While the pass law system directly regulated African movement in the city, it also threatened Africans' moral mobility by jeopardizing their access to heaven.

Although Saidi used moralistic language at times, his accumulated columns are better understood as an extended meditation on "fairness," whether in relation to women—"I'm all for preserving these members of the fair sex. But ARE they fair?"[162]—or capitalist enterprise in the townships. Saidi made this strategy plain in the Bits and Pieces from April 1961, when, in a rare instance, he discusses the arc of his column as a whole: "Some of you who have had the patience and sense to follow this column and are staunch disciples of the ORATOR will recollect that I'm against any unfair play. In fact, you will allow I don't go for these mugs who try to make a fortune out of us guys endowed with the respectability that goes with a good upbringing."[163] The "mugs" in this case are the bus company and the government, which continued to fail to address the issue of transportation in Harare and Highfield, which was "getting worse and worse like a cancer." Saidi suggests a simple solution: "Africans can get buses. They've got buses. And they can run them in the township just as well as anybody else." With such comments, Saidi continued African Newspapers' strategy of emphasizing the respectability of capitalism and urging the government to exercise "fairness" in allowing Black participation in the economy.[164]

This approach took on even greater salience as the Cold War progressed. Detecting no clear communist threat in the federation, the United States was content to allow Britain to continue to delay decolonization without fearing that African nationalists might turn to the Soviet Union for support.[165] As noted above, Saidi's and Dlamanzi's columns had a pro-US tenor, especially as compared to Motsisi's. Nevertheless, as an earlier column in *Parade* warned, Africans in the federation would not wait forever for support from democracies like the United States: "To leave the Africans too long suffering under economic, political, and social injustice is to drive them into the wily arms of Communism. A third World War between democracies and Russia will throw colonial Africa into chaos. To survive, democracy will very much depend on the loyal co-operation of the African people."[166] In a similar vein, the Orator evokes Western hypocrisy in his argument for the African ownership of pubs, writing, "I think it's hightime [*sic*] somebody told this City Council that we don't want all these nasty beer halls around us. . . . Everywhere you go you find them there, these stinking, muddy places which look like concentration camps. Why can't Africans with the money be allowed to build private bars."[167] Here Saidi sounds like Hughes's Simple. By suggesting that Africans in the federation were enduring conditions not unlike those the Allies fought to change in World War II, he condemned not only the Southern Rhodesian government but also, by extension, the Western democracies that failed to intervene in the region.

Despite these barbed critiques, Saidi's message of "respectability" and his ultimate advocacy of working within Southern Rhodesia's white-run capitalist system put him at odds with the broader, younger, and increasingly militant nationalist movement in Southern Rhodesia. Six months earlier, in a column from October 1960, published at a time when further rioting was following the earlier riots in Salisbury and Bulawayo in July, the Orator critiqued a friend he had learned was a "freedom fighter."[168] His pal thinks freedom "is something you eat or wear or take around to your sweet momma way down in Mabelreign," and when he tells a white soldier that "he wants freedom," the soldier hands him a tear-gas bomb. The Orator's friend takes a bite of it, and it bursts in his face. Saidi, in line with other relatively well-off nationalists, felt that African advancement should be achieved through more moderate means, such as including Africans in enterprise and allowing them to produce things that one could actually "eat or wear," rather than seemingly self-destructive militancy. In this respect, Saidi is emblematic of the African elite's "bumpy and somewhat less than fully executed journey from racial partnership to African nationalism."[169]

One of the last Bits and Pieces columns from 1962 demonstrates the Orator's willingness to manipulate his own subject position to his advantage—whether that meant congratulating the city council for their modest improvements and denouncing freedom fighters or arguing passionately for increased Black ownership rights in the township. In his January 1962 column, published just after the banning of the National Democratic Party in December, the Orator describes how a woman in a shebeen tricks him into holding a purse full of money she has stolen from a white woman so as to avoid being arrested. To emphasize his cosmopolitan awareness, he makes several references in the story that evoke global popular culture, including mentions of "Dr. Frankenstein's laboratory," "Tarzan," and "Aladin [*sic*] and his lamp"—all used to describe the police officers and their actions. Having successfully fooled the cops, the woman buys the narrator drinks until he passes out. In the morning, he comes "back to earth and its earthly problems . . . feeling that [he] had gone a cruise to Mars" and finds the woman has left behind a five-pound bill and a note: "They come and they go, don't they, Joe?" In response, the narrator makes his final and most interesting cultural reference: "For a fiver, I'll let anyone call me Joe or Robinson Crusoe. Even his Man Friday."[170] The Orator ultimately reveals himself to be, like Simple, a trickster figure. Although he insists on his worldliness, he will also maneuver into the position of a colonial subject (as represented by Friday) if necessary.

In their township tales, Saidi and Dlamanzi envisioned Harare and Bulawayo in similarly ambivalent ways. While Dlamanzi focused on morality and respectability in cultural affairs, Saidi imagined a future Black-owned and Black-operated township with the amenities and style of Hollywood. For members of the African elite like them, these townships served as pseudonationalist spaces of self-determination. Nevertheless, Saidi and Dlamanzi also pointed to Harare's and Bulawayo's restrictions and limitations, particularly when it came to issues of social, physical, and even moral mobility. Both columnists evoked outer space as a possible escape from earthly problems but mixed this imagery with visions of a moral terrain that extended from heaven to hell. Although Dlamanzi's column was relatively short lived, Saidi's continued into 1962. By this time, it was becoming more and more difficult for political moderates like Saidi, and African Newspapers more broadly, to straddle the divide between "ever-bolder nationalists" and a government that was rapidly moving toward the Rhodesian Front's hard-line white supremacy.[171] Saidi left Southern Rhodesia in 1963, not long after Winston Field of the Rhodesian Front assumed the position of prime minister, sounding the death knell of the federation. Saidi relocated to Zambia, one of the new nations that arose out of Britain's failed colonial project.

LUSAKA AFTER DARK AND ON THE EVE OF INDEPENDENCE

In 1963, Northern Rhodesia's nationalist aspirations were in the process of realization. In the legislative elections of October 1962, Kenneth Kaunda's United National Independence Party (UNIP) had received a majority of seats and moved to form a coalition government with the African National Congress. Together they called for Zambia's immediate withdrawal from the federation and complete independence from Britain. The chance to live and write in a soon-to-be independent African nation presented a unique opportunity for journalists from the region, particularly since Southern Rhodesia appeared to be going the way of South Africa and sinking deeper into white rule.

After arriving in Lusaka, Bill Saidi began working as a reporter for the *Central African Mail*, which was edited by Richard Hall and Kelvin Mlenga. At the *Mail* he was also reunited with his fellow Southern Rhodesian journalist Tim Nyahunzvi, who had worked with him at African Newspapers in Salisbury. It was Nyahunzvi who, "out of the blue," suggested that Saidi write a regular column based on his previous Bits and Pieces from Harare, only this time set in Zambia's capital.[172] In his memoirs online, Saidi reflects on this moment in his writing career:

> I hadn't realised, until then, that any body [*sic*] else had paid much attention to the column—apart from myself and the others working on the magazine. I was highly flattered. Tim had obviously enjoyed the column. What was more was that he had enough confidence in me as a writer to suggest I could try it here, in a foreign country on a newspaper, edited by two very professional journalists with so much experience at the job they would know a "dud" if someone tried to pass it off before their eyes as the "genuine article"?[173]

The question mark at the end of Saidi's statement is telling: he was not quite convinced that he could write as persuasively about a "foreign country" as he could about Harare township, which he knew "like the palm of [his] hand." Saidi's choice of the word "country" rather than "city" is also significant. Although the column was called Lusaka after Dark, Saidi frequently traveled to and wrote about other Zambian cities. This sprawling map of the newly forming Zambian nation stands in contrast to the vertical moral maps drawn by Saidi's and Dlamanzi's columns in *Parade*. Now Saidi was grappling with a nation on the cusp of realization, rather than the micronational space of Harare. On December 31, 1963, the federation was officially dissolved, and Kenneth Kaunda was elected prime minister of Northern Rhodesia the following month. On October 24, 1964, the Republic of Zambia achieved full independence. Lusaka after Dark records this political transition from colony to state, including its difficult racial, cultural, and economic dimensions.

A character that emerged from this column—Mr. Chite—is the nearest incarnation of Simple explored thus far. What is more, Saidi, who used his own name for the column rather than a pseudonym as he had for *Parade*, assumes a role similar to that of Hughes in the original Here to Yonder columns: he is a man of the world and a writer, while his "very esteemed friend, Mr. Chite" is of a "quaint mentality."[174] The relationship between Saidi as author and narrator and Mr. Chite is reminiscent of the interplay between Hughes and Simple, but whereas Hughes used Simple to speak for "an imagined African American nation,"[175] Saidi deploys a similar character to show the dangers of a "simple" African nationalism in a postcolonial context. Mr. Chite is emblematic of members of the working class with bourgeois ambitions, who, Fanon warns, "follow in the steps of their bourgeoisie."[176] Rather than compete with Europeans, however, these petty traders and workers turn their ire toward "non-national Africans," demonstrating the threat of deterioration from nationalism "to ultra-nationalism, to chauvinism, and finally to racism" in the postcolony.

In his memoirs, Saidi remarks that as a journalist, he benefited greatly from his time in Zambia and from the government's desire to "enhance our skills in the profession to match those of the rest of the continent."[177] However, he notes that many Zambian journalists resented him and other foreigners for "taking jobs that rightly belonged to them—even if some of them were not as qualified or as experienced." Saidi was able to fly under the radar for some time. He recalls that initially, "the 'Saidi' with which [he] signed off Lusaka After Dark in *The Central African Mail* was assumed to be a nom-de-plume. But it soon became clear that there was a real person behind the name, a man who, though with a name that was distinctly Malawian or even Zambian, was in reality a Rhodesian." Eventually, this led to Saidi being "targeted as a columnist" by local personalities, including at least one politician, who thought he had written about them unfairly,[178] and other times by readers who accused him of embellishing aspects of Lusakan nightlife. As one reader, whose letter Saidi addressed in his column, complained, "He should base his stories in facts or else call them 'fables.' His language and style should be suitable to news pages."[179] Having just left a bar where a drunk man was talking to a bird only to relocate to a café where a young white boy and girl aged eleven and ten are smoking cigarettes, Saidi "wonder[s] what CONCERNED READER would think about all this."

In an environment full of opportunity as well as numerous detractors, Saidi had to work hard to establish his writerly authority. One of his column's primary functions was to give himself street credibility as a journalist. As in all the township tales I have considered, much of this clout was derived from a demonstration of the author's knowledge of and mastery over the opposite sex. We find an example of this kind of posturing—as well as of Saidi's colorful language—in his column from September 7, 1963, where he writes, "You see, some guys are convinced that if they ever see me moving around the streets of Lusaka with a girl who looked as if she had been dissected by a drunken pathologist, they would resign from the human race. In other words, their confidence in my caliber as a connoisseur where girls are concerned is downright fantastic."[180] Here, Saidi couples his authority when it comes to women with his presence on the streets of Lusaka—a rhetorical move that emphasizes his authority in both realms. Similarly, when Saidi returns to Lusaka after a lengthy trip to the Copperbelt, the center of Northern Rhodesia's mining industry, he playfully laments that there was no welcome committee to receive him: "Everybody seemed to take it for granted that I am ALWAYS in Lusaka, which is all right by me. They will probably dedicate one of the streets to me one of these fine days."[181] By imagining a future "Saidi Street," he writes himself into Lusaka's geography. Given that so many of Lusaka's street names were changed following independence, this gesture also associates Saidi with Zambia's national liberation.[182]

During his trip to the Copperbelt, Saidi wrote a special edition of his column called the "Copperbelt Capers." Not surprisingly, many of the adventures he reports revolve around local women. His column from October 25, 1963, announces that his newest publication will be "THE ENCYCLOPAEDIA COPPERBELTIA. It's a manual for male travellers to the Copperbelt," detailing how to deal with "dames" in the area's various cities.[183] In this way, Saidi's column connected Lusaka with "the cosmopolitan Copperbelt," creating a map of the new nation based on the quality and supply of women.[184] For example, in Kitwe, which prior to independence was larger and wealthier than the capital,[185] Saidi warns other men not to "let any of the dames know you've got any dough" after a woman who thinks Saidi is a big shot tries to convince him that she too is a hot commodity not only in Zambia but in America: "You know, when I got to La Guardia Airport (that's in New York), there was FRANK SINATRA all ready to marry me. Imagine, he even had a priest with him. But I turned him down."[186] In contrast, in Chingola, "the only dames you CAN call dames are the nurses," and even worse, "[i]f there is a dump that hasn't any dames, it's BANCROFT just near the Congo border." The unrest in the Congo in the early 1960s and the secession of Katanga state just north of the Copperbelt had unnerved UNIP, which emphasized "One Zambia, One nation" and "drew on the experience of conflict in independent Congo to warn of the dangers of disunity in soon-to-be-independent Zambia."[187] In this context, Saidi's suggestion that the closer you get to Congo, the fewer quality dames you find indicates that, at least in his column, attractive women served as a key marker of Zambia's emergent national identity.

Saidi's column also indexed Zambia's racial divisions through the lens of women and dating. In a column published less than a year before independence, Saidi laments the eagerness of Black women to date "our white friends."[188] Though he insists he is not opposed to interracial dating in principle, he complains that when Black women "see a white guy they just go ga-ga. They completely ignore us black boys. Well, guys like me are not standing for that sort of thing." By "reclaiming" Black women, men like Saidi asserted their power in the new nation. A number of Saidi's columns also feature Coloured, or mixed-race, women who represent what Saidi perceives to be the Coloured view "that everybody else, particularly everybody who is black, is a no-account bum who should be shunned like the plague."[189] The contentious view of race relations that Saidi presented in his column contrasted with Kaunda's vision of Zambian Humanism, the new state's official ideology, which "centered on the unity of humankind and a spiritually minded rejection of racial and ethnic divisions."[190] In particular, Juliette Milner-Thornton points out that Kaunda urged Coloured Zambians to identify with Africans and to disavow European heritage.[191] Saidi, however, is less interested in mending racial divides than in cutting Coloured women down to size. When a Coloured girlfriend suggests they get married so that Saidi can get to know Coloured people better by living with her in a designated Coloured area, Saidi reports that he "was out of that place like an overshot rocket at Cape Canaveral."[192] As in Hughes's, Motsisi's, and Dlamanzi's columns, here outer space is coded as a refuge from racial tensions on Earth. However, in this instance, Saidi's escape seems designed to keep these spatialized racial barriers intact, or perhaps to show that racial divides could not be easily papered over with the one-party state's Humanist doctrine emphasizing unity.

Despite Kaunda's program for furthering Humanism, which included the creation of a socialist state,[193] class divisions also grew more pronounced following independence.[194] Much like Hughes, Saidi addressed the issue of class in his column through the introduction of his foil, Mr. Chite, who first appeared on August 24, 1963: "Ladies and gentlemen, I would like to introduce you to a friend of mine—Mr Chite. He insists on being called Mr Chite because omitting the prefix gives him a kind of inferiority complex. I don't blame him. This guy is so short, he would make Fulbert Youlou look like Sonny Liston."[195] Mr. Chite's name signals his bourgeois ambitions and status as a classic colonial "mimic man," who "functions as a kind of 'keep out' sign shared by elites on both sides of the colonial divide."[196] Through the invocation of the short-of-stature ex-president Youlou, whose attempt to turn the Republic of Congo into a one-party state was thwarted by political riots that very month, Saidi suggests that men like Mr. Chite, with their misguided illusions of upward mobility, help to prop up the worst forms of corruption in the postcolony.

Like Hughes, Saidi describes his "friend" with a mixture of condescension and appreciation. He writes, "It is just likely that without Mr Chite my life would be one long dreary and dull routine without any colour. But thanks to this man who is so resourceful the only thing he can't invent is a contraption to beat the cost of living, that is not so."[197] Mr. Chite, who is employed as a cleaner at the Criminal Investigation Department, is "ALWAYS broke." He also lacks education ("He says: 'Why be educated? Education means trouble'") and ends up in "all sorts of scrapes."[198] In the first column featuring Mr. Chite, he finds dagga in the police evidence room. One of the officers tells him that people smoke it to feel "as big as Ben-Hur."[199] Although Mr. Chite has never heard of Ben-Hur, he imagines him to be "quite some giant," and revealing his small-man inferiority complex once more, Mr. Chite smokes the dagga and lands in jail after trying to swim naked across a tarred road. To Mr. Chite's question as to whether he has ever tried to do the same, Saidi replies, "I didn't see any reason why anybody should do that. There were swimming pools after all . . . multi-racial, for that matter."

Most importantly, Mr. Chite represents Lusakans' class aspirations, or as he puts it to Saidi in another column: "This cancerous desire to keep up with the Joneses has now possessed the people of Lusaka."[200]

Mr. Chite relates his unfortunate episode with a "pirate taxi" that he hired to take him to work one day and that ultimately causes him to be three hours late, attributing the entire incident to the fact that the driver is "masquerading as a big shot" and "wants to be another Rockefeller." Saidi concludes that Mr. Chite will simply "have to buy a car of [his] own to avoid such inconvenience," thus becoming yet "another one of the people who want to keep up with the Joneses." In a voice that sounds like Simple's, Mr. Chite replies, "Hell, no. I would start off as a Jones myself."

Despite claiming a certain class-based status, Mr. Chite also eschews certain modern (read Western) practices when it suits him in favor of local customs. In a later column, we learn that Mr. Chite and his wife are not married because, according to him, "Marriage is not really compulsory or even necessary. My wife (and she IS my wife) says she wouldn't care less about the documents. After all, she says, what difference DOES it make?"[201] However, we see this difference, when, after an unfortunate accident involving a stolen pig's head, Mr. Chite's wife leaves him for another man. By standing outside Saidi's voice in the column, Mr. Chite serves a rhetorical function similar to Simple's, but to a somewhat different end. While Hughes used Simple to insert issues of race and African American nationalism into a planetary humanistic discourse, Saidi employs Mr. Chite to warn against the dangers of a "small man" African nationalism with its bourgeois aspirations and postured adoption of African elements of African "tradition." As a relative newcomer to Lusaka, Saidi was perhaps better able to move outside his own perspective than he was in Harare and thus to map the divisions that might threaten this new nation in the making.

Today, writers like Kadzitche continue to make use of the township tale to address pressing social issues and to navigate between local, national, global, and interplanetary imaginaries. It is not an accident that characters like Katakwe, Simple, Kid Booze, the Orator, and Pa Dlamanzi flourished in periodicals and still appear in them today. The immediacy of the weekly newspaper, and even the monthly magazine, allowed these characters to reflect on local and international events in a timely way, especially as compared to other print media such as novels and short story anthologies, which often took years to publish through government-sponsored bureaus and cash-poor publishers in southern Africa. Even in the United States, the publication of Hughes's first book of Simple stories was a long, arduous process that required the elision of many of the column's topical issues and current events.[202] By comparison, the embeddedness of these columns in their respective historical moments makes them particularly useful for mapping the ways authors envisioned new and lasting forms of affiliation from spaces that were originally designed to be both peripheral and temporary. In the eyes of these writers, the township was a highly individualized "place," as we can see in Motsisi's careful maps of Johannesburg, Dlamanzi's comparisons of Makokoba to Mpopoma, and Saidi's Encyclopaedia Copperbeltia. At the same time, Hughes, Motsisi, Saidi, and Dlamanzi presented Harlem, Sophiatown, Harare, Makokoba, and Lusaka as cosmopolitan centers that were steeped in global popular culture even as they actively transformed it. And while these writers glimpsed the future of their imagined nations in these townships, they also recognized the impediments to realizing these nationalist aspirations. Each thus turned to outer space to indicate the need for a more radically free location and, in many cases, to critique colonialism and neocolonialism in its various forms. At the very least, invocations of the interplanetary served to place the African continent in the widest possible frame, centering it not only in the world but in the cosmos. By reading the township tale as it traveled from Harlem to Lusaka, we can see how writers from across southern Africa have used this form to express a complex sense of belonging to here, yonder, and beyond.

CHAPTER 3

Weekend Stories

Gender, Mobility, and Form in the Malawi News

In 2012, Stanley Kenani's short story "Love on Trial," about a gay couple in Malawi, was short-listed for the Caine Prize, one of the most prestigious prizes for African writers today. In the story, Charles is publicly "outed" after an old man in his village catches him and his lover having sex in the public toilets. For a fee—usually a beer or a tasty meal—Mr. Kachingwe tells the story of what he saw to all who will listen, including, eventually, the national and international news media. In Malawi, where homosexuality is a punishable crime, this results in Charles being put on trial—in the court of law as well as the court of public opinion. His crime is compounded, it seems, by rumors that he has refused the romantic overtures of the president's own daughter and squandered the beautiful children they might have produced. Although Charles eloquently defends himself and his lover on a TV show against those who accuse him of going against the teachings of the Bible and of adopting a practice that is fundamentally "Western" and not "African" (a familiar accusation that has been routinely debunked by African gender rights theorists and activists), Charles is sentenced to twelve years in prison with hard labor—much to the horror of Malawi's Western donors, who cut off aid in response. In the widespread misery that follows, Mr. Kachingwe, who discovers he is HIV positive and in need of antiretroviral medication, suffers acutely.

After being short-listed for the Caine, Kenani and his story were also effectively put on trial. The story was harshly critiqued by international bloggers involved in the informal event of "Blogging the Caine Prize," some of whom criticized Kenani of writing about gay rights to pander to the Caine Prize's international audience, while others took issue with the form of Kenani's story, which many viewed as moralizing and simplistic.[1] In response, Kenani said that he "wanted to speak for a section of our society that have no time to tell their stories" and that he had written the story with a Malawian audience in mind.[2] Although "Love on Trial" was originally published in South Africa and became available in Malawi only after being short-listed,[3] its status as a nationally inflected love story and an HIV/AIDS story—genres that are exceedingly popular in Malawi's newspapers—would have made it familiar to Malawian readers. What is more, Kenani's story is straight out of the headlines of Malawi's national newspapers and cannot be fully understood without the intertext of Kenani's column, Memoirs of a Common Man, which was published in the *Malawi News*'s Weekender section.

Beginning in January 2010, a number of newspaper articles took on the growing issue of gay rights, centering on the nation's first "same-sex public 'engagement'" in Blantyre and the couple's subsequent arrest, suggesting that it was indeed a topic of interest to local audiences.[4] In June, Kenani argued in his column that Malawi should follow South Africa's example and repeal the colonial-era laws that had criminalized homosexuality in the first place. However, "On the Gay Pardon" is less a defense of gay rights than a reflection on how a nation's right to determine its sexual mores reflects its standing on the world stage:

> One lesson from the gay debacle: a poor nation cannot claim sovereignty. Our independence is an illusion. In America, they have just convicted a polygamist, whose five wives cried in court in support of their husband. No single person has raised a finger against America. . . . Why? This is because America is truly independent, rich and powerful. As for us, well, that would have been declared an abuse of human rights, first and foremost by America and Britain. Isn't it a monumental shame and a colossal disgrace?[5]

Similar sentiments are echoed in "Love on Trial," first in its depiction of the international community's outrage over Charles's conviction—"Britain is angry. America is annoyed. Norway is furious. France is outraged. Germany is livid"—and then more subtly in the fable with which the story ends.[6] Told to a dying Mr. Kachingwe by his last friend, the fable is simple on its face: a farmer inadvertently kills his entire family and then hangs himself as a result of his efforts to poison a single rat. Many readers understood this moral as a lesson to Mr. Kachingwe and the closed-minded society he represents, which, in hurting Charles, has ultimately hurt itself.

Writing in *The New Inquiry*, Aaron Bady locates the root of his dissatisfaction with the story in the way it forces readers to side with the "international community's morality police" in condemning Charles's oppressors.[7] However, a closer reading of the fable in light of Kenani's newspaper column reveals how we might understand the story differently: not as a moralistic story seeking international attention, but as a nationalist story that hasn't been recognized as such. In the fable, the rat, who has seen the trap set for him, pleads with the other farm animals to help him, arguing, "This is bad for us all."[8] The others, however, cannot see past their own self-interest. "It's a mousetrap, not a cock-trap," the cock replies. The small rat, powerless on his own, asks for solidarity with the other animals against the powerful farmer and is denied. This fruitless appeal echoes Kenani's assertion in his column that "a poor nation cannot claim sovereignty," for only "independent, rich and powerful" nations are able to do so.[9] Mr. Kachingwe, whose name in Chichewa means "small string," is thus the link in a larger chain, suggesting that Malawians must band together with their most vulnerable if they are to achieve national self-determination. That international critics missed the story's trenchant criticism of global power relations has an obvious irony, and we might easily extend the fable's moral to the international readers of "Love on Trial," who roundly condemned the story without knowledge of the conversations and conventions in Malawi's literary and media spheres.

"Love on Trial" can be taken as evidence of Pascale Casanova's assertion that writers on the "periphery" of international literary space are most acutely aware of its imbalances.[10] Indeed, Kenani says that there was virtually "no reaction" to his story in Malawi and that the few local critics who did eventually cover it were heavily influenced by its negative international reviews.[11] But Kenani's story does more than point to the inequities of the global literary field. In its attention to the intersections of storytelling and media, both in the story itself and in its indebtedness to the articles in the *Malawi News*, "Love on Trial" signals the centrality of the newspaper to producing and conceptualizing Malawian literature and its relationship to the rest of the world, even beyond its role as a venue of publication. Further, "Love on Trial" presents a vision of national sovereignty based on gender and sexual norms, thus tapping into a fundamental aspect of Malawian nationalism: namely, the efforts of Malawi's first president, Hastings Kamuzu Banda, to cast the nation as an extended kinship network with himself at the center. This nationalism has resulted in a particular kind of literature—one that, because it is both steeped in the domestic sphere and appears in venues like newspapers that lack international prestige, often fails to register to outside observers as either nationalist or literary.

Malawi's national literature has largely been built on poetry and short fiction rather than the novel, and anthologization is common.[12] Many of these short forms first appeared in the newspaper, even if it is not always acknowledged as their source. The *Malawi News*, which served as the mouthpiece for Banda's single-party state from 1964 to 1994, has published fiction in English every weekend since 1977, and more sporadically beforehand, yielding more than two thousand stories. From 1990 to 2010, it also published fiction in Chichewa, which Banda designated as Malawi's national language. This makes it the longest-running and most frequent secular publisher of Malawian fiction, rivaled only by the Catholic press Montfort's monthly magazine, *Moni*. Banda's state carefully controlled the media, banning television as well as many books and imprisoning dissenting writers. This rendered the single national daily, the *Daily Times*, which Banda purchased in 1972, and its weekend iteration, the *Malawi News*, the primary sources of information, literature, and entertainment for literate Malawians.[13] Although the short stories in the newspaper have sometimes been considered mere "weekend stories" that are "supposed to be read on boring weekends and then thrown away," they have gained longevity through their republication in other periodicals and seminal national anthologies.[14] These weekend stories, the subject of this chapter, have not traveled as widely as the other transnational forms considered throughout this book. Nevertheless, because of their extensive domestic mobility, they too benefit from a reading in motion. Feminist geographers have pointed out that women's mobilities are often overlooked because their "daily forms of mobility" occur on "'smaller' scales, such as the household and the body."[15] Similarly, the weekend stories in the *Malawi News*, which have yet to receive critical attention, move in a relatively small, domestic orbit and bridge the space between the home and the public sphere.[16]

While the name "weekend story" points most obviously to the temporal aspects of this form, including its ephemerality and the frequency of its publication, it also evokes the place where such stories were most often read "on boring weekends": the home. In this way, it indicates that Banda's gendered political discourse—a regular feature of the state-run newspaper—entered, engaged, and was transformed by the domestic space. Women have frequently served as symbols of the nation, the home, and the traditional in nationalist discourse and African literatures.[17] Conversely, in African women's writing, Susan Andrade identifies "the nation writ small."[18] These tropes took a unique form in Malawi, where "Life President" Banda, a member of Malawi's largest ethnic group, the Chewa, built his regime on a particular reinvention of the Chewa matrilineal system.[19] During his thirty-year rule, all Malawian women—whether or not they were ethnically Chewa—were cast as Banda's dependents, or *mbumba*, with Banda as the male guardian, or *nkhoswe*, responsible for them: the "Nkhoswe Number One." In rewriting tradition to consolidate Malawi's many ethnic groups and languages into one nation and to cement his own power, Banda effectively conflated the political and domestic spheres in a way that was both limiting and enabling for women's social, political, and economic mobility. The weekend stories in the newspaper explore love, marriage, and modern gender roles by focusing on the domestic and national home—whether their characters remain inside the home, build it, leave it, or return to it—and thus illuminating a complex and highly gendered picture of domestic space's relationship to physical, social, and political mobility and immobility. What is more, gender and the domestic served as primary lenses for the negotiation of Malawi's international relationships, as was the case in Kenani's story.

Banda's return to "tradition" took place against the backdrop of a century of missionary, colonial, and capitalist incursion that had gradually altered Malawian gender norms. Sylvia Tamale argues that colonialism produced "a new form of domesticity" by sharpening distinctions between the public and private spheres and commercial and domestic work that were more fluid in precolonial African societies.[20] Indeed, in the Malawian context, Kings M. Phiri demonstrates how missionary and colonial interventions eroded matrilineal systems that once afforded women power as the root, or *tsinde*, of their lineages, which entitled them to the ownership of children and inheritance of land.[21] The increase in migrant labor to mines and farms in South Africa and Southern Rhodesia also disrupted the matrilineal practice of uxorilocality, wherein a man went to live with his wife's family after marriage, and men increasingly requested that their wives join them elsewhere or live with their own families. This change tipped the balance of power away from a woman and her kinship network and toward the husband as the head of a nuclear family with "full control over both wife and children."[22] Banda, in his efforts to build a mass political movement that could win the support of rural chiefs, selectively reanimated aspects of the Chewa matrilineal system, fostering "mbumba culture" while ignoring the role of women as roots of their lineages.[23]

In this context, mobility was not necessarily empowering, nor was immobility disempowering.[24] Indeed, Malawian women's increased mobility could entail a loss of the matrilineal networks that were a product of rootedness and that had given women a measure of power and independence. Nevertheless, Banda argued that he had single-handedly liberated women from the oppression they faced in both their own homes and society more broadly and freed them to participate in Malawi's social, political, and economic development, an idea captured by the Chichewa song women sang at his political rallies, "Popanda a Ngwazi sindikadabwera pano," or "Without the Ngwazi (Hero) I could not have come here."[25] The irony of the song's title is that women were required to perform for Banda, who co-opted the role that women's dancing had played in the anti-colonial struggle for his own aggrandizement and political gain.[26] The way women were presented at these rallies also signaled many of the real limitations of their participation in the public political sphere. While men wore Western suits, women were clad in "'traditional outfits' made out of fabric covered with Banda's face."[27] Furthermore, the women sang in Chichewa, the language Banda had designated as Malawi's national language but that he himself refused to speak publicly, preferring English instead.[28] In all these ways, women were presented as "more closely related to African or 'traditional' cultures in a context in which access to European language and education was necessary for attaining power and money."[29] However, just as women achieved a degree of independence and mobility through these rallies (which, as the writer Norah Lungu told me, their husbands allowed them to attend because they couldn't say no to the Ngwazi), women did gain some social, educational, and political opportunities during Banda's rule—though not the total liberation that Banda touted.[30]

This chapter charts the way Malawi's national literature emerged on the pages of the newspaper, beginning with the earliest Chichewa and English fiction in the early 1970s and proceeding to its strikingly similar incarnations in the present. Based on hundreds of *Malawi News* stories in English and Chichewa from the past nearly half century, I explore how these weekend stories engage—in both their content and form—with the paradoxes of Banda's expanded domestic and national sphere, which created opportunities for women's physical and social mobility while also constraining it. As Lynda Spencer, Dina Ligaga, and Grace Musila caution, "surface readings" of African popular arts can make such forms appear either more conservative or more "transgressive and space opening" than they really are.[31] In reality, as Ruth Bush finds in her nuanced reading of the Francophone women's magazine *AWA*, "dominant discourse was both questioned . . . and at times reinforced."[32] The weekend stories in the *Malawi News* are not as didactic or closed as they might at first appear, nor were they able to open as much space as their writers might have liked, given Banda's tight control of the media. It is for this reason that these stories benefit from a reading in motion that is attentive to their retelling in various forms. With a new but similar story published every weekend, often featuring the same plots and stock characters, these weekend stories repeated and reinforced Banda's messaging about the roles women and men were expected to play in the new nation. At the same time, this repetition created space for ongoing discussion of these stories' content and form and, in some cases, for the subversion of Banda's message.[33] From the folds of the government newspaper, these weekend stories express sometimes surprising—and often coded—gestures to networks of female solidarity that contrasted with Kamuzu's *mbumba* network. By comparing these stories to more recent English and Chichewa stories from the Malawian Girls' Literary Competition, we can see how this domestic form of the short story continues to travel beyond the newspaper but, like Kenani's "Love on Trial," remains indebted to it.

Readers also engaged with these fictional stories in motion, as they navigated their way through the larger newspaper, taking in state-sponsored messages on the same or adjacent pages as literary and leisure materials.[34] If space is "a resource," as Tamale contends, the space of the page became one of the terrains on which constructions of the public and private spheres were negotiated, and choosing how to move through the paper gave readers a certain amount of agency, even as its editors used the space of the page to underscore political messages.[35] Tsitsi Jaji describes the "transsensory hermeneutic exercise" of taking in the entire page with its various forms of text, advertisements, and images as "sheen reading," emphasizing the way the glossy, advertisement-filled pages of magazines like South Africa's *Zonk!* and the West African *Bingo* catered to a wide range of readers and enabled feminist reading practices.[36] The *Malawi News* lacked the sheen of such magazines, and its readers were frequently reminded that even leisure reading was a nation-building exercise. Nevertheless, Malawian readers treated the *Malawi News*'s even more ephemeral pages with gestures similar to what Jaji describes, including preserving copies of the newspaper in home archives and carefully clipping out stories and articles to display on office walls. These are just some of the ways the stories in the *Malawi News* have outlasted the weekend on which they were published.

"WOMEN KEEP THE HOME": STORIES BY MALAWIAN WRITERS

On its cover in 1964, the *Malawi News* advertised itself as "The Only Newspaper in East, Central and Southern Africa owned, Printed and Published by Africans themselves at a Press that is owned and Managed by Africans themselves."[37] This spirit of independence—which echoes a similar assertion by *African Parade*, as discussed in chapter 1—reflects the newspaper's inception as an anti-colonial or "protest paper" in 1959 and belies its increasingly close association with Banda's single-party government postindependence.[38] Banda's control of the media was solidified by the 1968 Censorship and Control Entertainments Act, which established a censorship board with the capacity to "declare any publication 'undesirable'" and thus render its publication, distribution, or even possession illegal and punishable by law, effectively criminalizing the "expression of dissenting views, including literary ones."[39] In this environment, the *Malawi News* was able to circulate only because it was part of Banda's political apparatus. As Vail and White have argued regarding oral poetry in southern Africa, it was the poem that was "licensed," not the poet.[40] Here, the medium was sanctioned, not the individual journalists and writers associated with it, who were still subject to arrest on occasion.[41] Nevertheless, the fact that the newspaper was authorized as "Kamuzu's paper" meant that, like oral poetry, it could sometimes serve as a vehicle for complaint and critique.

In the early 1970s, when the first fiction appeared in the *Malawi News*, "Build the Nation" was the slogan on the paper's masthead, and writing for the paper was seen as "a contribution to [the] advancement of our country."[42] However, some of the paper's writers also understood its value to lie in its connection of the home to the wider world: it served as "a private study in every home" that equipped Malawian readers "to start writing books for the world" or, somewhat more modestly, as a means of sharing opinions and advice "even if someone lives far away" ("timakhoza kugwirizana m'maganizo ndi kupatsana nzeru ngakhale wina akukhala kutali").[43] Much of this advice related to marriage, and the paper received so many letters dealing with marital discord that the editor urged readers to send letters on other topics ("ndiponso nkhani zake zolembamo zisamakhala za mtundu umodzimodzi zokhudza kubvuta kwa maukwati").[44] These writers' border-crossing ambitions conflicted with Banda's nation-building agenda, which increasingly isolated Malawi from the international community, first when he refused to condemn South Africa's apartheid regime and Portuguese rule in Mozambique, and then when he abruptly suspended migrant labor to South Africa following a 1974 plane crash that killed seventy-four returning migrant workers.[45] Banda strategically positioned himself as Malawi's link to the outside world and encouraged Malawians to stay "at home" in Malawi to develop the nation through agriculture. Accordingly, the *Malawi News*'s earliest fictional stories, in both English and Chichewa, were used primarily to reinforce, in a more engaging fashion, Banda's messages to the nation in other parts of the paper. These weekend stories adapted a variety of oral forms—including oral tales, proverbs, rumor, and gossip—to the space of the printed newspaper page, exploiting them to convey Banda's insular nation-building philosophy.[46] They also, however, exposed some of its contradictions, particularly when it came to his reinventions of Malawian gender norms.

This strategy is particularly evident in the first fictional stories in the paper, the prize-winning stories from the newspaper's 1973 Chichewa story competition, which solicited "[n]khani zomveka bwino ndi zazifupi" ("[s]tories that are clear and short") to be published in the newspaper for a first prize of K10, second prize of K5, and third of K2.50.[47] Although *nkhani* has many meanings, including "news," "information," and "story," the competition's winners (aside from the first-place winner) have several key features in common: linear, fable-like structures, many beginning with "*kalekale*," or "long ago," and ending with a containing moral; rural, village settings; and extended time frames that often cover an entire lifetime or family history.[48] In these prize-winning stories, we can see how writers' adaptations of oral stories to print were heavily mediated by Banda's reinventions of Malawian tradition. The story that won third prize in the Chichewa competition, "Chikondi sachita choumiliza" ("Love Is Not Forced") by Ignatius V. Chidzulo, is notable for the way it presents women's adherence to "traditional customs" as key to prosperity and for its use of some of the resources of print to emphasize this moral. "Love Is Not Forced" is about a family with two beautiful daughters whose parents wish them to enrich the family by marrying wealthy men. While the elder daughter obeys, the younger daughter "has a great deal of courage in refusing" ("anachitabe khama pakukana") the man—a drunk—whom her father chooses for her, insisting that family wealth comes from the "courage" to work hard ("Chuma cha m'banja chimachita kubwera chifukwa cha khama la eni ake akakhala olimbikira kugwira ntchito"), a protest that echoes Banda's emphasis on working hard to build the nation.[49] As a result, her father kicks her out of his house, and she flees to her *gogo* (grandparent), who, rather than scold her for disobeying her father, applauds her for having "kept tradition" ("wasunga mwambo") by avoiding marrying a man who may have beaten her and ruined her reputation. "Wasunga Mwambo" is also the heading for this section of the story, underscoring the importance of presenting tradition as unchanging, even as it is reinvented.[50]

Chidzulo's story also demonstrates how Banda's reinvention of tradition disrupted family networks, affording women some greater freedom, so long as it was used to advance his nation-building agenda. While traditional Chewa marriages were negotiated by *ankhoswe*, or guardians, missionary and colonial intervention contributed to the growth of the "domestic authority" of fathers over their nuclear families.[51] In Chidzulo's story, Banda's nation-building rhetoric supersedes the girl's father's wishes, which is fitting given his self-proclaimed role as *nkhoswe* to all the women in Malawi. The girl's *gogo* urges her father to change his mind about disowning his youngest daughter, warning him with a proverb that is partially bolded in the text and then repeated at the story's end: "chifukwa za mawa sizidziwika mwina adzakupukutani malobvu kumbuyo" ("because tomorrow is not known perhaps she will wipe the spittle behind you").[52] In other words, you do not know who will take care of you tomorrow. Indeed, the younger daughter and the poor man she later marries become rich by working hard to make fallow land productive, and when the father ends up in jail because he has failed to pay his taxes, it is the younger daughter who helps him, not the older. This story clearly reiterates Banda's messaging to the nation about agricultural development, which he touted as the key to Malawi's advancement. However, it also dramatizes the way Banda, the Nkhoswe Number One, used women in his reinvention of Malawian tradition and inserted himself—at least rhetorically—into kinship networks. By "keeping tradition" and adhering to Banda's project of building wealth through farming, the younger daughter escapes her own father's tyranny and gains the freedom to choose a suitable partner and home for herself.

Stories like this one were read in the context of the newspaper as a whole, which in 1973 introduced a Women's Page that clearly demonstrates the merging of the national political and domestic spaces. Among its eclectic mix of news items, an opinion column by "Bernadette," baby advice, recipes "for people with taste," government tender notices, and advertisements for books, fashion, and community development courses, the page included Banda's advice to his *mbumba*, often voiced by one of his female deputy ministers.[53] In the lead-up to independence, when women had emerged as an important voting bloc, Banda assured women that he would include them in his Legislative Council since "women keep the home. Without women there could be no Nyasaland."[54] Although Banda did appoint a few women as junior ministers and nominated others to parliament beginning in 1977, Linda Semu suggests that these highly educated (and thus privileged) women were not necessarily interested in issues of gender equity once elected.[55] In some ways, then, postcolonial Malawi was what Amina Mama describes as a "femocracy," wherein a few politically powerful women draw their power from the patriarchal state and thus fully support it.[56] Instead of wielding "real political power," most Malawian women were called on to "keep the home" through a combination of grassroots Malawi Congress Party support and domestic work.[57]

While Tamale finds that in most cases, "the labour that [African women] perform in the domestic arena (e.g., mothering) is not inscribed into the construction of citizenship," Banda and his government insisted that for women, being good citizens entailed being good wives and mothers and vice versa.[58] On the Women's Page, one of Banda's junior ministers, Mrs. Effie Mtika, was quoted as asking women to attend government-sponsored homecraft classes "in order to raise the standard of living in their families and help in developing the country . . . Mrs. Mtika appealed to them to keep their homes clean all the time. She asked them to respect their husbands and remain loyal and faithful to them."[59] Similarly, in an article nestled between advice on a "Hundred and One Uses of Paraffin" and recipes for tea scones, Mrs. Margaret Mlanga, parliamentary secretary in the president's office, told women to "ensure that their domestic work is done and attend meetings [of the Malawi Congress Party]."[60] While Mlanga warned women against "petty jealousy and gossip" as "evils which caused confusion and disunity," she also asked them to be "the eyes and ears of their Nkhoswe Number One." Women's location in the home made them ideal informants on potential dissenters, even their own husbands—one of the more sinister ways women's task of "keeping the home" served Banda's autocratic state. As in Chidzulo's story above, women's loyalty to their families was necessarily subordinated to their loyalty to Banda and the MCP. Women received many such contradictory messages in the paper, and one might argue that the only difference between informing and gossiping was that the former served Banda, while the latter might threaten his power by creating competing narratives, as several later fictional stories suggest.

Women's duty to "keep the home" also extended to Malawi's international relationships. An article celebrating Mother's Day in 1972 pointed to women's role not only in "building the nation" but in changing its "relationship with other states" through helping to achieve independence, noting that Mother's Day that year coincided with Malawi's hosting of the Commonwealth Parliamentary Association Conference for the first time.[61] Another article from the same month suggested that housekeeping could serve as a tool of diplomacy: twenty-two women from the League of South African Housewives visited Malawi and reported having "learnt a lot" from the Ngwazi's counsel, in this case his advocacy of "dialogue between the people of all races."[62] Women also kept the home while Banda was away on international trips. Banda's presidential departures and returns at the international airport—which in many ways restaged his triumphant return to Malawi as the nation's liberator in the late 1950s—were key events in the "cycle of presidential rituals" that came to define Malawian politics.[63] Upon each of Banda's departures and arrivals, his *mbumba* lined the airport road and danced for him at the function, which also included political speeches. The *Malawi News* covered the president's comings and goings (usually on the front page), highlighting Banda's role in connecting Malawi to the rest of the world and suggesting that his ability to leave Malawi without fear of a coup or uprising was, in the words of the *Malawi News*'s later editor, Mike Kamwendo, "[p]roof of this nation's strength."[64]

The home is the focal point of many of the earliest stories in English in the *Malawi News*, which were published in 1974 under the suitably nationalist heading "Stories by Malawian Writers." Under the umbrella of "story," the editors included nonfictional accounts of various cultural practices, such as Rodrick Ndala's story on "Tchopa Dance—a Means of Expressing Love," as well as folktales and one narrative explicitly referred to as a "short story."[65] Despite this formal fluidity, most of these stories were structured simply, unfolding linearly with a clear moral that was sometimes conveyed using significant Chichewa names or proverbs. Of the twenty-two stories that were published in the newspaper in 1974, nine featured the wife as a character or the theme of marriage, and only two of the nine were told from a female point of view.[66] In some of these narratives, the home is synonymous with the wife herself, as was also the case in many traditional *chinamwali*, or girls' initiation, songs, where the woman's body was compared to a house to be entered.[67] Male movement to and from the home is central to the plots of many of these stories, and a number of them begin with a husband returning home to his wife, whether after a long night of drinking or a hard day's work in the fields.[68]

While men were often portrayed as having much greater physical and socioeconomic mobility in these early *Malawi News* stories, they too were encouraged to remain "at home" in Malawi to develop the new nation. Dymon Mosiya's "Why Are Men Driven into Crime and Women into Shame and Madness This Century?" depicts two educated, urbane men who, rather than migrate to South Africa, decide to stay in Malawi for the higher purpose of national development. Notably, the story appeared just a few months after the plane crash that supposedly precipitated Banda's prohibition of migrant labor to South Africa.[69] The narrator tells his friend, Makasu, whose name meaning "hoes" indicates his future profession, "The answer is: 'Let's be here in Malawi, till our gardens and make a good and honest profit from life. It has been done by many, many others without our academic background. We, with better education, can do even better. What we need is to work hard in the fields right here at home.'"[70] The nested quotations in Mosiya's "answer" lay bare the story's doublespeak—the way that it, like Chidzulo's story, gives voice to Banda's messaging without referring to him directly. In fact, the story's final line, "To others like the two of us, I say: 'There is wealth in Malawi soil,'" replicates almost verbatim Banda's frequent saying, "The soil is our wealth." In this story, Banda's rhetoric not only influences the story's moral but becomes the moral, attaining the status of a proverb. If Banda's messaging was not obvious enough to some readers, a letter to the editor on the same page titled "Ngwazi Thanked for Developing Country Following Independence" by James S. Makawa of Lilongwe relays this message in yet another form, praising His Excellency, whose "first concern is his people," for encouraging Malawians to grow crops. In reality, Banda's efforts to keep Malawian labor at home was not necessarily the boon to small farmers that Makawa's letter makes it out to be. Instead, many Malawian workers were funneled onto large-scale agricultural estates, at least one of which was owned by Banda.[71] In keeping with the official message, however, only one other story from the *Malawi News* in this period portrays international travel beyond Africa, and it suggests that failing to return to Malawi in a timely manner could have disastrous consequences—in this case, losing one's fiancée to another man.[72]

Given that women were charged with keeping the home, it is unsurprising that women's physical and social mobility is portrayed in the *Malawi News*'s weekend stories as potentially dangerous. Indeed, the very few stories that depict women leaving home end in hardship or death.[73] In Mary Matukuta Milanzi's "Enmity in a Village Because of Education," one of several stories published that year by a woman writer, a girl who leaves home to pursue her studies soon faces her entire family's demise. Asawilunda, whose father died several months previously, learns that her mother is ill and asks her headmaster if she can travel home. He initially refuses due to her impending exams, and when Asawilunda is finally allowed to leave, the journey she takes is marked by death. Asawilunda learns that she must take the "EXPRESS VIA MALIRO," or the bus via "funeral," because the stop "had just changed last week from Imfa [Death] stage"—indicating that she has come home too late to see her mother alive.[74] The girl's brother passes away shortly thereafter, and her mother's relatives, jealous of Asawilunda's education, blame her for her family's death, forcing her to leave the village and to marry a man from another district and lending credence to Banda's warning that jealousy fosters disunity. The story is accompanied by a drawing of a girl walking alone with her belongings on her head and the caption ". . . Asawilunda left home for good . . . ," which together suggest that mobility was not always advantageous to women, particularly when it resulted in the loss of the matrilineal networks that typically supported women after marriage.

The story ends with an initially puzzling two-part moral:

> A week after Amalembe's [her brother's] death Asawilunda left for school to resume her studies and from that time she never went back home because she was by then a "LONELY POOR GIRL" yet she could not have been a lonely girl but education had caused her father's, mother's and lastly brother's death. It is not only the education but ambition of the parents to make their children very useful citizens of the community.[75]

Here, the narrative classifies Asawilunda as a particular type, the "lonely poor girl," who leaves home to seek better opportunities elsewhere and ends up alone and vulnerable, evoking this stock character with eye-catching uppercase letters and quotation marks. However, the traditional ending of this kind of story, in which a girl learns a lesson about "bad behavior," is complicated by Milanzi's double moral. While the first part of this concluding paragraph blames the death of Asawilunda's family and her resulting loneliness on her education, the second part suggests that education is important for turning children, including girls, into "very useful citizens of the community."[76] Banda's conflicting rhetoric around women's role in national development registers visibly here: women were meant to "keep the home" by staying at home to care for their families while also pursuing educational opportunities outside the home that were important for national advancement. Milanzi seizes on this discord to simultaneously advocate for women's education and to express the social repercussions—including the loss of family networks—that women could face for pursuing such opportunities. Ruptured morals like this one, which created space for readers to reflect on and debate changing social norms, can be found in stories by Malawian women writers from the past nearly half century, including an uncannily similar one in a Chichewa story that received a special mention in the 2008 Malawian Girls' Literary competition, which I discuss below.[77]

While stories like Milanzi's and Chidzulo's build on Banda's rhetoric, from his warnings against jealousy to his emphasis on tradition, in their depictions of women's advancement, Angeline Dudu Kalizga's "The Wedding That Flopped" is striking for its treatment of gossip (against which Banda warned) as a means to foster female solidarity. The day before her wedding, Margarita receives an anonymous letter and then a phone call from a woman who claims to be her fiancé's wife. She decides not to broach the topic with Eddie, her husband-to-be, and to go forward with the wedding, but after the woman disrupts the ceremony, Margarita and her family become the subject of relentless gossip: "My mother could not do her shopping as she used to, because every time she went out, she could hear women still mumbling about my wedding flop and she could not stand the sight of women gossiping."[78] Eventually Margarita and Eddie are married, but when she arrives at her "new home," she finds this other woman and her children already living there. Although Margarita knows that "Eddie had cheated [her]," she feels she is also to blame for refusing to listen to her friends' advice: "I had thought it was always gossips, gossip, more gossip." Women's gossip turns out to be an important source of information and wisdom, and having failed to listen to it, Margarita finds herself unmarried with her parents "growing too old every day." The story suggests that by listening to other women in the future, Margarita will "tread on the right path" and gain the social mobility through marriage that she desires.

The earliest weekend stories in the *Malawi News* reinvented traditional literary forms in print alongside and through Banda's reinvention of Malawian tradition more broadly, particularly as it related to changing gender roles. Notably, the resources of print—from typography to layout—gave the page's writers and editors further means to not only reiterate Banda's rhetoric regarding national development but to also draw attention to some of the contradictions of Banda's vision of a domestic domain that encompassed the nation. Perhaps because it opened this space for critique, fiction was eliminated from the *Malawi News* in the mid-1970s during an enhanced period of censorship.[79] In the "brief period of relative liberalization" that followed, the newspaper's fiction page reemerged in a dramatically new form under the editorship of Mike Kamwendo.[80]

THE LITERARY PAGE: STORIES THAT "LIVE FOREVER"

The US-educated Mike Kamwendo arrived at the *Malawi News* from the state broadcaster, the Malawi Broadcasting Corporation, in 1976. First appointed features editor and then editor of the *Malawi News* only a year later, Kamwendo was tasked specifically with giving the page a new, more professional look. He had, in fact, gained his position by presenting the mock-up of a new layout. "It was a political paper, and I wanted it to be a social paper," Kamwendo explains. "How do we entice people not to feel that's just a political organ? So, we tried to make it as friendly as possible."[81] The establishment of the newspaper's "Literary Page" was a key part of this effort and certainly had something to do with the fact that Kamwendo was a fiction writer himself. In 1977, the *Malawi News* inaugurated its Literary Page with the publication of Kamwendo's serial story "Yaya." This new full page dedicated to fiction had its own logo, a feather quill placed over its title, and was designed to be eye-catching by playing with blank spaces, pull quotes, and even a cartoon rendering of the story's title—a far cry from the crowded, haphazardly organized appearance of "Stories by Malawian Writers" (fig. 3).

22 MALAWI NEWS/SUNDAY 2 OCTOBER 1977

THE STRANGE FEELING

Literary Page

PART 1

By Mike Kamwendo

YAYA sat in her office thinking back to her early days. This had become a habit each time her boss was out.

She had been confused by all that was happening around her. Her body had grown faster than her mind and she found herself at conflict as she tried to understand and reconcile the two growths. She needed help, advice, but who would talk to her about that? Indeed, when does a woman begin to experience the pangs of love while everyone else was calling her a child at the same time? The whole issue was frustrating. If the so called adults were going through what she was going through at that moment ...she did not wish to grow further.

Yaya was surprised that she was able to recapture the very feelings she had felt over eight years ago, two years before she went to secondary school. She was now a very sophisticated lady. An accomplished secretary. She could not believe that she was actually in the job which to her a few years ago was a dream. The irony of it all was that it was not the job per se which she had aimed for. Life really had funny twists.

She looked at her long fingers, and then at her fingernails. True, they were pretty. As she looked at her fingernails hot tears started filling her eyes, making everything in front of her typewriter go out of focus.

A few years ago. Why always look backward? She had to because it was a few years ago that seeds were sown but the harvest seemed never to come. A few years ago she was twelve years old. She was open and enjoyed the freshness of youth. A few years ago she lost her heart to a man. Yes, a few years ago she lost her identity and mind because her soul had been touched. Or was it all a cruel game her mind had played on her?

Everyone called her Yaya, a nickname she got because she could not say much as a child. She used to address her father and mother as Yaya, so they called her Yaya in- [illegible]. She loved her name because it was almost a gift from her parents. She kept it throughout school. She was Yaya. Forever she was going to be Yaya.

One day, someone mentioned her name with such tenderness that for a moment she didn't know it was her name. That was the moment. For some reason she could not understand why the name echoed right through her being. She had been helping her parents working in the fields. The rains had been generous this year and maize had grown very quickly, and with it...weeds. She had been weeding when he passed by and called her name. Utterly confused by the feeling, she just managed to smile. What even confused her more was that he was from the same village in Lunzu and she had seen him several times that year. Although he lived in the city, he was usually home during weekends.

Everything she did that day was done mechanically. She managed to burn the beans, and went to the market without money. She found herself easily startled each time anyone called her name. All of a sudden the sky was getting closer to earth and she could hear little noises made by the tiniest of insects. She was very sensitive indeed. She was open. Yes, she was a victim. A victim of love. Twelve years of age and she was in love, or whatever that feeling was. The worst part of it was that she could not discuss it with anyone. Why, she would be laughed at. Yaya in love, how unthinkable.

He was a friend of the family. He had seen Yaya grow. He was a bachelor. He had been engaged but broke it off because his fiancee had proved unfaithful on two counts. This was after three years of the engagement. She had been in college and he had wanted her to finish first before living together. He respected education. He was odd in many ways. It was known that he had vowed not to be involved with women again. His first love was his job as a laboratory technician. In a way he enjoyed retreating into his lab and worked quietly for hours on different specimens and prepared reports. He liked to be by himself most of the time. During weekends he went home to commune with nature... so to speak. He liked strolling by the riverside near his home. In a way, one could say he lived a simple life. His relationship to other human beings was as technical as his specimens. He was not going to be open to anyone... let alone women. It was from one of these strolls that he passed by his neighbour's garden and greeted Yaya. She cut a lonely but warm figure among the green of the maize. He was old enough to be her father. He was not aware of the tenderness in his own voice as he greeted the girl, or perhaps he felt no threat in her youthful innocence. After all, it was little Yaya. He dismissed the incident and by the time he was back in town he had forgotten it entirely.

Yaya dried her eyes with an embroidered handkerchief. Actually it was from a set she got by mail from an admirer. Admirers she had. She had also learnt the proper way of saying 'no' without actually saying so. She wished she could tell her story. Perhaps time was not ripe yet. Her boss had told her that he was going to be in later in the afternoon. She had done most of her work. Perhaps to kill time she had to take care of a few memories. Hers actually wasn't a memory....but a continuing saga of her life. The worst part of it was that she had made the choice. Although the greeting incident in her parents' garden was of no plan of her own, she accepted the hand offered by fate...for that was what it all seemed to be. She was going to see it through.

Having been taken by surprise by the incident at the garden, Yaya sought ways and means to shake the feeling. Because she had not understood it, she thought that it was a result of having been startled. Days turned into weeks, and weeks into months; still the feeling grew with her. In the meantime, for some unknown reason, it seemed that he had decided not to use the way leading to her parent's garden. She only saw him from a distance. This was odd. Why should she care that she was not seeing him? But she wanted to, very much. Sometimes she would walk towards his home and hope to see him at a closer range. Just see him. The thought frightened her as well as filled her with excitement. She was now thirteen. She had grown considerably. Her desire to see him was getting uncontrollable. She would get into tantrums over the most trivial things. She had to see him. But not here at home, no. She would follow him to the city. She had to think of a way, an excuse for seeing him. The thought of her possibility of seeing him in the city was scary as well as comforting. At least she would spend her days devising a plan.

Yaya was a growing woman. She did not know it. The following year she would be going to secondary school. Her plan should be executed before she left. She had come up with a good one. Yes, she would use her parents as an excuse. But in what way? Going to borrow money? But she had never heard her parents mentioning borrowing money, let alone from him. After days of thinking, as much as a thirteen year-old girl can think, she came up with a fool proof plan: she was going to take mangoes to him and say that it was her mother who had sent her with them. That was safe enough. Now for the preparations. The first thing to take care of was a story to her parents so that she could go to town. Secondly she had to have something impressive in which to carry the mangoes. A beautiful mpango would be suitable. Yes, she was going to sell some of the nuts and with the money, buy a mpango.

She bought a red silky looking mpango with blue and white designs. She looked at it several times and gave a smile of satisfaction. And now for the story to her parents so that she could go to the city.

Yaya was recalled from her thoughts by a knock on her door. It was the messenger. He was checking with her if she had anything she wanted because he was going to the post office. She wanted nothing. He closed the door and left her to her solitude.

Back to her approach. Yaya knew how much her parents valued education. She used that as an excuse. She was to go and visit a friend who had been already to secondary school so that she could get tips on early days at a boarding school. Mother was happy. She gave her transport money and begged her to be careful on the roads. She was to leave in two days time. The remaining problem now was the mango problem. Where would she get the best looking and tasting mangoes? Why, auntie of course, just across the stream. She had lovely trees of mangoes. Yaya hoped she would find the type known as India type mangoes. Those mangoes had a special taste and were very large indeed. They were good for a city person eating them with a knife. She would fetch them in the morning, let them stay for a few hours so that the gums ooze out, then she would wash them just before she took off for the city.

The journey from Lunzu to Blantyre that day was the shortest and the longest at the same time. She went over hundreds of times what she was going to say to him. Just in case he had surprising questions, she would be ready for them. If he was going to be hostile, that would just as well be, at least she wouldn't have to worry about that nagging feeling any more. Talking about that, she had actually forgotten or rather, she did not quite understand what she was going to do. Just see him, she tried to answer herself. And how was she dressed for the occasion? Her clothes were clean. As a matter of fact she almost burnt her dress with the coal iron. One thing she was glad about was that although she had lied to her parents about the purpose of her trip, she nevertheless had their blessings.

She arrived in Blantyre just a few minutes before half-past three. She changed buses and got onto one to Limbe, for she was going to Kanjedza. Yaya was in Limbe at twenty minutes to four. This meant that she had to be back very quickly in order to catch the five-thirty bus back home. Although she had never been to his house, she knew where to find it because it had been pointed out to her several times.

Clutching her mangoes in the red mpango like it was a fortune, Yaya made her way. As she neared the house, fear overcame her. All her planned defence simply evaporated from her head. She felt like turning around and going right back. Then another thought occurred to her, what if he was not home. What if it was a public holiday?

She reached the threshold, timidly knocked on the door. Nothing happened. She knocked again. She had waited for what seemed like a century. Then quietly the door opened. He was in his gown. He had been sleeping. He apologised for taking long in coming to the door. He ushered her in. She sat in a corner with the mangoes in her lap. He greeted her. He had not recognised her. Yaya. He got up and came towards her with his hand out [illegible] recognised [illegible] in manner. He [illegible] mangoes. [illegible]

CONTINUED

Fig. 3. *Malawi News*, Literary Page, October 2, 1977, 22, featuring "Yaya: Part 1" by Mike Kamwendo. Courtesy of Blantyre Newspapers Limited. Photo by Sam Banda Jr.

Already in its first several months, the Literary Page proved to be an important site for literary and critical exchange, particularly around "Yaya" and the review of it by Aubrey Kalitera, a writer who went on to publish numerous stories on the page and who ultimately became Malawi's most prolific self-published author. Kamwendo's narrative is the coming-of-age story of a young "sophisticated lady," Yaya, who falls in love with an older man when she is thirteen and marries him many years later.[82] The story is particularly interesting for what it can tell us about the intersection between medium, form, and constructions of gender in Malawi's emerging print literature. The format of the long serial provided Kamwendo with the opportunity to nuance some of his representations of Yaya, who epitomizes the possibilities and limitations of an expanded domestic sphere for women in Banda's Malawi. Equally significant, however, is Kalitera's critique of "Yaya" and his own story about modern gender roles, "Face Value," which appeared just after the publication of "Yaya." Both Kalitera's short story and his critique, which contains fictional elements, can be read as retellings of "Yaya." On the one hand, this reading points to the iterative quality of weekend stories, which retold many of the same stories over and over again. On the other, it elucidates the way literary form and representations of gender were intertwined on the page. While both Kamwendo's and Kalitera's stories explore the consequences for successful modern women when they move beyond the domestic sphere, including a loss of solidarity with other women, they also seek to contain women within the home. Kalitera's story suggests that this containment can happen not only in the story's content but also through its form.

"Yaya" is the longest story ever published in the *Malawi News*, appearing in nine parts from October 2 to November 27, and the first story to be published with a magazine style and layout, incorporating pull quotes and other eye-catching features. Kamwendo, who says he was inspired by British magazines and tabloids, argues that layout is important because "food is in the presentation."[83] In the late 1970s, Kamwendo was not the only editor experimenting with the style and layout of international magazines. *Star Stories*, produced by Blantyre Periodicals Limited, a subsidiary of Blantyre Printing and Publishing, began publication several months before the inception of the Literary Page.[84] *Star Stories* was also heavily influenced by British women's magazines, and the settings of its stories, filled with women who drink brandy with their in-laws and enjoy buttery scones, often bear a stronger resemblance to the UK than to 1970s Malawi.[85] In contrast, Kamwendo's "Yaya" combines an international layout with a story that is Malawian in its setting and cultural content and that was serialized in a way that was meant to cultivate Malawian reading habits. By using these spatial and temporal aspects of the page to entice readers, Kamwendo veiled some of his narrative's more politically inflected content, including Yaya's resemblance to Cecilia Kadzamira, Banda's longtime companion, known familiarly as "Mama."

Yaya represents a new kind of woman who marries "traditional" ideals of Malawian womanhood with "modern," urbanized characteristics. As a secretary for a large company, Yaya is extremely "efficient" and successful at her job, but she also shows more respect to men than do the other women at her hostel who grew up in the city. As a result, she lacks a sense of comradery with the other women, who laugh at her as she curtsies before each man she encounters: "The girls claimed they were civilized, equals to men and there was no need to curtsy, especially among the educated. To her, respect was intuitive."[86] Although she is cut off from other women, Yaya is figured as an ideal member of Kamuzu's *mbumba*: even as she is liberated from the domestic sphere to pursue her education and work in the city, she adheres to traditional gender roles and embodies Kamuzu's tenets of respect, obedience, and discipline. Like Kamuzu's actual *mbumba*, who were given a central role in "receiv[ing] and cheer[ing] visitors" to Malawi,[87] Yaya is selected as the head "hostess" at an international reception for her company, where she tells the others that they should consider themselves to be "representatives of their country."[88] She fulfills this role so successfully that "[o]ne would have thought she had been at it all her life. Or that she was a wife of a diplomat."[89]

In all these ways, Yaya bears an interesting resemblance to Cecilia Kadzamira, Banda's "efficient" personal secretary and Malawi's "Official Government Hostess."[90] Banda, who never married, was rumored to have had a romantic relationship with Kadzamira, who was forty years his junior. Although it is unlikely that Banda's censorship apparatus would have allowed Kamwendo to publish a story that seemed to comment on their relationship—even the Simon and Garfunkel song "Cecilia" was banned in Malawi—the similarities between Yaya and Kadzamira sharpen the story's message regarding the contradictory roles women were meant to play in the new nation, as simultaneously representatives of the traditional and the modern and as keepers of the home in both its domestic and national senses. Linda Semu argues that Kadzamira embodied the contradictions of the Banda era for women.

She was the highest-ranking and most visible woman in the public sphere, but she was not allowed to speak at public meetings: "She stood for what women could become if given a chance. And yet her silence confirmed the commonly held view that a woman should be seen but not heard."[91]

On a number of occasions, Yaya's role as a symbol of the ideal woman is linked to her role as a reader and interpreter. Given that the Literary Page was meant to entice readers to engage with what was otherwise a political paper, it is unsurprising that Kamwendo's story communicates the personal and social value of reading. When Fred, the older man she loves, sends her fifty tambala and a note that reads, "Little girls love sweets," Yaya is mature enough to interpret the simple message for what it is: "She read between the lines many times but the message was what it was."[92] As Yaya correctly understands, the letter must be taken at face value; there is no hidden message. Yaya is a little girl, and only time can change this. This scene might also be understood as a message to the censorship board not to "read between the lines" of the story's depiction of Yaya's relationship with Fred as an allegory for Banda and Kadzamira.

More broadly, reading is presented as one of Yaya's good habits, a practice that keeps her at home and away from the bad influence of other women in the city: "She did entertain female friends once in awhile [*sic*]. But most of the time she enjoyed reading. She loved novels a great deal, especially something epic . . . something that would take her weeks to finish. That made her look forward to something when coming home."[93] The kind of epic described here bears an obvious resemblance to "Yaya" the story, which was serialized over many weeks so that its readers could look forward to reading it each Sunday during their leisure time at home. With a new installment each week, serialized stories like "Yaya" were designed to give the stories on the Literary Page greater longevity than the single weekend on which they were published. Another moment in the story reinforces the importance of having an ongoing reading habit. Fred reflects on his respect for Yaya's father, who had passed away: "A man with great sense of humour, and probably the only one who ever lived in a village and sent out Yaya daily to get him a copy of the newspaper. He was a man who loved knowledge for its own sake."[94] In the late 1970s, the *Malawi News* was still read primarily in cities, where literacy rates were significantly higher than elsewhere. By gesturing to the potential value of the paper in rural areas, "Yaya" imagined a more expansive reading public. Nevertheless, reading was still a gendered activity in that women were encouraged to read to stay out of trouble in the city, whereas men were encouraged to read for "knowledge."

On two different occasions in the story, Yaya brings Fred a set of ripe mangoes, a symbol meant to convey that she is ready to marry him. The second time, she suffers a mental breakdown when she mistakenly believes he is already married, and she is sent to the Liquid Sunshine "rest and recreation centre."[95] Through Yaya's breakdown, Kamwendo illuminates the double standard to which modern men and women are held. Fred, who realizes he is in love with Yaya, at first wonders if she is not as virtuous as she appears: "Perhaps she had grown to be like many of the so-called urbanized girls, looking good in the city while burdening their mothers at home with their babies, the answer to a distorted version of good times."[96] Fred candidly wonders whether this would "mar her in his eyes" and realizes that as a woman, Yaya cannot gain the experience that would make her more emotionally mature without becoming damaged:

> There just were no short-cuts. Experience, perhaps, after which the human being assumes a better psycho-emotional mould. He had his experience, and by virtue of the fact that he was a man, he was blessed because he did not have to drag nor display trophies of his experience. Experience was him. But for the woman it was always a different story. Sometimes life simply wasn't fair.[97]

Men are both the subject and object of their own stories ("Experience was him"), but for women, their experiences always produce and signify more than themselves and must be carefully controlled to ascertain that the "right" kind of society is reproduced. The story's recognition of the inherent unfairness in this situation marks its most progressive moment, but it is quickly contained by the story's ending, in which Fred brings Yaya home, literally and figuratively: "She had been a homing pigeon, lost in another territory. He had come looking for her."[98]

Once Fred finally utters the words that Yaya has been waiting for eight years to hear, she does not speak again for the rest of the narrative—mirroring the way Kadzamira's "voice was muted," even though she stood next to Banda.[99] By remaining silent, Yaya returns to her earliest, most essential state: Yaya's name, we learn early in the narrative, was given to her "because she could not say much as a child."[100] Yaya returns to this prelinguistic state when Fred finally tells her he loves her: "She was no longer capable of language. . . . She shook her head to signify her statement."[101] The story then moves from its more psychological mode into a series of images (and senses) that suggests a traditional marriage scene:

> The two hearts paced a rhythm of their own. . . . The sound of drums filled her ears. She could see her father and mother spread banana leaves for welcome. She could hear many people ululate louder and louder and louder until the drum tore, and the sea rushed in amidst all this din. There was calm at the break of tide as tears of happiness flooded her face. They were slowly dried by the breeze fanned through the window by the flattering curtain.[102]

The sound of the two beating hearts of the couple travels outward to encompass her father and mother's home and the drums and ululations of the community, for this story has always been about more than just a woman's love for a man. It is a story about how to be a woman in modern Malawian society by respecting tradition, most importantly marriage, while also incorporating aspects of Westernized city life. It is also a scene that is framed quite literally by the window curtains of Fred's house, making the home once again the essential prism through which modern gender relationships are viewed. In this case, Yaya, brought home, goes silent, demonstrating that when nation and home overlap on the pages of the *Malawi News*, the expanded domestic sphere does not necessarily translate into female agency and mobility.[103]

Aubrey Kalitera's review of "Yaya" was published on the Literary Page a month after the story's conclusion. Kalitera writes that twice in the past week, he has seen a girl at the market buying mangoes, and on each occasion he thought of Yaya. "I was surprised. Because definitely if I am to remember Yaya each time I see a beautiful girl picking mangoes, then Yaya is going to live forever."[104] Kalitera is particularly concerned with whether Yaya is a story that "deserves" to live forever, as "every story that is worth the story-teller's while should." This standard for evaluating stories echoes a debate that occurred on the pages of a contemporaneous publication, the *Muse*, published by students involved in the well-known Writers Group at Chancellor College. Discussing divergent reactions to a story from the previous workshop, Charles S. Joyah, who went on to become Malawi's first internationally recognized filmmaker, argues, "It is for us Malawians to decide what to write: either weekend stories, one-year-lasting stories, or immortal stories like Dickens's."[105] A perennial concern of the Writers Group was the "commercial writers" who elected to write for popular publications rather than focusing on producing "Literature" that would stand the test of time. While Joyah argued for the latter, the *Muse*'s longtime editor and well-known short story writer Dede Kamkondo reasoned that the Writers Group needed to write works that would actually be read as a first step to gaining immortality. For Kamkondo, this meant publishing weekend stories in popular venues like the *Malawi News*. Writers "must invade M.B.C.'s Writers' Corner; they must shell Star Magazine; they must flood the Malawi News' Literary Page; they must kidnap popular publications, they must be felt by the reading public in Malawi."[106]

To assess "Yaya," Kalitera "rereads" the entire story. In fact, rereading becomes a simultaneously critical and creative practice, for it is by rereading that Kalitera intervenes in the narrative, much in the same way that audiences listening to an oral tale would actively contribute to it and perhaps retell a version of it later. In print, these processes are compressed, and Kalitera's rereading of "Yaya" is also a retelling, which in many cases alters Kamwendo's original. For example, in Kamwendo's story, we are told as a matter of fact that Yaya will be going off to secondary school soon. Kalitera, however, injects drama into this event and gives Yaya greater agency and a clearer internal voice:

> . . . Yaya's parents are making preparations to send Yaya to Secondary School.
>
> *No, please!* Yaya cries to herself. She is sure she will lose the man if she goes away. She has to ask him to marry her before they send her away. But how does a woman ask a man to marry her?[107]

Most of Kalitera's review is spent retelling the story in this way. Kalitera even imagines that when Fred goes to rescue Yaya from the Liquid Sunshine recreation center, "*[p]ossibly he has brought a mango or two*," giving the narrative a nice symmetry.

Toward the end of his review, Kalitera directly addresses the imagined readers of the story: "'Well, well,' I know most of you are saying, 'if that is the YAYA story, then definitely it isn't the way the author heard it.' Which means that you and I are on the same wavelength. All along the story I felt cheated. I had the impression that either the author hadn't been very attentive when the story was told to him or he was deliberately misleading us." Audiences of oral performances often respond in a similar way, shouting out "Satero! Mwalakwa! Mwasokoneza nthano! 'That's not the way the story goes! You are wrong there! You have mixed stories!'"[108] These interjections are not only about the veracity of the narrative but also about whether the story has been "well or badly told" and if it comports with cultural and social mores.[109] This is also the case in Kalitera's review, which ends with the following assessment:

> The story YAYA will live forever. What won't live with it is the uninteresting and unconvincing way it was told to us. That will die if it isn't already dead. . . .
>
> How will YAYA live while the way it was told to us will die?
>
> Because you and I will tell the story YAYA to our children and grandchildren in ways we will deem interesting and convincing. Each of us in his own way. But it will still be the same story. YAYA.[110]

Kalitera saw these ephemeral stories in the *Malawi News*, like the oral tradition, as having a certain mobility and longevity through their constant rewriting. In this way, stories like "Yaya" could be reworked through their retelling in different forms so as to better reflect social values and customs.

Kalitera's "Face Value," which appeared in the *Malawi News* in two parts in December 1977 (just before his critique of "Yaya" was published), is an example of just such a retelling. This much shorter story with a more obvious moral was compared directly to "Yaya" in both its form and content by other critics on the page, thus continuing the chain of creative and critical reproduction that helped to shape Malawi's emerging literature. It also demonstrates that literary criticism was often embedded in literary forms themselves, and I read Kalitera's story as a response to "Yaya" in narrative form. "Face Value" too is about changing gender roles, and it can be summarized by the first two lines of its introduction, which was bolded and centered on the page: "THE pace of modern life makes it a necessity that mom and dad work. But at the same time, family life must not be sacrificed at the expense of crossing that economic line."[111] The introduction continues to give away much of what will happen in the narrative: Steve and Lynda Manda hire a babysitter, Panda, to look after their child, but she "has her own ideas already—someone's nightmare." In the story, Panda's internal voice is expressed in italics in the text, much as Yaya's was in Kalitera's review of Kamwendo's story, suggesting an affinity between these two young characters and between Kalitera's critique and his story. Panda, who comes from a very poor family, is shocked by the Mandas' wealth. While watching Steve open a tin of milk for the baby, she thinks, "*There*, the whole of her inside screamed, *that milk could last her family a lifetime*." Like "Yaya," Kalitera's story contains some moments of progressive gender politics, with Steve showing himself to be a caring and engaged father in the story's opening, but when Panda robs them and leaves the baby alone and injured, it is Lynda who bears the blame for hiring a girl they barely know to watch their only child. Also like Yaya, who lacks a sense of solidarity with other women, Lynda and Panda are presented as antagonists whose different class positions preclude any form of mutual recognition as women.

While at work, Lynda senses that something is wrong and returns home to find the door locked and Panda nowhere in sight. Lynda returns twice more, the last time en route to a business meeting in Nchalo with her boss, who pointedly quips, "Between you and I this is the first time you've been concerned about your baby openly."[112] Each time, Lynda is locked out of her own house, and it is hard not to read this detail as a commentary on what happens to career-driven women who leave others in charge of their families. Eventually, the police find Lynda in Nchalo and inform her that Panda was seen leaving her home with a large suitcase and that her baby was found on the floor, knocked unconscious. The officer scolds her for taking the babysitter, a girl she barely knew, at "face value." Although Lynda tries to distribute some of the blame to her husband, she realizes that ultimately, as the baby's mother, she is responsible for what has happened, telling the officer, "'You can pick your stick, hold me by the hair and whip me.' And he felt that was exactly what she deserved."[113] The irony of the story's title is, of course, that you can't take anyone at face value. But whereas the title might appear playful, the story's moral about women's responsibility for what happens in the domestic sphere is startlingly unambiguous and meant to be taken at nothing other than face value.

While both Kamwendo's and Kalitera's stories explore the consequences that ensue when successful modern women move beyond the domestic sphere, they also seek to contain women within this sphere, and Kalitera's story is more successful in this regard because of its much shorter and more restricted form. George Kaliwo's review of the story on the Literary Page compares the two stories directly, locating Kalitera's success in some of the features that have long been associated with short fiction—namely, its shortness and its treatment of a single incident: "Aubrey Kalitera's 'Face Value' must have been an exhilarating experience for the fans of 'Malawi News' who complained that 'Yaya' was too long, but it was more than an exhilarating experience, it was I think, a well-balanced ordinary short story about an ordinary situation."[114] Moreover, Kalitera's story prefigures the type of "ordinary short story" that eventually became commonplace on the pages of the *Malawi News*. Like "Face Value," these stories were short (usually on a single page or spread), hinted at or even gave away their trajectories at the start, and finally came full circle to where they began. In this way, these stories embedded some of their critiques of changing gender norms, and the drive to contain women's social and economic mobility, in their very form.

"THE ELEMENT OF REALISING" IN WEEKEND FICTION

In the late 1970s and early 1980s, the Literary Page included fiction and criticism as well as essays and interviews about publishing, culture, politics, and journalism. In addition to addressing the state of Malawian publishing, censorship, and ways writers might reach larger publics on the African continent and beyond, a number of these essays were concerned with the form of African writing and its relationship to other traditions. For example, in 1978, the page published an interview with the Nigerian academic Theophilus Vincent, who argued that African writers should draw on local literary traditions but also make use of the European literary forms available to them rather than "go groping needlessly for completely new forms."[115] In another essay, Cuthbert Khunga, a Malawian writer published on the page, countered the idea that "African writers have tended to emulate the whiteman's style and subject matter," arguing that "[i]n fact, it is usually the whites when writing about African issues who tend to emulate what one would say African style," providing the example of Alan Paton's mimicry of Noni Jabavu to support his argument.[116] Articles and debates like these demonstrate the important role the *Malawi News*'s Literary Page played in developing a language in which to discuss African literary forms and indicate that its "weekend stories" were taken seriously as literature.

Initially, the editors and critics associated with the Literary Page used relatively flexible terms to categorize the stories it published, which were inconsistently called "short stories," "serial stories," and "prose fiction." This shifting terminology belies the real investment that the editors, critics, and writers associated with the page had in formal issues, which were often expressed using terms somewhat different from those common in Euro-American criticism. Warren Gunda's critique of "The Jailbird" by Themba Mbalazo (runner-up for Literary Man of the Year in 1979) is a good example of criticism that is concerned with form but that adopts its own literary terminology—here focusing on the "element of realising" within the narrative to discuss the story's temporal structure, realism, and ultimate progression toward a moral. In his critique, Gunda draws attention to the story's opening, in which the once-successful Mr. Nyatwa is released from prison and returns home after sixteen years, with the rest of the story promising to tell the reader how he was the "architect" of his own demise. Gunda finds that "the story was well begun, the flash back was very splendid; used tactifully [*sic*] as well as effectively."[117] As Gunda makes clear in his critique, the point of this prolepsis at the story's beginning is to give readers a preview of what is to come and to encourage them to read on: "From the very first paragraph you feel you are going to enjoy the whole story." The rest of the story is then told retrospectively, in the form of an extended flashback, before arriving again at the point where it began.

Gunda was not the only critic interested in flash-forwards and flashbacks as narrative devices.[118] As a literary technique, the flashback had grown in popularity since the Literary Page was first published, due in part, I argue, to the layout of the page itself. Following the publication of longer serialized stories like "Yaya," which had engaged readers with pull quotes from later parts of the installment, Kamwendo began placing the story's *beginning*, rather than an extract or teaser, in bold and offset from the text, seemingly to add interest to an otherwise linear narrative. By 1979, the most common layout for fiction was to have the first paragraph or two of a story bolded, with only its title in the center of the page. For many writers (about half, up from 40 percent in 1978), these opening paragraphs were used in the same way that pull quotes and introductions once were: to grab readers' attention with a scene from later in the narrative and to make them ask, what happened?

Gunda's critique of "The Jailbird," written at the end of 1979, thus comments on a shift in the form of the newspaper story that had been taking place over several years. Importantly, Gunda reflects on the way this "modern" story structure interacts with more traditional storytelling practices to disrupt what he calls the story's "element of realising." He spends much of his critique reflecting on the way the story's well-executed flashback is ruined by the author's choice of significant vernacular names, such as the protagonist's surname Nyatwa, meaning "hardship," and his tobacco estate called "Mabvuto ndi anga," or "Problems Are Mine":

> But alas! the names in the story remind you clearly that you are reading a mere story that never happened, pure fiction and no more. And when this fact is revealed by the writer's mistakes you are forced to lose interest in the whole story.
>
> The element of realising within fiction is suppressed. . . . While in real life we cannot question these names, in fiction we do question their essence and presence in a story. I mean that is all about fiction. We question some things normally acceptable in real societies.[119]

Gunda is not concerned only with the way these names give away the story's trajectory. Rather, the story's "element of realising" also has to do with its realism, which is compromised by its unduly obvious naming. The story's suspense and its ability to entice readers to read the "whole" story are thus tied to its ability to maintain the illusion that one is not reading "a mere story," because if this illusion is broken, readers may "lose interest" entirely.

Why such emphasis on the "whole story"? It stands to reason that without reading to the end, readers would be unable to appreciate the story's moral and social relevance. But taking this logic a step further, the element of realising might also lead the reader to "question some things normally acceptable in real societies." This is certainly the case in Gunda's own "Joe's Replica," which opens with a woman telling an unknown audience that perhaps she did not deserve her baptism, given what she has done. In the rest of the story, Mary recounts her life story, including her dismissal from school for becoming pregnant. Only at the very end do we realize that she is speaking to a group of men in a tavern, where she works to support Joe's child, or "replica," after he has left her.[120] Critics on the page praised both Gunda's style—including "the very compelling flashbacks told in the mouth of Mary herself"[121]—and the story's "element of realism" that was enhanced by its first-person confessional narration.[122] They also highlighted its social importance in shining a light on "the prevalent negative effects non-matrimonial boy-girl relations yield in society; and from an unexpected pub setting, the message radiates as to be felt by the attentive readership far and wide,"[123] leaving readers with "food for thought."[124] In these critiques, we can see many of the same concerns that Gunda expressed in his phrase "the element of realising": stories should have elements of both suspense and realism in order to engage readers to the end and reveal a strong social message. In Gunda's story, readers "realise" that the story is set in a pub at the same time that they recognize that social forces, not only Mary herself, are to blame for her situation.

In the early 1980s, during another political crackdown by Banda's government that saw Kamwendo leave the paper, the fiction page in the *Malawi News* underwent a number of changes that solidified this form of domestic realism and reinforced Banda's conflation of the domestic and political spheres on its pages. In the lead-up to the 1985 UN Women's Conference in Nairobi, Banda nominated a record number of women to parliament as part of his efforts to present his government "in a positive light regarding women's empowerment."[125] The *Malawi News* also touted its publication of fiction by more women writers. However, at the same time that the page celebrated women writers for ending its "monotonous domination by men," it also became a "Weekend Leisure" rather than a Literary Page, replacing lengthier stories and literary criticism with "short stories" of only one thousand words, most of which focused on love and relationships.[126] These stories were surrounded by other kinds of materials, including the "Newscope Stars" horoscope, a crossword puzzle, and the Radio Broadcast Programme, thus further embedding the newspaper's fiction in the world of domesticity and leisure.[127] By connecting its fiction to other forms of weekend leisure, the *Malawi News* presented reading as a leisure activity and appealed to readers of varying literacy levels. Both of these kinds of reading—for leisure and literacy—were depicted as important to national development in other articles.[128]

Due to the new word-count restrictions, which made the stories more accessible, the short stories on the Weekend Leisure page did not incorporate flashbacks into the narrative quite as frequently as before.[129] Nevertheless, they maintained a strong "element of realising" by building suspense via extratextual elements, including their titles and subheadings and the surrounding leisure materials. By engaging with these other parts of the paper, the Weekend Leisure page's short stories enhanced their own realism and naturalized the newspaper as a social space. Even though more women writers were now publishing on the page, the Weekend Leisure page often presented men (who were reading about women) as its imagined community of readers. Jonathan Kuntambira's "Namaluzi," the second-prize winner of the *Malawi News*'s short story writing competition in December 1982 and later collected in an anthology of the same title, opens with the narrator reading the newspaper when his wife angrily storms into the house. He quickly relates his current situation to that of Pewani, the character in a simple one-to-two-cell comic strip in the newspaper in front of him, who has just fallen into a manhole while ogling a pretty girl: "On any other day I would have laughed. But today I had the difficult task of trying to figure out what manhole I had unwittingly stumbled into myself in order to earn my wife's distemper."[130] Embedding the newspaper's fiction in the larger leisure world of the paper created its own element of realising. In Kuntambira's story and many others, references to other parts of the paper are incorporated into the story's opening, producing an element of suspense based on the act of opening the newspaper itself. This gesture drew readers into the shared world of the newspaper and naturalized the newspaper as the world through shared referents like Pewani. This world was populated by women but was often, as is the case in Kuntambira's story, presented from a distinctly male point of view.

As mentioned above, however, some women did write for the Weekend Leisure page in the 1980s and early '90s, and their work often offered a more nuanced picture of modern relationships. These stories were more likely to be told from a first-person female point of view, which was otherwise rare in the newspaper, though a handful of male authors wrote from a third-person female perspective.[131] While a number of these stories warned women of the costs of extramarital relationships, such as Grace Phiri's "Sugar-Daddy's Style" and Dorothy Ng'omba's "The Prodigal Daughter," they were also more likely than male-authored stories to depict instances of female solidarity.[132] In "The Prodigal Daughter," this solidarity takes the form of a woman caring for her childhood friend's children after the friend's life spirals downward following a teenage pregnancy. More comically, in "Meet My Aunt," another story by Grace Phiri, a woman realizes that her fiancé is dating her aunt behind her back, resulting in both women leaving him.[133]

As in the previous decade, the domestic home and the national space continued to be conflated in many of these narratives, and several women authors in this period wrote about the difficulties women encountered when attempting to leave home to pursue other opportunities—especially if this meant leaving the country.[134] Norah Lungu's "Rumours . . ." begins with the narrator standing alone on a cold street corner, filled with regret over events from six years ago when her husband watched her get arrested for nearly killing a woman (figure 4). The story's subheading provides a clue about what precipitated these events: "The note reported him 'HIV positive.'"[135] The rest of the story is told as a flashback, beginning with the narrator's acceptance of a scholarship to study in the fictionalized "United Calpenian States." Studying abroad is "what [she] wanted throughout [her] life"—even though it means leaving her husband Tony and four-month-old baby for three years. When Tony suddenly stops writing to her, the narrator fears the worst, particularly when she receives anonymous notes telling her that he has remarried and has HIV. She flies home and attacks the woman she finds in her house, only later learning that she is a distant relative, hired to help care for the baby after Tony was in a car accident. The story ends with the narrator having returned from her studies abroad, hoping that she will someday win back her husband and wishing she had not believed "evil malicious lies."

Lungu's story bears evidence of Banda's continuing tight grip on the media. Its moral about the consequences of believing rumors echoes Banda's warning to women regarding the evils of gossip. The story also uses fictionalized place-names to avoid the appearance of writing—or spreading rumors—about actual persons or events, a necessity

WEEKEND
The note reported him 'HIV positive'
Rumours...
by Norah M. Ngoma
LEISURE
The battle she won was soon lost
COFFEE TIME CROSSWORD
WEEK-END
SATURDAY
SUNDAY
FREQUENCIES
BOOKKEEPER
WANTED URGENTLY
The Lawn Tennis Association of Malawi Benson & Hedges Tennis Championships 1988
BENSON & HEDGES

Fig. 4. *Malawi News*, Weekend Leisure, October 8–14, 1988, 6–7, featuring "Rumours . . ." by Norah M. Ngoma. Courtesy of Blantyre Newspapers Limited. Photo by Sam Banda Jr.

for writers in Banda's Malawi, according to Lungu.[136] Banda's warnings to women of the dangers of gossip takes on additional meaning in the context of the many rumors that swirled around Banda himself—including the rumor that he was not Malawian at all, but rather an outsider merely posing as one, which was used to explain his refusal to speak local languages.[137] But while the story reiterates and even adheres to the Life President's maxim, it also uses rumor to, as Luise White puts it, "move between ideas about the personal and the political, the local and the national" and to express social contradictions.[138] In this way, "Rumours . . ." taps into a long history of Malawians using gossip and rumor to negotiate the perceived dangers of migration and mobility, including the risk of HIV infection, as Anika Wilson describes, although these migrants were almost always men.[139] In Lungu's narrative, the rumor about her husband's infidelity serves as a device to call the protagonist back home to Malawi, pointing to the conflicting rhetoric women encountered when it came to their personal, social, and political mobility postindependence. The continuing relevance of this story is evident in its republication in *WASI* magazine and, most recently, the Malawi Writers Union's 2018 anthology of women writers. Notably, the 2018 version of the story metes out a much harsher punishment to its protagonist, who loses her scholarship and is sent to prison to do hard labor—a change that is indicative of the backlash against recent drives for gender equity.

Love and relationship stories continued to be so popular in the *Malawi News* that after the publication of yet another story of a man who discovers his wife is cheating on him, this time ending spectacularly in a triple murder, the editors included the following note: "Authors are reminded to diversify themes. Love short stories are just too much, try other themes please."[140] Despite this appeal, the theme persisted, in English stories as well as in the Chichewa stories that were finally reintroduced into the newspaper in late 1990. Although material in Chichewa had been published in *Tikambe*, a supplemental section of the *Malawi News*, since the early 1980s, this section did not include fiction for its first decade. Instead, it was composed of letters from readers ("Makalata a awerengi athu"), Malawian news of the week ("Malawi sabata ino"), world news stories ("Dziko la pansi sabata ino"), and sometimes sections dedicated to health ("Thandizani—Red Cross"), farming, and village life that would have appealed to a broader, more rural audience than the English portions of the paper. Part of the impetus for publishing Chichewa fiction in the paper in the early 1990s came from the shuttering of several other outlets for Chichewa writing as well as the general loosening of restrictions on writers as Malawi moved toward multiparty democracy.[141]

When stories in Chichewa were reintroduced into the newspaper in *Tikambe*'s new fiction section "Ticheze," or "Let's Chat," in 1990, writers used many of the same devices popular in the English stories, including framing their stories with the scene of a male reader sitting down to read the newspaper so as to create an element of realising. In Nixon Mindano's "Ndinali 'Che uje'" ("I Was 'Mr. So-and-So'"), one of the first stories to be published in "Ticheze," the narrator decides to read the newspaper during his lunch hour since he lacks the money to buy even a banana to eat:

> M'malo mwake ndidaganiza zongokhala mu ofesi, nkumawerenga zina ndi zina pofuna kupititsa nthawi. Ndidapita mu ofesi ya sekeletale wanga kukayang'ana nyuzipepala yatsiku limenelo. Mwamwawi ndidayipeza pa tebulo pake. Ndidaitenga kupita nayo pa tebulo panga kuti ndikawerenge. Nditakhala pampando ndidayamba kuvundukula.
>
> Instead I thought of staying in the office, reading some more to pass the time. I went to my secretary's office to look for that day's paper. Luckily I found it on her desk. I took it and went to my desk so that I could read. After I sat on the chair, I started to open it.[142]

The story's frame of reading the newspaper has no real import to the narrative that follows. Rather, as in Kuntambira's "Namaluzi," simply opening the newspaper produces a suspense that draws the reader not only into this particular narrative but into the genre of the Chichewa newspaper story more broadly. This device aligned the story's narrator with its readers, who were also sitting with the paper open in front of them and the majority of whom were male. As in the English stories, this self-reflexive framing of the newspaper in the paper's fiction naturalized the newspaper, and the social world it contained, as *the world*.

Although the *Malawi News* had a near monopoly on the production of fiction and, as a result, on a particular vision of the social world for decades, the transition to a free press at the end of 1992 in the lead-up to the referendum on single-party rule had immediate consequences for the paper's approach and self-positioning.[143] With the advent of other news outlets, Banda and the MCP needed to work harder to control the national narrative, and Banda asked Kamwendo, who was living in Zimbabwe at the time, to return to Malawi and to use his knowledge of the media to "run our paper and run the campaign for us."[144] The *Malawi News* and the campaign against multiparty democracy were inseparable, and the paper ran numerous articles aimed unsuccessfully at convincing Malawians to vote against it. Many of these stories featured women's support for the Ngwazi, reiterating the familiar refrain that he had "raised their status from mere housewives to prosperous and industrious citizens."[145]

In this newly competitive media landscape, the *Malawi News*'s weekend stories had to do more to justify their social relevance. A story published in *Tikambe* in 1993 titled "Chidamupha nchiyani mwamuna wakeyo?" ("What Killed Her Husband?") comments on the growing number of newspapers in the country and dramatizes the central role of the media, and the newspaper in particular, in disseminating lifesaving information about, for example, the rapid spread of HIV/AIDS in the country.[146] Like the stories discussed above, this story opens with a man reading the newspaper. This time, however, he is not at home or at work, but in public, waiting for the bus. It is no accident that this story dramatizes the way newspapers were shared and read communally in public spaces at a moment when Banda's regime, along with his particular vision of the nation as a domestic space, was waning. The man reflects that he doesn't necessarily want to read the story about HIV/AIDS in the paper, but he does so because he feels that other people on the bus need to know this information. In fact, it turns out that the woman sitting next to him on the bus is ill, and it is only by reading the narrator's newspaper that she realizes that her husband likely died of AIDS. In this case, the story's "element of realising" contains a message with lifesaving consequences.

BURNING DOWN THE INITIATION CAMP: PUBLISHING BEYOND THE NEWSPAPER

After the end of Kamuzu Banda's reign in 1994, one might have expected the literary field to change substantially. But while new publications such as Steve Chimombo's *WASI* magazine provided additional outlets for literary production, the weekend editions of national newspapers like the *Malawi News* and the *Weekend Nation* have continued to serve as important venues for fiction and to outlive most other publications. Nearly thirty years after the advent of multiparty democracy, the *Malawi News* still contains short stories in English and Chichewa every weekend.[147] What is striking is how similar these more recent stories are in their form and representations of gender to those published in previous decades. Much like earlier fiction, contemporary stories in the *Malawi News*, particularly those in Chichewa, reanimate earlier tropes that associate women with the domestic sphere and Malawian "tradition." In contrast, the short stories written for the Malawian Girls' Literary Competition, which I helped the Malawi Writers Union launch in 2007, challenge these constructions of gender by rewriting popular narratives that have appeared in the newspaper over the past decades. Some stories, like Pamela Mithi's "Nambewe the Heroine," go so far as to take a story from the newspaper's headlines and turn it into fiction. In both kinds of stories, we can see that the newspaper continues to be an important intertext for Malawian writing, even as contemporary writers have lamented the declining quality of fiction published in the paper.

While the English and Chichewa stories in the *Malawi News* in 1973 and 1974 had many similarities, including linear, fable-like structures and the use of Chichewa proverbs, the exclusion of Chichewa fiction from the newspaper for the next twenty years meant that Chichewa short stories and their English counterparts developed in separate venues.[148] As discussed above, when Chichewa fiction was reintroduced into the paper in the early 1990s, it often borrowed techniques from English fiction, such as the use of teaser introductions that sometimes used the act of opening the newspaper as a device to build suspense and enhance the story's realism. However, what is most consistent throughout the Chichewa newspaper fiction from the 1970s to the present is the use of culturally significant proverbs and metaphors to carry the story's moral current. This phenomenon is unsurprising, since "Chichewa metaphors are pervasive in every day [*sic*] speech" and "give maximum meaning with minimum words."[149] In recent fiction in Chichewa in the newspaper, we can see how these culturally embedded proverbs and metaphors are used to connect women with traditional spaces and practices, such as the home and the initiation camp, in ways that are both containing and enabling.

"Ukatambatamba kumayang'ana kum'mawa," or "When Doing Witchcraft, Look for the Dawn," which was published in the *Malawi News* in September 2007, directs its most obvious moral to Bwansoso, who is having an affair with a married woman. This moral—the proverb of the story's title—suggests that one must be cautious when doing wrong. It returns at the story's end, when Bwansoso is beaten senseless by the woman's husband. At the same time, a subtler moral about the need to keep women aligned with tradition is folded into the narrative. When the woman and Bwansoso are about to be caught in the act by her husband, Bwansoso jumps into a drum to hide, while the woman goes to open the door for her husband:

> Bwansoso adadumphira mumgolomo ali njenjenje ngati mwanapiye wosowa make. Naye mayiyo momwe amatsegula mtima wake udali uli phaphapha ngati kuti waotcha dambwe.
>
> Bwansoso jumped into the drum, shaking like a chick that had lost its mother. As for the woman, while opening [the door], her heart was pounding like someone who had burned down an initiation camp.[150]

The two similes in this passage, both of which make use of an ideophone, or *mvekero* (from the root *mveka*, meaning "sound"), present Bwansoso's and the woman's culpability very differently. While Bwansoso trembles quietly with fear (*nje* meaning "quiet") like a lost chick, the woman's heart pounds (*pha* meaning literally "to hit one's hand against something") "like someone who has burned down an initiation camp." This familiar saying compares the woman's violation of the bond of marriage to an even more essential social bond created through initiation. Observing the drawing that accompanies the story, we can see that while Bwansoso is emasculated and beaten for this violation of social norms, the woman is shamed. She stands to the side, her brassiere slightly visible, struggling to cover herself with her *chitenje*—as though literally clinging to the threads of tradition. Until 1994, women were not allowed to wear trousers in Malawi. The *chitenje*, a brightly colored cloth that women wrap around themselves, particularly while doing domestic work, has long been a symbol of the traditional.

The same technique of using metaphorical language to carry the story's underlying moral is also used in "Masamu atsikana ena," or "Some Girls' Games," by Holyce Kholowa. In this story, a girl named Maliyana pretends to be ill with malaria and obtains a sick note from her concerned and sympathetic headmaster so as to secretly visit her boyfriend. Maliyana is eventually caught in her lie, and the moral of the story seems to be that girls should respect their elders rather than abuse their kindness and goodwill. However, as in the previous example, there is a single metaphor embedded in this story that explicitly binds gender to traditional practices, adding another layer of meaning: "Kumudzi nako . . . onsewa sankadziwa kuti mtsikanayu akutaya madzi pa khomo lina" ("Also in her village . . . no one knew that this girl was throwing water on another entrance [home]").[151] There are numerous metaphors in Chichewa that associate women and sexual activity with water.[152] Further, in songs taught to girls during female initiation, or *chinamwali*, Deborah Kaspin has found that sex is linked to the image of water. As Kaspin summarizes it, "These songs use the imagery of the house to remind girls to refuse the sexual advances of their husbands during menstruation: the vagina is the door, sex is a pot of water, and an unresponsive girl is a wall with no opening."[153] In "Masamu atsikana ena," there is a strong suggestion, only three paragraphs before the metaphor of "throwing water on another entrance," that Maliyana and her boyfriend, Milimita, are engaging in variety of inappropriate behaviors, including premarital sex: "Tinyimbo tachikondi tidaperekeza awiriwo mpaka ku nyumba ya Milimita kumene kudali kudya, kumwa, kumwerera ndi kusangalala kolapitsa" ("Love songs guided the two on their way to Milimita's house where there was eating, drinking, boozing, and enjoyment to waste oneself with"). *Kusangalala* which can mean variously "happiness," "enjoyment," "feeling pleasure," and "entertainment," takes on clearly sexual undertones in light of the metaphor "throwing water on another entrance" that occurs several paragraphs later.

"Throwing water on the entrance" also refers to a wife's customary household duties.[154] According to this reading of the metaphor, no one in Maliyana's village knew that while pretending to be ill, she was in fact acting like a wife in another man's house, in another village. In this way, the focus of the story shifts away from the wrongfulness of Maliyana's deceit (although this reading does not fall away entirely) to her failure to respect the social customs regulating relationships between young men and women. As discussed previously, matrilineal societies such as the Chewa are traditionally uxorilocal. By going to "throw water on another entrance," Maliyana violates the cultural practices put in place to keep a woman and her husband's labor in the matrilineal network, an issue that is addressed in many of the stories discussed above. In the passage here, it is not only Maliyana's immediate family that does not know her whereabouts but the entire village, underscoring the fact that her irresponsible behavior impacts the community as a whole. In this way, Maliyana shows her parents, as well as her village, the ultimate form of disrespect: she becomes sexually active, and thus essentially marries, without their knowledge or consent.

In "Masamu atsikana ena," as in the previous story, ideas about gender and tradition are co-constructed through a metaphor that occurs in the midst of the narrative, rather than being offered as a fixed moral. However, there is an interesting resonance between the metaphor of "throwing water on the entrance" and the story's ending. Finally wise to Maliyana's plans, the headmaster and Maliyana's teachers and parents go to the bus stop—where Maliyana's boyfriend will drop her off—to catch her in the act. Maliyana is shocked when she sees her parents in the headmaster's car, and the story seems to end abruptly without a meaningful resolution: "'Amayi!' adafuula Maliyana ndikuterezuka popanda matope mpaka pansi thii! Kukomoka kudali komweko" ("'Mother!' Maliyana cried and slipped as though she was in mud and fell to the ground, thump! That was how she fainted"). This ending may feel jarring to a reader who was looking forward to seeing Maliyana meet her just punishment. Nevertheless, it may tell us more than we think, given the connection of the "mud" Maliyana slips in to the water in the previous metaphor. In Kaspin's account, when Chewa women finished menstruating, they were required to smear a layer of mud on the hut floor. Since traditional songs use various parts of the house as euphemisms for parts of the female body, Kaspin shows that "the whole of the house becomes the whole of the woman when she smears mud on the floor at the end of her period, cooling the house to reflect the coolness of her body."[155] In Chewa cosmology, "newborns are cold, children are cool, and adults of childbearing age are warm."[156] By literally returning Maliyana to the coolness of mud, the story brings her back to childhood—to the appropriate, non–sexually active state for her current age.

In comparison to these stories in Chichewa, the narrative of "This Is Man to Man," a story published in English in June 2010, must work harder to contain the presence of strong but ultimately despised female characters. A married man who suspects he has a sexually transmitted disease goes to the clinic, where he is shocked to find it staffed entirely by young female nurses. He is further mortified and insulted when they plug their noses while examining his genitals and condemn him for cheating on his wife. Making it clear that he does not deem this attitude to be their place, he recounts, "I silently told her the Reverend already imparted similar advice the day I took Eliza to the altar."[157] The story is told in a conversational style, as though by a man speaking to another male friend, and the narrator insists over and over, "Man, this is between you and me. This is man to man. . . . So I implore you to tell no one." The man's general anxiety over his health is ultimately conflated with an anxiety over the power of the female nurses to administer or withhold care and to judge him socially. In particular, the man is disturbed by the nurses' unreadable, scribbled diagnoses: "I gave her the piece of paper on which her colleague had scribbled something illegible. You know their handwriting resembles that of standard one pupils but all the same they communicate effectively among themselves. They all went through the same initiation ritual in college." In this instance, we find a different kind of initiation camp—the modern form of initiation that is education, symbolized by the college. Rather than turning women into obedient members of society, this initiation camp has been co-opted by women. While initiation camps were (and still are) used to communicate secret knowledge among women, this narrative conveys a deep-seated fear that women will use modern education, and particularly writing, to gain social power and move beyond the confines of domestic spaces like the home. This story thus acknowledges and laments that the binary of male/modern and female/traditional constructed during Banda's rule is beginning to break down and insists on privileging male interlocutors as a means of reestablishing patriarchal dignity and control.

These stories from the *Malawi News* stand in stark contrast to those written by young female writers for the Malawian Girls' Literary Competition in 2008. The competition's stories rewrite many of the narratives popular in newspaper fiction in ways that show the full, and as of yet incompletely realized, possibilities of an expanded domestic sphere. In Tiseke Chilima's "Be Careful What You Wish For," a young girl leaves her village in Malawi to fight on Africa's side in an imagined World War III. This story expands the scope of women's influence to global affairs—something intimated by *Malawi News* articles like the one on Mother's Day in 1972—and is all the more groundbreaking given how infrequently stories have depicted women leaving Malawi. The competition's winning story, "Nambewe the Heroine" by Pamela Mithi, also rewrites the familiar narrative of a man returning home to his village to develop it.[158] Mithi was inspired by a story she read in the newspaper about a girl who fled her village rather than take part in *chinamwali*, during which she would be forced to sleep with an older male in the village called a *fisi*, or hyena.[159] Once in the city, Nambewe is taken in by one of her teachers and continues her education. She eventually earns a degree in community and rural development, and fifteen years later, she returns to her village to help develop it. The story ends with Nambewe confronting "her parents in their old, small hut. They thanked her for every little thing she was doing and apologized for what they had done. Nambewe was declared the Heroine of Namkumba village."[160] Unlike earlier female characters like Asawilunda, who are permanently exiled from their homes for pursuing their education, Nambewe not only returns to her village but also marshals the power of modern education to challenge traditional practices that are presented as harmful to young girls.

It is instructive to compare these stories in English to the stories that were submitted to the Malawian Girls' Literary Competition in Chichewa. The competition's judges, like the well-known author Prince Shonga, suggested that overall the Chichewa stories were less original than those in English and were often based on familiar folktales.[161] Linda Mulera's "Mwana Wotayidwa M'chimbudzi" ("The Child Thrown Out in the Latrine"), which received a special mention in the Chichewa category, rewrites the well-known narrative of a newborn baby abandoned by a teenage mother.[162] After being rescued from the pit latrine, Mwayi, or "Lucky," is adopted by a kind, barren woman who provides her with everything she needs to pursue her studies. Mwayi is an excellent student, and when she finishes school she is given a top position at the Reserve Bank. Her very comfortable financial situation enables her to care for both her adoptive mother and her real mother, whom she eventually locates. Despite this success, the somewhat confusing and polysemic moral of Mulera's story is reminiscent of earlier narratives like "Enmity in a Village Because of Education":

> Kuyambira apo mbiri ya Mwayi, mwana wotayidwa m'chimbudzi ndi mayi wake, koma lero ndi bwana wa ku banki yaikulu inabuka ponse-ponse niipereka [*sic*] phunziro lozama kwa amayi ankhalidwe wonyasawu.
>
> Starting from there, the tale of Mwayi—who was abandoned in a pit latrine by her mother as a child, but who is today a boss at a huge bank—spread everywhere and gave a significant lesson to women with this detestable behavior.[163]

Another translator of the story omitted this line because it does not seem to fit with the story of female empowerment that the rest of the story attempts to tell.[164] Still, it is important to think about why this young author chose to end her story in this way. Who is learning the lesson against "detestable behavior"? Mwayi's mother is now living in a comfortable house thanks to the daughter she abandoned. Through this indeterminacy, this contemporary story about gender roles, much like those from the *Malawi News* in the 1970s, gives readers an entrance into the narrative and asks them to participate in debating, or "realising," these issues. The ending of Mulera's story also registers the way Banda's conflicting messages about an expanded domestic sphere continue to inform gender politics in Malawi today. Though the Chichewa stories for the competition were dismissed by the judges as less creative, Mulera's story is important for the way its language and form wrestle with inherited images and story structures, many of which crystallized over decades on the pages of the *Malawi News*. Overall, these stories from the Malawian Girls' Literary Competition both engage with and rewrite many of the narratives that have been made familiar by Malawi's national newspapers, giving new power to the idea of "burning down the initiation camp."

The newspaper, and the *Malawi News* in particular, has helped to produce a particular form of the Malawian short story that has been dominant domestically but that has rarely traveled beyond Malawi's borders. It is still the case that very few Malawian writers have received international recognition. Those who have won international success have often done so by bypassing a domestic audience, either by publishing in international anthologies or online on sites like authorme.com. Even so, the imprint of the Malawian short story's domestic form is often visible in these internationally published stories, which has led in some cases to their dismissal by international critics, as is evident in the reception of Stanley Kenani's "Love on Trial" in 2012.

Nevertheless, many Malawian writers lament the poor quality of newspaper stories today, suggesting that increasingly restrictive word limits, a lack of good editors, and even a lack of censorship have led to uninspired and unimaginative writing.[165] While Kenani has argued that "it is high time Malawian writers moved beyond the frontiers of being satisfied with having their works in the local papers if they are to compete on the international level," others have pointed out that the writers who have achieved a measure of international success, including Kenani himself, began their careers by winning domestic writing competitions and publishing in local magazines and newspapers.[166] As Bright Molande, a lecturer in creative writing at Chancellor College, argues, "It would be impossible to expect our writers to impress on an international stage when they have not yet done so at home."[167] Indeed, when the veteran writer Benedicto Wokomaatani Malunga was attempting to restart his writing and publishing career in 2018, he turned to the newspaper to do so.

Other young writers, some of whom have attempted unsuccessfully to publish in the newspaper, have gone on instead to use, and even to create, new forums and social spaces that are increasingly replacing the newspaper, even in a domestic context. In 2017, two young women writers, Ekari Mbvundula and Wonawaka Gondwe, successfully launched Storytelling Sessions in Blantyre and Lilongwe, which drew both established and new writers to read their short stories to a live audience. Mbvundula went on to found Story Ink Africa, which has published several anthologies from the Storytelling Sessions in both print and ebook versions. Others, like Juniah Ngwira, have taken a different tack, turning to virtual social networks such as Facebook to publish their serialized fictions, as I discuss in chapter 5. In both cases, young women writers are pioneering fictional forms that can travel new routes both domestically and globally. As they do so, these forms may finally give female mobilities the full scope of an expanded domestic and national sphere.

CHAPTER 4

Time Machines

Pan African Imaginaries in the Chimurenga Chronic *and* Jungle Jim

In this chapter, I explore contemporary literary endeavors that model themselves on some of the iconic print media forms I have considered throughout this book. As I demonstrated in the previous chapters, southern African writers have used the traveling forms in magazines, newspapers, and other periodical media to produce complex spatial imaginaries, ranging from the township to the nation, region, diaspora, and outer space. Some of these alternative geographies were complicit with colonial space-making endeavors, and many of their more radical elements were never realized: the large African state envisaged by some of *African Parade*'s writers failed to materialize as Southern Rhodesia descended further into white minority rule, and writers like Langston Hughes and Casey Motsisi did not live to see a Black man travel into outer space. Nevertheless, the forms published in mass-produced periodicals generated new ideas of space, community, and belonging—sometimes against the grain of the publications in which they appeared.

Building on these arguments, this chapter considers digital-age publications that have taken up popular print forms from earlier eras, a trend that can be observed across the continent. In 2017, two successful online magazines—Nigeria's *Saraba* and *Jalada*, an online pan-African writers' collective based in Kenya—published print versions of what were previously strictly online publications, the latter through a collaboration with the famed Ugandan magazine *Transition*, currently housed at Harvard. Why this return to print, when the digital space seems to offer unfettered access to the globe? While print continues to afford more prestige, as well as the possibility of remuneration, these are not the only factors driving this phenomenon. Focusing on two contemporary South African publications, the *Chimurenga Chronic* and *Jungle Jim*, I argue that these magazines have reanimated the periodical print form because of its ability to produce multifaceted spaces and its as yet unrealized potential to usher in alternative futures. These present-day publications are explicitly "pan African" or "African" in scope, and by using twentieth-century print forms and genres as "time machines," they chart new pan-African affiliations for the twenty-first century. They are also notable for their robust digital presences and use of the virtual space to cultivate this print pan-Africanism.

An editorial in the *Chimurenga Chronic*'s first issue, written as a poem, asks, "Is the newspaper a time machine? / Have all the images been exhausted? / Have all the words been disinfected? / If all news is old news how do we go forward?" As these lines intimate, periodicals like the *Chronic* "go forward" into the future, somewhat paradoxically, by returning to the past. By using older print media forms as "low-tech time machine[s]," these literary magazines not only travel in time but, as the editors of the *Chronic* suggest, "produce" time: the past, the present, and the future.[1] This is done most explicitly in the *Chronic*'s first issue, which is designed as a "fictional pan African newspaper" that travels back in time from when it was published in October 2011 to May 18–24, 2008, a period of xenophobic violence in South Africa.[2] The entire newspaper and its accompanying *Chronic Life* magazine and *Chronic Books* are meticulously backdated to this moment in South Africa's recent history to challenge the reductive way such violence is typically represented in mass media and to connect it to broader trends in African and global history. *Jungle Jim* magazine, which also began publication in 2011, similarly engages in low-tech time travel via the pulp magazine. The "pulps"—so named because they were produced on cheap wood pulp paper—gained popularity at the height of the imperial era and were often set in various locations in the Global South, including Africa.[3] Styling itself as an African pulp magazine, *Jungle Jim* decolonizes various pulp genres, from detective stories to science fiction. By using these genres as time machines, *Jungle Jim* centers Africa in imaginations of the global past, present, and future.

These time-traveling forms provide a new lens through which to understand African ways of being and belonging in the world that have previously been explored through the frameworks of Afrofuturism and Afropolitanism. In their disruption of linear, progressive time through time travel[4] and their "focus on the past as an instrument for survival in the future," these publications are in many ways deeply Afrofuturist projects.[5] However, the *Chronic* and *Jungle Jim* also make important interventions in conceptions of space, particularly when it comes to representations of the African continent and its relationship to the rest of the world. In this respect, they marry what Sofia Samatar identifies as Afrofuturism's emphasis on time with Afropolitanism's focus on space, which takes the form of "claiming the world for Africans."[6] Fittingly, the trope of time travel itself "conflat[es] time and space," treating time as though it were a three-dimensional space in which one can move in any direction.[7] Though time travel may signal a denial of history or historical determinism in other contexts, I argue that the *Chronic* and *Jungle Jim* use time travel's conflation of time and space purposefully—to expose the way they have consistently been treated as interchangeable in Western imaginations of Africa (i.e., Africa as the West's "past") and to actively think about time and space differently on a global scale. In other words, these publications harness time travel's seemingly problematic conflation of time and space to claim *both*.

And yet, while the *Chronic* and *Jungle Jim* engage with elements of Afrofuturism and Afropolitanism, these terms are inadequate to describe these projects' interventions. Both Afrofuturism and Afropolitanism have their roots in the diaspora, leading some African speculative fiction writers to insist on different designations for their work, including "Africanfuturist" and "pan-African."[8] Africanfuturism and recent articulations of pan-Africanism are notable for their explicit focus on the African continent and insistence on thinking the future from this space, often in relation to indigenous ways of being and knowing. Although only the *Chronic* explicitly calls itself "pan African," both it and *Jungle Jim* are invested in thinking about the African continent from their locations of production in South Africa and in repurposing twentieth-century pan-African aspirations for the present and future. Through their use of various print forms as time machines, the *Chronic* and *Jungle Jim* produce what I call "pan African spacetime." The concept of spacetime usefully captures the inseparability of time and space in these publications' deployment of pan Africanism and alludes to the use of their time travel to generate affiliations across the continent and the globe.

In spacetime, identity is not fixed, as it is in absolute space, but rather "becomes open, fluid, multiple, and indeterminate."[9] Similarly, "small 'p'" pan-Africanism signifies a relatively "eclectic" and "ephemeral" cultural solidarity, as opposed to the "formal organizations comprising capital 'P' Pan-Africanism."[10] Indeed, the latter was often co-opted by nationalist governments in the postindependence period[11] and has been seen by some to have a "one-dimensional" focus on race and racism that "could not sustain Pan-Africanism after the demise of colonialism, segregation, and apartheid."[12] Recent pan-African endeavors like those considered here are still attentive to anti-Black racism and forms of colonial and neocolonial oppression and alienation, but also seek to address the neoliberal world order's particular forms of subjugation through "a different way of thinking internationalism and radical aesthetics."[13] The gap between the terms in "pan African" indicates an African transnational solidarity that leaves space—quite literally—for the different ways these issues have been experienced across the continent and in the diaspora. Following the *Chronic*, I refer to this self-reflexive project of engaging with earlier pan-African imaginaries as "pan African." Ultimately, by producing pan African spacetime, the *Chronic* and *Jungle Jim* demonstrate that they are not interested in simply reanimating past iterations of Pan-Africanism, which scholars like Mbembe have critiqued as "ossified" and racialized and no longer useful in the present.[14] Instead, they enact a contemporary, flexible, and agential form of pan African engagement with the continent and globe.

In the *Chronic* and *Jungle Jim*, this pan Africanism takes a dual form: reexamining South Africa's place in Africa and the African continent's place in the diaspora and the world. Due to its history of apartheid, its celebrated transition to democracy long after most of the continent had achieved independence, its liberal constitution, and its relative economic power, South Africa is often considered (and has considered itself) "exceptional"—as "in, but not of, Africa."[15] In the early apartheid era, this view took the form of looking northward to the rest of Africa, as Prime Minister D. F. Malan put it, as "a reserve, if I may call it that, for the future development of the Western European Christian civilization."[16] During the struggle against apartheid, many South Africans imagined that the new South Africa "would be able to solve the problems of development (and maldevelopment or underdevelopment) experienced by other African states" and, after apartheid ended, the South African government aimed to develop neighboring states as part of its African Renaissance.[17] It is precisely with such ideas in mind that the first issue of the *Chimurenga Chronic* travels back in time to the 2008 violence against African foreign nationals. As *Chimurenga*'s associate editor Stacy Hardy explains, this was "a time where there was a disruption of a lot of South African thinking, where our ideals of the rainbow nation were for once and for all really killed off and one was forced to engage with this country as an African country and as a postcolonial country."[18] Similarly, one of *Jungle Jim*'s founders, Hannes Bernard, describes *Jungle Jim*'s "message" as: "Connect with the places that have shaped your environment today. We have a lot more in common with the rest of African [*sic*] than the rest of the world."[19] South Africa has not been immune to the issues that have faced other African states following decolonization, including the failure of the nation's liberation party, the African National Congress (ANC), to address issues of corruption and inequality, or to the problems faced by "any other democracy" in the neoliberal age, including "economic inequality, labor rights abuses, corporate irresponsibility."[20] Rather, South Africa's exceptionalism among African states might be seen in its unprecedented level of violence against Black foreign nationals, which David Mario Matsinhe argues is rooted in the apartheid state's particular logic of group relations and white supremacy.[21] Others have suggested that the apartheid state's anti-Black and consequently anti-*rural* bias was extended to the rest of Africa in the postapartheid period.[22]

The authors and editors of the *Chronic* and *Jungle Jim* are keenly aware of their connections to the African continent, as well as the inequalities that structure the relationship between South Africa and other African nations, particularly its closest neighbors in southern Africa. This attention to regional and continental disparities and to the outsized cultural and literary influence that South Africa has wielded marks a significant break from earlier publications like *Drum*, as discussed in the book's first two chapters. South Africa's most iconic popular magazine might have been pan-African in its reach and distribution, but it purveyed a notion of African modernity rooted in South Africa's cities that sometimes alienated its readers from other parts of the region. In the *Chronic* and *Jungle Jim*, we find important contemporary counterpoints to this attitude. Indeed, as Madhu Krishnan highlights, by forging partnerships with other Africa-based publishers, including Kwani Trust and Cassava Republic Press, Chimurenga aims "to circumvent the systems of distribution which silo and divide Africa's many geographies."[23] Just as South Africa is often seen as distinct from the continent of which it is a part, Africa itself is frequently elided in discussions of the African diaspora and pan-Africanism or romanticized as "a site of origin to which all journeys aim to return."[24] Challenging these perceptions, the *Chronic* and *Jungle Jim* insist on Africa's coevality in time as well as its imbrication in global space by treating African mobilities as exemplary of contemporary forms of mobility on a global scale.[25]

CHIMURENGA'S PAN AFRICAN ARCHIVES

Chimurenga, South Africa's longest-running literary magazine in the postapartheid period, takes its name from the Shona for "struggle for freedom." Founded in 2002 by the Cameroon-born Ntone Edjabe, the Cape Town–based magazine marries political and aesthetic aims, describing itself on its website as "a pan African platform of writing, art and politics" for the expression of "free ideas and political reflection about Africa by Africans."[26] *Chimurenga*'s agential form of pan African engagement is succinctly captured by the magazine's tagline "who no know go know," the title of a song by the iconic Nigerian artist and political activist Fela Kuti. Released in 1975, the song deplores the decline of African unity in the postindependence period with lines such as, "Nkrumah shout for Afrika, we no hear." Fela would shout out "who no know go know" during his performances at the Afrika Shrine, and the chant served as a provocation to listeners, a kind of call-and-response that brought audience members into the performance and turned them into engaged participants. In an interview, Edjabe explains, "I hear Fela signaling that knowledge is something that one makes (or takes) rather than merely receive [*sic*]—an active rather than passive process. This guides how we approach the editorial aspect of the publication."[27]

By reanimating aspects of Fela's art and activism in South Africa after the turn of the millennium, *Chimurenga* situates South Africa as a postcolonial nation and places itself in Fela's tradition of critical pan-Africanism.[28] In a 2004 essay, Edjabe comments on the similarities between postcolonial Nigeria and postapartheid South Africa. In such "new nations," Edjabe suggests that what *Transition* magazine founder Rajat Neogy calls "a culture of *don'ts*" prevails: "artists and creators must be given direction and shown how to mobilise their activity to social good—to the country's good, that is, or, better still, the party's good. There are a number of things you should not and often cannot do."[29]

Fela was famously critical of the Nigerian state postindependence and even ran for president himself. He also boycotted the 2nd World Black and African Festival of Arts and Culture (FESTAC), which was held in Lagos in 1977, pointing to its co-optation of a more radical pan-African vision to advance the military government's nationalist agenda.[30] Edjabe argues that writers and artists in the new South Africa have been subject to similar pressures to "[b]e pragmatic. Be practical. Be realistic. Build the nation."[31] Fela's refusal to "play by the rules of those who guard the gates of the nation's 'best interest'"[32] informs *Chimurenga*'s approach to radical and critical dissent in the postcolony, where "the common enemy has disappeared or, more precisely, has mutated into a series of phantoms."[33] These phantoms might be considered to include South Africa's embrace of economic policies that benefit international capital rather than its people, including the privatization of state services and infrastructure, and the various means by which South Africa's neoliberal engagement with the rest of southern Africa is rebranded as "development."[34]

To combat these less visible and more mutable forms of oppression after the formal ends of colonialism and apartheid, *Chimurenga* shape-shifts, inhabiting various forms and media and embodying Edjabe's maxim that "the most radical art (whatever the medium) isn't 'protest art' but work that envisions a different way of seeing, of feeling, of being."[35] To this end, the magazine, which is available in print and digital formats, plays between the registers of the popular and the elite, fashioning itself in various issues as a curriculum report, a sci-fi magazine, and a graphic novel before taking the form of the newspaper in the *Chronic*. Chimurenga is also the umbrella name under which a host of other projects operate, including an online radio station dubbed the Pan African Space Station; an ongoing exploration of African urbanism, "The African Cities Reader"; "Chimurenganyana," a "pavement literature project" that prints single articles from the journal and makes them available at a low cost;[36] and the Chimurenga Library.[37]

The oldest part of the library, a virtual archive of "independent pan African paper periodicals from around the world," is essential to our understanding of *Chimurenga*'s contribution to this history in the form of the *Chronic*.[38] The digital archive currently includes thirty-three popular, arts-based, and more academic publications whose places of origin span the globe.[39] There is South Africa's anti-apartheid, community-based magazine *Staffrider*; Kenya's *Joe*, which was aimed at youthful urbanites in the 1970s; and *Third Text*, the scholarly journal published out of London that has sought "to challenge the West's position as the ultimate arbiter within arts and culture."[40] An earlier version of the library's website, which was active when the *Chronic* was first published, encouraged readers to approach this diverse, admittedly "subjective" collection as an archive of *Chimurenga*'s influences, rather than as "a comprehensive bibliography."[41] These publications were imagined in geographic terms, as "an archipelago of counter-culture platforms that impacted on our concept of the paper-periodical, the publishable even"—imagery that evokes the wider African diaspora. In addition to mapping pan African geographies through these periodicals, the earlier version of the site made a clear claim to pan Africanism's literary historical roots, locating a common lineage for these publications in African print periodicals from the 1950s and '60s: "All these projects built on the work of *Drum*, *Présence Africaine*, *Transition*, *Black Orpheus* and so on but are also alternatives to those monuments."[42] The current archive continues this practice by including a "Family Tree" below the description of each magazine. In this way, the periodical archive records the global history of print pan Africanism: the *Chronic*'s family tree. Importantly, the mapping of this print history has only been possible in the digital space. As Edjabe explains, "[s]ince we couldn't collect the print publications themselves—they're locked in the vaults of the Euro-American academy and the Internet does not know about them—we collected and circulated our memories and imaginations about them."[43]

In mid-2017, the library expanded to include ongoing research projects and global in-person exhibitions that foreground the complexity with which Chimurenga engages with pan Africanism in its various forms, including its state-sponsored iterations. Through one of these projects, Panafest, Chimurenga explored the ideals and contradictions of the continent's major pan-African festivals of the 1960s and '70s, including FESTAC '77.[44] Though it was funded with state oil money and had nationalist aims, it also provided an important space for forging solidarity between various African and African diaspora resistance groups and "for a myriad of personal and artist encounters that allows for an understanding of diaspora less as a historical condition than a set of practices."[45] Like the periodicals archive, Panafest recovers the history of this festival by making documents housed in largely inaccessible archives available online (and in person at various exhibitions). In this way, these projects turn readers into potential knowledge producers and adhere to Chimurenga's core principle of "who no know go know." Alice Aterianus-Owanga argues that through such archives,

Chimurenga creates "a virtual space which allows (South) Africa to imagine its global solidarities, including different times, different spaces and different worlds."[46] These virtual archives of print history encourage readers to understand the power of the past, not only in terms of its direct effects on the present but also in its unrealized possibilities, asking, "Can a past that the present has not yet caught up with be summoned to haunt the present as an alternative?"[47] Returning to the past is thus a way of moving forward, of creating new presents and futures. We might think of archives like the Chimurenga Library and Panafest as their own kinds of time machines that mobilize the resources of the virtual space to produce an agential, print pan Africanism. These projects both predate and extend the *Chronic*'s inaugural issue in which the newspaper is turned into a time machine, pointing to this first issue's genesis and its continuing significance for Chimurenga's interventions.

THE NEWSPAPER AS "TIME MACHINE"

On May 20, 2008, the *New York Times* published an article on the violence against African foreign nationals taking place in South Africa. Under the headline "South Africans Take Out Rage on Immigrants," a photograph appears in which a man dressed in black swings a golf club at a shack against the backdrop of another makeshift structure that has been set ablaze.[48] As a viewer, it is hard to read the image as anything other than an example of the destruction and "rage" of the article's title. Apparently, an earlier version also included a misleading caption under the image. A correction at the bottom of the *Times* article, issued the following day, clarifies: "Because of an editing error, the caption may have left the mistaken impression that the man was a rioter, and should have made clear he was trying to prevent the spread of a fire."

This elision of context and nuance is not limited to the article's photograph and its caption. The article begins with a grim four-paragraph description of a man near death surrounded by a "jaded crowd," and it limits its assessment of the "contagion" of xenophobic violence to one city—Johannesburg—and its diagnosis to the nation's recent history. Specifically, it locates the anger of poor, Black South Africans in the failures of the Black-led, postapartheid state to benefit more than "a small percentage of the nation's black population—the highly skilled and the politically connected," leading many to "tak[e] out their rage on the poor foreigners living in their midst." This, certainly, is part of the story, but like the image that accompanies the article, the article's framing limits our understanding of the other historical and geographical contributors to this moment of violence.

It is precisely to counter news coverage like this that the *Chimurenga Chronic* uses the newspaper as a time machine. The editors explain, "The *Chronic* imagines the newspaper as a producer of time—a time-machine—which travels backwards and forwards, to place these events within a broader context and thereby to challenge the logic of emergencies and immediate needs that characterize contemporary African media."[49] The cover of the *Chronic*'s first issue even recalls the *Times* article's image, with the bright fire at its center framed by darkened shacks on the sides (fig. 5). The *Chronic*'s cover, however, immediately introduces a temporal element, depicting a succession of images of a house—twenty in all, arranged in seven rows of three—much like a photographic proof sheet or even a photocomic strip. The house is small and plain, surrounded by dirt, pavement, and other similar structures. It resembles the Reconstruction and Development Programme (RDP) houses built by the South African government after the end of apartheid. While the program was successful in providing housing for millions, the occupation of these homes by foreign nationals is cited in a 2008 Human Sciences Research Council report as "[o]ne of the most important triggers of the recent violence."[50] Over the course of the first three photographs, a man and woman exit the house carrying a washing bucket between them. After they have left, perhaps to go about their daily chores, the house begins to burn from the inside, the flames growing until they consume it. By introducing a sense of time into an image that is otherwise similar to the one in the *Times*, the *Chronic*'s cover depicts the "before" of the violence: the normal life that is often left outside the frame. In so doing, it both humanizes the victims of the attacks and points to attacks on Black foreigners as "an everyday problem."[51] South Africa's 2008 xenophobic violence may have seemed particularly remarkable, but as Matsinhe argues, the difference between it and previous outbreaks was only one of "magnitude."[52] By treating May 2008 as exceptional, the media response hid the "slower" everyday violence experienced by foreign nationals and Black South Africans alike in South Africa's townships.[53]

What makes the image on the *Chronic*'s cover even more striking is that, upon closer inspection, it is not the house that is burning but rather the *paper* it is printed on. The image is a trompe l'oeil that works in reverse: instead of creating the impression of three dimensions, the

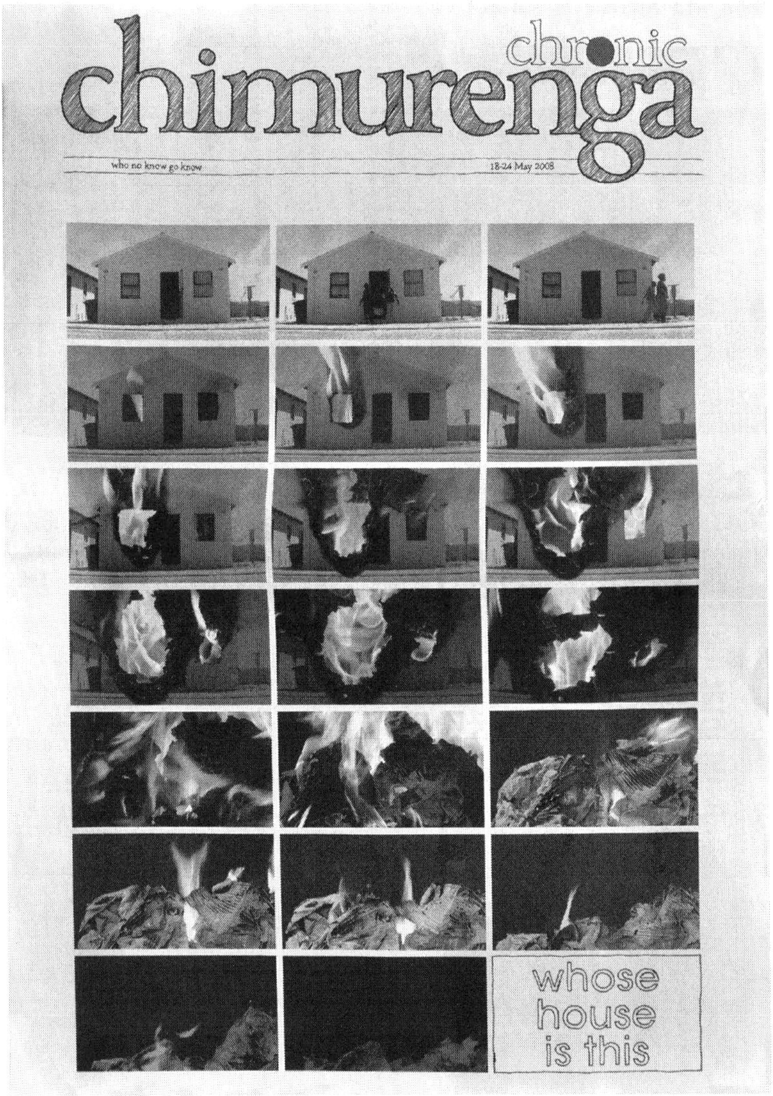

Fig. 5. *Chimurenga 16: The Chimurenga Chronic*. Courtesy of Chimurenga.

illusion purposefully flattens the image to two dimensions. Across the twenty images, the house is swallowed by the gaping, burning hole in the newspaper and is eventually reduced to a pile of singed paper, to ash, next to the words "whose house is this." In this way, the cover foregrounds the materiality of the *Chronic*, asking readers to think about it as a printed newspaper, which is shown here to be a particularly ephemeral medium that nevertheless travels widely through time and space. More than this, the cover's succession of images draws attention to the relationship between time and space in a way that encourages active engagement from readers. A later *Chronic* project on African comics called "Lower Frequencies" suggests a grammar of the comic that can be usefully applied here: "[The comic's] reliance on visual substitution to suggest continuity, the representation of time through space, and the fragmentation of space into contiguous images, demands an active participation on the part of the reader."[54] From this first image on the cover, readers of the *Chronic* are asked to understand reading the newspaper as travel in both time and space in which they are immediately implicated. Whose house is this? Perhaps it is our own.

This image on the newspaper's cover is one of many examples of the *Chronic*'s playful engagement with its materiality. While the *Chronic* is available in both print and digital formats, which can be ordered through Chimurenga's elaborate website, its reflexivity about its own form is most obvious in its physical version.[55] Printed on cream-colored paper the size of a regular newspaper, the *Chronic* is somewhat unwieldy. To read it properly requires folding pages over, taking sections out—in other words, deconstructing it to some degree. Like an actual newspaper, it bears the marks of the reader: worn, softened edges, small tears in the page, creases throughout. It yellows with age and lacks the durability of a book or even a magazine, and in consuming it, one becomes aware of this ephemerality. At the same time, readers likely hold on to the *Chronic* because, after all, it is not a cheap "one-day bestselle[r]," as Benedict Anderson describes the modern newspaper, but rather a pricier literary magazine that most purchasers intend to keep.[56] Furthermore, its backdated articles, which are already out of step with time, do not "expire" in the same way that an average newspaper's do. In this way, the *Chronic* materializes our paradoxical conception of the newspaper as both disposable and lasting, a medium associated with both the fleeting present and "[o]ur sense of history, our sense of what is important and our sense of record."[57]

By including a fictionalized date at the top of nearly every spread, the *Chronic* also gestures to one of the newspaper's essential fictions. Anderson describes the newspaper's date as "the single most important emblem on it," for it "provides the essential connection" between its various stories.[58] Since the *Chronic* is backdated, it is able to step outside "the steady onward clocking of homogenous, empty time" to reveal the average newspaper's sleight of hand: it is not an objective account of the (infinite number of) events that occur on a given date, but a human product, composed subjectively.[59] The *Chronic* emphasizes its contingency by being purposefully fragmented and non-linear, with many of its sections labeled only "Another Section," and readers are invited several times to "[p]lease re-order this newspaper as per your wishes, needs, wants, fears and/or desires." As a result, readers of the *Chronic* travel through the time and space of the paper with a simultaneous awareness of their own "agency" and "liminality," a condition shared by many of the actors described in the issue.[60]

As discussed above, our "medial ideology"[61] of the newspaper—as ephemeral and durable, contingent and routine—is also an "ideology of temporality."[62] One of the *Chronic*'s aims is to draw attention to the temporalities embedded in the modern newspaper as a form. The first is a temporality of "newness" and "emergencies," as evidenced by the domination of today's news cycle by "breaking news"—the value of which lies in its instantaneousness rather than its ability to provide a full or nuanced understanding of events, exemplified by the *Times* article above.[63] The second temporality is what we might call "nation time." Anderson famously links the development of the modern nation to the newspaper form, which generates a sense of connection among a nation's citizens, all of whom engage in the same "mass ceremony" of reading the newspaper each morning.[64] Though it might seem that, unlike a time of emergency, nation time maintains some sense of history, it also mythologizes the nation-state as an "origin" and thus inscribes it with "a dehistoricized and circular logic."[65] As Bhakti Shringarpure helpfully argues in her own conception of it, "nation time" is "the deeply layered, complicated chronopolitics that newly formed nations struggle with."[66] In Shringarpure's model, "nation time" binds in several ways. In the colonial period it relegates the colonized nation to a time outside history. However, as it is taken up by anti-colonial revolutionaries, it is equally binding in its emphasis on putting aside internal differences for the purposes of national liberation, an idea that resonates with Edjabe's reflections on the pressure put on artists in postapartheid South Africa to "build the nation."

Perhaps most importantly, these temporalities are associated with certain kinds of space, which the *Chronic* likewise seeks to disrupt. In Bakhtin's concept of the chronotope, or "time-space," the "primary category" is time, but the temporality of a genre—the "adventure time" of the ancient Greek novel, for example—produces a particular kind of space. In the case of the adventure novel, this space is as empty and abstract as its sense of time, "[f]or any concretization—geographic, economic, sociopolitical, quotidian—would fetter the freedom and flexibility of the adventures and limit the absolute power of chance."[67] Regarding the typical newspaper, a temporality of crisis and immediacy results in a space that is equally incomplete and hastily sketched. It is in such a chronotope that Africa becomes "a country" and that the particularities of its many regions, nations, and people are reduced to just a few stories: warring tribes, starving children, and corrupt governments, all of which make it a place ripe for Western aid and "development."[68] Similarly, nation time—whether envisioned, as it is by Anderson, as calendrical "homogenous, empty time" or as "the time of action and urgency" in the struggle for national liberation, as it is by Shringarpure—produces the idea of the nation as a singular, uniform entity, a "solid community moving steadily down (or up) history."[69] The *Chronic*, however, seeks to "challenge the newspapers' [*sic*] history as a tool of nationalism," using it instead to write a pan African history that breaks free from both the bounded time-space of the nation and the broad generalities that elide the specificities of particular African contexts.[70]

Time travel creates a unique opportunity for the *Chronic* to disrupt both time and space because of its "'time as space' chronotope."[71] Time travel not only connects time and space but treats time as though it *were* space, so that "[t]ime and space become a single frozen *space-time*, isotropic and capable of being navigated in any direction one chooses."[72] Although time travel seems to promise the ability to alter time and history, Elana Gomel observes that its conflation of time and space "requires the equivalence of the past and the future," rendering both "determined and immutable."[73] For Gomel, who is concerned with the enduring importance of time in postmodern theory, the popularity and ubiquity of time travel as a trope "exposes the paradoxical kinship between the postmodern denial of history and the extreme forms of historical determinism." Time travel, however, looks different through a postcolonial lens, where an emphasis on time and history is necessary to address colonial and neocolonial forms of oppression. The *Chronic*, for instance, plays on time travel's "spatialization of temporality" to draw attention to the way Africa, as a geographic space, has consistently been used to signify time.[74] Africa has long been depicted as the prehistory of Western civilization, and for one infamous example we need only look to Conrad's *Heart of Darkness* and its descriptions of boating up the

Congo River as time travel into the primordial past. This trend continues in contemporary Western genre fiction, particularly science fiction, which has often cast Africa as the site of apocalyptic futures and "the *zone* of absolute dystopia."[75] More than simply pointing out this problematic treatment of time as space, however, the *Chronic* exploits it, employing time travel to produce a pan African spacetime.

PAN AFRICAN SPACETIME

The *Chronic*'s use of time travel as space travel is evident throughout its inaugural issue, beginning with its representation of time through space on the cover. It also appears in the final lines of the issue's poem-cum-editorial, which, echoing the words that appear on the cover, is titled "Whose House Is This?":

> Forget tomorrow.
> Sun Ra said: Linktime has officially ended.
> We'll work on the other side . . .
> we'll bring them here somehow
> through either isotope
> internal linkteleportation
> transmolecularisation . . .
> Maybe newspapers should be written by aliens?[76]

Several of these lines are from the film *Space Is the Place*, in which Sun Ra uses his music as a means of time and space travel to transport Black people to a new planet and "altered destiny" untouched by white supremacy.[77] The film's language—"we'll bring them there somehow," "linkteleportation," and "transmolecularisation"—is just as, if not more, spatial than temporal, and Ra's suggestion that "we'll work on the other side" easily refers to both time ("Linktime has officially ended") and space in the context of his interplanetary travel.

By sampling Sun Ra, the *Chronic* signals its connection to Afrofuturism, which it transforms for its own ends. The last line of the editorial is particularly notable given the issue's focus on the violence against foreign nationals in South Africa. Here, the word "alien" slips between registers. It belongs at once to the lexicon of Afrofuturism—Sun Ra famously claimed that he was an alien—and to the dehumanizing language of government bureaucracy that categorizes people who belong as "citizens" and those who do not as "aliens." This is the kind of language that undergirds, if not sanctions, the "us versus them" mentality that culminated in violence in South Africa in 2008. In asking whether "newspapers should be written by aliens," the *Chronic*'s editors gesture to the two aims of their project: to publish a newspaper that gives voice to those who were victims of the attacks and to use the newspaper as a means to "work on the other side" of time and space as we know it to create a pan African spacetime.

In pan African spacetime, South Africa's xenophobic violence is situated within the frameworks of global apartheid, colonialism, and racial capitalism. Across its 252-page issue, which it urges readers to navigate at their discretion, the *Chronic*'s articles range widely across time and space. While the first section, "Burnin' and A-Lootin,'" deals most directly with the 2008 attacks, the magazine also features "Trade Routes," which looks at issues of "ethnic capital" and the "business of migration," as well as more standard sections that could be found in any typical newspaper, including Arts, Sports, Media & Technology, and Health. The articles in these sections—all of which are carefully backdated to May 2008—cover topics as diverse as cybercrime in West Africa and the Institute for Naturopathy and Yogic Sciences outside Bangalore. The result is that the 2008 attacks are not, as the *Times* article suggests, a South African aberration: they are woven throughout the fabric of global spacetime.

The first section of the *Chronic*, "Burnin' and A-Lootin,'" best demonstrates what a time-traveling "alien" newspaper can achieve. By using time travel to create a broader temporal frame for the 2008 attacks, which according to mainstream news coverage began in Johannesburg, this section facilitates a new spatial understanding of the violence. Kwanele Sosibo's "The Warm-Up" challenges the media's coverage of the violence in May as a "sudden phenomena," instead "dat[ing] the origins of this wave to March, in a township of Pretoria."[78] The article includes the accounts of two victims, Moses Mhlanga and Thomas Moyana, and one alleged perpetrator, Jeff Ramohlale, moving backward and forward in time with respect to the attacks to highlight the complex geographies of migration and political power in the area. Before this earlier wave of violence began on March 18, for example, Mhlanga and other business owners in Atteridgeville were squeezed for protection money by Ramohlale, who told them that attacks on "foreigners" had already started elsewhere and were coming to the area. Sosibo points to the power of actors like Ramohlale to displace and dispel their own culpability by shifting the time frame of the events and drawing alternative maps of the violence: "From Winterveld it went [south-eastwards] to Soshanguve. From Soshanguve, [north-eastwards] to Hammanskraal. From Hammanskraal [southwards] to Mamelodi. From Mamelodi [westwards] to here in Itireleng. From Itireleng, there was a meeting there in block K in Jeffsville."[79] Nevertheless, the violence in Jeffsville, named after Ramohlale himself, could not have occurred without Ramohlale's knowledge and complicity.

Sosibo's article also foregrounds the experiences of Mhlanga and Moyana, who were attacked, describing their lives both before and after the violence from close third-person perspectives and highlighting not only hardship but also the pleasures and more mundane parts of their lives. By extending our time frame to encompass more than the attacks, we can also see the complicated geography of home for migrants like Moyana and a more comprehensive map of simultaneous refuge and alienation. Following Moyana to KwaNyamazane in Nelspruit where he is still recovering in May, the article moves forward in time and back toward "home" in Mozambique. Displaced from Atteridgeville—"what he had thought home was for a while"—Moyana feels physical, psychological, and linguistic estrangement: "A slight chill was starting to set in even in subtropical KwaNyamazane. He felt discomfort, despite the closer proximity to Mozambique."[80] His body is bruised, and he suffers from nightmares; he is "closer to home but further away from himself." Taken as a whole, Sosibo's article illuminates a different spacetime in relation to the attacks—both in terms of the time line and trajectories of the attacks and the various places migrants like Moyana and Mhlanga called home before and afterward.

The issue travels back even further in time to place the attacks within South Africa's history of apartheid. Jacob Dlamini's "The Death of Jacob Dlamini" returns to the mid-1980s, when a deputy mayor was murdered by neighboring residents over a rent increase, demonstrating that the violence of 2008 is not new and in fact has its roots in apartheid-era logic. Though Jacob Dlamini—the present-day author—is clearly not the same man as the subject of the piece, the past and present are entwined through their shared name in addition to the similarities of their respective moments. It is almost as though Dlamini-the-mayor is a time traveler from the past, coming with the message that repeating the same actions will not lead to a different future. In 1984, he was stoned, beaten, and eventually burned to death in Sharpeville. The residents, in publicly executing Dlamini, "saw their actions as expressing 'the will of the people,'" a justification that bears a striking similarity to the way South Africans who participated in the 2008 violence against foreign nationals rationalized their actions.[81] Dlamini-the-author understands the incident as "a contest about legitimacy" between the Sharpeville residents and the apartheid government over who has the right "to decide on who may live and who may die," but he critiques the dehumanizing logic of this struggle that reduces human life to a means to an end, reminding the reader that the earlier Dlamini "was also a father, a neighbour, a teacher and many things besides." By positioning 1984 as an "overlapping time-space" in relation to the violence against migrants in the postapartheid era,[82] Dlamini suggests that if the struggle against apartheid has a lesson to offer the present moment, it is that while the provision for basic needs, like housing and toilets, is essential, it cannot be the only measure of a democracy:

> But surely the struggle against apartheid was not about who—between the liberation movement and the apartheid state—could build better toilets for black people. Yet, it is these totems—RDP houses, toilets, tarred roads, affirmative action and BEE [Black Economic Empowerment]—that have become the measure of our freedom, a measure that marks a serious failure of the imagination on our part.[83]

Through this imagery, Dlamini's essay connects powerfully to the image of the burning RDP house on the *Chronic*'s cover and the question that resonates throughout the issue: "Whose house is this?" Not only is this house possibly our own—a nation burning itself from the inside—it is also a reminder that a more radical vision of freedom is necessary to combat oppression past and present.

Dlamini's return to the apartheid past illuminates not only the connection between South Africa's xenophobic violence and the struggle against apartheid but also the need for a more capacious imagination of freedom on a pan African scale. This broader pan African vision, Dlamini argues, was essential to defeating apartheid. Traveling even further back in time to the 1960s, just before the anti-pass protests in Sharpeville, Dlamini recalls the words of Robert Sobukwe, founder of South Africa's Pan Africanist Congress, to demonstrate the reach of this pan African imagination of the time: "This is not a game. We are not gambling. We are taking our first step in the march to African independence and the United States of Africa. And we are not leading corpses to the new Africa. We are leading the vital, breathing and dynamic youth of our land. We are leading the youth, not to death, but to life abundant."[84] In the "new" South Africa, which continues to see itself as a leader for the African continent, Dlamini laments South Africans' willingness to rest on the legacy of figures like Nelson Mandela and to accept little individual responsibility for creating a freer society for all. In the wake of the death and destruction of 2008, the time-traveling Dlaminis remind us of this unfulfilled pan African dream by asking questions that continue to haunt the rainbow nation: "Who exactly are we leading? And where are we leading them to?" In this and other articles throughout the issue, the *Chronic* asks whether a pan African future can be produced in South Africa today.

The *Chronic* examines South Africa's relationship to Africa in a variety of ways throughout the issue. In "Questions & Some Answers," which plays on the letters section common to many newspapers and magazines, various writers situate the 2008 violence relative to other African contexts. Kofi Agyemang from Accra sees the attacks in South Africa as "a repeat" of the expulsion of Ghanaians from Nigeria (known as "Ghana-Must-Go") in the mid-1980s.[85] And well-known writer Petina Gappah, writing from Harare, reflects on the fact that Kenya, which had always "seemed achingly normal" compared to her native Zimbabwe, is now infamous for its 2007–2008 postelection violence.[86] Kenya, like South Africa long a darling of the West, is now talked about by "stern-faced British prime ministers, European Union observers and American presidents" in much the same way that Zimbabwe once was. While pointing to the rotating failed states that contribute to the patterns of migration, violence, and expulsions that fueled attacks like the ones in South Africa in May, these letters also share a different vision based on mutual support among African nations as well as intracontinental mobility.

We see this in particular in a letter by Marc Gbaffou of Johannesburg, which refashions the "spirit of May 2008" to include not only xenophobic violence but also the newly organized diasporic community that grew out of it.[87] Gbaffou, one of the founders of Johannesburg's new African Diaspora Forum, reflects on the fact that although he had lived in the city for many years, 2008 was the first time he found himself concerned about the darkness of his skin. Frustrated by the government response to the violence, Gbaffou and Rayban, "a Zimbabwean-born South African—who insists on being identified as 'African' only," formed a new "pan African forum, where all African migrant organisations could speak with one voice to engage government and communities." The "Africa Diaspora Forum," as it came to be called, chose its name as a way to signal a sense of community based on mobility: "We did not want 'Foreigners'—that we found derogatory; we did not want 'migrants'—that was ambiguous. 'Diaspora', although improper, was capturing our sense of being far away from home, permanently mobile, and strongly connected to one another. This is also the spirit of May 2008." It is by time traveling back to 2008 that this alternative vision is uncovered, a vision that would otherwise have been lost in the traditional reportage of the events, like the *Times* article, which focused on the violence alone. In traveling back to this moment, the *Chronic* identifies yet another past that the present has yet "to catch up to."[88] This, in turn, reveals an alternate geography of interconnection across the continent, a pan African spacetime born of shared experiences of permanent mobility.

The fluid vision of pan African or diasporic identity envisioned by Gbaffou and Rayban is impeded by the many barriers to movement across the continent and globe. As a time-traveling, alien newspaper, the *Chronic* makes visible these many barriers past and present through mapmaking and data visualization. Many of these maps are hand drawn and thus call attention to the humanness and contingency of mapmaking. Some of these maps also represent time through space, much like the image on the *Chronic*'s cover. "Mourir aux portes de l'Europe" ("Death at the Gates of Europe") depicts the EU's official borders as well as its "pre-border and EU buffer zone"—such as detention camps in North Africa—overlaid with red circles sized to account for the number of migrant deaths in various areas over three decades.[89] The largest circle encompasses much of Portugal and Spain as well as parts of Morocco and Algeria and represents the six thousand deaths that have occurred around Gibraltar. In this way, this new map makes visible the extended space of Europe's borders—many of which are located on the African continent—and the enormous migrant death toll over time. Just as time travel made visible alternate geographies of the 2008 violence in Sosibo's article, these maps spatialize ongoing violence related to migration and border crossing on a global scale.

Through maps like this one, the *Chronic* situates the violence in South Africa in May 2008 within the framework not only of South African apartheid but also of a global apartheid order. "Les frontières les mieux gardées du monde" ("The Best-Guarded Borders in the World") is drawn in rough colored pencil and resembles a child's drawing. States and regions with both extensive legislation to curtail migration and physical barriers have bright red lines with jagged teeth drawn around them.[90] South Africa, one of these states, is severed from the rest of the African continent by a toothy, vicious smile. These border walls represent a "failure of the imagination," and maps such as this are in dialogue with Dlamini's assertion that South Africa has failed to imagine democracy as accomplishing more than the provision for basic needs.[91] Indeed, based on this and similar maps, South Africa is exceptional not in its potential to lead the continent but in its resemblance to other wealthy, heavily bordered states.

One might guess that it was the overwhelming success of the *Chronic*—designed originally as a "once off"—that led Chimurenga to continue publishing issues and, indeed, to having the *Chronic* eventually *become* Chimurenga, supplanting other iterations of the magazine, at least for the time being. The decision, however, had more to do with the belief that a single issue would essentially freeze time and therefore reify Africa in much the same way that articles like the one in the *New York Times* do. Edjabe recalls that he was still enjoying the many praises that had been lavished on the publication, including the *Financial Times*'s description of it as "better than *The New Yorker*," when he realized that the project had become "a spectacle that came dangerously close to perpetuating the very thing it sought to critique. It presented Africa as a land of never-ending present and instant, where today and now matter more than tomorrow, let alone the distant future."[92] As a result, Edjabe established the *Chronic* as a quarterly magazine. Though it no longer deliberately time travels, it continues to use not only the newspaper but also a host of other print genres, from Onitsha market literature to photocomics, as time and space travel machines.

GENRE AS TIME AND SPACE MACHINE

On the cover of the *Chronic*'s next issue, published in April 2013, its characteristic tagline "who no know go know" is accompanied by another descriptor: "now-now, a quarterly pan African gazette." The *Chronic*'s new temporal marker, or "time-zone," of now-now indicates its practice of "documenting historical events in real time."[93] Derived from the Afrikaans *nou-nou*, now-now is sometimes used "to indicate a more immediate present" in South African English, as compared to "just now" and "now," which can mean "later" or "in a while."[94] While now-now's use of reduplication gives it a somewhat greater urgency, its contemporary usage indicates a fluid temporality spanning from "right now" to "never." In writing history "now-now," the *Chronic* continues to signal its liminality and contingency. It moves between the past and the present to write new histories and thus to create alternative futures and presents—endlessly traveling this temporal Mobius strip. It is, as Samatar suggests of Afrofuturism more broadly, "always about all times: past, present, and future."[95]

As this new temporality implies, subsequent issues of the *Chronic* do not use the same conceit of time travel in that they are not backdated as the first issue was. They do, however, use a variety of other print forms to produce pan African spacetime. Specifically, later issues of the *Chronic* take twentieth-century print genres that had, or were imagined as having, a pan-African scope, and adapt them in ways that reveal both their embeddedness in particular times and places and their ability to forge solidarities across the continent and the globe. These mass-produced popular print forms, such as the photocomic magazine *African Film* published by South Africa's Drum Publications, were designed to travel seamlessly across the African continent and the diaspora. In an article in the June 2014 issue of the *Chronic Books*, which is designed to look like an issue of *African Film*, Uzor Maxim Uzoatu reflects that he and many other Nigerian readers never realized that *African Film* was a South African publication.[96] Often lacking dates or other place-based markers, these genres were meant to travel without the need for cultural translation. In adapting these twentieth-century pan-African genres for the twenty-first century, the *Chronic* reinvests these forms with time and place so that they are attentive to temporal *décalage* and spatial difference while still forging a sense of solidarity, producing a more critically informed pan African spacetime.[97]

The *Chronic*'s August 2013 issue, for example, includes a *Chronic Books* section that styles itself as an Onitsha market literature pamphlet. Nigerian Onitsha market literature is one of Africa's most iconic forms of popular literature. Published in the 1950s and '60s in the town of Onitsha in southeastern Nigeria and sold out of its famed market, the largest one in West Africa, these pamphlets were written primarily in English and were often instructional in nature, with titles like "How to Speak to Girls and Win Their Love" and "How to Get Rich Overnight."[98] Newell finds the temporality of many such publications, and of West African self-help literature more broadly, to be "future-oriented" with "a kind of aggressive, or absolute, contemporaneousness."[99] Often lacking issue numbers or dates, these publications were meant to be eternally relevant to readers, no matter when they were picked up, and Newell notes that Onitsha pamphlets from the mid-twentieth century can still be purchased at the market decades later.[100] Similarly, such publications have been read as more or less placeless. Coulon argues that "[t]he vision of Onitsha authors is either local or pan-African; it is hardly ever *national*. The writers of popular market literature are interested in teaching their readers to cope with an urban environment, in cautioning them about the evil effects of the big city. Their warnings could, in truth, be valid for any African city, anywhere on the African continent."[101]

This issue of the *Chronic* uses the form of the Onitsha pamphlet as a vehicle for time and space travel, in the process exposing some of the assumptions about the genre's timelessness and pan-African scope in much the same way that the *Chronic*'s first issue reveals the medial and temporal ideologies embedded in the newspaper form. The issue's cover, which bears the title "How to Be a Nigerian," looks like an Onitsha market pamphlet, with its decorative borders and black-and-white photos of a quality akin to that of a Xerox. Yet this particular low-resolution photo is of someone immediately recognizable to most readers: the Nigerian novelist Chimamanda Ngozi Adichie. Adichie is a renowned but controversial figure, and it is fitting that she appears under this particular title.[102] Globally, Adichie is the most well-known contemporary African author, and probably the most well-known Nigerian cultural figure in the West—a status cemented by Beyoncé's sampling of Adichie's TEDxEuston talk "We Should All Be Feminists" in her 2014 song "Flawless." Given her position of power and influence in the African literary field, Adichie sparked controversy in July 2013 when she suggested that the Caine Prize—for which several of her former students had been short-listed—was "not the arbiter of the best fiction in Africa."[103] When asked where she goes to look for the best African fiction, she replied, "I go to my mailbox, where my workshop people send me their stories. . . . They're not on the Caine Prize short list." The shortlistees who were also former students of Adichie's were incensed by her comments.[104] The quote that appears below Adichie's image on the *Chronic Books* cover is suggestive of these contemporary events. Taken from Peter Enahoro's (a.k.a. "Peter Pan") infamous 1960s book *How to Be a Nigerian*, it reads: "Every other Nigerian has a small dagger in his pocket, hoping to draw blood. Get your own dagger! Be on your guard. And may the Lord be with you." In the photo on the cover,

Adichie stands with her hands clasped in front of her, raised so they are just below her breasts. It does indeed look as though she is holding a small, invisible knife as she stares confidently into the camera, her lips in a slight, knowing smile.

Beginning with its cover, which juxtaposes Adichie's image with classic Onitsha pamphlet aesthetics, this issue of the *Chronic Books* is not so much timeless as it is *timefull*, moving seamlessly between the past, present, and future, as its time zone of "now-now" suggests. This strategy of producing overlapping temporalities continues throughout the issue, which also includes a similar image of Elnathan John, one of Adichie's former students with whom she clashed over the Caine Prize, on the cover of an imagined chapbook, *How to Be a Nigerian Writer*, and Tolu Ogunlesi on another titled *How to Be Nigerian Today*, which takes Peter Enahoro's *How to Be a Nigerian* into the digital future.[105] The overall effect of these various rewritings and homages to the Onitsha pamphlet, a genre that aimed to retain its currency in a never-ending present, is to make visible time's various layers rather than erasing it.

By treating time in this way, the issue also gestures to a more complex understanding of space. The issue's first article, a review of Adichie's *Americanah* by Yemisi Ogbe, asserts that Adichie's novel is "about definitions," and particularly about what it means to be Nigerian. However, in a story where Nigeria serves only as "preamble" to Adichie's protagonist's self-discovery in America, Adichie has failed to capture the complexity of the "Nigerian world," let alone a broader African one: "Africa is immeasurable. It is a living, muscular bricolage flexing and expanding backward and forward through all the manifestations of time and space. . . . The African continent is not just a part of the world. Conceptually it is the same size as the world."[106] Ogbe seems to suggest that Adichie might do better to embrace uncontainableness rather than the tidiness of definitions. In seeking to "tur[n] the definition[s] on the definers,"[107] Adichie's novel becomes too rigid, unable to account for an Africa that claims not only "all times" but also all spaces.[108]

Adichie's presence in the issue contrasts with that of the "novelist, poet, playwright, rapper, singer, visual artist, clothes designer, dressmaker" and "priestess" Werewere Liking, the only other figure in this issue to be given the full-page Onitsha pamphlet treatment.[109] On the simulated cover, she is pictured sitting, holding a staff as though she were on a throne, over the title "La Puissance de Werewere Liking" ("The Power of Werewere Liking"). Notably, Liking embraces the kind of bricolage that Adichie supposedly eschews. In addition to her many forms of art practice, the Cameroon-born Liking established a theater troupe and community arts center in Côte d'Ivoire called the Ki-Yi Mbock (Ultimate Knowledge) Village.[110] In all these ways, Liking resembles Fela, the *Chronic*'s foundational pan African exemplar. Critiquing South Africa for its cultural isolationism, Liking emphasizes cultural connections across the continent in order to bridge the divides between languages and literary traditions. Embracing bricolage, which Samatar refers to as a "time-traveling practice,"[111] Liking describes her simultaneous existence in multiple temporalities: "I am a repository of traditional African culture. I also consider myself to be one of the moderns, somebody who goes toward the future. My vision is that Africa must be modern, Africa must go into the future, but mustn't get there empty-handed."[112] The *Chronic*, too, might be thought of as traveling into the future with the Onitsha pamphlet and other popular print forms in hand. While many of these genres were designed to be timeless and broadly applicable to audiences across the continent, the *Chronic* reinvests such forms with time and attention to the nuances of space—of South Africa's insularity, Nigeria's "size and complexity"—in order to create a pan African spacetime that is expansive enough to account for difference and *décalage*.

JUNGLE JIM'S AFRICAN PULP FICTION

Jungle Jim magazine (2011–2016) described itself as an "African pulp fiction magazine" for "genre-based writing from all over Africa."[113] The magazine's playful title immediately conjures up stereotypes of Africa from pulp fiction's golden era in the 1920s and '30s. The pulps were inexpensive magazines that published short and serialized fiction in a variety of genres, including adventure, crime, horror, science fiction, and romance. These stories were frequently set in "exotic" locations and thus, in addition to their Western, white, and usually male heroes, included a cast of locals, who served as villains, native informants, and other supporting characters. *Jungle Jim* shares its name with one such publication, a comic strip (1934–1954) set in Asia featuring Jim Bradley, a hunter, and his sidekick, Kolu.[114] In the late 1940s, the story's setting shifted to Africa when the comic was turned into a series of movies (1948–1956) and a TV show, both of which starred Johnny Weissmuller, best known for playing the role of Tarzan.[115] Today's *Jungle Jim* draws on and reconfigures such narratives. As Jenna Bass, the magazine's cofounder and editor, explains regarding the choice of the magazine's title, "We wanted a title that acknowledged the role that Africa has played in Western pulp and genre writing in the past—the exotic, the other, the place where anything happens—and sort of recolonize that, if that's possible."[116]

Jungle Jim uses the pulp magazine as a time-travel machine, in much the same way that the *Chronic* used the newspaper and other popular print genres, both to draw attention to the role this form has played in colonial and neocolonial projects and to reimagine the global past, present, and future from a pan African perspective. Whereas twentieth-century European and American pulps contained racist depictions of Africans that often relegated them to an unchanging past devoid of modern technology, South African *fotoboeke*, or photo comics, aimed at whites frequently did not portray Black South Africans at all, appearing to elide Blackness from the genre entirely.[117] Though *Jungle Jim* does not time travel explicitly by backdating its content in the way that the first issue of the *Chronic* did, it does engage in a form of time travel through its reanimation of a wide spectrum of pulp genres, from the pirate story to hard-boiled detective fiction, romance, and science fiction. Additionally, *Jungle Jim* time travels through its material form, which is produced using simple printing techniques reminiscent of the pulps. Finally, and also like the *Chronic*, *Jungle Jim* plays with time travel's conflation of time and space, using these stories not only to rewrite the "temporal logics that condemned black subjects to prehistory," as Eshun puts it, but also to reimagine space in a way that transcends the colonial spatial logics imposed on the continent.[118] These logics include the borders that artificially divided ethnic and linguistic communities as well as the ideas about who belongs as a "citizen" and who is tolerated as a "subject" that continue to haunt postcolonial Africa and to erupt in xenophobic violence.[119] Through stories that deal with alienation—not only from time and history but also from space and the right to mobility—these stories produce a pan African spacetime that centers Africa in global space and history while drawing attention to questions of belonging, migration, and xenophobia past and present.

Jungle Jim began as a collaboration between Bass, an award-winning South African writer and filmmaker, and Hannes Bernard, a South African illustrator and designer, on a small budget of 1,500 rand (US$150). It expressly solicited work by African nationals living on the continent as well as in the diaspora, and it "consider[ed] stories by writers of African descent/parentage."[120] *Jungle Jim*'s first twenty-four issues, published between 2011 and 2014, included the work of writers from fifteen African countries from West, North, East, Southern, and Central Africa.[121] *Jungle Jim* also gained an international platform in 2012, when one of its stories, "Hunter Emmanuel," written by Bass under the pen name Constance Myburgh, was short-listed for the Caine Prize. The magazine has published some of the most prominent names in African genre fiction, including South Africa's S. L. Grey (the pen name under which authors Sarah Lotz and Louis Greenberg write horror novels), the crime writer Kwei Quartey of Ghana (currently based in California), and the Nigerian American writer Nnedi Okorafor, the most well-known writer of African speculative fiction today.

Jungle Jim's materiality is a key facet of its evocation of an iconic print form, and it serves as a marker of its potential exclusiveness. While presenting itself as an "African" magazine, *Jungle Jim* is conceptualized, produced, and distributed out of Cape Town. South African writers also authored approximately half of the magazine's stories from 2011 to 2014. Sold for only R15 (about US$1.50), a price that allowed it to barely break even, *Jungle Jim* is printed on low-quality paper and must be opened by cutting or ripping off its top with a pair of scissors.[122] This, according to Shaun Swingler, the magazine's managing editor, was primarily a cost-saving measure, but it also enhanced the magazine's DIY (do-it-yourself) quality and its "rough, raw, cheap, shitty pulpiness."[123] The magazine was printed at the cheapest printer in the Woodstock area, which also published local prayer materials, among other things, and Swingler describes how the magazine's cheap ink tended to stain one's hands: after picking up a new issue, his hands would be covered in red and blue for days. All these material aspects of the magazine, Swingler says, were crucial to its message and its subversion of pulp as a genre and aesthetic.

Nevertheless, the magazine did not fully embrace the mass-produced "aspect of pulp publishing," resulting in a publication with pan African ambitions but little ability to reach African audiences beyond South Africa.[124] Even in South Africa, purchasing a physical copy of the magazine was possible only in Cape Town and Johannesburg, where it was sold at small, independent bookshops. One of the ways *Jungle Jim* compensated for its limited physical circulation was by maintaining a relatively robust online presence. Many, though not all, issues of the magazine can be purchased online through Amazon and read on Kindle—a literary form that Bass calls "kindlepulp."[125] Still, as Swingler points out, the experience of engaging with an ephemeral object does not quite translate on an iPad. And while digital distribution may have afforded the magazine a wider international audience, many parts of the continent were still unreachable via platforms like Amazon and PayPal in 2014.[126] All of this has led some critics to wonder whether *Jungle Jim*'s aesthetic has fostered a sense of "exclusivity" that might "ultimately impede itself from reflecting incisively upon an Africa beyond the borders of the Cape's particular urban jungle?"[127] In other words, *Jungle Jim*, like the *Chronic*, raises an important question: whether a magazine produced and distributed under these material conditions and in this location can foster an inclusive pan Africanism.[128]

While purchasing a copy of *Jungle Jim* may have been difficult both on- and offline, parts of its project were freely accessible, including its website and Facebook page. Both of these sites came to serve as an archive of African pulp, much like Chimurenga's archive of pan African publications, demonstrating once again the important role of the digital space in preserving ephemeral print forms. These archives map the pulp genre's antecedents and possible futures, demonstrating the tropes it is writing against as well as its globality. While it was active (and still today on the Internet Archive's Wayback Machine), *Jungle Jim*'s website featured thumbnail images of each of the magazine's own covers, followed by those of pulp publications from the 1950s to 1980s. Although a number of these publications are *fotoboeke* published in South Africa and Rhodesia, others, like many of the publications in Chimurenga's archive, were not published on the continent at all. Instead, these magazines demonstrate the central role that Africa and other similarly exoticized spaces have played in Euro-American genre fiction.

The covers of the publications that *Jungle Jim* includes in this archive feature dark-skinned monsters, aliens, or villains rather than the white heroes most commonly associated with them. We find, for example, several covers of the American comic *Blue Bolt*, none of which feature the series' eponymous hero, a Harvard football star who gains superpowers after being struck by lightning twice.[129] Instead, one cover from the earliest version of the series depicts Edison Bell—a teenage inventor who was a recurring character in the magazine—being attacked by brown-skinned "headhunters" wearing garish masks and loincloths. Looming above the scene is a multiarmed monster. As the caption at the bottom of the cover tells us, "Edison Bell's pal, Jerry, saved the day by hiding in the headhunters' mechanical idol!" This cover is consistent with a pervasive narrative in the series in which Blue Bolt wages war against the natives of "exotic, fabulous, sf [science fiction] kingdoms" that are technologically advanced but otherwise primitive—a paradox given visual form by the mechanized, multiarmed idol.[130] Covers like this one stand in contrast to the South African and Rhodesian *fotoboeke*, which exclusively featured white actors.[131] On most of these covers, powerful-looking white men hold pistols at the ready, facing down an unseen enemy, indicative of the way *fotoboeke* constructed their audiences around bounded notions of race and language, in this case white Afrikanerdom.[132] Stephanie Marlin-Curiel writes, "Images of blacks never tainted the pages of these comic books. Instead, the Cuban and Soviet troupes assisting the independence movements stood in for the black 'communist enemy'—Angolan, Namibian, or South African."[133] By creating its own archive of covers like these, *Jungle Jim* showcases the misrepresentations and erasures that have characterized pulp fiction, and genre fiction more broadly.

Although *Jungle Jim* highlights the covers of Euro-American and South African publications on its website, its Facebook page creates a more global archive of pulp fiction. Between August 2012 and June 2013, *Jungle Jim* posted 232 examples of what it calls "Pulp of the Day," featuring the covers of pulp fiction magazines from around the world, from Onitsha market literature and *African Film* to Ghanaian movie posters, Mexican pulp art, Chinese science fiction, and Urdu pulp. Bass says that the "moralistic fable style/purpose" of the Onitsha pamphlets resonates with the didacticism of many of the submissions that *Jungle Jim* received, particularly from other parts of Africa.[134] Aside from these Onitsha pamphlets and *African Film*, however, most of the examples of African pulp are movie posters rather than magazines—once again, from the perspective of *Jungle Jim*, demonstrating the necessity of African pulp fiction as a category. *Jungle Jim* makes this point clear in a "Pulp of the Day" post from February 11, 2013, featuring a movie poster for *Macumba Love*, a 1960 American film starring June Wilkinson.[135] On the poster, a woman with a skeleton mask holds a crying baby over a fiery cauldron around which men and women dance and play drums. Some of its text reads, "Weird, Shocking, Savagery in Native Haunts . . . It's Happening Today!" The post reads, "I think next time we get asked 'Why a pulp magazine in Africa?' I will take out this picture and say . . . ['Blood-Lust of the Voodoo Queen!']." Much like Chimurenga's archive of pan African publications, *Jungle Jim*'s online archive curates publications that have inspired its editors to intervene in this particular literary canon. *Jungle Jim*'s archive of print and film culture simultaneously demonstrates the role Africa and Africans have played in the global pulp tradition and contests those representations.

By drawing attention to the complicity of the pulps in colonial and imperial projects, *Jungle Jim* presents itself as a pulp publication capable of addressing these legacies as well as neocolonial oppression through its reimagination of various pulp genres.

"AFRICAN PULP TAKES ON COLONIALISM"?

The cover of *Jungle Jim*'s first issue features a line drawing of a black-and-white skull, a red snake darting in and out of its gaping eyes and mouth. Echoing many classic pulp publications, bold blue and red font proclaims enticing elements from the issue's contents: "Murder! Voudou! Aliens! Pirates!" Aside from the tiny image of the African continent placed next to the issue number and the name of the publishing company, Afreak Press, there is little on the magazine's cover to suggest that it is an African or African-focused publication. In Bass's words, "Genre can be a universal language, allowing us to share stories and challenge popular conceptions between the very different countries in Africa—and giving African stories a potentially broader audience internationally, allowing foreign readers a familiar access point to a culture they may not be at all familiar with."[136] This accessibility, however, is somewhat deceptive. Many of *Jungle Jim*'s narratives draw readers in with the shared language of the pulp genre, but then proceed to bend genre conventions so as to force a confrontation with the genre's deeply rooted histories of violence and exclusion, from the slave trade to the global refugee crisis. Time traveling via these pulp genres reveals these histories and produces accounts from African perspectives as well as new maps of global and interplanetary spaces.

"The Lonesome Ballad of Easter Jack" by the South African comic artist Nikhil Singh is written in the style of an old sea yarn, told from the perspective of "a lowly sugar smuggler."[137] In its first lines, the story rapidly deploys the language and images typically associated with such pirate adventure tales. Easter Jack recalls "[r]iding the endless spice routes to exotic climes and hunting down big red X's on deserted beaches. Drinking out the bottoms of endless banana rums with me cutlass in me belt . . . cutting the heads off of many a jooby joob native."[138] The language is thick with the clichés of the genre, which the story mimics and mocks with gusto. Language play is an important key to the story's intervention in the pulp genre as well as its upending of expected geographies. In Easter Jack's account, the globe's center is the

South Pole, which he describes as "[t]he ice-plugged furry belly-button of the funndygurry world we float like hot, spicy clams upon."[139] It is here that Jack—whose tale also upsets many of the gender roles associated with the pirate and adventure genre—finds love with his "Eskimo baby," with whom he enjoys "that rarely appreciated sanctimonious state of monogamy and marital bliss."[140] However, the lovers' happiness is threatened as they sail through the tropics: "in a strange twist of latitudes," Jack's ship "r[uns] aground in a Sargasso Sea."[141] In much pirate lore, the Sargasso Sea is known as a graveyard for ships. The dangers are largely mythical: this sea takes its name from *sargassum*, a kind of seaweed that can entangle vessels but is usually found in more northern parts of the Atlantic. As Easter Jack notes, geographies do indeed seem to have been turned upside down in this tale—a "twist of latitudes" that also marks a decline in Jack's good fortune.

While trapped in the Sargasso Sea, Jack is bewitched by a beautiful siren, a seductive mermaid whom he follows willingly to the bottom of the ocean. This is a familiar trope in many seamen's yarns, but in this case, the sexual encounter that takes place is driven entirely by the mermaid, whose sex organs are described as androgynous and fearsome: "Twas a flickering and finned aperture, unfolding in a China fan of spiky membranes . . . I was suddenly enveloped in a cloud of milky fluid which caught in me eyes. Them tendrils coiled about me manhood, and she drew me into her unholy body."[142] The mermaid holds Jack underwater and demands that he transport a load of "Bad Sugar," which ends up sinking his ship. In the end, angry because "her Bad Sugar had not never reached its unlawful destination," the mermaid emasculates Jack by turning his Eskimo lover into a plastic doll and taking his good eye, leaving him to "[put his] love into the crusted case of a plastic doll."[143] Although playfully written, "The Lonesome Ballad of Easter Jack" touches on colonial themes through its attention to the lucrative sugar trade. Sugar was a staple of the British and French colonial economies and was produced in the Caribbean using slave labor. Sugarcane was a particularly labor-intensive crop and spoiled quickly after it was harvested, thus creating the need to off-load "bad sugar," as we find in Singh's tale.[144] When Jack fails to bring the sugar to its destination, the mermaid comes after him with "a private army of octopi, and sharkmen in shades and cheap suits," language that nods to neocolonial forms of retribution and control.[145] Overall, "The Lonesome Ballad of Easter Jack" twists not only language and genre but also geography as it reorients the globe's center to the Global South.

Another story that "twists" its genre to reveal alternative spacetimes is Shabnam Mahmood's hard-boiled detective story "The Most Beautiful Place," published in *Jungle Jim*'s fourth issue. While local settings have always been a key feature of the crime genre,[146] in Mahmood's story, a detective's journey through the city of Jinja, Uganda, to discover why a woman committed an initially unnamed crime also becomes a form of time travel, uncovering layers of the city's history. Further, with little information revealed in the story's opening, readers must use their own detection skills to deduce not only the woman's identity and what she did but also the story's historical moment: Uganda's infamous Asian expulsion in the 1970s.[147] In various ways, then, travel through space and time is a key mode of detection in Mahmood's narrative, linking the tragedy of one woman—who throws her three daughters and then herself into the river at Owen Falls Dam—to spatial projects and ideologies of division rooted in the colonial period.

Having exhausted all other leads in his mysterious case, Detective Otoni decides to retrace the woman's final journey by taxi through Jinja. In this way, Otoni's detective work is based on a method of "deduction" that is closely related to the term's archaic meaning: to "trace the course of." In other words, travel is crucial to his attempt to crack the case: "Otoni wanted to know why this route? Would it answer his question as to why she did it?"[148] For Otoni, the woman is indistinguishable from the landscape of Jinja itself: "Jinja was not like small and friendly Iganga or bustling cosmopolitan Kampala. Otoni couldn't place Jinja anymore than her."[149] However, the narrative does "place" Jinja in a broader geographic frame, describing its location on the banks of "*Nalubaale*," or Lake Victoria, "the source of the river Nile," whose route it also traces: "The inlet embraces the southern part of Jinja, where the Nile begins ascending north through Uganda, Sudan, and Egypt."[150] Placing Jinja in this way evokes the scramble by various colonial powers to secure the Nile's source. In addition to locating Jinja in relation to the continent, the narrative draws attention to Jinja's local geography, particularly its segregation along racial and ethnic lines, another legacy of its colonial history.

Otoni travels from the lush green areas of the European sector—"*Luxuriant opportunities for the select few* thought Otoni bitterly"—to Main Street, with its shops, houses, and brightly colored flowers.[151] He stops outside a particular house on Main, with many cars parked outside, where it seems the woman lived: "Aromas of curry wafted out. A gaggle of Asian women stood outside, animatedly whispering amongst themselves. '*Oooh, eh-eh*!' Otoni grimaced. The house was bordered by a dress shop on one side and the other by another two-storey home with more Asians gawking out the window. *Yeye pekeyake, bado kwenda injeh* (she was alone, never went out)."[152] Through these details, we deduce that the woman in question was also Asian, which in the Ugandan context refers to people from the Indian subcontinent.[153] We also sense Otoni's own prejudices in his perception of the scene, in his grimace at the women's whispering and the description of the "gawking" Asians—and we note that in both instances, people are described as groups, rather than as individuals.

While Otoni's movement through space organizes the first part of the narrative, this scene, including Otoni's reaction to the women, raises new questions about the story's time period. There are a number of clues, including a Beatles song playing on the radio as Otoni drives, to suggest that the story is set in the early 1970s, around the time of Idi Amin's expulsion of Ugandan Asians in 1972. Otoni notes the makes and colors (but does not give the years) of the many cars parked outside the house where the woman lived—a description that plays an important part in helping to solve the crime (we learn at the end that one of the cars likely belongs to the woman's husband, who has also disappeared) and that aids readers in their own detective work of dating the story. All the cars described—the Fiat 1500, Ford Cortina, Peugeot, and Volvo 164 E—were popular in Uganda in the 1970s.[154] The Volvo 164 E, in particular, is a model that was produced beginning in 1972. In August of the same year, Uganda's president, Idi Amin, issued an order giving all Asians, including citizens, ninety days to leave the country. Otoni's reaction to the women can be read within the context of the hostility toward Asians in Uganda in this period, particularly among the African working class and small businessmen.[155] Jinja was in fact home to the country's largest Asian population,[156] many of whom were "shopkeepers, artisans and petty bureaucrats," positions that gave them greater economic mobility than Africans.[157]

Though Amin may have issued the decree, Mahmood Mamdani locates the roots of the Asian expulsion in the colonial authorities' racialization of the economy and their fundamental strategy of divide and rule.[158] Throughout the story, the spatial divisions revealed by Otoni's travel through Jinja also uncover its history of colonial and postcolonial exclusion. Revealing these overlapping spacetimes becomes more essential to uncovering the story's mystery as it nears its conclusion.

Otoni's journey through the city ends at the Owen Falls Dam with a short history lesson:

> Owen Falls Dam, the brainchild of Sir Charles Westlake who in 1954 became the first chairman of the dam after its completion. It was to provide hydroelectric power to Uganda and neighbouring Kenya. The resulting dam submerged not just the natural Rippon Falls, but the memories of many a youth, including Otoni, who had spent their holidays swimming and catching tilapia, relishing *machuzi* and *oogali*.[159]

In this description, we are given a sense of how the colonial project changed Jinja's landscape, turning the idyllic Rippon Falls, where Otoni spent his childhood, into a place where something terrible has happened. The story's title, "The Most Beautiful Place," subtly reflects this history of appropriation and erasure. John Hanning Speke, the first European to observe Rippon Falls, the source of the Nile, wrote in his notes, "Though beautiful, the scene was not exactly what I expected; for the broad surface of the lake was shut out from view by a spur of hill and the falls, about twelve feet deep and four to five hundred feet broad, were broken by rocks. Still it was a sight that attracted one to it for hours."[160] The dam later played a gory role in Amin's rule. Hannington Sengendo writes, "It is said that so many bodies were dumped in Lake Victoria that they often blocked the hydroelectric intake channels at the Owen Falls Dam."[161] Mahmood's story hints at this grisly aspect of the place's history through Otoni's observation that "some points along the bank were waves of swaying grass, large slender blades of green bending in the wind, dense enough to hide a person."[162]

In this way, the story's ending reveals layers of history at the Owen Falls Dam, suggesting that only by moving between these different historical moments might we come closer to the truth of why the woman threw her three young children into the river before drowning herself. One officer reports to Otoni that the woman's mother-in-law "is now saying there *might* have been domestic disturbances."[163] Given the story's keen attention to place, and the many clues about its historical moment, "domestic disturbances" alludes once again to the expulsion of Ugandan *citizens* based on their race. Perhaps the woman did not know what would become of her or her family, or where they would go, once they were forced to leave. When Otoni is asked what he found along his route through the city and why the woman had chosen this place in particular, "Otoni blew smoke out from his nostrils forlornly recalling what the taxi driver told him and what he deduced: *Because she said it was the most beautiful place*."[164] Through its time travel, "The Most Beautiful Place" returns to the past in order to illuminate the present, confronting colonial and postcolonial legacies of violence through the lens of the Asian expulsion. However, it is also a story that relates intimately to South Africa's history, and specifically the apartheid logic of "privileged insiders and demonic outsiders" that is evident in South Africa's contemporary immigration policies.[165] Stories such as this one point to *Jungle Jim*'s investment in understanding postapartheid South Africa in relation to the African continent and as a belatedly postcolonial nation.

Many other stories in the magazine, of a host of different genres, take up the issue of alienation, from both space and history. Not surprisingly, these themes are often explored through science fiction stories that take place in outer space or feature actual aliens, reconfiguring the familiar sci-fi trope of the alien invasion. The cover of *Jungle Jim*'s "South African Sci-Fi" edition (issue 16) evokes the stereotypical image that Western audiences—especially pre–*Black Panther*—have of science fiction in an African setting (fig. 6). Printed in the magazine's characteristic red and blue colors, this image depicts tiny Zulu warriors casting toothpick-sized spears at the Goliath of an alien bearing down on them. As the Kenyan science fiction writer Wanuri Kahiu points out, citing the scene in *Independence Day* of Masai warriors fighting the alien ships with spears while the rest of the world deploys missiles, Western pop culture still frequently relegates Africa to a technological Stone Age.[166] In contrast, the science fiction stories in *Jungle Jim* employ futuristic technology, especially technology that is connected to past modes of African resistance. Further, these alien stories reflect on past and future forms of alienation and exclusion.

These themes are explored in "Here Be Cannibals" by Masimba Musodza, a story included in *Jungle Jim* 23, an issue titled "African Pulp Takes on Colonialism." Set in outer space, the story is told as a dialogue between Dr. Ama Agos, director of the Interplanetary Security Bureau, and Yulios Kadzeka, a scientist who has found evidence that "the Commonwealth," comprised of "[h]undreds of autonomous communities scattered over seven planets and 14 satellites," is about to be invaded by "a technologically superior branch of humanity."[167] The Commonwealth, a product of colonialism and imperialism in our own world, isn't described at length in the story, though we do learn that it has vast natural resources and living space as well as a large labor force.

Fig. 6. *Jungle Jim* 16: The South African Sci-Fi Edition. Courtesy of Dale Halovrsen (a.k.a. JOEY HI-FI).

In these respects, it resembles precolonial Africa: "The Commonwealth was wealthy. 'Is this how the nations of Africa on the ancient Home Planet felt when they learnt that their lands were about to be invaded?' [Dr. Ama Agos] wondered out loud."[168] To survive, Agos and Kadzeka use a form of resistance that dates to the precolonial period. Deciding to make it appear as though the Commonwealth has already been subject to a radioactive attack, Kadzeka muses, "It is said that one way the smaller nations could dissuade invaders was to spread rumours of cannibals or monsters."[169] Agos "smile[s], savouring the visualization of the Commonwealth appearing on any charts from outside the system as FORBIDDEN, or better, HERE BE CANNIBALS."[170] In calling this collection of communities the Commonwealth, the story is not suggesting a future pan African utopia but rather acknowledging the history of colonization and its lasting impact on the Earth even as it confronts new, and in some ways similar, forms of intergalactic oppression. On the most basic level, the universe as we knew it is now facing the kind of oppression that Africa once did. More importantly, it is learning to use pan African strategies of resistance as well.

"San Junction" by Thembisa Cochrane also uses the familiar alien invasion story to draw parallels to various moments in South African history and to suggest that in the future, apartheid will be a global and interplanetary phenomenon. In Cochrane's narrative, the Pahnan, a technologically advanced species descended from humans, return to Earth after millennia of space travel. Finding their home planet nearly destroyed by a burgeoning human population, the Pahnan seek to restore balance by massacring many, issuing "Earth Permits" to those who are allowed to remain, and evicting "illegal residents" to the "lunar colony," where conditions are brutal.[171] There are many similarities to various moments in South African history, including the first encounters between the San and European colonists in the 1600s, apartheid-era restrictions such as the pass laws, and even contemporary court cases in which the San are fighting for their rights to land of which they were dispossessed.[172] Under apartheid, Black South Africans had to hold a pass, linked to their employment, to remain in white-controlled cities. Similarly, in "San Junction," those who work for the Pahnan are allowed to remain on Earth, while those who are unemployed or unemployable are sent to the lunar colony, which we can liken to the independent homelands or reserves to which Black South Africans were "repatriated." In Cochrane's narrative, the lunar colony, like the South African reserves, is self-run, with the Pahnan, like the apartheid government, refusing to take any responsibility for its poor conditions while passing off the burden of social reproduction to such areas. Ultimately, like Mahmood's "The Most Beautiful Place," "San Junction" mixes temporalities, moving between the precolonial, colonial, apartheid, and postapartheid periods in order to show the enduring phenomenon of forced migration and displacement. Though set in San Junction, the story compares experiences there to similar ones across the globe, thus showing how apartheid has become a global phenomenon in this imagined future.

Though it projects South African experiences on to a global scale, the story also implies that South Africa has failed to serve as an example of resistance for the world. The narrative is told largely through the diary of a fourteen-year-old girl, Maya, who was born in the lunar colony and is about to be deported from Earth because she lacks employment. Maya's grandfather, Dr. Gamchani, a community leader, begs Lady Ixmucane, a seemingly benevolent member of the Pahnan Royal Council, to allow his granddaughter to remain. When Maya is permitted to stay, some members of the community suggest that Dr. Gamchani and other leaders have sold out the community to protect their own families, lamenting: "This was an opportunity to re-awaken our old resistance—and we failed. We failed because we followed corrupt leaders. We had a chance to become an icon of resistance for the entire globe."[173] Much like "Here Be Cannibals," this story that takes place in the future is attuned to history and past expressions of resistance. In this case, however, the San Junction resistance fails due to corruption, in what is apparently a reference to postapartheid South Africa. As in the *Chronic*, stories like this one question South Africa's ability to serve as a model of pan African cooperation for the continent and the world.

Both "San Junction" and "Here Be Cannibals" are science fiction stories that rewrite the reductive and racist tropes that are pervasive in mainstream science fiction, from the black, otherworldly beasts depicted in *Blue Bolt* to the films that present Africa as devoid of modern technology. Notably, in both stories, what is necessary to defeat alien threats of species-wide annihilation is not advanced technology but strategies that resemble anti-colonial forms of resistance dating back to the precolonial and colonial periods. Most importantly, these stories make it clear that using past modes of African resistance is essential to the future survival of not only Africans but also people across the world and even beings from other planets. It is in this sense that these narratives depict the global future as pan African.

As magazines, the *Chronic* and *Jungle Jim* embody this project in their form. By using the newspaper, pulp magazine, and other iconic print forms as time machines, they reimagine literary survival in the present and future. However, both publications are also aware of their inability to fully transcend their location of production in South Africa. By drawing attention to these limitations, the *Chronic* and *Jungle Jim* make space for disjunctures and divisions within pan African spacetime. As I have argued throughout this book, the fictional forms in African newspapers and popular magazines were never wholly aligned with one kind of political or social imaginary. Rather, these forms moved across borders and languages and pushed the boundaries of genres to produce new ones, creating the space for writers to engage with multiple entangled geographies of affiliation.

CHAPTER 5

Digital Diaries

The World of Facebook and Beyond

As of 2019, there is a new South African book genre—the "diary chronicle," or "diary chron," a term coined by journalist Lesedi Setlhodi and Tiisetso Maloma, founder of Bula Buka publishers.[1] The diary chron is "digital born," beginning online as a blog or Facebook page before being published in a more traditional book format.[2] These narratives are written in the style of a personal diary, but they also include elements of popular soap operas and other serialized print forms, and most chapters end with a tantalizing cliff-hanger. Other hallmarks of the genre include its focus on the lives of young adults, chronicling their "actions and relationships during the era of social media, exploring themes such as blessers, blessees, slay queens/kings, players, as well as indulgence in expensive champagne and whiskey."[3] Mike Maphoto, whose *Diary of a Zulu Girl Part 1* was published by Bula Buka in 2015, claims to be "the father" of the genre.[4] Other diary chronicles by the same publisher include Lesego Maake's *Diary of a Side Chick—Makhwapheni* (2018), Londiwe Xaba and Siphelele Masango's *Diary of a Cheating Wife* (2020), and Maphoto's latest, *Confessions of a Sugar Baby* (2021).

Much like popular online fictions from other parts of the world that gained a sizable following online before winning book deals—a well-known example is E. L. James's 2011 *Fifty Shades of Grey*—the South African diary chronicle demonstrates the seemingly fluid relationship between print and digital forms and the growing influence of the latter.

Without the interest and support of thousands of readers online, the books of the diary chronicle genre would not have made it to print. Like *Fifty Shades*, these novels often contain graphic sexual content that has otherwise been taboo in mainstream publishing.[5] Further, although the published versions of these diaries differ from their digital originals, the imprint of their online lives is often evident in their language and form.[6] Many "digital diaries," as I have called them elsewhere, are multilingual, moving seamlessly between English and African languages as well as linguistic registers—incorporating ample amounts of slang and text speak.[7] They are also peppered with spelling and grammar mistakes that irritate some readers and that others find to impart a certain realism, given the diaries' youthful narrators. The print versions of such texts rein in a good deal of this linguistic mobility, limiting language- and code-switching and editing out grammatical errors.[8] They also often alter the form of digital diaries by combining many short online posts into longer chapters, thus shifting aspects of the original narrative's temporality and reliance on suspense. In the case of Maphoto's *Diary of a Zulu Girl*, 168 online chapters (and twenty final chapters that Maphoto held back to publish in book form) were condensed into eighty-eight chapters published in two separate books. The hundreds of reader comments that appeared below each of Maphoto's posts online, which ran as a kind of parallel diary to Maphoto's, are not included in the print version—though some of the material from these discussions was incorporated into Maphoto's *Confessions of a Sugar Baby*. Even after being excised from the digital space, however, aspects of the diary chronicle's digitality remain in its language and form, which, like the stories' contents, have helped to reshape South African publishing norms.

If the diary chronicle is a product of the mobility between digital platforms and print, it is also a concerted effort on the part of its publishers to popularize fictional texts nationally and to globalize South African literary forms. Bula Buka says that part of their impetus for naming the diary chron genre was "to promote local books."[9] On the shelves of South African bookstores like Exclusive Books, the bestseller and fiction sections are filled mostly with books by non-African writers. "Pan-African Writing," which includes work by South African authors, occupies its own smaller section of the store. Bula Buka also seeks to bolster South African fiction specifically, given the much wider popularity of nonfiction books in the country. If fiction better reflects the lived experiences of average South Africans, it will become more popular, they reason. However, the publishers also indicate a desire to reach broader audiences with the genre, which they suggest has "a chance of penetrating the international market." Indeed, as it is presented in the Macmillan dictionary online and in the Urban Dictionary—entries that may have been made by the publishers themselves—the diary chronicle is a literary genre that "emerged as fictional diary-like posts on Facebook around 2013 and 2014 in South Africa," but that, presumably, may now also be identified elsewhere.[10] In other words, naming this new, digitally inspired genre both locates it in South Africa and enables it to travel.

Print publishing, however, is only one route via which digital diaries have circulated—and a less traveled one at that. Whereas Bula Buka has published only a handful of diaries, and a few others have been self-published by their authors, thousands of diaries on Facebook alone have followed much different, and much more difficult, itineraries.[11] While Bula Buka has plucked several diaries from the dense web of Book Series pages on Facebook, others, even those with many followers, have been pirated by other Facebook or web pages, moved by their authors to personal websites or writing platforms like Wattpad, transitioned to WhatsApp groups, or abandoned by their authors entirely. They have also forged communities that transcend the virtual sphere, leading to real-world meetups and book clubs. Their history is far from a simple story of easy mobility through a global, placeless cyberspace. On the contrary, the ways these digital diaries travel highlight the chaos of digital networks and their nuanced relationships to material realities and geographies. These fitful mobilities have produced equally complex reading communities that coalesce around different kinds of affiliations, including national, regional, and diasporic ones, as well as various cultural, gender, and linguistic identities.

The communal and spatial imaginaries of these diaries thus differ quite substantially from that of the platform on which they appear. Facebook sees itself as building "the world" online and lauds connectivity as a universal good and even a "human right."[12] Until very recently, however, Facebook has been a Western-dominated space, with one study finding that in a sample of the most popular media posts shared on the site in 2013, 90 percent originated in the United States or UK and 95 percent were in English.[13] This situation is particularly striking given that North American and European users comprised less than half of Facebook's global usership around this time.[14] In some ways, then, Facebook's ethos and content resemble recent approaches to and canons of world literature. Despite its global ambitions, world literature has largely remained a Western-focused and Western-sanctioned body of texts written or translated into English in forms such as the novel that are familiar to Western readers and critics. Similarly, recent approaches to digital literature cast the web as a singular, global space and often treat Western online practices as normative, a problem exacerbated by the dearth of research on "non-Western Internets."[15] These approaches have obscured the ways context shapes virtual engagement and the various kinds of digital world making that are being practiced around the globe.[16] In this chapter, through a consideration of various Facebook diaries and their later iterations, I will show how these digital forms have produced nuanced mobile worlds online and offline and a more expansive vision of literature for the world. As Keguro Macharia argues in relation to Kenyan queer blogging practices, these diaries must be read "not as frozen artifacts or passive objects awaiting a critical intelligence that will grant them legibility, but as living acts of self- and collective-making, living and powerful interventions into the collective worlds we share."[17]

FACEBOOK'S "WORLD"

A social network of nearly 3 billion monthly active users, Facebook is the world's most used social media platform and third most visited website, following Google.com and YouTube.com.[18] While Facebook users are declining in some European and Asian countries and younger Americans are eschewing Facebook in favor of sites like Instagram (also owned by Meta) and TikTok, Facebook usage continues to grow in many parts of the globe.[19] In fact, younger people in "developing economies" remain some of the site's "heaviest users."[20] India, with 367 million Facebook users as of July 2023, has far surpassed the United States (188 million) as the country with the largest number of users on the site, followed by Indonesia (135 million) and Brazil (112 million).[21] In some parts of the world, including Trinidad and Indonesia, Facebook has come to be synonymous with the internet itself.[22] This conflation is not surprising, given that Facebook has made a concerted effort to make Facebook *as* the internet a reality. Since 2010, Facebook has partnered with local internet providers to offer data-free (often text-only) access to Facebook and other sites that vary by country, including health information and government websites. While there have been several iterations of this endeavor, it is known broadly as "Free Basics."[23]

This Facebook-curated internet prompted swift backlash in places like India over the issue of net neutrality, but Facebook's model of offering piecemeal, corporately determined internet has spread across much of the world, including the African continent.[24] This strategy has proven successful. In 2020, Facebook users grew the fastest in three African countries: Nigeria, Egypt, and South Africa.[25] In 2022, there were about 290 million Facebook users in Africa, up from just over 40 million users a decade prior.[26] These users are also overwhelmingly mobile in that they access the site from cell phones rather than desktop or laptop computers. Notably, actual users are only part of the story of Facebook's influence, and Facebook's reach stretches far beyond those who are on the social media site. Even people who have never seen Facebook have an "imagined" idea of the site, as a recent study in rural Zambia found.[27] In addition to the platform's perceived economic opportunities, non-users associated Facebook with "spatial expansion" and saw it as enabling one to find and keep in touch with friends "throughout the world," from "neighboring villages, to bordering countries, to the United States."[28]

Facebook capitalizes on this desire for connection and the "cultural fantasy" of an equally accessible cyberspace, where everyone in the world can meet on equal footing.[29] Further, Facebook sees itself as the architect of this new world online. In a letter posted on Facebook on February 16, 2017, the site's founder and CEO Mark Zuckerberg wrote, "On our journey to connect the world, we often discuss products we're building and updates on our business. Today I want to focus on the most important question of all: are we building the world we all want?"[30] As Zuckerberg makes clear, Facebook is intended to produce much more than a web of global connections. It is actively involved in a project of world making, or "worlding," with both temporal and spatial aspects. Ainehi Edoro-Glines argues that social media produces "a new sense of the literary, but one that is legible only when we take into account the rules governing knowledge-making on social media platforms."[31] We can extend this idea to take into account the world-making aspects of such platforms. Indeed, examining the ways Facebook *worlds*—a process that Eric Hayot describes as "to enclose, but also to exclude"—reveals both Facebook's problematic single-world vision and possibilities for new literary worlds on and beyond the platform.[32]

To begin, we can see how Facebook engages in a normative process of world making through temporalization, thus dovetailing in interesting ways with recent approaches to world literature that have deemphasized the spatial circulation that characterized earlier models like those of David Damrosch, Pascale Casanova, and Franco Moretti. In *What Is a World?*, Pheng Cheah argues that the conflation of "globe" and "world," or the purely spatial with a category of belonging, obscures world literature's potential to act as an "ethicopolitical" force.[33] Drawing on Heidegger's *Being and Time*, Cheah suggests—in language that sounds uncannily like Facebook's own—that worlding is primarily a temporal process: "We can only create normative value if we exist in a world with other beings and have access to them. The unifying power of temporalization is precisely a force of worlding, the precipitous ushering into a world, a meaningful whole that brings all beings into relation."[34] Although we often think of Facebook in terms of its spatial reach, the platform also relies on the "unifying power of temporalization." Facebook's most distinguishing features are based on time rather than location, including a user's personal profile, or "timeline," and their home page or "news feed" (now "feed"), which regularly updates with new posts from friends. Facebook also functions as a calendar, reminding users of friends' birthdays and holidays as well as highlighting the users' "memories" based on previous Facebook posts. Through these temporal markers, Facebook creates the sense of a community moving through linear, calendrical time together, in much the same way that the newspaper fosters a sense of the nation in Anderson's account, but now at the scale of the "world." In *This Thing Called the World*, Debjani Ganguly argues that the contemporary novel has absorbed and adapted its ability "to imagine the human condition on a scale larger than ever before in history" from global information and communications technologies like Facebook.[35] Looking closer, however, it seems clear that the novel's chronotope of "world" built on digital technologies might exist only through the prism of the novel itself (and in Facebook's marketing materials). When we look at the ways Facebook fictions imagine their audiences and their connections across time and space, a more nuanced and less totalizing sense of worldedness emerges.

Foregrounding time when it comes to Facebook also obscures the enduring importance of space to the platform, which engages in "worlding" endeavors in Gayatri Spivak's sense of the term in that it seeks to create a world where none exists, "upon what must be assumed to be uninscribed earth."[36] Although Facebook is used and engaged with differently in various parts of the globe, its unifying concept of time tends to conceal this fact, producing a similarly unified concept of space. In other words, digital worlding, as I use it here, is the process by which digital spaces are constructed by and in the West with Western internet platforms and their forms of usage, knowledge production, and ways of imagining the world taken as normative. The world that Facebook is committed to building elides the many different material realities that structure access to the site as well as the global labor that maintains it (for example, the many low-paid workers around the world who watch and remove pornographic and violent videos from users' news feeds).[37] It also hides Facebook's own space-making projects. Facebook is currently building a network of undersea cables around the African continent, and it opened its first African headquarters in Johannesburg, South Africa, in 2015. Facebook and other companies are also beginning to look to the African continent as a site for data centers, in part because many African governments have relatively few regulations on the corporate mining and storage of personal data. Notably, one article cites the global centrality of places like Nigeria—located between the Western and Asian time zones, but outside Europe's stricter internet regulations—as the factor that makes it the ideal site for such data storage operations.[38] Here we can see that Facebook's project of building "the world" online has real material implications for African spaces and geographies, which in turn impact the ways such spaces are imagined globally.[39] Africa might become the physical center of global digital mining, but how much input will African producers and consumers have in this project, and how much will it resemble colonial and neocolonial models where the continent serves as a site of extraction?

Ultimately, as Aamir Mufti cautions in relation to world literature, we cannot "speak of 'literature'" or, in this case, the internet "as a single world-encompassing space without reference to these material and ideological features of the structures of mobility, and therefore also *immobility*."[40] In the case of Facebook, its promise of connectivity and access—a kind of digital mobility—has always operated under different conditions and assumptions in African contexts than it does in wealthier, mostly Western markets, as the Free Basics program demonstrates. Facebook has also worked diligently to buy its competitors, reducing the options for alternative, affordable platforms for African consumers. In these respects, Facebook's world-making project and "structures of mobility" bear a resemblance to the many earlier hegemonic spatial endeavors described throughout this book. The Central African Federation, for example, promised greater social and physical mobility for Africans living in its three territories, but it quickly worked to contain, and eventually curtail, this mobility. *African Parade* played an important role in both selling this fiction of the benefits of a unified African state and presenting alternative ideas of mobility that undermined it. The same can be said of the *Malawi News* under the auspices of Banda's one-party state. While the paper touted Malawian women's emancipation from the home and their new mobility in social and political spheres, its fiction in English and Chichewa simultaneously circumscribed women within this expanded domestic and national space. However, just as writers in the federation and in Banda's Malawi used state-affiliated and state-run outlets in ways that both supported and contested colonial and autocratic space-making projects, writers on Facebook demonstrate the allure as well as the limitations of Facebook's one-world imagination.

FACEBOOK FICTION

Following the runaway success of Mike Maphoto's *Diary of a Zulu Girl* blog, writers from across southern Africa began publishing their own digital diaries. While some of these diaries were published on blogs, including *Diary of a Guji Girl* and *Diary of a Harare Girl*, many writers turned to Facebook. As a social media site designed to make sharing content as simple as possible, Facebook is even easier to use than blogging platforms like WordPress and comes with a built-in network of potential readers. It is also somewhat better at hiding the many advertisements that populate the free versions of most social media and blogging sites and, thanks to programs like Free Basics, is sometimes cheaper for readers to access than personal blogs. In this section, I consider the mobile communities that have emerged in this new form of fiction, focusing on the Facebook diaries of the South African Thulani Lupondwana and Juniah Sophie Ngwira from Malawi. These young women, both in their twenties at the time, accrued an impressive number of followers on Facebook. Unlike many diary writers, Lupondwana and Ngwira produced work that evolved beyond their personally inspired diaries—*Diary of a Cheating Husband* and *Diary of a Single Mum*, respectively—to include narratives that are more overtly fictional. These stories feature a larger cast of characters and demonstrate these writers' continual adaptation of Facebook fiction as a form.

Most of the early diaries on blogs and Facebook, like Maphoto's, were male authored, though many included female perspectives. Lupondwana and Ngwira are representative of a second phase of online diary fiction, one in which young women are, according to Lupondwana, "taking back the power."[41] These works center discourses of tradition and modernity around female experiences and shift literary language toward an appreciation for accessibility to non-native English speakers. They also mix the intrigue and drama of soap operas with didactic intent: they are Facebook "pulp," we might say, that is highly conscious of its potential social impact. This feature aligns them with a continent-wide tradition of socially oriented popular print forms, from the Pacesetter series to the many stories in newspapers and magazines explored elsewhere in this book.

Thulani Lupondwana's experience as one of the top diary writers on Facebook is emblematic of both the power and limitations of Facebook as a platform for African writing. Lupondwana began her Facebook Book Series page, *Diary of a Cheating Husband*, when she was only twenty years old. Like many young women from southern Africa who start Facebook diaries, Lupondwana was initially motivated to write by the painful breakup of her relationship. A Facebook Book Series page was easy to set up without assistance and afforded her anonymity. It also provided an immediate outlet for her anger: Lupondwana posted three "inserts," or chapters, on the first day. As Emma Segar points out, the flexibility of publishing online allows writers to manipulate time and to use it as a central narrative feature.[42] Writers are able to post their stories at intervals that match readers' sense of the passing of time, thus creating an even greater sense of intimacy with readers, but also setting up the expectation that writers will post frequently. As a result, the temporality of digital writing is characterized by what Macharia describes as "interruption, deferral, manic production, the micro-narratives of labor . . . and the macro-narratives of intimate events (weddings, funerals, relationships, a pet's death)."[43] As I discuss further below, delayed posts (and posts that are perceived to be too short) are a source of constant tension between writers and their readers on Facebook Book Series pages.

Like many diary writers, Lupondwana was inspired by Maphoto's blog, going so far as to say that without Maphoto, "the rest of us wouldn't have started writing." She was also a follower of several other male-authored Facebook diaries that emerged immediately after Maphoto's, including Thabang Machona's *Diary of a Kasi Taxi Driver* and Mbasa Yona's *Diary of iCherrie Yomjaivo*, both set in and around Lupondwana's home of Port Elizabeth. There are obvious similarities between the first installments of Lupondwana's diary and Maphoto's *Diary of a Zulu Girl*, both of which can be seen as part of the region's longer tradition of "Jim or Jane Comes to Joburg" stories, discussed in chapter 1. Like Maphoto, Lupondwana chronicles a young girl's move from rural South Africa, in this case the Eastern Cape, to study at an urban university.[44] Also like Maphoto's protagonist, Thandeka, Entle is unprepared for the fast life of the city, here Port Elizabeth, which involves clubbing, drinking, and having sex with older men. The early chapters of *Diary of a Cheating Husband* mirror Maphoto's diary in both their informal writing style and plot, as many readers pointed out in their comments on Facebook. Like Thandeka, Entle arrives at her dorm, meets her city-savvy roommate, changes into the best clothes she has, and goes out clubbing.

Despite these similarities, Lupondwana found some of Maphoto's representations of female characters to be limiting, and I read Lupondwana's and others' appropriations of the digital diary as an important example of "reworlding" in the digital space, one that creates a fuller sense of African women's worlds and lived experiences, online and off. For example, as Dina Ligaga observes in the Kenyan context, the internet has allowed young women to rewrite the trope of the "good time girl" in a more agential way.[45] Lupondwana's diary similarly addresses issues of cultural relevance while seeking to expand readers' worldviews to encompass topics such as mental health, female empowerment, and albino rights, among others. Although Lupondwana's first diary fit the mold of the diaries that came before it, her later fictions have married social activism with new experiments in form. For example, her 2017 diary *When the Lights Are Off* explores the subject of mental health, which Lupondwana says Black South African communities do not discuss often enough. Lupondwana herself suffers from clinical depression, which she writes openly about on Facebook.

In *When the Lights Are Off*, Lupondwana combines the theme of mental health with that of traditional marriage through a story about multiple personality disorder. Inserts alternate between the perspectives of what seem to be two different characters, Sethu and Zipho. The former young woman is forced into an arranged marriage because of a debt her father owed, while the latter attends college, writes a blog, and lives with her boyfriend. In a plotline that could have been taken from a soap opera, we eventually learn that Sethu and Zipho are the same person. Sethu suffers from multiple personality disorder, and whenever she consumes alcohol, she transforms into the more liberated Zipho and leaves the constraints of her other life behind. Lupondwana's story is particularly self-reflexive in its meditations on blogging. For Zipho, blogging becomes a form of freedom. In a clear reference to Maphoto, who gained such a large following that he hired other writers to write diaries for him on his website, Zipho dreams of a time when she too will be famous enough to have her own team of writers. Unlike Sethu, who is bound by tradition, Zipho finds a new life through the blog, a theme that resonates with recent literature such as Chimamanda Adichie's *Americanah*.

Another key facet of Lupondwana's world-making activities in *Diary of a Cheating Husband* and subsequent diaries is her emphasis on isiXhosa. Lupondwana followed the strategy of her fellow Eastern Cape diarists Yona and Machona in writing her diary in a mix of English and isiXhosa. Based on data from Facebook, for which she had to pay, Lupondwana learned that her readers clustered around the areas in South Africa where isiXhosa is spoken most widely, including the Eastern Cape, home to 20 percent of her audience, as well as major cities such as Johannesburg, Durban, and Cape Town. Lupondwana also had readers from Malawi and Zimbabwe and even one from England, who eventually stopped reading because of the large amount of isiXhosa in the narrative. While Lupondwana expressed excitement about having readers from outside South Africa, she found it not only taxing but also detrimental to her work to have to translate. Some things, particularly swear words, were simply better said in isiXhosa, and she felt that inserting translations into such scenes lessened their impact. Instead, she hoped that non-isiXhosa readers could "catch up in the comments," where readers sometimes provided translations for one another. When I interviewed Lupondwana in Port Elizabeth in 2017, she surmised that she probably would never be published in print because she planned to continue writing in isiXhosa, and this did not bother her. In many ways, Lupondwana's approach to writing is what Taylor Eggan has described as "introverted." Compared to Eileen Julien's theorization of the "extroverted," outward-looking African novel, the introverted text is, Eggan observes, "open to the outside but motivated primarily from within."[46] Lupondwana's digital diary is a good example of what happens when introverted texts are published online, where the intimacy of the diary form meets Facebook's mission of absolute connection. Indeed, although—or perhaps because—it is primarily motivated by "inward" concerns, from issues of mental health to the pleasures of writing in a particular language, Lupondwana's diary forged not only a virtual community of thousands but also real-world connections with her readers, creating a literary and social world with online and offline dimensions.

Like Lupondwana, Juniah Sophie Ngwira wrote *Diary of a Single Mum* "out of passion because of the experience that [she's] had in her life."[47] Similarly, Ngwira changed or omitted aspects of her personal story in the diary, which she published in seventy-eight episodes over a little more than one year. In the diary, which began in December 2014, Ngwira tells the story of Wangu, who is sent away from her rural home in Nkhata Bay to live with her aunt and uncle in Lilongwe, Malawi's capital city. After being raped by her uncle, Wangu flees his house and lives with a kind *gogo* (granny) until she finds employment in a local shop. It is here that she meets and falls in love with her coworker, Ben, who eventually dumps her for another woman, leaving her alone and pregnant at the age of sixteen. In many ways, *Diary of a Single Mum* is rooted in the Malawian milieu: it names Malawian cities and incorporates small amounts of Chichewa. Malawi is predominantly Christian, and it is not surprising that Ngwira's first two diary entries begin with a religious reflection. In fact, in the first entry, Wangu reflects on her relationship to God before introducing herself to readers.

Beyond its cultural significance, Ngwira's choice to begin her diary in this way can be read as a particular way of writing in and for what danah boyd refers to as "networked publics," a term that encompasses the digital space as well as "the imagined collective" produced through engagement in this space.[48] In her commentary, boyd outlines various dynamics that distinguish networked publics from "unmediated publics," essentially arguing that online—as opposed to in shared, physical space—one's audience and social context are not entirely visible or knowable and the public and private are thus blurred.[49] By introducing her diary in the way she does, Ngwira establishes the framework within which her diary is to be read, no matter who may come across it or where it may circulate online beyond her control. Perhaps for a similar reason, Ngwira's diary explicitly troubles the boundaries between herself as author and her character, particularly in her responses to reader comments. Initially, when readers commented on various aspects of the story—such as the way Wangu always forgives and goes back to the man who left her—Ngwira responded by referring to her character in the third person, establishing some distance between herself and these critiques. Later, however, she replied "in character," writing in a comment on episode 28B, where it is revealed that Wangu's new boyfriend has impregnated another girl, "feels lyk trouble is my middle name."[50] Tellingly, in another comment on the same episode, Ngwira writes, "don't know where this is heading anymore," implying that she does not, in fact, have control of the narrative but that her disruptive character, who is always getting in "trouble," might.[51] Although Ngwira seems to admit to a lack of authorial control in this moment, she uses the already blurred distinction between the public and private online to her advantage. By asserting multiple, overlapping identities, Ngwira regains a measure of authority over her narrative and socially mediated identity. She is and is not her character, just as online, we are and are not our digital avatars.

This fluidity between writers and their characters is a key part of the digital diary's appeal and forges close, if sometimes fraught, relationships between diary writers and readers. Facebook writers like Ngwira are sometimes referred to as "admins," short for administrators, which suggests an organizational rather than a creative role. Similarly, Segar thinks of fictional blog writers as "curators."[52] However, because Facebook connects people as "friends," the network of strangers brought together by a particular Facebook story also becomes enmeshed in this concept of friendship and even of love and family, something that did not occur on Maphoto's blog.[53] As Edoro-Glines argues, intimacy is "a formal principle on Facebook" that arises from the platform's "information structure . . . built on giving users the sense of sharing something deep and felt with people they imagine they know."[54] Lupondwana said of her readers, "I like thinking those people are my friends, so their opinions really count and it's no use writing about what matters to me and what doesn't matter to them." While her page was active, she read every comment and crafted her stories relative to reader responses, sometimes even sending private messages to readers who said they didn't like aspects of a story to ask them for further clarification. (In this respect she is very different from Maphoto, who went out of his way to avoid plot spoilers predicted by readers and who sought to distract readers by posing questions at the end of each chapter on topics from relationships to xenophobia.) Similarly, Ngwira often responded to comments that readers left on her stories. In several instances, she encouraged comments by promising readers that if they responded with "an exciting saying, proverb, advice," and so on, she would include it in her next installment of the story and credit the contributing reader.[55] Although Ngwira gave her real name to readers on March 14, 2015, when she announced that it was her birthday, most continued to address her as Wangu in their comments. On August 27, 2015, Ngwira celebrated that the page had reached nearly seven thousand likes and thanked her readers for encouraging her to continue writing when she had nearly given up: "I will always be indebted to you in my journey as a writer, God will surely bless you. I feel humbled and I love you all so much."[56] While this post prompted many readers to ask for her real name (apparently having missed the earlier post), others simply replied to Wangu as though she were the writer: "It's because you a good writer Wangu," "U r an inspiration wangu," and "we love you loads Wangu, keep up the good work!"[57] This suggests a dynamic similar to the one described above. Just as Ngwira exploits the fungibility between her "real" identity and that of her character, her readers also embrace the mobility between writer and her character. Indeed, to many of Ngwira's readers, "Wangu" is an author—not just an informant—who goes on to write other fictions.

When she finished *Diary of a Single Mum*, Ngwira began experimenting with more "literary" fiction on the same Facebook page. As compared to her original diary, *The Veil*—which she began publishing only a day after the diary's final episode in early 2016—uses less slang and textspeak and is more carefully edited. The story's first insert received 656 likes and 76 comments, about two to three times as much engagement as installments of *Diary of a Single Mum*. Readers began referring to this story as a "short story" due to its perceived literariness, and Ngwira posted the story in "chapters" rather than "episodes," language associated with print publishing rather than television. *The Veil* alternates between the perspectives of more than ten characters, focusing on a woman named Loveness; her daughter Flora, who is dating Jack, a boy five years her senior, and who ends up pregnant at fourteen; and Naomi, a college student who leaves her newborn baby in a basket outside the home of a pastor and his wife. While the narrative centers on these women, it also incorporates the perspectives of their friends, families, and lovers. Readers appreciated the complexity of the narrative, with one reader from Botswana commenting on the third chapter, "Your diary is not as simple as many, very strong and interesting."[58] Another, also from Botswana, commented that *The Veil* had "depth" compared to the many stories about young girls who date wealthier older men, ending their post on the story's seventh chapter with "#proudreader."[59] The web of relationships that *The Veil* describes works particularly well on Facebook, which as a platform is based on integrating different voices into what appears to be a larger unfolding narrative.

Ngwira's diary has drawn a loyal fan base of female readers from across southern Africa.[60] Unlike Lupondwana, the majority of whose followers were based in South Africa, Ngwira told me that most of her readers were from outside Malawi, including Botswana, Eswatini, Namibia, and South Africa as well as Zimbabwe and Zambia. She also had a few readers from Tanzania and some Malawian readers in the UK. Otherwise, her followers were mostly located in "the southern part of Africa." Ngwira attributed the popularity of her diary in South Africa to the fact that "we have many diary writers" from there. However, her largest and most active contingent of readers hailed from Botswana. When I interviewed Ngwira in 2016, she told me that this was because the Botswanan writer of another Facebook page that she was following asked readers to send her their stories. The other writer liked Ngwira's story and posted it on her page, suggesting that Ngwira start a page of her own, which she did. Nevertheless, Ngwira still struggled to gain likes and traction until she made this other writer an administrator on her page so that she could help Ngwira to advertise and share the blog, resulting in a jump from ten likes a week to ten thousand. "People were saying we love you from Botswana. That gave me the drive. I would write at home in my free time." In a Facebook post on February 26, 2015, Ngwira wrote a special thank-you to her readers from Botswana: "good morning readers. thank you very much for being part of this journey with Wangu. you guys are amazing. special thanks to my Botswana fans. you are the best."[61] A number of other readers corrected Ngwira, arguing that she should in fact say, "THANK YOU MY AFRICAN READERS."[62] Others chimed in with their own locations, which included South Africa, Zimbabwe, and Namibia. Nevertheless, "#teamBotswana" soon appeared in a number of comments.

From exchanges such as these, we can see that particular national spaces are still salient in diaries like Ngwira's, in terms of both the diary's content, which draws heavily on its Malawian setting and context, and its readers' points of identification. Nevertheless, these nationalisms appear within a larger framework of regional exchange and virtual friendship. Lupondwana paid forward the help she originally received in promoting her diary by recommending diaries from other writers in the region, including *Diary of a Harare Girl*, the South African *Diary of a Deflowered Campus Girl*, and *Baring It All*, another South African Facebook diary that was published as a book in 2016. Ngwira often provided links to these other diaries to appease her readers at times when she had failed to post a new insert. It is evident that Ngwira saw herself as part of a regional network of writers and readers, a network that had been born in the digital space but was a product of physical, cultural, and linguistic proximity.

Ngwira's regional popularity may also explain why she chose to write almost exclusively in English, incorporating virtually no Chichewa into later installments of *Diary of a Single Mum* or subsequent narratives like *The Veil*. Her highly engaged readership asked for translations even when a story included only a single word of untranslated Chichewa, as was the case in the second installment of the first chapter of *The Veil*, in which Loveness refers to *nsima*, a maize porridge that is one of Malawi's staple foods. After Ngwira provided an explanation in the comments, other readers chimed in with regional equivalents including *pap*, as it is referred to in South Africa and Botswana, and *sadza*, its name in Zimbabwe.[63] Based on the minimal use of Chichewa in this chapter of the story (which also included a single line of dialogue that was translated in text), another reader commented that she hoped to learn Ngwira's language. These small moments of recognizing regional similarities and differences are an important facet of Ngwira's diary that connects it to earlier print fiction in magazines like *African Parade*, which acknowledged the need to translate literature and culture even when traveling relatively short distances between neighboring countries. What did not require any translation in Ngwira's diary, however, was heartbreak. Just below the translations of *nsima*, many readers expressed their sympathies for Loveness, who has just found out that her husband is cheating on her. Other chapters of *The Veil* elicited similar responses, with readers often lamenting the poor behavior of men and the many burdens women must bear as a result. The community that formed around Ngwira's Facebook fictions thus has characteristics of both a deterritorialized virtual community—one that has united around shared personal experiences and interests—and what Alonso and Oiarzabal have referred to as a "digital diaspora," which, unlike a virtual community, is rooted in its connections to physical geographies.[64]

As I've observed in relation to other digital fictions like Maphoto's, online relationships with readers sometimes find their way into the real world. Lupondwana says that she only received her first "like" on her diary when she was on chapter 29, after writing for about a year. Living in Johannesburg at the time, she befriended this reader "because she was the only person that was actually interested in what [she] had to say." Later, when she had more followers, she recounts being recognized at a shopping center in Port Elizabeth by a reader who approached her to convey her criticisms of the diary (specifically the fact that her character, Entle, was always sad). Lupondwana herself confessed to approaching the writer of *Diary of iCherrie Yomjaivo*, of which she was a huge fan, at a bar in Port Elizabeth. Lupondwana's second serialized story, *Life without My Husband*, which follows Entle after the death of her husband, even earned Lupondwana an invitation to the wedding of a reader who said this story had reaffirmed her belief in love. Ngwira too recounts being approached by readers after she posted her picture on the page.

Elsewhere I have referred to these kinds of networks as "paravirtual": literary networks that are mediated in significant ways but that also operate "offline."[65] Paravirtual networks fit under the umbrella of what Jenny Kennedy describes as "networked space," which includes "all sites both physical and digital in which interactions occur,"[66] but the term is more useful for describing networks and genres, like the diary chron, that function "*alongside* and *beyond*" the virtual sphere.[67] Meeting people through her stories was a central reason Lupondwana enjoyed writing on Facebook, and in 2017, when she had more than sixty thousand followers, she began planning meetups with readers in cities across South Africa. A reader "roundtable" had previously offered to pay for her to attend a "high tea" in another city, but she had to refuse due to her school schedule. The only event that came to fruition was held in Port Elizabeth in September, with fewer readers in attendance than she had originally anticipated. Lupondwana met about a dozen readers, some of whom had traveled six hours from a neighboring city, at a restaurant in Greenacres shopping mall. Readers dressed up in "tea" outfits or wore traditional Xhosa attire and gathered around a beautifully decorated table to eat, talk, and play games related to *Diary of a Cheating Husband*. Lupondwana hired a professional photographer, who took more than six hundred pictures of the event, the best of which were posted to Facebook several days later.[68]

While Lupondwana primarily spoke about her readers in the language of friendship in our interview in March 2017, the idea of *Diary of a Cheating Husband* as a "family" emerges in the lead-up to these in-person events. On May 7, 2017, Lupondwana posted:

> Yesterday I cried after reading some comments and the inboxes I received. Not because I pity or I like carrying other

> peoples [*sic*] burdens, but because we are so broken as Black Women.
>
> Now I realized why that reader thought us meeting, in one room and sharing each other [*sic*] stories could somehow help to show omnye [one another] you are not alone.[69]

She ended this reflection with "I Love you family," which prompted her readers to leave many expressions of love for her in return. A new closeness seems to have developed between Lupondwana and her readers during this period. Shortly afterward, when working on ideas for a new story, Lupondwana again shared her own battle with depression and invited readers to share a bit about themselves on the page. Dozens of readers responded with stories of sexual abuse and other struggles, demonstrating how the page could operate as a collective space for mutual support among women both online and off. The language of family also comes into Ngwira's diary when she as a person surfaces more prominently in the diary, such as when she wrote in a post on March 14, 2017, "Help me family to celebrate my 28th birthday."[70]

In these paravirtual communities, forms of virtual and real friendship, and even kinship, do not preclude mutual irritation, particularly when it comes to the frequency of posting and "liking." Ngwira and Lupondwana apologized to their readers when they failed to post as often as the readers would have liked. Lupondwana also became increasingly frustrated with her "silent" readers, who read but did not comment on or like her posts. While writing *When the Lights Are Off*, Lupondwana told readers that she would only post a new insert once the current one had reached one thousand likes.[71] Despite these frustrations, in a reading and writing environment like South Africa's, where "fiction authors consider themselves fortunate if they sell one thousand copies of a novel," Lupondwana's popularity was remarkable.[72] Malawi's publishing environment, where most publishers today struggle to publish any books that are not textbooks, is even more challenging. In other words, the kind of reach that both of these amateur writers gained would have been impossible without Facebook, which Lupondwana describes as "one of the most powerful platforms ever." For these young female writers, Facebook provided the opportunity to re-world on their own terms, creating mobile worlds that toggle between geographic scales, linguistic codes, and real and virtual relationships.

"CHICHEWA STORIES"

A somewhat different model of Facebook fiction has emerged around specific language communities. While both Lupondwana and Ngwira incorporated African languages into their work—Lupondwana much more so than Ngwira—other Facebook pages like "Chichewa Stories" are primarily language based. Before the original "Chichewa Stories" page was removed from Facebook several years ago, it had accrued more than 33,000 followers.[73] In 2016, the same admin started two related Facebook pages, "Chichewa Stories Page 2," with 19,000 followers to date, and "Chichewa Stories HD" (which presumably stands for "high definition"), with about 8,900 followers. While these subsequent pages do not have as many followers, they had relatively active readerships when they were still posting fictional content, receiving more than 400 likes and comments on some posts. Neither of these pages, however, has posted fiction recently.[74]

While Lupondwana and Ngwira began by writing diaries that were—or appeared to be—personal accounts before branching out into more explicitly fictional content, these Chichewa pages capitalized on fictionalization from the start. New fictional series were regularly produced on these sites, often accompanied by images that resemble movie posters. One for the second "season" of *Kumbali Ya Mitambo* ("The Silver Lining") depicts the story's two characters back-to-back, surrounded by fiery, sunlit clouds and the words "Chichewa Stories HD presents" at the top. The story's title is written across the bottom half of the frame in large, blockbuster movie letters with the logo of IGraphix, which designed the cover, in the lower right-hand corner. Much like the Western movies that circulate in southern Africa but retain their titles in English, the titles of some of these series are in English, although the stories themselves are usually written entirely in Chichewa. In these ways, such pages tap into the aesthetics and language of global popular culture while catering to local and regional language speakers.

Often, Chichewa stories pages operate more like older communication technologies than like personal blogs or other single-author Facebook pages such as Lupondwana's and Ngwira's. (Maphoto, whose blog later featured the work of multiple other writers, is an exception.) Many Chichewa pages post stories by several different (sometimes rotating) authors and maintain more rigorous and time-specific posting schedules than writers like Lupondwana and Ngwira. The original

"Chichewa Stories" page, for example, promised readers that a new chapter of *The Painful Life* would be posted Monday at noon so that "podya nkomaliro mukuwelenga nkaniyi" ("while you are eating lunch you can read this story").[75] Page admins and writers also regularly tell readers when they can expect the story's next installment, sometimes incorporating the release time at the end of an episode.[76] In the specificity of these schedules, which sometimes include both a date and time, these Chichewa pages resemble other kinds of media programming familiar to readers such as TV and radio, the latter of which remains a widespread and important medium of communication in a country with relatively low literacy rates. Having multiple writers writing stories for a single page also becomes a way to keep up with readers' demands for a steady stream of content.

Like Lupondwana's and Ngwira's diaries, the Chichewa stories pages also attract readers from across the region and even some from other parts of the globe, many of whom are likely members of the Malawian diaspora. The regional and diasporic imaginary of such Facebook stories is particularly evident in stories like *Facebook Love* by Sir Jim Chiona, which was published on "True Love Stories with Charity," one of the many Chichewa story pages to have emerged more recently. The "True Love Stories with Charity" page began in April 2016 and in 2023 had twelve thousand followers. *Facebook Love*, which appeared in twenty-one parts from May 29 to August 11, 2021, tells the story of Fatsani, a twenty-eight-year-old married Malawian man living in South Africa who uses Facebook to create an alternate identity in order to meet women. Going by "Cartel Mathews," Fatsani begins a relationship with Alicia Adams, a Malawian of a "higher class" than his who works at the American Embassy in Lilongwe.[77] Fatsani begins building a house in his home village of Chiladzulu for himself and Alicia and sends her money to finish the house and to buy a minibus to generate income. However, Fatsani's plans, and his attempts to conceal his true identity, are thrown into disarray when he is abruptly deported from South Africa for overstaying his visa and finds himself at home in Malawi—with both a name and a face that Alicia does not recognize.

Much of the story's plot revolves around aspects of Facebook as a platform, particularly the way it can be used to create false or misleading identities. When Fatsani is deported, he loses his phone, and with it all his contacts as well as his access to Facebook. To make matters worse, he has forgotten his Facebook password, so he can't access the site from elsewhere. Unable to connect with Alicia, Fatsani finds himself at a loss regarding how to find her and then convince her that he is Cartel. In the story's second part, Fatsani is in a shop buying a radio when he hears the voice of a woman who sounds just like Alicia but looks nothing like her. Alicia, too, it appears, has a fake Facebook photo. This development prompted a number of responses from readers affirming that this is indeed what happens on Facebook: "Ndipo zikuchitikadi PA FB pompa eeee" ("and these things happen here on FB [Facebook]") and "yaaaaaaaaaaa kunama sibwino komaso kupaza mkax pa fb ndichonch" ("yeah lying is bad but you find it all the time on fb [Facebook]").[78]

In its plot as well as its language, the story exploits the opportunity for linguistic mobility that platforms like Facebook afford. Having finally convinced Alicia that he is Cartel—not someone who is impersonating Cartel to steal his money—and that she should give him a second chance, Fatsani runs into Alicia in Blantyre while he is with his wife, Sithanda, who has traveled to Malawi to bring him home to South Africa. Fatsani uses his fluency in multiple regional languages, a product of his travels, to his advantage in this situation. In Afrikaans, he tells Sithanda that Alicia is his cousin, while in Chichewa, he tells Alicia that Sithanda is his sister-in-law.[79] Since neither woman understands the other's language, Fatsani is able to capitalize on his linguistic mobility for a while. This strategy works until Sithanda asks Fatsani's brother what "ndimakukonda" means in the story's sixth part and, learning that it translates to "I love you," wonders who Fatsani is really speaking to every day on the phone.[80] Just like his character, the author of *Facebook Love* displays linguistic fluidity, peppering his Chichewa with small amounts of English. In this way, the story resembles South African soap operas, in which characters move between several languages, often within the same sentence.

While South African audiences are accustomed to such mixing of languages—as Lupondwana's diary also demonstrates—Malawian readers appear to be less so. Most Facebook fiction from Malawi that I have found is monolingual; Ngwira writes almost exclusively in English, and the Chichewa stories pages are in Chichewa. It is therefore not surprising that this narrative's (relatively minimal) movement between languages upset at least one of Chiona's readers. After the story's third episode, a reader asks indignantly if the story is in English or Chichewa: if it's in Chichewa he should write in Chichewa, and if it's in English, he should write in English. The author replies, "ngati zikuvuta ndi bwino musamawerenge nkhani zanga or else ubwerere ku school" ("if it is difficult it's better if you don't read my story or else go back to school").[81] In a story attentive to issues of class and in a context where a command of English has long signaled one's social status, this comment makes it clear that the author's use of language serves multiple functions, including as an indicator of the story's own worldliness and "class."

Facebook Love is also instructive in its regional imaginary and its commentaries on the issue of migration. After Sithanda agrees to permanently relocate to Malawi to be with Fatsani, one reader describes how she "shows international love" for her man.[82] Given the story's emphasis on language, it is not surprising that Sithanda's expression of her transnational love takes the form of her learning some Chichewa, as Fatsani is surprised to find when he picks her up from the airport. Sithanda also defies some of the stereotypes of South African women—as one friend bluntly tells Fatsani, "Anthu amati akazi a Jon ndioyipa" ("People say women from Joburg are bad").[83] For example, when Sithanda finally realizes that Fatsani was having an affair with Alicia, who claims to be pregnant, she is ultimately forgiving, telling him in English, "Dear, my love for you will never fade koma [but] please try to control your feelings, HIV Aids is real."[84] Fatsani remarks that Sithanda "ndi mkazi omvesetsa akulu akulu ndipo ndi wa chikhalidwe ngati si waku south Africa" ("is a very understanding woman and with behavior as if she isn't from South Africa"). Indeed, Sithanda goes out of her way to adopt Malawian customs after she moves to Blantyre, learning to cook Malawian dishes like okra and instructing a friend from South Africa who comes to visit to cover her miniskirt with a cloth wrap or *chitenje* because they are in Malawi "komwe thupi limalemekezedwa" ("where the body is respected").[85]

Facebook Love reanimates many of the stereotypes of South African culture that were prevalent in the 1950s in *African Parade*. In both publications, South Africa (and Johannesburg in particular) is depicted as modern and Westernized as well as dangerous and corrupt. The same fear of *tsotsis*, or gangsters, also reemerges in *Facebook Love*, where they once again represent the policing of South African cultural boundaries in their use of violence to protect South African women from foreigners. However, whereas many of *Parade*'s stories (and subsequent crime fiction from the region) imagined a "*tsotsi* invasion" of the former federation's territories, the gangsters in *Facebook Love* are a menace that remains contained within South Africa's borders. In this way, the *tsotsi* is envisioned specifically as a threat that lurks on the other side of the border. When Sithanda first hears Fatsani saying "I love you" to someone else in Chichewa on the phone, she tells him, "Uli ndi mwayi poti ndili ku dziko lakwanu ukanakhala kwathu nkanakupha" ("You are lucky that I am in your country if you were in our country I would kill you").[86] A female reader, speaking directly to the character, reiterates this threat: "Iwe ukapita kujoni akakupha" ("You, if you go to Joburg they are going to kill you").[87] Later, when Sithanda has returned to South Africa with the expectation that Fatsani will join her, he uses his fear of being killed by *tsotsis* as an excuse for his delayed return.

Like many stories in *Parade*, *Facebook Love* uses the figure of the *tsotsi* as a symbol of the dangers migrants face in South Africa's cities. However, *Facebook Love* also suggests that Malawian migrants have only their own behavior to blame for their persecution. When Sithanda finds out that Fatsani gave Alicia money for both a house and a minibus, she describes his behavior as part of a larger phenomenon wherein Malawian men come to South Africa and lie about having families at home in order to find a South African wife and gain citizenship. She concludes, "That's why mumafa imfa zowawa za mpeni or mfuti, mumakhala kuti mwatitayitsa nthawi ("That's why you are dying a painful death by knife or gun, you are wasting our time").[88] Fatsani agrees with her assessment, reflecting that it is true that when Malawian men "or even ladies" arrive in Joburg to make a life, they often say that they are single so as to live freely.

The gangster was a popular figure in *Drum* because of his perceived mobility, and many of *Parade*'s writers sought to recast the migrant as having a similar ability to travel both through space and across categories. In particular, the magazine's later crime stories depicted the Malawian "gentleman gangster" as a man who remained at home in Malawi but who had the intelligence and sophistication previously attributed to the *tsostsi*. Fatsani aspires to be like the latter, but while he acquires the physical, social, and even linguistic mobility associated with the gangster, he does so through nefarious means. In other words, Fatsani is hardly a "gentleman." Rather, he uses a new kind of mobility at his disposal—a digital mobility facilitated by platforms like Facebook—to dupe women in both South Africa and Malawi. In this sense, Fatsani resembles other digital scammers, whose online activities James Yékú theorizes as "an agential reiteration of the Afropolitan capacity for mobility."[89] Fatsani's embrace of a kind of digital tsotsism is a means of asserting agency in the context of southern Africa's repressive border politics, where, as discussed in the previous chapter, mobility and belonging are policed by legal and extralegal means, including violence against Black foreign nationals. Sithanda's threats of *tsotsi* violence are thus more than a euphemism. Faced with various forms of corporeal immobility and violence, Fatsani is pulled again to the virtual sphere and, despite swearing again and again to Sithanda that he will change, he pursues yet another woman he has met on Facebook in real life.

Overall, the story's sympathies, as well as those of most readers, lie with Sithanda rather than with Fatsani or Alicia, who in the end is pregnant by another man but tries to trick Fatsani into thinking that her baby is his in order to extort more money from him. However, readers' allegiance to Sithanda is not, as was the case in other stories, the result of a sense of solidarity among female readers for female characters. In fact, unlike Lupondwana's and Ngwira's stories, which had audiences comprised mainly of women, *Facebook Love* and many other Chichewa Facebook pages drew many male readers as well. This can be attributed to the fact that nearly two-thirds of Malawi's Facebook users are men.[90] Many of the most active commenters on *Facebook Love* presented as men (based on their names and photographs), and these commenters overwhelmingly sympathized with Sithanda: "Sithandi Ndi Gulu La Akazi Omwe Ku Malawi Kuno Amasowa" ("Sithanda is of a class of women that is missing in Malawi") and "Sithanda ndi real wife" ("Sithanda is a real wife").[91] In response to the same chapter, a female reader chimed in, "I wish I could be like sithanda,(golden heart)."[92]

Despite the different demographics of its readers, *Facebook Love* ultimately encountered many of the same issues as the other Facebook diaries discussed above. Readers of *Facebook Love* were dissatisfied with having to wait more than two days for the next part of the story and complained if Chiona was late in posting. Though Chiona rarely responded to readers the way he initially did—when he told the one reader to go back to school if he couldn't read English—he sometimes provided readers with insights into his own life, contextualizing his failure to post in much the same way as Lupondwana and Ngwira did. Sometimes he simply apologized for a late post because he was busy with work, but in one instance, he gave readers a bit more information, explaining that the story was late because he worked as a welder and his eyes hurt from working so much the previous few days ("Pepani dzana ndi dzulo zinandivuta kamba koti ndine welder nde dzana ndi dzulo ndinaotcherera kwambiri nde maso. Amawawa").[93] In another case, he made readers aware of the monetary difficulties involved in Facebook writing by naming and thanking a particular reader for providing him with airtime (data) in order to post.[94] In the end, just as Fatsani's love dramas spill over from the virtual world into the material one, so too do aspects of the writer's life outside the platform become part of its larger story.

DIFFICULT MOBILITIES

Facebook users around the globe have become increasingly aware that the social network's accessibility and ease of use come with a price and that its lack of obvious advertising is meant to conceal the fact that the consumer is the product. Unlike platforms like YouTube, Facebook only began offering users the opportunity to monetize their content recently, and many creative writers who initially turned to Facebook to publish their work have since migrated to other platforms, especially WhatsApp, which is owned by Facebook's parent company, Meta.[95] Other writers, like Lupondwana, have tried to move their Facebook stories to other venues like personal blogs and Wattpad, with varying degrees of success.

Lupondwana had her Facebook diary pirated several times: first by another blog that she eventually managed to shut down and again in 2015 by *Mzansi Stories*, a tabloid-like website that posted news, "gossip," and fiction in the form of stories, jokes, and poems. Although *Mzansi Stories* claimed to be a page promoting South African writers and said that what made it unique was that it didn't "copy and paste other people's work which is known as plagiarism Unless [*sic*] if agreed," Lupondwana did not give permission to the site to republish her diary from Facebook.[96] Until late 2023, Lupondwana's and Ngwira's original diaries and subsequent ones (*Life without My Husband* and *The Veil*, respectively), were available in their entirety on *Mzansi Stories* alongside a handful of diaries by other Facebook writers. *Mzansi Stories* appeared to earn advertising revenue from these writers' work, and the page was filled with "promoted content" articles, many of which related to weight-loss strategies. Lupondwana was frustrated by this situation but nevertheless provided the link to *Mzansi Stories* on Facebook, in part because she did not want to be accused of plagiarizing her *own* work.

While Ngwira very occasionally returns to Facebook to post new stories—an unfinished story, *Road to Forgiveness*, appeared in three parts in April 2019—Lupondwana has continued to post stories on Facebook, despite attempts to leave the platform. In 2017, Lupondwana started her own web page, storiesbylani.co.za, with the aim of posting some of her new work there rather than on Facebook. This move may have been precipitated by yet another person copying her work, this time on another Facebook page. Facebook provided little help or support, suggesting she block this user but offering no other protection for her content, as she explained in a Facebook post and comment on the same post on August 22, 2017.[97] On Facebook the following month, Lupondwana further clarified her reason for starting a blog by citing plagiarism and the desire to earn a little bit of money from her writing. "We don't get paid on Facebook, we write for the love of it . . . DOACH has been plagiarised too much on these streets," she posted on September 23, 2017.[98] Lupondwana directed readers to her blog to read the continuation of *Diary of a Cheating Husband* but, in the spirit of compromise with her Facebook family of readers, said that she would still post some material on the social media site. Lupondwana acknowledged that data was expensive for readers, suggesting that she understood that Facebook was often cheaper to access, but she explained she could earn around R50 (less than four dollars in 2017) for each post if "all of you go read" on the web page.

The blog, however, was short lived. It appears to have last been updated in March 2018 and has since been removed.[99] Instead, Lupondwana began writing on Wattpad, a "webnovel platform," under the handle "UglyLani."[100] In 2017, Lupondwana told me that she would never start a Wattpad or Goodreads page even though there is potential to make money on those sites since "it requires a lot of technology," and at the time she was "comfortable on Facebook." However, she has since had success with Wattpad, where she has 930 followers and thirteen published stories to date. *The Inheritance (Book 2)*, which began in June 2020, is her most viewed and most liked work with nearly 49,000 "reads" and 3,400 "votes." As of October 14, 2023, it is the fourteenth most popular book in Wattpad's "Lessons" category, which includes nearly 6,000 stories.[101]

When writing on Wattpad, especially as compared to her earlier stories on Facebook, Lupondwana writes much more in English than in isiXhosa. Eight of her stories are currently ranked in the top forty "Xhosa stories" on the site, but while these narratives are about Xhosa characters, many include only a small amount of dialogue, if any, in isiXhosa. Readers sometimes write their comments on the story in isiXhosa, demonstrating that readers continue to be a driving force in African-language writing online, although there are far fewer comments on Lupondwana's Wattpad site than she used to enjoy on Facebook.

Like the Chichewa story *Facebook Love*, Lupondwana's Wattpad story *The Other Side of Love* contains a metacommentary on language use and barriers. This story about dating across South African ethnicities follows the relationship between Xolisa, a Xhosa woman, and Khathu, a Venda man, who is engaged to be married to someone else. Though he was warned against Xhosa women when he moved to Port Elizabeth, he soon falls for Xolisa, a student he meets at party. After they have been dating for a while, he begins telling her "Ndi a ni funa" in Tshivenda, to which she replies, "You are so annoying because you know I don't understand your language."[102] At first, he teases her that it means "go take a bath," but eventually he confesses that he is telling her that he loves her. "I kept on saying it in TshiVenda because I thought you were not where I am but I think you love me too." In other instances, Xolisa is next to Khathu while he speaks to someone from home on the phone in Tshivenda, a setup that Lupondwana uses to draw attention to the fact that Xolisa knows little about this man, the woman is he marrying, or his family in Limpopo. Ultimately, Lupondwana's use of language in this and other stories on Wattpad is largely situational. Except for moments where linguistic disconnections and translations are purposefully highlighted to alternately demonstrate distance and closeness in their relationship, Xolisa and Khathu largely converse with each other in English. When Xolisa is speaking to her friends and especially to her parents, however, most of the dialogue is in isiXhosa.

Unlike Facebook, Wattpad offers Lupondwana and other writers some minimal protection for their work under the Digital Millennium Copyright Act (DMCA). If writers find that their work has been copied and reposted on Wattpad or another website, they can submit a DMCA takedown notice. Wattpad also disables copy-and-paste functions on its site so that it is somewhat more difficult to pirate another writer's material. Given the difficulties inherent in protecting the copyright of the "hundreds of millions of story uploads on Wattpad and upwards of hundreds of thousands of new uploads" each day, Wattpad has recently enabled users to anonymously report plagiarism to the original author of the work.[103] Nevertheless, the company warns writers that if they want to ensure the maximum legally defensible protection for their content, they must register it with the copyright office in their home country.[104]

Just as Wattpad does a better job of protecting writers' original content than Facebook, which makes no such efforts at all, it also provides some limited means for writers to be compensated for their work. While Lupondwana's perception in 2017 was that, in general, writers could earn money on the site, the platform's "Paid Stories" program (replaced in October 2023 by "Wattpad Originals") was available by invitation only. For the limited number of stories that became part of the Paid Stories program, readers could buy coins on the site and pay to read individual chapters or an entire work, and writers shared their profits with Wattpad. While Wattpad once promoted itself as a place where writers could gain an audience and visibility in order to win book deals—touting the fact that "[t]here are thousands of writers on Wattpad who have transitioned to traditional publishing from Wattpad and have had readership north of six figures"—this highly optimistic language no longer appears on the site.[105] Nevertheless, Wattpad's own publishing ventures appear to be doing well. In 2019, the site began operating as a publisher, selecting forty to fifty books to publish each year, and as of 2023, Wattpad's publishing arm includes four imprints that publish more than a hundred books per year.[106] Further, the site's Wattpad WEBTOON Studios seeks to create a pipeline from the platform to the entertainment industry.

With its suggestions that it will provide the opportunity for writers to move from the site into traditional publishing and even TV and film, Wattpad appears to provide more literary mobility than it does. In fact, its vision of the world is much like Facebook's, prizing a vague sense of connectivity above all else. It suggests, for example, that "Wattpad writers create some of the most-read stories in the world."[107] In reality, the number of writers who have been published as a result of posting on Wattpad is a very small fraction of its 4 million "monthly active writers" and 665 million "unique story uploads."[108] In other words, Wattpad writers find themselves in much the same situation as the Facebook writers in southern Africa who hope to be plucked from obscurity and published as part of the "diary chronicle" genre. Platforms like Wattpad and Facebook are ultimately still designed for consumers rather than producers of content, and in 2021, active monthly readers on Wattpad outnumbered writers twenty to one. It is therefore not surprising that in its description of its former Paid Stories program, Wattpad assured readers that "the majority of the millions of stories on Wattpad will always be free."[109] For creators, this means that Wattpad will continue to rely on their desire to "share [their] story with the world at any time, from anywhere on Wattpad," language that reflects a one-world imagination that ultimately benefits the platform itself.[110]

In contrast to Lupondwana's and Ngwira's Facebook pages, many of the Chichewa story pages have migrated away from Facebook to groups on the popular messaging platform WhatsApp. Purchased by Facebook in 2014, WhatsApp has been rapidly adopted by internet users on the African continent, where the app's penetration rates were the highest in the world in 2020: 97 percent of Kenyan internet users, 96 percent of South Africans, and 95 percent of Nigerians on the internet used WhatsApp monthly in the last quarter of that year.[111] WhatsApp enables users to share text, voice, pictures, videos, and even documents. The platform is cheap to use thanks to internet provider data bundles that are made specifically for WhatsApp (similar bundles are available in Malawi for both WhatsApp and Facebook). A further benefit for fiction writers is that WhatsApp allows users to send longer messages than can be sent via SMS.[112]

Across the continent, WhatsApp has become a means to discuss social and political issues, though governments have increasingly sought to regulate its usage.[113] In Malawi in 2016, several political opposition leaders were arrested for treason based on WhatsApp messages they sent criticizing the government and discussing how to mobilize the country's youth in protest—charges that were subsequently dropped.[114] More recently, a Malawian woman was arrested for sharing a video on a WhatsApp group for "comedy fans" supposedly mocking President Lazarus Chakwera.[115] Although the security of WhatsApp is being called into question by events like these, many writers may still feel a greater sense of privacy and control over their fictional content on WhatsApp groups, where writers add users individually to their groups, than on Facebook, where Book Series pages are usually visible to anyone with an account. In an effort to stem the spread of misinformation, WhatsApp has recently introduced "forwarding limits" for messages, perhaps also helping writers to limit the unwanted distribution of their stories.[116]

There is some evidence that readers prefer WhatsApp to Facebook for reading fiction.[117] The admin for the "Chichewa Stories Page 2" asked readers in August 2019 what they thought of the prospect of the site moving to a WhatsApp group. Most followers simply replied "good decision" and provided their mobile number in order to be added.[118] A few days later, the admin followed up with some of the reasons stories had been delayed or suspended on Facebook, citing the lack of comments on stories from readers, the fact that they had been busy with other things such as work, and the lack of any kind of sponsorship on

Facebook. The admin proceeded to ask for money for airtime to be sent via WhatsApp so that they could continue to post. The ease of sending money via WhatsApp may also be an incentive for writers to transition to the messaging app.

Ultimately, despite this move away from Facebook, the vast majority of writers still struggle to earn money from their creative work via digital or more traditional publishing channels. Maphoto, who now writes for a nationally aired television show, *Makoti*, is once again the exception. Maphoto's most recent story on his blog, "Origins," concluded its second part in September 2020. Despite telling readers that he would be taking "a few days off so lets [*sic*] hope next week there will be more content," he has yet to return.[119] Nevertheless, as soon as it appears that the moment of blog and Facebook fiction may finally have passed, new diaries from new perspectives emerge to take the places of those that have run their course. In particular, there are several recent diaries from queer perspectives—including *Diary of a Tswana Gay* and *A Ndebele Gay Diary*, which began in 2019 and 2020 and the latter of which is still active. Though these pages have yet to garner the number of followers that Maphoto, Lupondwana, or even Ngwira once did, they demonstrate the continuing malleability and mobility of the digital diary as a form despite the difficult itineraries it travels.[120]

DIGITAL WORLDS

Facebook's idea of the world has come under increasing scrutiny in recent years. The platform's ability to spread false and misleading information has received widespread condemnation, and its users in general have a greater awareness of the ways Facebook has captured and capitalized on users' personal data. It is more difficult, however, for users to fully appreciate the degree to which Facebook leverages this data against them. As Roger McNamee puts it, "When we check a news feed, we are playing multidimensional chess against massive artificial intelligences that have nearly perfect information about us."[121] As a result, the world that Facebook creates for each individual user is uniquely tailored to that person, making it increasingly difficult for users to encounter ideas that differ from their own on the platform. Facebook's echo chamber effect is produced by the platform's algorithms that populate users' news feeds with more of the kind of content they "like," essentially creating the illusion of an external world perfectly aligned with users' own worldviews. This illusion is heightened by the fact that our real-life social networks often overlap with those on the site. Since Facebook's "Core Values" prioritize content from friends and family, we often see the same things on Facebook that those closest to us in real life see, and this naturalizes the world of Facebook as "the world." Perhaps most disturbingly, even though Facebook users have become much more aware of the site's "filter bubbles," they are increasingly comfortable with not seeing alternative views, thus moving from filter bubbles to "preference bubbles."[122]

The communities that form on Facebook are therefore much more individualized and fragmented than Facebook's grand vision of connecting "the world" suggests. These niche groups take myriad forms, the most disturbing iterations of which are the many hate groups that have populated the site. However, as I have described throughout this chapter, the platform has also provided space for unique writing and reading communities to form around languages and identities that have been marginalized in mainstream publishing. Once formed, these mobile communities have continued to travel through various digital and real-world networks, sometimes moving to different online platforms, and in other cases, being published in print or finding expression in face-to-face interactions and conversations. Read in motion, such forms point us to a different kind of world literature, one that is more closely tied to various life worlds around the globe in both their real and virtual dimensions.

In other words, the permeability between virtual and material worlds—wherein one's mobile phone, and therefore one's book, is always in one's pocket and readers can run into their favorite author at a shopping mall or a club—is changing the relationship between the world and literature. One way to see this difference is to compare the reading communities discussed above to predigital ones. In an essay published in 1994, for example, Sarah Nuttall found a significant disconnect between the ways South African women writers and readers conceived of the relationship between the world and texts. While Black women writers sought to present reading "as a shared community of 'taste'" so as to "break down boundaries between world and text, readers generally subscribe[d] to a kind of realism in which the two—readers and texts by black women—remain intact and separate entities."[123] Many of South Africa's female writers had been writing about the harsh realities of apartheid, often for audiences abroad due to state censorship at home. In contrast, the women readers Nuttall interviewed generally avoided what they saw as "serious," political writing in favor of more escapist material such as romance and adventure novels. In many cases, their reading histories were eclectic, comprising British "classics" they read at school and popular genre writers like James Hadley Chase, Sidney Sheldon, and Danielle Steel. In the online communities discussed in this chapter, the difference in taste between writers and readers has diminished substantially, with both writers and readers preferring stories that are entertaining as well as socially oriented. And while the women readers Nuttall interviewed did not generally imagine themselves as writers, many readers on Facebook do, in part because of the platform's ease of use and accessibility and its blurring of the boundaries between content producers and consumers. While these are also features of many of the print periodical forms considered throughout this book, the boundaries between world and text are becoming even more porous online. As these digital diaries travel—albeit fitfully—across virtual and material networks, they produce reading communities at multiple scales and more capacious ideas of both the world and literature itself.

EPILOGUE

Old and New Forms of Mobility

In November 2021, the United States, Europe, and much of the world banned travel from southern Africa based on the discovery of a new variant of COVID-19 by South African scientists. Omicron, the name given to this "variant of concern" by the World Health Organization, caused a fresh spike of cases in South Africa, particularly in the Gauteng region. The travel bans, however, were applied much more widely, with the United States prohibiting travelers not only from South Africa and Botswana, where a few cases of the variant had also been discovered, but also Eswatini, Lesotho, Malawi, Mozambique, Namibia, and Zimbabwe. Britain banned travel from these nations as well as from Angola and Zambia. These bans were implemented before Omicron cases were identified in most of these countries, and they remained in place even after the variant was detected across most of the globe.[1] What is more, American and British citizens were still free to travel to and from southern Africa, further undermining the idea that travel restrictions are about viral transmission alone.

I point to this most recent case of restricted mobilities in relation to southern Africa not to emphasize the ineffectiveness of travel bans, which over the course of the coronavirus pandemic has been well documented, but rather as an example of what Achille Mbembe has identified as a new form of "mobile sovereignty."[2] In this new regime, the border is no longer understood as "a particular point in space," but rather as "a new global partitioning between potentially risky bodies vs. bodies that are not."[3] These classifications, as Mbembe argues, are increasingly based on large quantities of biometric and other data (although such data was scant when it came to the Omicron travel bans in southern Africa) but are equally the product of racist ideologies and institutions, including the racism built into these technologies themselves. Understanding "bodies as borders" is particularly crucial in this situation where terrestrial borders cease to exist for bodies with the right passports. Borders themselves are in motion, flexing and adapting to contain bodies deemed undesirable.[4]

The southern African travel ban also points to the fact that the many other countries in the region of southern Africa continue to be perceived in the global geopolitical imaginary as South Africa's appendages or "peripheries." Certainly there are historical and economic reasons for understanding the region as closely interconnected, including the vast numbers of people, texts, goods, and ideas that circulate through it, but as I have demonstrated throughout this book, South Africa and southern Africa are not interchangeable. South Africa has increasingly wielded its own form of mobile sovereignty in southern Africa in its efforts to exclude and contain undesirable and risky bodies, despite its postapartheid rhetoric of opening to the rest of the continent and its progressive constitution that affirms that "South Africa belongs to all who live in it."[5] The pandemic intensified South Africa's efforts to control its borders through more traditional means—including fortifying its northmost border with Zimbabwe with additional fencing[6]—as well as new measures that essentially extend the border into everyday life, a hallmark of the "new mobility regime."[7]

During the pandemic and South Africa's subsequent lockdown, many undocumented migrants and refugees lost their already-contingent jobs, were forced by police to close their shops, remained confined to overcrowded housing, and were often afraid to access health services for fear of deportation.[8] Most strikingly, they were also excluded from the many social support services offered to South African citizens to help them weather the national lockdown, including grants for the unemployed and for those with children, tax subsidies and other support for businesses, and even food relief programs.[9] Often stranded without the ability to return to their countries of origin, many migrants found themselves in increasingly dire living conditions and at a greater risk of contracting COVID-19, further compounding the stigmas attached to migrancy.[10] Since the start of the pandemic, it is estimated that ten thousand Malawians have returned home. Those who tested positive for the coronavirus were quarantined in various locations, including Kamuzu stadium and a prison training school, due to fears that returning migrants were spreading the disease in Malawi.[11]

Anna Bara observes the deep irony of the fact that 2020, designated the "year of mobility" for the African continent based on a number of recent measures meant to improve intracontinental travel and migration—including the African Union Free Movement Protocol and the establishment of the African Continental Free Trade Area—ended up being characterized by even greater efforts to curtail such movement.[12] Borders and other forms of containment within the continent have proliferated in the past decade. Several years ago, South Africa abandoned its policy of integrating asylum seekers into South African society and began operating detention centers for the first time since the end of apartheid.[13] Similarly, Malawi recently announced that refugees, many of whom have been living in Malawi for years, will be forced to relocate to the country's Dzaleka refugee camp, which houses thousands of migrants from eastern and Central Africa.[14] In South Africa, some of these camps are effectively located outside its borders, as migrants who are trying to reach South Africa are frequently arrested and detained in Zimbabwe.[15] In this way, the border situation in South Africa resembles the recent attempts by European countries to externalize their borders by setting up migrant detention camps in North Africa, much as the United States has used Mexico as a buffer zone for migrants from Central America.

Despite their seeming newness, these "advanced" or "pre-territory borders" of the "new mobility regime" should be understood in relation to earlier colonial and imperial projects. To this end, we too, like the *Chimurenga Chronic* and *Jungle Jim* discussed in chapter 4, must engage in a bit of time travel. The first issue of the *Chimurenga Chronic*, which uses the newspaper as a time machine, includes several full-page hand-drawn maps of Europe's extra-territorial borders in its "Boundaries and Territorialities" section. Alongside these maps, which visualize a contemporary global apartheid order, articles in this section situate the contemporary migrant crisis in relation to efforts to control and contain mobilities across various times and spaces. One such article begins with several lines from a letter, which I have described in this book as a quintessential migrant form, but that here marks travel across not only space but time. In this letter, the Libyan intellectual Abi Elkafi implores the Libyan ambassador in Rome to see the Berlusconi government's efforts to set up migrant detention camps in Libya—a prototypical advanced border—in relation to their precursors in the early colonial period: "How can you forget the concentration camps built by Italian colonists in Libya into which they deported your great family—the Obeidats?"[16] The article goes on to suggest that it was only by curtailing mobility in this way—through such concentration camps as well as a fortified border with Egypt—that the Italians finally broke the Libyan anti-colonial resistance, pointing once again to the centrality of mobility to forms of control and resistance both then and now.

Such detention camps and pre-borders constitute "the 'virtual' extension" of wealthy nations' actual borders.[17] But it is important to remember that virtual borders of all kinds, including the ones Mbembe describes, continue to work in tandem with actual, physical borders. Today's internet-dominated world has often been understood through the lens of Gilles Deleuze's "control society," wherein subjects are virtually tracked and controlled by "invisible rules and systems of regulations, such as our credit scores, web history, and computer protocols."[18] These systems rely on huge quantities of personal data and "follow him or her even when 'outside' an institution as such."[19] The control society resembles Mbembe's idea of mobile sovereignty in that it flexibly adapts to and travels with each body, following them across and within spaces that exceed institutional or national borders. However, as Tung-Hui Hu persuasively argues, virtual networks ought to be understood not in terms of the control society but rather as an amalgamation of new and old forms of sovereignty that are "graft[ing] control onto an older structure of sovereign power, much as fiber-optic cables are layered or grafted onto older networks."[20] While the recent global pandemic has in many ways exposed the regime of new mobilities that Mbembe describes, it also emphasizes that mobile sovereignty is built on older ideas of national sovereignty. Indeed, the pandemic has caused the border to reemerge as precisely a fixed line on the map, even as it shows the many ways "borderization" now travels.

Like new forms of mobile sovereignty, digital forms and networks are often "grafted" onto analog ones, using many of the same structures and terminologies as print ("diaries," "chapters") while also inventing new ones ("inserts," "admins"). Virtual forms like the digital diary replicate some of the features of print periodicals, including an emphasis on serialization, multilingualism, and reader engagement. And yet, while virtual networks like blogs, Facebook, and Wattpad have provided writers with alternative venues for publication outside the orbit of traditional gatekeepers such as agents, publishers, and editors, they also, as the emergence of the South African diary chronicle suggests, reinforce the power of these same actors to select a few digital diaries for traditional publication. Meanwhile, digital platforms reap the benefits of publishing thousands of writers' work without paying a cent and, in cases like Wattpad, have become print publishers themselves. Other publications like the *Chimurenga Chronic* and *Jungle Jim*, which adopt popular twentieth-century print periodical forms but are widely available in PDF and "Kindlepulp" form, graft older technologies on to new networks, in much the same way that they seek to remake pan-Africanism for a global digital age.

This book has examined space-making projects and efforts to control and contain African mobilities since the mid-twentieth century. From the Central African Federation and the colonial township to South Africa's exploitative relationship with migrants throughout the region and Kamuzu Banda's efforts to keep Malawian labor at home, space and mobility have been essential to struggles over sovereignty in the region. Each of the literary forms I have considered here reimagines mobilities in ways that make visible these different workings of power as well as a complex set of alternative geographies and itineraries. If, as Mbembe suggests, "a key issue of the 21st century will be the management of human mobility," literary forms such as these are a central place to look for the ways migrants and other people on the move understand their own mobility, or lack thereof.[21] Much as the letter by "an African Pioneer" in *Vyaro na Vyaro*, republished in the *Manchester Guardian* in 1937, contested many of the ways African movement was being imagined by European missionaries and colonists, so too do these traveling forms express more capacious ideas of mobility and, in turn, new communities and geographies. As I have argued here, these forms are best read in motion as they move within and across real and virtual borders via various periodical publications, print books and anthologies, and digital networks. By reading in motion, we can stay attuned to new and old forms of mobile sovereignty while recognizing the ways writers have used these same spaces and platforms to envision forms of mobility that exceed them.

Notes

INTRODUCTION

1. Maweh Mbambo KaMageza, May 22, 2013, comment on Maphoto, *Diary of a Zulu Girl*, chapter 58. Following other recent book-length studies of digital and social media forms (see Adenekan, *African Literature in the Digital Age* and Yékú, *Cultural Netizenship*), I have included some readers' comments posted on blogs and social media in cases where they are publicly available because they shed valuable light on digital literatures. In many ways, these comments are similar to the readers' letters and comments published in the print publications considered throughout this book. Nevertheless, I am aware that what is "public" online is sometimes different from what is considered public offline (see Zimmer, "'But the Data Is Already Public'" and Proferes et al., "Studying Reddit"). This is an important issue that serves as a useful prism for comparing print and digital media and their publics and that deserves further attention.

2. Lupondwana, in conversation with author, March 25, 2017.

3. babalwa luhabe, June 12, 2013, comment on Mike Maphoto, *Diary of a Zulu Girl*, chapter 67.

4. ZEE, September 5, 2013, comment on Mike Maphoto, *Diary of a Zulu Girl*, chapter 101.

5. Hu, *Prehistory of the Cloud*; Kitchin and Dodge, "'Placing' Cyberspace: Geography, Community and Identity."

6. Bosch Santana, "From Nation to Network."

7. Maphoto, *Diary of a Zulu Girl*, chapter 40.

8. Barber, *Anthropology of Texts*, 145.

9. See also Barber, "Introduction: I. B. Thomas and the First Yoruba Novel."

10. Mbeba, "Rhodesia Road," *African Drum*, March 1951, 16.

11. Fasselt, "Decolonising the Afropolitan," 78; Iheka and Taylor, *African Migration Narratives*, 2.

12. Mohutsiwa, "I'm Done with African Immigrant Literature."

13. Armillas-Tiseyra, "The African Novel at the Vanguard," 248.

14. See Anderson, *Imagined Communities*; Ganguly, *This Thing Called the World*, 2; Goyal, *Runaway Genres*.

15. Ouma and Krishnan, "Small Magazines in Africa," 196.

16. Harris, *Afropolitanism and the Novel*, 20–21.

17. Barber, *Print Culture and the First Yoruba Novel*; Hofmeyr, *Portable Bunyan* and *Gandhi's Printing Press*; Newell, *Ghanaian Popular Fiction*, *Power to Name*, and *Newsprint Literature and Local Literary Creativity in West Africa, 1900s–1960s*. See also Adejunmobi, "Abiola Irele and the Publicness of African Letters"; Bush, "'Mesdames, il faut lire!'"; Bush and Ducournau, "Introduction: African Audiences: Making Meanings across Media"; Harris and Hållén, "African Street Literature"; Helgesson, *Transnationalism in Southern African Literature*; Hofmeyr, Nuttall, and Michael, "The Book in Africa"; Kalliney, "Modernism, African Literature, and the Cold War"; Odhiambo, "Inventing Africa in the Twentieth Century"; Ouma and Krishnan, eds., special issue, "Small Magazines in Africa"; Peterson, Hunter, and Newell, eds. *African Print Cultures*; Suhr-Sytsma, *Poetry, Print, and the Making of Postcolonial Literature*; Wallis, "How Books Matter."

18. See, for example, Askew, "Everyday Poetry from Tanzania"; Barber, "Introduction: I. B. Thomas and the First Yoruba Novel"; Jones, *At the Crossroads*; Mokoena, "Assembly of Readers"; Ogude, "Vernacular Press and the Articulation of Luo Ethnic Citizenship"; Reuster-Jahn, "Newspaper Serials in Tanzania" and "Sex and Relationship Education on the Streets."

19. Krishnan makes this point about the West African novel, demonstrating that it both reproduces imperial cartographies and contests them at the same time (*Writing Spatiality in West Africa*).

20. Bulson, *Little Magazine, World Form*, 8. Some of the publications considered here are comparable to what Bush and Ducournau call "big magazines," which mixed "popular" and "literary" materials and envisioned their readerships at the scales of the nation as well as the continent and diaspora ("'Small Readers' and Big Magazines," 46, 54–56).

21. In the 1940s, the Northern Rhodesian Colonial Information Office "estimated that each paper was seen by ten people; some of these would have been illiterate villagers who had the paper read to them" (Smyth, "War Propaganda," 352). In the twenty-first century, Cagé suggests that the number of people who read a single issue is between ten and twenty ("The Economics of the African Media," 618).

22. See Hofmeyr, *Portable Bunyan* on the imagination of travel and circulation that extends into the spiritual world.

23. See for example Bush and Ducournau, "'Small Readers' and Big Magazines," 64; Helgesson, *Transnationalism in Southern African Literature*; Odhiambo, "Inventing Africa in the Twentieth Century"; Ouma and Krishnan, "Small Magazines in Africa," 198; Quayson, "Kòbòlò Poetics"; Suhr-Sytsma, *Poetry, Print, and the Making of Postcolonial Literature*.

24. On curation as a critical practice, see Bush and Ducournau, "'Small Readers' and Big Magazines," 51. See also Adesokan, *Everything Is Sampled*,

for a productive account of the ways that African writers and artists have engaged in methods of "curation, adaptation, remix, platform and composition" across media over the past several decades (3).

25. Young, "The 'Native' Newspaper," 63.

26. The first "known African newspaper in southern Africa" was published in Xhosa by Wesleyan missionaries in South Africa in 1837 (Switzer, "Introduction: South Africa's Alternative Press in Perspective," 23), and Nyasaland's first "native paper," *Kalilole*, was published by the Church of Scotland Mission in 1890 in English, Chichewa, and Yao (Namponya 176). Dombo points to mission newsletters as an early example of such publications in Southern Rhodesia, the earliest dating to 1913 (*Private Print Media*, 7).

27. Dombo, *Private Print Media*, 8.

28. Young, "The 'Native' Newspaper," 66.

29. Young, "The 'Native' Newspaper," 66.

30. Young, "The 'Native' Newspaper," 67.

31. Young, "The 'Native' Newspaper," 70.

32. Manda provides this translation of the title ("Journalism Education and Training in Malawi," 38). Others, including Young, translate it as "Other Lands."

33. D. D. Phiri notes that while *Vyaro na Vyaro* was primarily published in English and Tumbuka, it also included some pages in Chinyanja for reading in schools ("National Language and Smaller Languages," *Nation*, July 16, 2013, https://www.mwnation.com/national-language-and-smaller-languages/).

34. Derek Peterson and Emma Hunter observe this to be a trend in African newspapers across the continent ("Print Culture in Colonial Africa," 4).

35. See Adejunmobi, who argues that "publicness" does not always equate to "visibility" for African literary forms ("Abiola Irele and the Publicness of African Letters").

36. On the composition of the migrant workforce on the Copperbelt during the colonial period, see Money, "'Aliens' on the Copperbelt," 864–66.

37. "African Pioneer," *Manchester Guardian*, November 22, 1937, 11.

38. On the Mfecane, the catalysts of which continue to be debated, see Carolyn Hamilton, "'The Character and Objects of Chaka.'"

39. Mbembe in conversation with Bregtje van der Haak, "The Way I See It," 2.

40. See Edwards, *Practice of Diaspora*; Goyal, *Romance, Diaspora, and Black Atlantic Literature* and others who have built on and extended Paul Gilroy's seminal *The Black Atlantic*.

41. See Desai, *Commerce with the Universe*; Hofmeyr, *Dockside Reading*; Bystrom and Slaughter, *Global South Atlantic*; and Samuelson, "Coastal Form."

42. For important examples of intra-African textual circulation and travel, see Hofmeyr, *Portable Bunyan* and Jones, *At the Crossroads*.

43. Odhiambo, "Inventing Africa in the Twentieth Century"; Ouma and Krishnan, "Small Magazines in Africa"; Bush and Ducournau, "'Small Readers' and Big Magazines."

44. Southern Africa is a diverse and variously defined region of at least ten countries, with different though not entirely dissimilar colonial experiences, and thousands of languages. It is usually considered to include South Africa, Leso-

tho, Eswatini, Botswana, Zimbabwe, Mozambique, Angola, Namibia, Zambia, and Malawi. However, the Southern African Development Committee also includes the Democratic Republic of Congo, Tanzania, the Seychelles, Comoros, Madagascar, and Mauritius.

45. Mphande, "Ngoni Praise Poetry and the Nguni Diaspora," 100.

46. Groves, *Malawian Migration to Zimbabwe*, 21.

47. van Onselen, *Chibaro*, 119–20.

48. Crush et al., "Migration in Southern Africa," 1.

49. Groves, *Malawian Migration to Zimbabwe*, 12.

50. Cohen, *Politics and Economics of Decolonization in Africa*, 36–37.

51. Cohen, *Politics and Economics of Decolonization in Africa*, 39.

52. James Griffiths quoted in London Committee of the United Central African Association, "Central African Federation: The Only Way to Partnership between the Races," 3.

53. London Committee of the United Central African Association, "Central African Federation," 7.

54. Slinn, "Commercial Concessions and Politics during the Colonial Period," 379; Gwande, "Political Economy of American Businesses in British Central Africa," 80.

55. Cohen, *Politics and Economics of Decolonization in Africa*, 37, 42.

56. James Johnson quoted in Cohen, *Politics and Economics of Decolonization in Africa*, 67.

57. Helgesson, "Southern Africa," 198. See, for example, Chapman's useful and ambitious survey, *Southern African Literatures*, which nevertheless gives much greater space to South Africa, as well as Emmanuel Ngara's *New Writing from Southern Africa*.

58. As Primorac and Chan observe, South Africa's earlier "visibility as a *literary* nation-state" was the result of the admittance of white South African authors into global literary canons ("*Gwebede's Wars*," 553). Olive Schreiner's 1883 *The Story of an African Farm* is usually considered to be the first South African novel.

59. Chapman, *Southern African Literatures*, 205.

60. The first Shona novel, *Feso*, was published by Southern Rhodesia's literary bureau in 1956 (Primorac, "The Novel in a House of Stone"). Malawi is an exception in terms of having its first vernacular novel published somewhat earlier: Samuel Y. Nthara's *Nthondo*, the winner of an International Institute for African Languages competition in 1933 (Chimombo, *A Guide to Malawi's Literature*).

61. Primorac counts eleven novels published by six Black Zimbabwean authors in exile in the 1960 and '70s ("The Novel in a House of Stone," 54).

62. Lazarus, "South African Ideology."

63. Dombo, *Private Print Media*, 14.

64. Helgesson, *Transnationalism in Southern African Literature*; see also Jackson, "*Reading for the Region in New African Novels*," and Sacks, *Networked Poetics*, which appeared while this book was in the final stages of production.

65. Primorac, "At Home in the World?"

66. Switzer, "Bantu World," 352.

67. Switzer, "Bantu World," 360; Dombo, *Private Print Media*, 16. The *Native Mirror* was edited by an ex-missionary, F. L. Hadfield, and published in four languages—English, Karanga, Zezuru, and Sindebele. It included fables and cultural stories with educational aims (Dombo, *Private Print Media*, 12). For more on *Imvo Zabantsundu*, see Mkhize, "'To See Us as We See Ourselves.'"

68. Dombo, *Private Print Media*, 23.

69. Dombo, *Private Print Media*, 22.

70. Banda, "Ruling Minds," 318.

71. Veit-Wild, *Teachers, Preachers, Non-Believers*, 70.

72. Chapman, *Southern African Literatures*, xix. Achebe also draws a distinction between "ethnic" literatures in African languages and a Nigerian national literature in English ("English and the African Writer").

73. Mchombo, "Politics of Language Choice in African Education," 193–94.

74. Marten and Kula, "Zambia," 313.

75. Paas, preface to *English-Chichewa/Chinyanja Dictionary*, 3rd ed., 3.

76. Lionnet and Shih, *Minor Transnationalism*.

77. Casanova's model, for example.

78. Edwards, *Practice of Diaspora*, 7.

79. Moretti, *Distant Reading*, 111.

80. The single exception I have found is Zambian writer Andreya Sylvester Masiye's *The Lonely Village* (1951).

81. Mandelbrot, quoted in Dimock, "Genre as World System," 88. Dimock argues for a practice of reading that moves between the "very small" scale of the individual word and the "very large" scale of genres such as the epic as a way of doing broad literary analysis that can still account for the "jagged" and "random" features one finds when close reading individual texts.

82. Owuor, "Imagined Waters," 10.

83. Owuor, "Imagined Waters," 13, 10.

84. Levine, *Forms*, 7.

85. Warner, *Publics and Counterpublics*, 95.

86. Pfalzgraf, *Mobility in Contemporary Zimbabwean Literature in English*, 5.

87. Toivanen, *Mobilities and Cosmopolitanisms*, 1, 5. For a seminal study on automobility see, Green-Simms, *Postcolonial Automobility*.

88. Toivanen, *Mobilities and Cosmopolitanisms*, 1.

89. Distinguishing movement from mobility, Cresswell argues that movement is "mobility abstracted from contexts of power" (*On the Move*, 2).

90. Robolin, *Grounds of Engagement*, 8–9. See also Said, *Culture and Imperialism*; Soja, *Seeking Spatial Justice*; Massey, *For Space*.

91. See Robolin, *Grounds of Engagement*, and Krishnan, *Writing Spatiality in West Africa*.

92. Cresswell, *On the Move*, 3, 5. De Certeau also argues that "space is composed of intersections of mobile elements" (*Practice of Everyday Life*, 117).

93. Mbembe, "Idea of a Borderless World," 4.

94. *Chimurenga Chronic*, 2018.

95. Hofmeyr, "Transnational Circulation," 13.

96. Suhr-Sytsma, *Poetry, Print, and the Making of Postcolonial Literature*, 10, 8.

97. Ouma and Krishnan, "Small Magazines in Africa," 199, 198.

98. Sacks, "Moving Forms"; Adesokan, *Everything Is Sampled*, 6.

99. Laachir, Marzagora, and Orsini, "Significant Geographies," 294.

100. Laachir, Marzagora, and Orsini, "Significant Geographies," 297.

101. Apter, "Untranslatables," 583.

102. De Certeau, *Practice of Everyday Life*, 121.

103. De Certeau, *Practice of Everyday Life*, 120.

104. Nakao, "Convivial Multilingualism as a Modern African Ethos," 21.

105. Nakao, "Convivial Multilingualism as a Modern African Ethos," 21; Nyamnjoh, "Incompleteness," 264.

106. Damrosch, *What Is World Literature?*, 288; Gikandi, "Contested Grammars," 259, 267.

107. Gikandi, "Contested Grammars," 269.

108. Ngũgĩ wa Thiong'o, *Decolonizing the Mind*, 74–75.

109. Apter points to a "fluid" model of "*mobile* decipherment" elaborated by Robert Young ("Untranslatability and the Geopolitics of Reading," 198). Drawing on Nikolai Trubetzkoy, Young suggests a mode of translation that is attentive to languages not as rigid, discrete entities but as malleable and graded, "continually reacting and interacting, colliding and combining . . . in a dialectical movement of centripetal and centrifugal forces" ("That Which Is Casually Called a Language," 1215).

110. Helgesson and Kullberg, "Translingual Events," 145, 144.

111. Asinakufunda, "Tinoda Cizezuru Ciwande," *African Parade*, January 1954, 32.

112. "Uneducated," "Mapeji Acinyanja Acuruke," *African Parade*, January 1954, 29.

113. While numerous translation theorists have discussed the inadequacy of understanding translation in this way, see Warner for a particularly nuanced view of translation in an African context (*Tongue-Tied Imagination*); Levine, *Forms*, 7.

114. Apter, "Untranslatability and the Geopolitics of Reading," 198.

115. Lindfors, *Loaded Vehicles*; Chinweizu, Jemie, and Madubuike, *Towards the Decolonization of African Literature*, xiv.

116. Mphande, "Ngoni Praise Poetry and the Nguni Diaspora," 101.

117. Mphande, "Ngoni Praise Poetry and the Nguni Diaspora," 101; Coppan, "World Literature and Global Theory."

118. Moretti, *Graphs, Maps, Trees*, 77.

119. Balogun, *Tradition and Modernity in the African Short Story*, 3.

120. Pressman argues that digital literature "pushes comparative analysis to move from text to process . . . from work to network" ("Electronic Literature as Comparative Literature").

121. Helgesson, "Shifting Fields," 40.

122. This is how Mike Kamwendo, the paper's former editor, refers to it. Kamwendo, in conversation with author, August 6, 2018.

123. I take inspiration from the fact that Moretti's term "distant reading," seen by many to elide individual texts in favor of data—was initially modified by another adjective: "serial" (*Distant Reading*, 44). Serial reading suggests an

entirely different critical practice from distant reading alone. However, it was edited out of the final version of Moretti's text.

124. Owuor, "Imagined Waters," 10.

CHAPTER 1

1. For readability, I refer to the magazine from this point forward as "Parade." *African Parade* was the magazine's official title until June 1962, when it became simply *Parade*. Thompson Publications purchased *Parade* and published it as *Parade and Foto-Action* from 1967 to 1990 and *Parade* from 1990 to 2004. *Parade* was relaunched from 2012 to 2014 as a Zimbabwe Publishing House publication by Padare reNhau.

2. Angolo, "Parade Is Read," *African Parade*, August 1961, 70. See also L. M. C. Phiri, "In Defense of Vernaculars," *African Parade*, August 1954, 25.

3. "Between You and Me," *African Parade*, January 1954, 5. See also "Vernacular Controversy," *African Parade*, November 1957, 2. In October 1961, the editors announced that all vernacular language material would henceforth be "transferred" to *Parade*'s "newly-born sister" publication, the *Popular Post* ("Air Your Views," 37).

4. Veit-Wild, *Teachers, Preachers, Non-Believers*, 28.

5. Mtepuka, "Central African Federation: The Attack," *Africa South*, July 1957, 73–74.

6. For relatively brief accounts see Dombo, *Private Print Media*, 27–28, 35; Kahari, *Search for Identity and Ufuru*, 198–214; McLoughlin, "Zimbabwean Short Stories by Black Writers," 79–81; and Veit-Wild, *Teachers, Preachers, Non-Believers*, 68–75.

7. Behdad, "Postcolonial Theory and the Predicament of 'Minor Literature,'" 224.

8. *Parade* appropriated some of its materials directly from other publications, including excerpts that seem to be taken from George Birmingham's *Famous Murders* (1935) and C. T. Bedford's *Livingstone of Africa* (1925). Like many newspapers from around the globe, *Parade* often "cut-and-pasted" material directly from other periodicals, a practice that Hofmeyr and Peterson describe as "an infrastructure of textual exchange that made newspapers into assemblages of texts from elsewhere" ("The Politics of the Page," 3).

9. Saidi, in conversation with author, August 6, 2012.

10. While *tsotsis* were just one of the types of gangsters found in South Africa's urban centers, they were the "[m]ost notorious and common" ("Inside Johannesburg's Underworld," *Drum*, October 1951, 7). In its strictest sense, the term *tsotsi* referred to younger criminals, who were as infamous for their violence as their fashion—"tight-fitting zoot trousers, wide-brimmed hats, loud shirts and ties" ("Inside Johannesburg's Underworld," 7).

11. See Benjamin, quoted in Edwards, *Practice of Diaspora*, 8; Lindfors, *Loaded Vehicles*; Lewis et al., "John Lewis: Profile of a Civil Rights Legend."

12. Odhiambo, "Inventing Africa in the Twentieth Century."

13. Helgesson, *Transnationalism in Southern African Literature*, 40.

14. Fleming and Falola, "Africa's Media Empire."

15. I take inspiration from Apter's term "*mobile* decipherment" to describe a "fluid" form of translation ("Untranslatability and the Geopolitics of Reading," 198).

16. *African Parade*, November 1953, 3.

17. "Kuyenda Mtsogolo," *African Parade*, November 1953, 27.

18. Rabkin, "Drum Magazine (1951–1961)," 57–58.

19. Cowling, "Echoes of an African Drum," 18; Helgesson, *Transnationalism in Southern African Literature*, 38–39.

20. Dombo, *Private Print Media*, 40.

21. Dombo, *Private Print Media*, 29.

22. "We," *African Parade*, June 1955, 5.

23. Vambe, *From Rhodesia to Zimbabwe*, 254. Both Dombo (*Private Print Media*, 106–8) and Veit-Wild (*Teachers, Preachers, Non-Believers*, 55–65) discuss whether Vambe, Saidi, and other journalists affiliated with *Parade* actually believed in the multiracial project. Both cite evidence to suggest that they did, but Dombo ultimately concludes that "a stooge was one in the eyes of the beholder" (*Private Print Media,* 108).

24. "Ngwazi of Malawi!" *Parade*, August 1964, 3.

25. "Parade," *African Parade*, November 1955, 5.

26. On these improvements, see Roscoe, *Columbia Guide*, 26. While Africans did have representation in the federal and territorial legislatures, the federal parliament of fifty-nine members included only twelve African representatives, who Chiume observes were "elected in such a way that only those acceptable to Europeans [could] win," and the situation was not much better in the territorial legislatures ("Commentary," 24).

27. Chiume, "Commentary," 24.

28. "Between You and Me," *African Parade*, August 1956, 3.

29. "Between You and Me," *African Parade*, June 1956, 5.

30. *African Parade*, January 1955, 5; H. S. Gathigira, "The African Parade Comes to Kenya," *African Parade*, September 1957, 36.

31. Saidi, in conversation with author, August 6, 2012.

32. Laachir, Marzagora, and Orsini, "Significant Geographies," 294.

33. For extended treatments of the relationship between African American and South African writers, see Nixon, *Homelands, Harlem, and Hollywood*; Graham and Walters, *Langston Hughes and the South African Drum Generation;* and Robolin, *Grounds of Engagement.*

34. D. D. Phiri, in conversation with author, January 23, 2012.

35. Vambe, *From Rhodesia to Zimbabwe*, 261–62.

36. For a discussion of the complex relationship between regional imaginaries in Central and East Africa, see Milford, "Federation, Partnership, and the Chronologies of Space in 1950s East and Central Africa."

37. In a 1955 article, Vambe wrote: "We must forge a common citizenship, a common loyalty to a system in which no individual, be he White, Black, Brown or Yellow, is handicapped by reason of his colour, race or creed. That implies that every man should be given equal justice, equality of opportunity and the enjoyment of all the rights of civilization" (quoted in Veit-Wild, *Teachers, Preachers, Non-Believers*, 29).

38. Vambe, *From Rhodesia to Zimbabwe*, 261.

39. "Between You and Me," *African Parade*, June 1956, 62.

40. As Man to Man, *African Parade*, September 1957, 42.

41. Helgesson, *Transnationalism in Southern African Literature*, 33.

42. Edwards, *Practice of Diaspora*, 13.

43. Vambe, "From near the Bush to New York," *African Parade*, September 1957, 20, 25.

44. Dube, "America as I Saw It," 89.

45. Professor Kilimanjaro, "And So the World Turns," *African Parade*, May 1956, 44.

46. *Uncle Tom's Cabin*, *African Parade*, September 1954, 25.

47. Sollors, *Ethnic Modernism*, 13.

48. Sollors, *Ethnic Modernism*, 62.

49. "Meet the Rural African of S Rhodesia," *African Parade*, June 1954, 8–9.

50. Saidi, in conversation with author, August 6, 2012.

51. "A Glimpse into the Protectorate of Nyasaland," *African Parade*, June 1954, 18.

52. "A Glimpse into the Protectorate of Nyasaland," *African Parade*, June 1954, 18. This vision echoed earlier calls for Central African solidarity. A young Hastings Kamuzu Banda, who returned to the federation to lead the Malawian fight for independence in 1958, argued in a 1938 letter, "We have to begin to think in terms of Nyasaland, and even Central Africa and Africa as a whole, rather than of Kasungu. We have to look upon all the tribes in Central Africa, whether in Nyasaland or in Rhodesia, as our brothers" (quoted in Dee, "Central African Immigrants," 323).

53. Veit-Wild, *Teachers, Preachers, Non-Believers*, 30.

54. "In Clash with the Colour Bar," *African Parade*, July 1961, 80–81; Tinos Guvi, "Malcolm the Man and His Ideas," *African Parade*, June 1965, 50–51; William Wannamaker, "American Crisis," *African Parade*, September 1965, 45–47.

55. "The Year 1960 and the Changing Face of Africa," *African Parade*, December 1960, 19, 25. See also "The New Africa and the New America," which ends with an emphasis on nonalignment in the Cold War (*African Parade*, June 1961, 16), and an editorial from several months later that identifies Pan-Africanism as key to successful independence struggles in North and West Africa. In the face of growing "tribalism" in the nationalist movement in the federation, the editorial complains that both the Zimbabwe National Party (ZNP) and the National Democratic Party (NDP) "claim to represent pan-Africanism in this part of Africa. . . . This is despite the declared policy of pan-Africanism: 'No division before, but after independence'" (*African Parade*, November 1961, 3).

56. Editorial, *African Parade*, August 1964, 70.

57. "Opinion," *African Drum*, March 1951, 3.

58. "Introduction to 'Rhodesia Road,'" *African Drum*, March 1951, 16.

59. Under the impression that the story was originally written in English, Rafapa argues that "Mbeba purposely distorts the conventional word order of English" and draws on African proverbs and "vernacular words" to present an "African cultural identity" ("South African Drum Writers of Fiction," 254–56).

60. "Introduction to 'Rhodesia Road,'" *African Drum*, March 1951, 16.

61. Deleuze and Guattari, *Thousand Plateaus*, 381.

62. Gray, "Third World Meets First World," 65–66.

63. Gray, "Third World Meets First World," 70. Gray charts the history of the genre, whose name derives from a 1949 film of the same title, suggesting that it "record[s] not only how 'Jim Comes to Joburg,' but why he stays there" ("Third World Meets First World," 62).

64. Fenwick, "'Tough Guy, Eh?,'" 619.

65. In his unpublished dissertation on *Drum*'s Black writers, Rabkin observes, "African writers had no such illusions" that the rural areas constituted a "viable alternative" to the white cities (95). Therefore, he argues, "it would be a mistake to suppose that the similarity in form of the stories by black writers to the 'Jim' variety by white authors, extended to an identity of content" ("Drum Magazine (1951–1961)," 95).

66. Sampson, *Drum: An African Adventure—and Afterwards*, 20.

67. However, later editions of *Drum* produced specifically for the federation beginning in 1960 included more articles on its increasingly tense political situation.

68. Gray also observes this shift, finding that the Jim genre extends into the "late 60s as a recognizable, pristine form," and is finally "laid to rest" when a "new hero," the urban gangster, emerges in Athol Fugard's *Tsotsi* ("Third World Meets First World," 77–78). However, Gray focuses primarily on the novel, drama, and short story collections rather than more immediate periodical genres. I argue that the transition from migrant-hero to *tsotsi* can be observed earlier in *Drum*'s fiction than in these other forms.

69. Nxumalo, "Birth of a Tsotsi," 18.

70. Vaughn, quoted in Manase, "Making Memory," 61.

71. "Act," *Union Gazette Extraordinary*, June 27, 1952, 93.

72. See Nixon, *Homelands, Harlem, and Hollywood*; Fenwick, "'Tough Guy, Eh?'"; Morris, "Style, *Tsotsi*-Style, and *Tsotsitaal*."

73. Morris, "Style, *Tsotsi*-Style, and *Tsotsitaal*," 88–89.

74. Morris, "Style, *Tsotsi*-Style, and *Tsotsitaal*," 88–89.

75. Morris, "Style, *Tsotsi*-Style, and *Tsotsitaal*," 87.

76. Lewis Nkosi quoted in Nixon, *Homelands, Harlem, and Hollywood*, 33. Nixon expands on Nkosi's use of the term "intellectual tsotsi" to describe Can Themba in Nkosi's introduction to Themba's *The Will to Die* ("Obituary," x).

77. Maimane, "Hot Diamonds," *African Drum*, April 1953, 36. Maimane wrote under the pseudonym "Arthur Mogale."

78. Fenwick, "'Tough Guy, Eh?,'" 623.

79. Sidayiya, "Ntombo Gets a Job," *Drum*, March 1952, 29.

80. Gray, "Third World Meets First World," 77.

81. Morris, "Style, *Tsotsi*-Style, and *Tsotsitaal*," 108.

82. Mphahlele, "Lesane [The Lesanes of Nadia Street]," 134.

83. Mphahlele, "Lesane [Fanyan]," 143.

84. Molamu, "Wietie," 147–48.

85. Themba, "'Baby Come Duze,'" 109.
86. Mphahlele, "Lesane," 143.
87. Saidi, in conversation with author, August 6, 2012.
88. D. D. Phiri, in conversation with author, January 23, 2012.
89. Canana, "The Man with a Beard," *African Parade*, January 1954, 19. Veit-Wild suggests that "Canana" was the pen name of Lawrence Vambe (*Teachers, Preachers, Non-Believers*, 69).
90. See "My Experiences: A True Story" by a woman named Sophie who journeys to Bulawayo alone, loses her job, and ends up being forced to work as a prostitute. In introducing the serial, the editor wrote, "This story is published for one reason only, that is to drive one point home—PROSTITUTION DOES NOT PAY" (*African Parade*, March 1956, 11).
91. See Groves, *Malawian Migration to Zimbabwe*, 166, and Scott, "Migrant Labor in Southern Rhodesia," 29.
92. Scott, "Migrant Labor in Southern Rhodesia," 29.
93. Groves, *Malawian Migration to Zimbabwe*, 148–49.
94. Groves, *Malawian Migration to Zimbabwe*, 148–49.
95. Daimon, "Settling in Motion as Consciousness."
96. Coplan, "Power of Oral Poetry," 21.
97. Crush, "Vulcan's Brood," 240.
98. Mala, "Kwelani Galimoto Wa Ulere," *African Parade*, March 1955, 41.
99. Mala, "Kwelani Galimoto Wa Ulere," *African Parade*, March 1955, 41. In this instance, the past continuous *ma* is used.
100. Carter, quoted in Crush, "Vulcan's Brood," 230.
101. Mala, "Kwelani Galimoto Wa Ulere," *African Parade*, March 1955, 41.
102. Scott, "Migrant Labor in Southern Rhodesia," 36.
103. Scott, "Migrant Labor in Southern Rhodesia," 36.
104. Scott, "Migrant Labor in Southern Rhodesia," 32–33.
105. Daimon, "Settling in Motion as Consciousness," 6.
106. Daimon, "Settling in Motion as Consciousness," 1.
107. See Shili, "From Cape Town to Pointe-Noir," and Godsman, "The Distant Place," in which a witch doctor prophesies and then attempts to prevent his own death by sending his son on a journey from Northern Rhodesia's Bangweulu swamps into the Congo.
108. Daimon, "Settling in Motion as Consciousness," 10.
109. Pambana, "A Race with Chance: Part 1," *African Parade*, November 1954, 32.
110. Pambana, "A Race with Chance: Part 2," *African Parade*, December 1954, 44.
111. Daimon, "Settling in Motion as Consciousness," 8–9.
112. Gates, *Signifying Monkey*, xxv.
113. For example, "The Gub-Gub Peas" from Jamaica tells an inverted version of this tale. In it, Anansi—who often takes the form of a spider—tricks an illiterate watchman using a letter that is supposedly written by his master, instructing him to tie Anansi up in the pea fields and allow him to eat his fill (Parkes, "Gub-Gub Peas," 4–5).

114. The Nyanja version is slightly simplified at the story's end, suggesting that perhaps it is a translation of the English version. Further, whereas the English version in one instance refers to the white man as "his master," the Nyanja version refers to him only as Mzungu, meaning white man or European.

115. Cancel, *Storytelling in Northern Zambia*, 199.

116. Manduli, "Kasumbalala and the Letter," 25; "Kalata Ndi Kasumbalala," 27.

117. Manduli, "Kasumbalala and the Letter," 25.

118. Manduli, "Kalata Ndi Kasumbalala," 27.

119. Bwelezani, "Kanthu Konama," 37.

120. Bwelezani, "Kanthu Konama," 37.

121. Mtima, "Kuceza Kwanga Ku Rhodesia," 37.

122. Mudeka, "Gendered Exclusion and Contestation," 26, 31.

123. Mtima, "Kuceza Kwanga Ku Rhodesia," 37.

124. See, for example, Maganga, "Zufeyo Mwana Wokonda Kusaka," or "Zufeyo the Child Who Loves to Hunt," 56.

125. Mudeka, "Gendered Exclusion and Contestation," 30.

126. Groves, *Malawian Migration to Zimbabwe*, 152.

127. Barber observes a similar connection between letters in the newspaper and their appearance in West and East African fiction ("Introduction: Hidden Innovators in Africa," 17–18).

128. See, for example, Francis, "'The Meanest Devil of the Pit'"; and Quinn and Schleh, "Popular Crime in Africa," 39.

129. Schwarzbach, "Newgate Novel to Detective Fiction," 240.

130. Bollen and Ingelbien, "An Intertext That Counts?," 410.

131. From 1915 to 1924, African migrants to Southern Rhodesia comprised an average of only 5.1 percent of the total immigrant population each year, with the rest recorded as British, British South African, Dutch South African, other Europeans, and "Asiatics" (Willcox, "Statistics of Migrations," 1067). The fact that a relatively small number of Black South Africans migrated to the federation for any purposes, including work or school, is reflected in an August 1954 letter to *Parade*'s editor by a South African reader, Jane Moshaapalo, who recounts her somewhat unusual trip to Southern Rhodesia. She writes, "It is not often that one hears of a young lady or gentleman, born and bred in the Union of South Africa, crossing the Limpopo with its greyish waters, to further her or his studies in Southern Rhodesia" (21).

132. "The African in the Union Through the Eyes of a Southern Rhodesian," *African Parade*, February 1954, 17.

133. "Between You and Me," *African Parade*, April 1954, 5.

134. Zizi, "Man with Missing Fingers," *African Parade*, November 1953, 10.

135. Zizi, "Man with Missing Fingers," *African Parade*, January 1954, 14.

136. Kynoch, "Urban Violence in Colonial Africa," 643n88.

137. Zizi, "Man with Missing Fingers," *African Parade*, February 1954, 14.

138. Zizi, "Man with Missing Fingers," *African Parade*, February 1954, 14.

139. Zizi, "Man with Missing Fingers," *African Parade*, March 1954, 14.

140. "An African Policeman," *African Parade*, March 1954, 11.

141. Morris, "Style, *Tsotsi*-Style, and *Tsotsitaal*," 86.

142. "The Man about Town," *African Parade*, August 1955, 11.

143. Editor, "Murder Stories," *African Parade*, July 1955, 13.

144. Chanda, "Death of the Stranger," *African Parade*, February 1961, 30; Chanda, "Death of the Stranger," *African Parade*, April 1961, 27.

145. Chanda, "Death of the Stranger," *African Parade*, February 1961, 31.

146. "Mrs. Kisosonkole," *African Parade*, August 1955, 9.

147. Chanda, "Death of the Stranger," *African Parade*, February 1961, 33.

148. Shonga and Zulu, *Matsotsi*, 4.

149. For another contemporary example, see Primorac, "At Home in the World?."

150. Makokha, "In the Spirit of Afropolitanism," 14.

CHAPTER 2

1. Steven Paas, *Online Dictionary of Chichewa (or Chinyanja/Cinyanja) with English*, s.v. "katakwe\a-," accessed October 14, 2023, https://translate.chichewadictionary.org.

2. Kadzitche has collected these stories in several volumes, including *Katakwe: M'dzina La Yesu* (*Katakwe: In Jesus's Name*) (2020), *Katakwe Kumudzi* (*Katakwe in the Village*) (2017), and *Katakwe Kutauni* (*Katakwe in Town*) (2010). For more on the Katakwe stories, see Lipenga, "Imagining the Malawian Urban Space in Lawrence Kadzitche's *Katakwe Kutauni*."

3. Kadzitche, "Mgodi Uvuta," 4.

4. Steven Paas, *Online Dictionary of Chichewa (or Chinyanja/Cinyanja) with English*, s.v. "hule\ma-," accessed October 14, 2023, https://translate.chichewadictionary.org.

5. Bond, *Against Global Apartheid*, 61, 63–64.

6. Machingaidze, "Agrarian Change from Above," 570.

7. Leslie James suggests that "The Owl" is an early example of the "flying newspaperman" character, who appeared in columns such as Tom Tinkle's Here, There, and Yonder in the *West African Pilot* (1938–1941) and the Roving Hobo in the *Comet* in the late 1940s. Through their fantastical travels, these figures commented on a changing Nigeria, British colonialism in Nigeria and beyond, and Black internationalism more broadly (James, "The Flying Newspapermen and the Time-Space of Late Colonial Nigeria").

8. Sandwith, "Well-Seasoned Talks," 106.

9. Dombo, *Private Print Media*, 27.

10. Vambe, *From Rhodesia to Zimbabwe*, 227.

11. For a comparison of the tale and the short story as forms, see Julien, "Of Traditional Tales and Short Stories in African Literature."

12. Harper, *Not So Simple*, 23–24, 40–41; Smethurst, "Adventures of a Social Poet," 54.

13. Moore, "Local Color, Global 'Color,'" 60. Recent scholarly work has explored the connection between Hughes and South Africa's *Drum* generation of writers. See Graham, *Cultural Entanglements*; and Robolin, *Grounds of Engagement*.

14. Shringarpure, *Cold War Assemblages*, 150–51.

15. Moretti, *Distant Reading*, 50; Damrosch, *What Is World Literature?*, 4. Moretti turns an observation made by Fredric Jameson into a "law of literary evolution" that he tests further, ultimately arguing that such evolution occurs as a compromise between "foreign form, local material—and local form," or more specifically, "foreign plot, local characters, and then local narrative voice" (*Distant Reading*, 57).

16. On the township as a site of "spatial control," see Barnard, *Apartheid and Beyond*, 6–7.

17. Vambe, *From Rhodesia to Zimbabwe*, 195.

18. Dlamini, *Native Nostalgia*, 153–54.

19. Newell, "Local Cosmopolitans in Colonial West Africa," 114.

20. Dlamini, *Native Nostalgia*, 153, 147, 8.

21. Baucom, "Township Modernism," 241–42.

22. Baucom, "Township Modernism," 237.

23. Baucom, "Township Modernism," 241–42.

24. Armah quoted in Baucom, "Township Modernism," 236.

25. See Robotham on the limitations of Paul Gilroy's "planetary humanism" to address racial inequality ("Cosmopolitanism and Planetary Humanism," 577).

26. *Space Is the Place*, directed by John Coney. Sun Ra composed the music for the film, which he also co-wrote.

27. Sexton, "Social Life of Social Death," 28.

28. Fawaz, "Space, That Bottomless Pit," 1104.

29. See Blum, *Other Modernism*, 2.

30. Barnes, "'To Raise a Hornet's Nest,'" 42–43.

31. Hughes, "Why and Wherefore."

32. Hughes, quoted in Harper, *Not So Simple*, 41.

33. Hughes, "Why and Wherefore."

34. However, as Harper suggests, there are hints of Simple in the first Here to Yonder column in the figures of the truck driver and older man (*Not So Simple*, 44.)

35. Harper, *Not So Simple*, 40.

36. Hughes, "Conversation at Midnight."

37. Hughes, "God, War, and Swing."

38. Rampersad, *Life of Langston Hughes*, 2: 62–64.

39. Greenberg, "Politics of Disorder," 424–25.

40. Greenberg, "Politics of Disorder," 422.

41. Hughes, "Simple Looks for Justice."

42. Hughes, "Simple Looks for Justice."

43. See Jackson Jr. for a contemporary account of why "Harlem is not Manhattan" (*Harlemworld*, 1).

44. Matlin, "'Something Apart, Yet an Integral Part,'" 501.

45. Matlin, "'Something Apart, Yet an Integral Part,'" 509.

46. Matlin, "'Something Apart, Yet an Integral Part,'" 502.

47. Hughes, "Simple and Harlem."

48. Greenberg, "Politics of Disorder," 424.

49. For an extended discussion of this phrase, see Matlin, "'Something Apart, Yet an Integral Part,'" 504–5.

50. Hughes, "Toast to Harlem," 31, 33.
51. Hughes, "Simple and Harlem."
52. Hughes, "Simple Rocks a Rocket."
53. Hughes, "Simple Rocks a Rocket."
54. Hughes, "Feet Live Their Own Life," 4. The earlier column, "Simple Says with Four Feet He Could Have Stood in More Places," has a weaker connection between sitting to drink and sitting to rest and think (*Chicago Defender*, July 9, 1944, 6).
55. Hughes, "High Bed," 108. "High Bed" was formed out of two columns, "Simple Rocks a Rocket," *Chicago Defender*, January 24, 1948, 14, and "Simple in the Hospital," *Chicago Defender*, December 9, 1944, 12.
56. Williams, "Physics Made Simple," 133.
57. Graham and Walters, *Langston Hughes and the South African Drum Generation*.
58. Matthews, "South African Judiciary and the Security System," 199.
59. Smethurst, "Adventures of a Social Poet," 61.
60. Editor, "Landladies!" *Africa!*, April 1954, 20.
61. "Your Author," *Africa!*, April 1954, 21.
62. Editor, "Ball of String!" *Africa!*, September 1954, 41.
63. "Your Author," *Africa!*, April 1954, 21.
64. "Your Author," *Africa!*, April 1954, 21, my emphasis.
65. Beginning with "Landladies!" the editors published more stories about women than on any other topic, including: "Jealousy!" (August 1954), "After Hours!" (October 1954), "Vacation!" (December 1954), "Explain That to Me!" (January 1955), "Baltimore Womens!" (February 1955), "Simply Heavenly!" (March 1955), "Morals Is Her Middle Name!" (April 1955), and "On the Warpath!" (July 1955).
66. Ostrom, *Langston Hughes*, 36; Harper, *Not So Simple*, 158.
67. Hughes, quoted in Graham and Walters, *Langston Hughes and the South African Drum Generation*, 96.
68. Driver, "Drum Magazine (1951–59) and the Spatial Configurations of Gender," 228–29.
69. Driver, "Drum Magazine (1951–59) and the Spatial Configurations of Gender," 229.
70. Hughes, "Landladies!," 20.
71. Hughes, "Landladies!," 20.
72. Nosy, "Low Down: On Rooms to Let." The article echoes Simple's concerns about housing conditions but presents an even direr picture of some landlords' unreasonableness, including one landlord who limited the amount of water tenants were allowed to drink.
73. Hughes, "Explain That to Me!," 45, 47. The excised portion reads: "Her white folks was crazy about Mabel because she never missed being at work in time to cook breakfast for their children and get them off to school. Then she got breakfast for the old man to get him down to the office. Then she made toast and coffee for the Madam about ten. By that time she had been at work a long time. And she worked hard" (Hughes, "Explain That to Me," *Simple Takes a Wife*, 25).

74. Hughes, "Banquet in Honor!," 38.

75. Hughes, "Matter for a Book!," 59.

76. Whether Motsisi's column was pure fiction has frequently been debated. Zander has emphasized its blend of real township personages and incidents with fictional elements. Most studies of *Drum* give brief mention to Motsisi's column, and several offer more detailed accounts. See Dodson, "Four Modes of Drum"; Rabkin, "Drum Magazine (1951–1961)"; Zander, *Fact-Fiction-"Faction"*; and Manus, *Emerging Traditions*.

77. Casey Motsisi to Langston Hughes, 25 March 1961, Langston Hughes Papers, James Weldon Johnson Collection in the Yale Collection of American Literature, Beinecke Rare Book and Manuscript Library, Yale University.

78. Gopnik, "Talk It Up."

79. Harper, *Not So Simple*, 174.

80. Dodson, "Four Modes of Drum," 324.

81. See La Hausse, *Brewers, Beerhalls and Boycotts*.

82. Harper describes how Hughes's publisher insisted on substantial rewrites to the columns when they were published in book form, including a clearer dichotomy between the voices of Simple and the foil and reducing the foil's prominence in the narrative (*Not So Simple*, 40).

83. Lindfors, "Post-War Literature in English by African Writers from South Africa," 56.

84. Manus, *Emerging Traditions*, 93.

85. Motsisi's original column did not include these titles. Mutloatse seems to have given these names to the columns based on each one's central character.

86. Motsisi, "Kid Playboy," 27.

87. Motsisi, "Mattress," 17.

88. Motsisi, "Kid Newspapers," 33.

89. Motsisi, "Kid Newspapers," 34.

90. Motsisi, "Confessions of an Illicit Boozer," 66.

91. There are, however, very brief mentions of the South African political landscape in On the Beat, including the Treason Trial (February 1960), British prime minister Harold Macmillan's visit (March 1960), the emergency regulations (June 1960), and the Liquor Act (June 1962). Notably, these columns were not chosen for the *Casey & Co.* anthology.

92. Motsisi, On the Beat, *Drum*, April 1958, 69.

93. Fawaz, "Space, That Bottomless Pit," 1103–4.

94. "Drum on the Moon!" *Drum*, June 1954, 10–11.

95. Motsisi, On the Beat, *Drum*, February 1960, 51.

96. Motsisi, On the Beat, *Drum*, May 1960, 51.

97. Smethurst, "Adventures of a Social Poet," 56.

98. "Will There Be a US of Africa?" *Drum*, January 1959, 20.

99. Motsisi, On the Beat, *Drum*, May 1958, 51; Motsisi, "Kid Malalapipe," 44.

100. Unlike On the Beat, which quickly developed a regular format, Makokoba Park Talk and Bits and Pieces from Harare went through several iterations. Early installments of Bits and Pieces from Harare are often more similar in structure to Can Themba's *Drum* column Talk O' the Town in that they

include several subfeatures and a "footnote" (instead of Themba's playful "tailpiece") at the end.

101. Dlamanzi, Makokoba Park Talk, *African Parade*, July 1959, 20.

102. Anderson describes the cosmograph as "a series of supraterrestrial heavens and subterrestrial hells wedged in the visible world along a single vertical axis. It was useless for any journey save that in search of merit and salvation" (*Imagined Communities*, 174–75).

103. West, *Rise of an African Middle Class*, 214.

104. Somerville, "Central African Federation," 391; Butler, "Britain, the United States, and the Demise of the Central African Federation," 132.

105. Roscoe, *Columbia Guide*, 26; "Discrimination: Part 2," *African Parade*, December 1956, 16–17.

106. Dombo, *Private Print Media*, 34.

107. Vambe, *From Rhodesia to Zimbabwe*, 229.

108. Vambe, *From Rhodesia to Zimbabwe*, 142.

109. Vambe, *From Rhodesia to Zimbabwe*, 146; West, *Rise of an African Middle Class*, 102, 107.

110. Vambe, *From Rhodesia to Zimbabwe*, 151.

111. Raftopoulos, "Nationalism and Labour in Salisbury 1953–1965," 82–85.

112. Vambe, *From Rhodesia to Zimbabwe*, 177. While Africans could not own homes in Harare, the government eventually built houses that could be leased for ninety-nine years in New Highfield in Salisbury and Mpopoma in Bulawayo. These homes became available in 1956 (West, *Rise of an African Middle Class*, 113).

113. Vambe, *From Rhodesia to Zimbabwe*, 143.

114. What appears to be a trial version of the column by "A Correspondent" appeared in September 1958.

115. Vambe, *From Rhodesia to Zimbabwe*, 235.

116. Saidi, Bits and Pieces from Harare, *African Parade*, December 1958, 18.

117. Vambe, *From Rhodesia to Zimbabwe*, 144. My emphasis.

118. Saidi, Bits and Pieces from Harare, *African Parade*, December 1958, 71. The column refers to the Foreign Migratory Labour Act of 1958, which was part of the Southern Rhodesian government's attempt to limit foreign workers in Salisbury, largely, it seems, to deal with the unemployment of workers from Southern Rhodesia. See Raftopoulos, "Nationalism and Labour in Salisbury 1953–1965," 87.

119. Ranger, *Bulawayo Burning*, 208.

120. Somerville, "Central African Federation," 393.

121. Saidi, Bits and Pieces from Harare, *African Parade*, March 1959, 59.

122. Saidi, Bits and Pieces from Harare, *African Parade*, April 1959, 34.

123. Vambe, *From Rhodesia to Zimbabwe*, 216.

124. Saidi, Bits and Pieces from Harare, *African Parade*, March 1959, 59.

125. Saidi, Bits and Pieces from Harare, *African Parade*, April 1959, 34.

126. Saidi, Bits and Pieces from Harare, *African Parade*, April 1960, 84.

127. Saidi, Bits and Pieces from Harare, *African Parade*, November 1959, 24.

128. Saidi, Bits and Pieces from Harare, *African Parade*, March 1960, 85.

129. Butler, "Britain, the United States, and the Demise of the Central African Federation," 132.

130. Raftopoulos, "Nationalism and Labour in Salisbury 1953–1965," 90.

131. Saidi, Bits and Pieces from Harare, *African Parade*, June 1960, 21.

132. Saidi, Bits and Pieces from Harare, *African Parade*, March 1960, 85. New Highfield was where more recently arrived, mostly Southern Rhodesian residents and leaseholders lived, although it, too, came to have slum-like conditions. It was also a center for nationalist activity (West, *The Rise of an African Middle Class*, 115).

133. Saidi, Bits and Pieces from Harare, *African Parade*, February 1960, 31, 79.

134. Dlamanzi, Makokoba Park Talk, *African Parade*, January 1959, 9.

135. Samkange belonged to Zimbabwe's first generation of writers and was a "historian, journalist, businessman, educationist, political activist" who published a history of Southern Rhodesia, the *Origins of Rhodesia*, in 1968 (Veit-Wild, *Teachers, Preachers, Non-Believers*, 17).

136. Dlamanzi, Makokoba Park Talk, *African Parade*, March 1959, 14.

137. Ranger, *Bulawayo Burning*, 2.

138. Ranger, *Bulawayo Burning*, 3.

139. Ranger, *Bulawayo Burning*, 3.

140. See Yoshikuni, "Notes on the Influence of Town-Country Relations on African Urban History, before 1957," 119, and Stern, "How Movies Move," 203.

141. Ranger, *Bulawayo Burning*, 9.

142. Ranger, *Bulawayo Burning*, 9.

143. Ranger, *Bulawayo Burning*, 174–75.

144. Ranger, *Bulawayo Burning*, 186.

145. Ranger, *Bulawayo Burning*, 174.

146. Ngcebetsha quoted in Ranger, *Bulawayo Burning*, 175.

147. Motsisi, "Kid Hangover," 16.

148. Dlamanzi, Makokoba Park Talk, *African Parade*, March 1959, 14, 69. The latter term, "stalk fella," is a transliteration of "stokvel"—the name of community savings schemes in southern Africa, which were often funded through these types of parties.

149. Dlamanzi, Makokoba Park Talk, *African Parade*, March 1959, 14.

150. Hughes, "House-Rent Parties Returning; Simple Sees Depression Coming," 11.

151. Dlamanzi, Makokoba Park Talk, *African Parade*, June 1959, 34.

152. Dlamanzi, Makokoba Park Talk, *African Parade*, April 1959, 85.

153. Dlamanzi, Makokoba Park Talk, *African Parade*, July 1959, 15.

154. Alexander, "'Hooligans, Spivs and Loafers'?" 349–50.

155. Ranger, *Bulawayo Burning*, 221–40.

156. Ranger, *Bulawayo Burning*, 234.

157. Dlamanzi, Makokoba Park Talk, *African Parade*, April 1960, 94.

158. Ranger, *Bulawayo Burning*, 220.

159. Dlamanzi, Makokoba Park Talk, *African Parade*, October 1960, 28, 32.

160. Saidi, Bits and Pieces from Harare, *African Parade*, July 1959, 63.

161. Saidi, Bits and Pieces from Harare, *African Parade*, September 1959, 28.

162. Saidi, Bits and Pieces from Harare, *African Parade*, May 1962, 43.

163. Saidi, Bits and Pieces from Harare, *African Parade*, April 1961, 43.

164. Vambe, *From Rhodesia to Zimbabwe*, 208.

165. Butler, "Britain, the United States, and the Demise of the Central African Federation," 140.

166. "Parade," *African Parade*, January 1957, 5.

167. Saidi, Bits and Pieces from Harare, *African Parade*, March 1961, 20.

168. Saidi, Bits and Pieces from Harare, *African Parade*, October 1960, 68.

169. West, *Rise of an African Middle Class*, 220.

170. Saidi, Bits and Pieces from Harare, *African Parade*, January 1962, 51.

171. West, *Rise of an African Middle Class*, 227.

172. Saidi, "How a Column Can Change Your Life."

173. Saidi, "How a Column Can Change Your Life."

174. Saidi, Lusaka after Dark, *Central African Mail*, September 14, 1963, 19.

175. Miller, "Reinvention and Globalization in Hughes's Stories," 73. While Miller is describing Hughes's work of the 1920s and '30s, this idea also applies to the Simple stories.

176. Fanon, *Wretched of the Earth*, 156.

177. Saidi, "Zimpapers."

178. Saidi, "Nearly Killed in Combat."

179. Saidi, Lusaka after Dark, *Central African Mail*, January 31, 1964, 17.

180. Saidi, Lusaka after Dark, *Central African Mail*, September 7, 1963, 19.

181. Saidi, Lusaka after Dark, *Central African Mail*, November 8, 1963, 17.

182. Hansen, *Keeping House in Lusaka*, 1.

183. Saidi, "Copperbelt Capers," *Central African Mail*, October 25, 1963, 19.

184. Larmer, "Nation-Making at the Border," 152. For an extended treatment of the relationship between localism and cosmopolitanism on the Copperbelt, see Ferguson, *Expectations of Modernity*.

185. Hansen, *Keeping House in Lusaka*, 25.

186. Saidi, "Copperbelt Capers," 19.

187. Larmer, "Nation-Making at the Border," 154–55.

188. Saidi, Lusaka after Dark, *Central African Mail*, January 3, 1964, 15.

189. Saidi, Lusaka after Dark, *Central African Mail*, November 15, 1963, 21.

190. Larmer, "Nation-Making at the Border," 154.

191. Milner-Thornton, "Absent White Fathers," 195.

192. Saidi, Lusaka after Dark, *Central African Mail*, November 22, 1963, 21. Coloured Zambians were marginalized in white society and often cut off from Black society, a segregation they contributed to in some degree by asking the colonial government for separate housing in the 1950s. See Milner-Thornton, "Absent White Fathers," 201–2.

193. Kaunda, *Humanism in Zambia*, 23.

194. See Shaw, "Zambia."

195. Saidi, Lusaka after Dark, *Central African Mail*, August 24, 1963, 18. An article on Youlou's downfall, "Youlou: Short Reign of the Short Man" by Nora Beloff, appears in the same issue (*Central African Mail*, August 24, 1963, 9).

196. Newell, "Local Cosmopolitans in Colonial West Africa," 111.
197. Saidi, Lusaka after Dark, *Central African Mail*, October 18, 1963, 17.
198. Saidi, Lusaka after Dark, *Central African Mail*, August 24, 1963, 18.
199. Saidi, Lusaka after Dark, *Central African Mail*, August 24, 1963, 18.
200. Saidi, "This Life," *Central African Mail*, May 15, 1964, 21.
201. Saidi, Lusaka after Dark, *Central African Mail*, 14 September 14, 1963, 19.
202. Harper, *Not So Simple*, 116.

CHAPTER 3

1. Ikheloa, "#Caineprize—The Thirteenth Caine Prize Shortlist: Love on Trial."
2. Stanley Kenani, "Caine Prize Workshop," July 4, 2012, King's College, Anatomy Museum, London. At the same workshop, and in opposition to many other reviewers, Ranka Primorac argued that the inclusion of Kenani's story on the Caine Prize short list suggested that the prize had in fact matured since its beginnings in 2001. Primorac pointed to the way that Kenani's story speaks to multiple audiences simultaneously: to Malawian audiences who are used to reading moralistic stories in national newspapers as well as to international readers.
3. Kenani, Facebook message to author, October 16, 2018.
4. Felix Mponda, "Malawi Gays Pick Up the Baton to Fight for Rights," *Malawi News*, January 2–8, 2010, 2–3. On the cover of the *Malawi News*'s Chichewa supplement, *Tikambe*, Steve Gulumba interviewed people about their reactions to the story ("Mphongo Ziwiri Zikwatirana" ("Two Males Marry"), *Malawi News*, Jan. 2–8, 2010). A profile on the couple also appeared on the front page of the *Sunday Times* (January 3, 2010). A follow-up article from March covered Amnesty International's "adoption" of the couple, who were eventually pardoned by Malawi's president, Bingu wa Mutharika, after pressure from the United States and UK (Dickson Kashoti, "Amnesty International Adopts Alleged Gay Couple," *Malawi News*, March 20–26, 2010, 6).
5. Kenani, "On the Gay Pardon," *Malawi News*, June 5–11, 2010, 2.
6. Kenani, "Love on Trial," 63.
7. Bady, "Damning with Faint Prize."
8. Kenani, "Love on Trial," 65.
9. Kenani, "On the Gay Pardon," 2.
10. Casanova, *World Republic of Letters*, 43.
11. Kenani, Facebook message to author, October 16, 2018.
12. Chimombo, quoted in Lee, "Malawian Literature after Banda and in the Age of AIDS," 34.
13. Barton, *Press of Africa*, 155.
14. Joyah, "Truth about Chapweteka's Fiction," 15.
15. Silvey, "Geographies of Gender and Migration," 67.
16. While numerous studies have considered Malawian poetry—asking in particular how its opaque language made it possible to conceal anti-government rhetoric (Vail and White, *Power and the Praise Poem*)—and even newspaper

poetry (Chalamanda, "'Pressing Literary Expressions'"), no work has yet been done on the short fiction in the *Malawi News*.

17. Samuelson, "'Home and the World,'" 32. Among the significant works on this topic see Boehmer, "Stories of Women and Mothers"; McClintock, *Imperial Leather*; Ogundipe-Leslie, *Re-Creating Ourselves*; and Stratton, *Contemporary African Literature and the Politics of Gender*.

18. Andrade, *Nation Writ Small*, 1.

19. On the relationship between Banda's appropriation of Chewa traditions and the representation of women in several well-known Malawian novels, see Chirambo, "'All Men Do Is Love Love,'" 16, 24, 36–37.

20. Tamale, "Gender Trauma in Africa," 52.

21. Kings M. Phiri, "Some Changes," 258. See also Semu, "Kamuzu's Mbumba," 81.

22. Kings M. Phiri, "Some Changes," 272.

23. Semu, "Kamuzu's Mbumba," 82.

24. Gilbert, "'Race,' Space, and Power," 596.

25. "Nkhoswe Number One Gives Mbumba Zeal," *Malawi News*, Convention Supplement, September 17–23, 1988.

26. Gilman, *Dance of Politics*, 5.

27. Gilman, "Traditionalization of Women's Dancing," 45.

28. Mphande, "Dr. Hastings Kamuzu Banda and the Malawi Writers Group," 88.

29. Gilman, "Traditionalization of Women's Dancing," 45.

30. Power, *Political Culture and Nationalism in Malawi*, 192, 204.

31. Spencer, Ligaga, and Musila, "Gender and Popular Imaginaries in Africa," 4–5.

32. Bush, "'Mesdames, il faut lire!,'" 226.

33. Similarly, Newell argues that authors use stock female characters not because they lack artistic creativity but in order "to create ethical debates among their readers" ("Introduction," 6).

34. In her article on "newspaper poetry" in the *Malawi News*, Chalamanda argues that "newspaper literature" constitutes "a specifically local, participatory literary genre which goes some way to dissolving the formal binary distinction between newspaper reader and newspaper writer" ("'Pressing Literary Expressions,'" 380). Specifically, she suggests that newspaper poetry is a "genre of reception" that engages with, reproduces, and reinterprets aspects of the larger form of which it is a part.

35. Tamale, "Gender Trauma in Africa," 53.

36. Jaji, *Africa in Stereo*, 116–17.

37. See, for example, the front page of the *Malawi News* from December 1, 1964.

38. Lwanda, "Paper Tigers," 4.

39. Mphande, "Dr. Hastings Kamuzu Banda and the Malawi Writers Group," 81.

40. Vail and White, *Power and the Praise Poem*, 56.

41. Kamwendo was arrested numerous times. Kamwendo in conversation with author, August 6, 2018.

42. Msowoya, "Writing Is a Contribution to Advancement of Our Country," 7. Although it did not publish short fiction before this, the newspaper did occasionally include humorous columns, such as Our Man, Mister Squeeze and Ndakulapa nkulinga utayenda naye.

43. Msowoya, "Writing Is a Contribution to Advancement of our Country"; Mapala, "Kodi mtsikanayo anali ku khitchini?," 4.

44. "Tilembereni makalata ambiri," *Malawi News*, October 10, 1972, 4.

45. Chirwa, "Malawian Government and South African Labour Recruiters," 623.

46. Banda was adept at using cultural resources such as the oral tradition to his benefit (Chirambo, "Protesting Politics of 'Death and Darkness' in Malawi," 207).

47. "Mpikisano wolemba nkhani m'Chichewa," *Malawi News*, January 12, 1973, 6.

48. The first-prize winner of the competition takes a somewhat different tack, one that we might read as delegitimizing aspects of the oral traditiion that did not serve Banda's agenda and might even be used to critique it. In a story that is a mix of reportage and oral history, F. D. Tulumbwa recounts the myth of the destructive Napolo river, which many Malawians believe is a large snake, and encourages readers to question these "rumors" given that no one has ever seen the snake and experts say the legend is false. Nevertheless, the myth has persisted and was used by the writer Steve Chimombo to critique Banda's destructiveness more than a decade later (Chirambo, "Protesting Politics of 'Death and Darkness' in Malawi," 210).

49. Chidzulo, "Chikondi sachita choumiliza," 4.

50. Gilman suggests that using tradition as a means of oppression requires that people perceive these practices as "static and superorganic artifacts that *should* not be altered and that *should* be transmitted over time" (2004, 35). In other words, "tradition" must be understood in light of Terence Ranger's and Eric Hobsbawm's observation that all traditions are "invented" by those who stand to benefit from certain cultural formations (*The Invention of Tradition*).

51. Kings M. Phiri, "Some Changes," 260, 273.

52. Chidzulo, "Chikondi sachita choumiliza," 4.

53. See Women's Page, *Malawi News*, June 1, 1974, 5; Women's Page, *Malawi News*, June 22, 1974, 5; and Women's Page, *Malawi News*, August 31, 1974, 13.

54. Banda, quoted in Power, *Political Culture and Nationalism in Malawi*, 145.

55. Semu, "Kamuzu's Mbumba," 83.

56. Mama, "Feminism or Femocracy?," 41.

57. Semu, "Kamuzu's Mbumba," 84.

58. Tamale, "Gender Trauma in Africa," 54.

59. "Benefits of Homecraft Classes Explained by Junior Minister," *Malawi News*, June 22, 1973, 5.

60. "Women Asked to Act as Eyes and Ears for Nkhoswe No. 1," *Malawi News*, June 1, 1974, 5.

61. "Great Day for Mothers," *Malawi News*, October 17, 1972, 2.

62. "South African Women Take Leave of Ngwazi," *Malawi News*, October 5, 1972, 1.

63. Vail and White, "Of Chameleons," 35.

64. Kamwendo, "A Nation Indivisible," *Malawi News*, July 6, 1980, 7. In the article, Kamwendo rails against the international media for misrepresenting Malawi's postindependence success.

65. See Lipande, "To Kill or Not to Kill Is the Question."

66. The figure of the wife features prominently in "Riches through Murder Foiled" by Stan Nyirongo, "The Mysterious Man That Never Was" by J. W. Kalua, "He Was Not among Them" by Bob Chayenda, "Dirika Gets Wages of Disobeying" by D. F. Grey Njakwa, and "A Story by a Malawian Writer" by Ester Solomoni. Marriage is a key theme in these stories: "Where Did We Go Wrong?" by Themba Mbalazo, "Rise and Fall of a Pretty Girl" by Bertrand Salima, "The Wedding That Never Was" by Elliot Phwitiko, and "The Wedding That Flopped" by Angeline Dudu Kalizga. Only Mbalazo's and Kalizga's stories are told from a female perspective.

67. Kaspin, "Chewa Cosmology of the Body," 571. In Nyirongo's "Riches through Murder Foiled," Joseph Phiri's wife wakes him up after a long night of drinking, shouting at him to go work in the fields. She begins to weep and threatens to leave him for another man, which finally prompts Joseph to rise and tell her, "I will do something for you, I mean, for the house."

68. See Edward Phiri's ". . . Almost Home . . . ," Nyirongo's "In Riches through Murder Foiled," and Kalua's "The Mysterious Man That Never Was."

69. Chirwa, "Malawian Government and South African Labour Recruiters," 629.

70. Mosiya, "Why Are Men Driven into Crime," 7.

71. Chirwa, "Malawian Government and South African Labour Recruiters," 628. Englund, "Village in the City," 138.

72. Phwitiko, "Wedding That Never Was."

73. Njakwa, "Dirika Gets Wages of Disobeying," 10.

74. Milanzi, "Enmity in a Village Because of Education," 7.

75. Milanzi, "Enmity in a Village Because of Education," 7.

76. In 1972, Banda introduced a quota system for secondary schools that reserved a third of the spaces for girls, but relatively little else was done to promote girls' education. Swainson, Bendera, and Kadzamira, *Promoting Girls' Education in Africa*, 37.

77. "Journey's End" by Cuthbert Khunga, which appeared in the *Malawi News* several years later, features a woman who dies on her journey home to Malawi from England, where she was completing her medical degree. The story gives voice to the villagers' conflicting views on women's education, including pride in her accomplishments and even satisfaction with her death, which for some signifies that "[b]lack magic had triumphed over the whiteman's wonders" (*Malawi News*, May 6, 1979, 18).

78. Kalizga, "Wedding That Flopped," 6.

79. During this period, which coincided with the end of Albert Muwalo's time as the MCP's secretary-general, "journalists faced almost absolute censor-

ship" as a result of "Muwalo and other MCP barons' own agendas competing with those of Dr. Banda" (Lwanda, "Paper Tigers," 6).

80. Lwanda, "Paper Tigers," 6.

81. Kamwendo, in conversation with author, August 6, 2018.

82. Kamwendo, "Yaya: Part 1," *Malawi News*, October 2, 1977, 22.

83. Kamwendo, in conversation with author, August 6, 2018.

84. Mwiyeriwa, "Printing Presses and Publishing in Malawi," 44.

85. *Star Stories* was born out of an entertainment magazine, *Star*, which received more stories than it could print. Many of the stories in the first issue were attributed to female authors and were likely copied from other sources. This places the magazine firmly in the English periodical tradition, where in the eighteenth and nineteenth centuries "[w]ell over half of these stories were plagiarized, or adapted or translated without payment" (Orel, *The Victorian Short Story*, 6). By *Star Stories*' second and particularly its third issue, the layout, form, and content of its stories had all changed substantially to highlight locally produced, mostly male-authored stories with Malawian settings.

86. Kamwendo, "Yaya: Part 5," *Malawi News*, October 30, 1977, 22.

87. "Blessings Start from Mothers," *Malawi News*, October 16–22, 1982, 7.

88. Kamwendo, "Yaya: Part 5," 22.

89. Kamwendo, "Yaya: Part 6," *Malawi News*, November 6, 1977, 22.

90. Lwanda, *Kamuzu Banda of Malawi*, 91.

91. Semu, "Kamuzu's Mbumba," 83–84. Lwanda, however, recounts that Kadzamira and her uncle, John Tembo, wielded a great deal of power behind the scenes. See Lwanda, *Kamuzu Banda of Malawi*, 91–99.

92. Kamwendo, "Yaya: Part 2," *Malawi News*, October 9, 1977, 22.

93. Kamwendo, "Yaya: Part 3," *Malawi News*, October 16, 1977, 22.

94. Kamwendo, "Yaya: Part 9," *Malawi News*, November 27, 1977, 28.

95. Kamwendo, "Yaya: Part 8," *Malawi News*, November 20, 1977, 22.

96. Kamwendo, "Yaya: Part 9," 28.

97. Kamwendo, "Yaya: Part 9," 28.

98. Kamwendo, "Yaya: Part 9," 30.

99. Semu, "Kamuzu's Mbumba," 84.

100. Kamwendo, "Yaya: Part 1," 22.

101. Kamwendo, "Yaya: Part 9," 30.

102. Kamwendo, "Yaya: Part 9," 30.

103. Levine, in contrast, argues that when the bounded forms of the home and the nation intersect, "the formal equivalence of the two containing shapes itself undermines rather than reinforces the social power of gendered spheres" (*Forms*, 44).

104. Kalitera, "Criticism of Yaya," *Malawi News*, December 25, 1977, 22.

105. Joyah, "Truth about Chapweteka's Fiction," 16.

106. Kamkondo, "Editorial," 1.

107. Kalitera, "Criticism of Yaya," 22.

108. Muvala, quoted in Chimombo, *Malawian Oral Literature*, 64.

109. Chimombo, *Malawian Oral Literature*, 65.

110. Kalitera, "Criticism of Yaya," 22.

111. Kalitera, "Face Value," *Malawi News*, December 4, 1977, 22.

112. Kalitera, "Face Value: Conclusion," *Malawi News*, December 11, 1977, 22.

113. Kalitera, "Face Value: Conclusion," 31.

114. Kaliwo, "Face Value: An Appraisal," *Malawi News*, December 25, 1977, 22.

115. Coppola, "African Writers Influence Society," 13.

116. Khunga, "Criterion for Writing Should Be Competence in the Language . . . ," *Malawi News*, June 24, 1979, 7.

117. Gunda, "Critique of 'The Jailbird,'" 12.

118. See *Muse* 36, 42, and 50 as well as the third issue of *Star Stories*.

119. Gunda, "Critique of 'The Jailbird,'" 12.

120. Gunda, "Joe's Replica," 12.

121. Mankhomwa, "Poking at Society," 12.

122. Hauya, "Imaginative Portrayal of Social Reality," 12.

123. Hauya, "Imaginative Portrayal of Social Reality," 12.

124. Mankhomwa, "Poking at Society," 12.

125. Semu, "Kamuzu's Mbumba," 85.

126. Ngulube, "Malawian Women in Literature," 19.

127. A number of these stories make references to the radio, an essential medium for reaching a broader section of Malawians, particularly in rural areas.

128. Zingani, "Booked for Reading Pleasure," 11; "Malawi Gives New Drive to Literacy," *Malawi News*, August 7–13, 1982, front page.

129. From 1984 to 1986, the short stories in the *Malawi News* were once again accompanied by pull quotes from the text, which were bolded in the center of the left page. Like the short stories from the previous few years without pull quotes, these stories were mostly linear and relied on the extracts from the text alongside the story's title and subheading to serve as teasers. The paper returned to incorporating flashbacks directly into stories more frequently in 1988.

130. Kuntambira, "Namaluzi," 6.

131. See Gondwe, "When the Spirits Beckoned"; Hanke, "Shut Up"; Kadzuwa, "The Mask Fell Off"; Mwalwanda, "It All Happened in Room 20."

132. Grace Phiri, "Sugar-Daddy's Style," 6–7; Ng'omba, "Prodigal Daughter," 6–7.

133. Grace Phiri, "Meet My Aunt," 6–7.

134. See Mlenga, "Bed no. 13," 6–7.

135. Ngoma, "Rumours . . . ," 6. The story is published under the author's maiden name, Ngoma.

136. Lungu, in conversation with author, January 30, 2012.

137. See Marmon, "Fallout from the Fallacious Accusation of Hastings Kamuzu Banda's West African Origins."

138. White, *Speaking with Vampires*, 62. White distinguishes between gossip and rumor, arguing, "The power of any particular piece of gossip lies in the importance of the contradictions it reveals; the power of a rumor lies in the contradictions it brings together and explains" (*Speaking with Vampires*, 70).

139. Wilson, "Of Love Potions and Witch Baskets," 150–51, 163.

140. "Editors [*sic*] Note" to Zumani Kondowe's "Gatehouse Man," 8.

141. Chikoti, in conversation with author, October 4, 2018.
142. Mindano, "Ndinali 'Che uje,'" 5.
143. Lwanda "Paper Tigers," 1, 13.
144. Kamwendo, in conversation with author, August 6, 2018.
145. "Women Will Vote," *Malawi News*, January 2–8, 1993, 4.
146. Nkhoma, "Chidamupha nchiyani mwamuna wakeyo?," 3. This story appears in the section "Phukusi la Moyo" ("The Parcel of Life"). The title refers to the proverb "The parcel of life is not kept by others," which Paas translates as "You have to take care of yourself."
147. From around 2010 until at least 2018, the *Malawi News* did not publish stories in Chichewa. Steve Gulumba, former editor of *Tikambe*, said this occurred when the total number of pages of *Tikambe* were reduced as a cost-saving measure. Gulumba, in conversation with author, August 9, 2018.
148. *Moni* magazine did include fiction in both English and Chichewa.
149. Mbaluko, "Interpretation of Chichewa Metaphors," 51, 44.
150. Singano, "Ukatambatamba kumayang'ana kum'mawa," 6.
151. Kholowa, "Masamu atsikana ena."
152. In a study of the metaphors Malawian youth use to describe sex, Undie, Crichton, and Zulu note that water is a recurring image. The phrases "hitting water" and "putting water on the beans" are both used to describe sexual intercourse ("Metaphors We Love By," 228, 230).
153. Kaspin, "Chewa Cosmology of the Body," 571.
154. I would like to thank Chidzero Nkumba for his help in explicating this cultural reference.
155. Kaspin, "Chewa Cosmology of the Body," 571.
156. Kaspin, "Chewa Cosmology of the Body," 569.
157. Mgunda, "This Is Man to Man," 3.
158. Ndala, "Wrestling with Fate," 8.
159. Mithi, in conversation with author, May 3, 2008.
160. Mithi, "Nambewe the Heroine," 7.
161. Shonga, in conversation with author, April 28, 2008.
162. See "Mother Dumps Newborn in Toilet, Arrested," which appeared in the *Nyasa Times* on August 22, 2009.
163. Mulera, "Mwana Wotayidwa M'chimbudzi," 56.
164. Sambalikagwa Mvona, former president of the Malawi Writers Union, ends the story on the previous line, which reads, "Mwayi and her mother, relatives and good Samaritan Lady Patsogolo led a very happy life ever after."
165. Chikoti, in conversation with author, January 29, 2012.
166. Namusanya, "While Neighbors Rake in Awards," 4.
167. Molande, quoted in Namusanya, "While Neighbors Rake in Awards," 5.

CHAPTER 4

1. "Chimurenga 16—The Chimurenga Chronicle (October 2011)," Chimurenga, September 3, 2020, https://chimurengachronic.co.za/chimurenga-16-the-chimurenga-chronicle-october-2011/Chimurenga-16-The-Chimurenga-Chronicle-October-2011-p109265996; *Chimurenga Chronic*, *Chimurenga* 16, 10.

2. Edjabe, "Diagnosing," 63.
3. See Robinson and Davidson, *Pulp Culture*, 33.
4. Eshun, "Further Considerations of Afrofuturism," 297.
5. Samatar, "Toward a Planetary History of Afrofuturism," 187.
6. Samatar, "Toward a Planetary History of Afrofuturism," 186.
7. Gomel, "Shapes of the Past and the Future," 335.
8. Okorafor, "Africanfuturism Defined"; Bosch Santana, "Review Essay."
9. Harvey, "Spacetime and the World," 14.
10. Jaji, *Africa in Stereo*, 3. Jaji is drawing on George Shepperson, "Pan-Africanism and 'Pan-Africanism.'"
11. Eshun, Gordon, and Pethick, "Navigating Pan-Africanisms," 84.
12. Falola and Essien, "Introduction," 1.
13. Krishnan, *Contingent Canons*, 88. On the necessity of understanding neoliberalism as a fluid concept, see Krishnan, 37.
14. Mbembe, "Afropolitanism," 26.
15. Magaziner and Jacobs, "End of South African Exceptionalism"; Klotz quoted in van der Westhuizen, "Popular Culture, Discourse and Divergent Identities," 50.
16. Malan quoted in Barber and Barratt, *South Africa's Foreign Policy*, 37.
17. Lazarus, "South African Ideology," 610–11.
18. Hardy quoted in Valley, *Chimurenga: Who No Know Go Know*.
19. Bernard quoted in Alix-Rose Cowie, "Young South Africa."
20. Magaziner and Jacobs, "End of South African Exceptionalism."
21. Matsinhe, "Africa's Fear of Itself," 295.
22. Neocosmos quoted in Matsinhe, "Africa's Fear of Itself," 298.
23. Krishnan, *Contingent Canons*, 81.
24. Jaji, *Africa in Stereo*, 9.
25. In *Critique of Black Reason*, Mbembe refers to a similar phenomenon as the "becoming black" of the world (5–6).
26. "About," Chimurenga, accessed October 14, 2023, chimurengachronic.co.za/about.
27. MacViban, "Q & A with Ntone Edjabe on Chimurenga, Fela, and Politics."
28. Fela's life, music, and activism are clear inspirations for *Chimurenga*, which is published by the Kalakuta Trust, named after Fela's commune, the Kalakuta Republic. The magazine also held a "Felasophy" session in Johannesburg in 2005 to launch *Chimurenga* 8, "We're All Nigerian!," which included live performances of Fela's music.
29. Edjabe, "Dour Rhetoric," 60.
30. Aterianus-Owanga, "A Pan-African Space in Cape Town?," 263.
31. Edjabe, "Dour Rhetoric," 60.
32. Edjabe, "Dour Rhetoric," 60.
33. Edjabe quoted in Fraser, "'Who No Know Go Know,'" 64.
34. Lazarus, "South African Ideology," 614–15, 617–18.
35. Edjabe, "Dour Rhetoric," 60.
36. "Chimurenganyana," Chimurenga, http://www.chimurenga.co.za/publications/chimurenganyana (page removed). Captured by the Internet Archive's Wayback Machine on July 4, 2017, https://web.archive.org/web/20170704151141/http://www.chimurenga.co.za/publications/chimurenganyana.

37. To distinguish the magazine from the larger Chimurenga collective, I italicize the name of the magazine.

38. "The Chimurenga Library," Chimurenga, accessed October 14, 2023, https://chimurengachronic.co.za/about-the-chimurenga-library/.

39. "Periodicals," Chimurenga Library, Chimurenga, accessed October 14, 2023, https://chimurengachronic.co.za/periodicals/.

40. "Third Text," *Chimurenga*, July 11, 2019, http://chimurengachronic.co.za/periodicals_posts/third-text/.

41. "About," Chimurenga Library, Chimurenga, http://chimurengalibrary.co.za/about (page removed). Captured by the Internet Archive's Wayback Machine on October 10, 2016, https://web.archive.org/web/20161010180439/http://chimurengalibrary.co.za/about.

42. "About," Chimurenga Library, Chimurenga.

43. Edjabe in conversation with Morris, "Performing Pan-Africanism," 283.

44. See Apter, *Pan-African Nation*; Aterianus-Owanga, "A Pan-African Space in Cape Town?"

45. "Panafest," Chimurenga, July 23, 2019, https://chimurengachronic.co.za/research_posts/panafest/.

46. Aterianus-Owanga, "A Pan-African Space in Cape Town?," 266.

47. "Panafest," Chimurenga.

48. Bearak and Dugger, "South Africans Take Out Rage on Immigrants."

49. *Chimurenga Chronic*, *Chimurenga* 16, 10.

50. Pillay et al., *Citizenship, Violence and Xenophobia in South Africa*, 9.

51. Matsinhe, "Africa's Fear of Itself," 306.

52. Matsinhe, "Africa's Fear of Itself," 306.

53. See Nixon, *Slow Violence*.

54. "Comics & Lower Frequencies," Chimurenga, July 23, 2019, https://chimurengachronic.co.za/research_posts/comics-lower-frequencies/.

55. The digital version is a PDF and otherwise identical to the printed version save a few hyperlinks.

56. Anderson, *Imagined Communities*, 35.

57. "About: The Chimurenga Chronic," Chimurenga, https://www.chimurenganewsroom.org.za/chimurenganewsroom/about/ (page removed). Captured by the Internet Archive's Wayback Machine on February 2, 2024, https://web.archive.org/web/20240202073720/https://www.chimurenganewsroom.org.za/chimurenganewsroom/about/.

58. Anderson, *Imagined Communities*, 33.

59. Anderson, *Imagined Communities*, 33.

60. "The Chronic," Chimurenga, accessed October 14, 2023, https://chimurengachronic.co.za/about-the-chronic/.

61. Kirschenbaum, *Mechanisms*, 36.

62. Gomel, "Shapes of the Past and the Future," 334.

63. *Chimurenga Chronic*, *Chimurenga* 16, 10.

64. Anderson, *Imagined Communities*, 35.

65. Mongia, "Interrogating Critiques of Methodological Nationalism," 201.

66. Shringarpure, *Cold War Assemblages*, 15.

67. Bakhtin, *Dialogic Imagination*, 100.

68. See *Africa Is a Country* (https://africasacountry.com), a well-known blog on African events, politics, arts, and media, and Chimamanda Adichie, "The Danger of a Single Story," TEDGlobal, October 2009, https://www.ted.com/talks/chimamanda_ngozi_adichie_the_danger_of_a_single_story/comments.

69. Anderson, *Imagined Communities*, 26; Shringarpure, *Cold War Assemblages*, 64.

70. "About: The Chimurenga Chronic," Chimurenga.

71. Gomel, "Shapes of the Past," 345.

72. Gomel, *Postmodern Science Fiction and Temporal Imagination*, 17.

73. Gomel, "Shapes of the Past," 335.

74. Gomel, *Postmodern Science Fiction and Temporal Imagination*, 17.

75. Eshun, "Further Considerations of Afrofuturism," 292, my emphasis.

76. "Whose House Is This?" *Chimurenga Chronic*, *Chimurenga* 16, 10.

77. *Space Is the Place*, directed by John Coney.

78. Sosibo, "Warm-Up," 2.

79. Sosibo, "Warm-Up," 3. Brackets in original.

80. Sosibo, "Warm-Up," 2.

81. Dlamini, "Death of Jacob Dlamini," 4.

82. "Chimurenga 16—The Chimurenga Chronicle (October 2011)," Chimurenga.

83. Dlamini, "Death of Jacob Dlamini," 4.

84. Dlamini, "Death of Jacob Dlamini," 4.

85. Agyemang, "Repeat of Ghana-Must-Go," 10.

86. Gappah, "How Kenya Exploded in My Heart," 11.

87. Gbaffou, "Spirit of May," 11.

88. "FESTAC at 45: FESTAC '77, A Mixtape by Chimurenga," Chimurenga Library, Media & Propaganda, Music, Chimurenga, July 29, 2020, https://chimurengachronic.co.za/festac-77-a-mixtape-by-chimurenga/.

89. "Mourir aux portes de l'Europe," 4.

90. Rekacewicz, "Les frontières les mieux gardées du monde," 5.

91. Novosseloff and Neisse, "Walls Make Us Strangers, Not Stronger," 5.

92. Edjabe, "Diagnosing," 63.

93. "The Chronic," *Chimurenga*.

94. Watermeyer, "Afrikaans English," 112.

95. Samatar, "Toward a Planetary History of Afrofuturism," 178.

96. Uzoatu, "Impossible Death of an African Crimebuster," 15.

97. Another later issue of the *Chronic* from June 2016 also reanimates the photocomic with a contemporary "Jabu Comes to Joburg" story that seeks to provincialize contemporary Johannesburg, poking fun at its pretentions to being the center of the continent.

98. Uzoatu, "Onitsha Republic," 30.

99. Newell, "Corresponding with the City," 21.

100. Newell, "Corresponding with the City," 16.

101. Coulon, "Onitsha Goes National," 304.

102. Adichie has been criticized for her comments on trans women; see Fischer, "Trans Responses to Adichie."

103. Bady, "Varieties of Blackness."

104. In response, Abubakar A. Ibrahim, one of her students who was shortlisted that year, tweeted, "So the best African fiction is in Chimamanda Adichie's inbox? I hail thee, queen-god mother. Go fuck yourself, Chimamanda. Nonsense!" (Ainehi Edoro, "African Literary Feud," *Brittle Paper* (blog), July 15, 2013, https://brittlepaper.com/2013/07/african-literary-feud-adichie-ibrahim/).

105. Enahoro's text was based on newspaper columns that the author published in the 1960s in the *Daily Times* and itself mimics Onitsha market literature (MacPhee, "226: Small Press Africa").

106. Ogbe, "*Americanah* and Other Definitions of Supple Citizenships," 11.

107. Ogbe, "*Americanah* and Other Definitions of Supple Citizenships," 9.

108. Samatar, "Toward a Planetary History of Afrofuturism," 178.

109. Kozain, "La Puissance de Werewere Liking," 41.

110. There is also a clear contrast between Adichie's consumerism—she is a product that sells—and Liking's pan African communalism.

111. Samatar, "Toward a Planetary History of Afrofuturism," 178.

112. Liking quoted in Kozain, "La Puissance de Werewere Liking," 43.

113. *Jungle Jim*'s website, http://www.junglejim.org/, appears to have last been updated in early 2018. Captured by the Wayback Machine on February 21, 2018, https://web.archive.org/web/20180221043126/http://www.junglejim.org/.

114. Backer, *Gripping Chapters,* 40.

115. Backer, *Gripping Chapters,* 40.

116. Bass quoted in Reid, "Q&A: (Pt 1) Jenna Bass."

117. As Lily Saint observes, the racial divisions in South African photocomics—wherein white characters featured in comics for whites, and Black characters in those for Blacks—were often undermined by the ways readers engaged with texts that weren't "meant" for them (*Black Cultural Life in South Africa*, 90–93).

118. Eshun, "Further Considerations of Afrofuturism," 297.

119. See Mamdani, *Citizen and Subject.*

120. "Submit to Jungle Jim!" *Jungle Jim,* http://www.junglejim.org/?cat=13 (website discontinued). Captured by the Wayback Machine on February 22, 2018, https://web.archive.org/web/20180222220241/http:/www.junglejim.org/?cat=13.

121. Most of these issues were published between 2011 and 2014. The magazine tapered off as Bass's, Bernard's, and Swingler's careers took off, and the last issue of the magazine that I can find, issue no. 27, was published in December 2016, although it is not available on Kindle. Swingler believes that another issue may have been published sometime in 2019.

122. Swingler, in conversation with author, October 15, 2019.

123. Swingler says that although he was the magazine's editor, this role was informal.

124. Bass quoted in Cowie, "Young South Africa."

125. Bass quoted in Reid, "Q&A: (Pt 2) Jenna Bass."

126. Bernard quoted in Cowie, "Young South Africa."

127. Charlton, "Jim in the Urban Jungle."

128. For its part, the *Chronic* sold issues of its inaugural issue via street hawkers and at Somali-owned shops in Cape Town (Krishnan, *Contingent Canons*, 89). Nevertheless, Edjabe admits that there is more work to do to connect

the magazine to its own locality (Aterianus-Owanga, "A Pan-African Space in Cape Town?" 264).

129. Yanes, "Graphic Imagery," 55.

130. Grost, "Blue Bolt."

131. These covers include *Swart Luiperd* ("The Black Leopard"), *Die Speuder* ("The Investigator"), *Beau: Die Ontembare* ("Beau: The Untamable"), and *Grensvegter* ("Border Fighter").

132. The cover of *Grensvegter*, or "Border Fighter," for example, depicts a white man in a khaki shirt, which, although unmarked, suggests the uniform of the South African Defense Force. This was Rocco de Wet, or "Rocco the Law," whose mission was to protect the (white) nation and its borders from "communist terrorists" (Marlin-Curiel, "Rave New World," 157).

133. Marlin-Curiel, "Rave New World," 157.

134. Bass quoted in Reid, "Q&A: (Pt 2) Jenna Bass."

135. *Jungle Jim*, "I Think Next Time We Get Asked," Facebook, February 11, 2013, https://www.facebook.com/junglejimmag/photos/a.185843501467319/516672321717767.

136. Bass quoted in Reid, "Q&A: (Pt 2) Jenna Bass."

137. Singh, "Lonesome Ballad of Easter Jack," loc. 4.

138. Singh, "Lonesome Ballad of Easter Jack," loc. 4.

139. Singh, "Lonesome Ballad of Easter Jack," loc. 8.

140. Singh, "Lonesome Ballad of Easter Jack," loc. 8.

141. Singh, "Lonesome Ballad of Easter Jack," loc. 26.

142. Singh, "Lonesome Ballad of Easter Jack," loc. 44.

143. Singh, "Lonesome Ballad of Easter Jack," loc. 63.

144. Houston, *Food Culture in the Caribbean*, 11.

145. Singh, "Lonesome Ballad of Easter Jack," loc. 63.

146. Kahora, "Authority Stealing," 18.

147. Ranka Primorac argues in her introduction to a special volume of the *Journal of Postcolonial Writing* on African thrillers that "detection is a form of reading" (2013, 71).

148. Mahmood, "Most Beautiful Place," loc. 162.

149. Mahmood, "Most Beautiful Place," loc. 185.

150. Mahmood, "Most Beautiful Place," loc. 162.

151. Mahmood, "Most Beautiful Place," loc. 162.

152. Mahmood, "Most Beautiful Place," loc. 185.

153. Mamdani, *From Citizen to Refugee*, 9

154. Kato, "45 Years of the Car Business in Uganda."

155. Mamdani, *From Citizen to Refugee*, 42–43.

156. Mwakikagile, *Ethnicity and National Identity in Uganda*, 46.

157. Mamdani, *From Citizen to Refugee*, 15.

158. Mamdani, *From Citizen to Refugee*, 15.

159. Mahmood, "Most Beautiful Place," loc. 208.

160. Speke, *Journal of the Discovery of the Source of the Nile*, 369.

161. Sengendo, "Urban Geography of Uganda," 152.

162. Mahmood, "Most Beautiful Place," loc. 208.

163. Mahmood, "Most Beautiful Place," loc. 229.

164. Mahmood, "Most Beautiful Place," loc. 229.
165. Landau quoted in Hofmeyr, "African History and Global Studies," 349.
166. Kahiu quoted in Beukes, "Is Science Fiction Coming to Africa?"
167. Musodza, "Here Be Cannibals," loc. 474, 444.
168. Musodza, "Here Be Cannibals," loc. 474.
169. Musodza, "Here Be Cannibals," loc. 499.
170. Musodza, "Here Be Cannibals," loc. 499.
171. Cochrane, "San Junction," 10–11.
172. It is notable that this story was published in late 2012. In February of that year, the Khoisan brought a case to the courts in South Africa arguing for the restitution of their lands, which were not protected under the Land Restitution Act of 1994. This act sought to return only lands that were confiscated after the Land Act of 1913, whereas Khoisan lands were appropriated centuries before then. See Van Wyk, "Indigenous Rights, Indigenous Epistemologies, and Language," 39.
173. Cochrane, "San Junction," 15.

CHAPTER 5

1. "About," Bula Buka Publishers, accessed October 11, 2023, http://bulabuka.co.za/about/.
2. Hayles, "Electronic Literature: What Is It?" *Electronic Literature Organization* 1, January 2, 2007, https://eliterature.org/pad/elp.html.
3. For a discussion of "blessers" (sugar daddies/mommies) and "blessees," "those who receive gifts and intangible rewards from 'blessers'" see Ligaga, *Women, Visibility and Morality in Kenyan Popular Media*, 100–101.
4. "About Mike," *Diary of a Zulu Girl*, accessed December 22, 2021, https://diaryofazulugirl.co.za/about/.
5. See de Lange, *Muzzled Muse*.
6. On the ways print is influenced by digital languages and genres as well as how it confers literary value on them, see Wallis, "How Books Matter," 40.
7. Bosch Santana, "From Nation to Network."
8. Yékú, "Deference to Paper," 14.
9. "A new book genre for South African books, 'Diary Chronicles'—Please support these local books," Bula Buka Publishers, May 6, 2019, http://bulabuka.co.za/a-new-book-genre-for-south-african-books-diary-chronicles-please-support-these-local-books/.
10. *Macmillan English Dictionary*, s.v. "Diary Chronicle," entry by Shackd, May 4, 2019, https://www.macmillandictionary.com/dictionary/british/diary-chronicle (site discontinued); Mcdsh. *Urban Dictionary*, s.v. "Diary chronicle," entry by Mcdsh, May 4, 2019, https://www.urbandictionary.com/define.php?term=Diary%20chronicle.
11. Qaanitah Hunter self-published her *Diary of a Guji Girl* about a young Muslim woman in South Africa.
12. Zuckerberg, "Building Global Community"; Nothias, "Access Granted," 331.
13. Tremayne, "Facebook Agenda," 31.

14. In March 2012, Facebook had just over 173 million North American users and nearly 233 million European users, together 48.6 percent of the world total of just over 835.5 million. "Facebook Users in the World," Internet World Stats, https://www.internetworldstats.com/facebook.htm. Earlier iteration of the page captured by the Internet Archive's Wayback Machine on April 23, 2012, https://web.archive.org/web/20120423155110/https://www.internetworldstats.com/facebook.htm.

15. Hu, *Prehistory of the Cloud*, 7.

16. On the uses of Facebook in Trinidad, see Miller, *Tales from Facebook*.

17. Macharia, "Blogging Queer Kenya," 105.

18. Kemp, "Digital 2023: Global Overview Report."

19. Williamson, "Global Facebook Users 2019."

20. Kemp, "Facebook Users, Stats, Data and Trends."

21. Kemp, "Digital 2023 July Global Statshot Report."

22. Miller, *Tales from Facebook*, 202–4; Mirani, "Millions of Facebook Users Have No Idea They're Using the Internet."

23. As Nothias recounts, the first of these programs, Facebook Zero, began in 2010 as a market-expanding initiative. In 2013, however, Internet.org took a philanthropic approach to what was essentially the same project, arguing that connectivity is a "human right" ("Access Granted," 331).

24. Nothias, "Access Granted."

25. Williamson, "Global Facebook Users 2020."

26. "Facebook Users in the World," Internet World Stats, page updated June 15, 2022, https://www.internetworldstats.com/facebook.htm. An earlier iteration of the page was captured by the Internet Archive's Wayback Machine on April 23, 2012, https://web.archive.org/web/20120423155110/https://www.internetworldstats.com/facebook.htm.

27. Wyche and Baumer, "Imagined Facebook."

28. Wyche and Baumer, "Imagined Facebook," 1100–1101.

29. Hu, *Prehistory of the Cloud*, xxiv.

30. Zuckerberg, "Building Global Community."

31. Edoro-Glines, "Unruly Archives," 523.

32. Hayot, *On Literary Worlds*, 40.

33. Cheah, *What Is a World?*, 5–6.

34. Cheah, *What Is a World?*, 9.

35. Ganguly, *This Thing Called the World*, 2.

36. Spivak, "Three Women's Texts and a Critique of Imperialism," 260.

37. Roberts, "Digital Detritus."

38. Idris, "Why Is Facebook Really Coming to Nigeria?"

39. Massey, *For Space*, 96.

40. Mufti, *Forget English!*, 8.

41. Lupondwana, in conversation with author, March 25, 2017.

42. Segar, "Blog Fiction and Its Successors."

43. Macharia, "Blogging Queer Kenya," 111.

44. There may also be a connection between these blogs and earlier nonfictional blogs like *Diary of a Kenyan Campus Girl*, as described by Ligaga, "Mapping Emerging Constructions."

45. Ligaga, "Mapping Emerging Constructions," 259.
46. Eggan, "Regionalizing the Planet," 1303.
47. Ngwira, in conversation with author, July 4, 2016.
48. boyd, "Social Network Sites as Networked Publics," 39.
49. boyd, "Social Network Sites as Networked Publics," 49–50.
50. Juniah Sophie Ngwira, April 18, 2015, reply to Khanyi Leus's comment on *Diary of a Single Mum*, Facebook, https://www.facebook.com/diaryofasinglemum19892009/posts/pfbid02VpNMNtX8B3BViPKpb6uH7jCLb1GJrqXp1FrrNbiE43DRMSe873LXE04HuSF8sCHFl.
51. Juniah Sophie Ngwira, April 18, 2015, reply to Ndu Fenny Morafe's comment on *Diary of a Single Mum*, Facebook, https://www.facebook.com/diaryofasinglemum19892009/posts/pfbid02VpNMNtX8B3BViPKpb6uH7jCLb1GJrqXp1FrrNbiE43DRMSe873LXE04HuSF8sCHFl.
52. Segar, "Blog Fiction and Its Successors," 28.
53. Adenekan, "Transnationalism and the Agenda of African Literature in a Digital Age," 140.
54. Edoro-Glines, "Unruly Archives," 528–529.
55. Juniah Sophie Ngwira, "Hello Darlings," *Diary of a Single Mum*, Facebook, July 15, 2015, https://www.facebook.com/diaryofasinglemum19892009/posts/pfbid0212KRxqu5Gxuh3ezYVq2csaDf4wzbyfiw4Arrkt5hdkY9d3vTJoaC4FNgCYEUqNTyl.
56. Juniah Sophie Ngwira, "woow I don't know how to thank each one of you for the support you have always rendered to me," *Diary of a Single Mum*, Facebook, August 27, 2015, https://www.facebook.com/diaryofasinglemum19892009/posts/pfbid02kFnq7xNbTz7D6P2sZiqtn6Cgw9Li3wbf3NMfd3EkhxwTXpDTqbKat3gwSt3Jgicl.
57. Lucky Mlambo, August 27, 2015, comment on *Diary of a Single Mum*, Facebook; Juliet Mailole Luxylady, August 27, 2015, comment on *Diary of a Single Mum*, Facebook; Nondi Nkonzo, August 27, 2015, comment on *Diary of a Single Mum*, Facebook, https://www.facebook.com/diaryofasinglemum19892009/posts/pfbid02kFnq7xNbTz7D6P2sZiqtn6Cgw9Li3wbf3NMfd3EkhxwTXpDTqbKat3gwSt3Jgicl.
58. Lethabo Raykops, January 27, 2016, comment on *Diary of a Single Mum*, Facebook, https://www.facebook.com/diaryofasinglemum19892009/posts/pfbid0VPoCHGxtt2zbfAFhhpgy8vCwifE1kKQrPYeUFgpPNY24FFGJaMhnXnDcqEZXhagrl.
59. Chedza Molefe, February, 13, 2016, comment on *Diary of a Single Mum*, Facebook, https://www.facebook.com/diaryofasinglemum19892009/posts/pfbid05NVftshJaeTJAKSX11vBgRerw6acaJNDiHcfBg3PqkHvHfcoYQKoKFjrRJA5JSTdl.
60. Bosch Santana, "From Nation to Network," 204–5.
61. Juniah Sophie Ngwira, *Diary of a Single Mum*, Facebook, February 26, 2015, https://www.facebook.com/diaryofasinglemum19892009/posts/pfbidoGjFTY8ckfiw4Qi2xRC6qQJDsgmScNAwjYiMNwt7CBQKFtLBovBUmyejaoCMLAw67l.
62. Abonga KaJoleks Ngongoshe, February 26, 2015, comment on *Diary of a Single Mum*, Facebook, https://www.facebook.com/diaryofasinglemum1989

2009/posts/pfbidoGjFTY8ckfiw4Qi2xRC6qQJDsgmScNAwjYiMNwt7CBQK FtLBovBUmyejaoCMLAw67l.

63. Responses to LuluPrecious Mofokeng, "What is nsima?" *Diary of a Single Mum*, Facebook, January 16, 2016, https://www.facebook.com/diaryofasinglemum19892009/posts/pfbidopD2PGLGy9cbhyP7tb7NbSDShkmtca6JArXyJRMdH87HjcPNR71hWZ86yNdv2sRmml.

64. Alonso and Oiarzabal, "Immigrant Worlds' Digital Harbors," 11.

65. Bosch Santana, "Story Club."

66. Kennedy, "Conceptualizing Social Interactions in Networked Spaces," 27.

67. In formulating this concept, I draw on Stephanie Newell's idea of "paracolonial" literary networks that exist "*alongside* and *beyond*" colonial formations ("'Paracolonial' Networks," 350).

68. Thulani Lupondwana, "High tea part 1," *Diary of a Cheating Husband*, Facebook, September 26, 2017, https://www.facebook.com/ShortstoriesbyLani/posts/pfbidowxCwcNnDDPXUtv2JJEMJAupUugi8xz6Dos5GgiZ9837cmAWAoTAVCeLzbrxP2D3Ql.

69. Thulani Lupondwana, *Diary of a Cheating Husband*, Facebook, May 7, 2017, https://www.facebook.com/ShortstoriesbyLani/posts/pfbido26qMGs8E2VSR3ha7tBsANFRoiozuqfN9kxPBr3V3CMA5WLCh3nVwAH3nHMAxEtZ3Ul.

70. Juniah Sophie Ngwira, "I just want to thank God," *Diary of a Single Mum*, Facebook, March 14, 2017, https://www.facebook.com/diaryofasinglemum19892009/posts/pfbido2mpmGbmXEF2pM7kc6yEMYEcXuougWcVaUxWniY4p3KgqKHyi5BNiYfUeCTLvSjZ9fl.

71. Thulani Lupondwana, "Posting chapter 2 soon," *Diary of a Cheating Husband*, Facebook, March 4, 2017, https://www.facebook.com/ShortstoriesbyLani/posts/pfbidojKqqepFMtPCjKx26N4skUMgtDQGTdAF1TWyPefSsBbd7Ke5i95boK8nFKzf7PPMzl.

72. Frassinelli and Treffry-Goatley, "Digital Media, Literacies, Literature, and the African Humanities," 77.

73. The page is once again available on Facebook as of April 9, 2024: https://www.facebook.com/Chichewastories.

74. "Chichewa Stories HD" appears to have last posted fictional content on Nov. 24, 2016, and "Chichewa Stories Page 2" in January 2020.

75. "Story imeneyi ifika mawa," "Chichewa Stories," Facebook, July 23, 2015, post removed.

76. See *Facebook Love* for examples.

77. This term appears in English in the text, which is otherwise written in Chichewa.

78. Fatima Lloyd, May 29, 2021, comment on "Facebook Love Part 2," "True Love Stories with Charity"; Benjamin Nyirenda, May 29, 2021, comment on "Facebook Love Part 2," "True Love Stories with Charity," https://www.facebook.com/permalink.php?story_fbid=pfbidoomFYMjoFtwBRymRUVorYExux6jS44XTUQiuMvPrWiPU73JMub54ejsdVtdZheTAyl&id=1686883804911365.

79. Sir Jim Chiona, "Facebook Love Part 4," "True Love Stories with Charity," Facebook, May 31, 2021, https://www.facebook.com/permalink.php?

story_fbid=pfbid023AcFj6MxByY7XGsNGt9mw7jdaWm23SS4kQvNVG6D1XpWbiJQ5Bjn7xEmBS5czQQxl&id=1686883804911365. Afrikaans is not actually represented in the text. On multiple occasions, the reader is told that Fatsani is speaking Afrikaans to his wife, but the dialogue is rendered in Chichewa or English.

80. Sir Jim Chiona, "Facebook Love Part 6," "True Love Stories with Charity," Facebook, June 3, 2021, https://www.facebook.com/1686883804911365/photos/a.1687302568202822/2917844758481924.

81. Sir Jim Chiona, reply to Wyson Sandram, "Facebook Love Part 3, " "True Love Stories with Charity," May 31, 2021, https://www.facebook.com/permalink.php?story_fbid=pfbiddDZmGbXa6aT4UHQBuUbFoHtQkcQVTiPG2RQvMm58Wa6jHGYWdu2iqSjpYegLndUsl&id=1686883804911365.

82. Mathewz Bzyakulima, June 10, 2021, comment on "Facebook Love Part 8," "True Love Stories with Charity," Facebook, https://www.facebook.com/1686883804911365/photos/a.1687302568202822/2920808291518904.

83. Sir Jim Chiona, "Facebook Love Part 8," "True Love Stories with Charity," Facebook, June 7, 2021, https://www.facebook.com/1686883804911365/photos/a.1687302568202822/2920808291518904.

84. Sir Jim Chiona, "Facebook Love Part 13," "True Love Stories with Charity," Facebook, June 18, 2021, https://www.facebook.com/permalink.php?story_fbid=pfbid024UBY4aH6TgRgnTbHK7RSLgAm4thr8U6zJ7VJHbs2ozdszthSLfDKZtF64dZN6jzUl&id=1686883804911365.

85. Sir Jim Chiona, "Facebook Love Part 13."

86. Sir Jim Chiona, "Facebook Love Part 6."

87. Mirriam Jiya, June 3, 2021, comment on "Facebook Love Part 6."

88. Sir Jim Chiona, "Facebook Love Part 17," "True Love Stories with Charity," Facebook, July 9, 2021, https://www.facebook.com/permalink.php?story_fbid=pfbid02LqexAZwhhqh1RPbKxZ4pGrBw9yrgSmxkkBAmmaECrEbLf95d2gxQny95fSoPPEDPl&id=1686883804911365.

89. Yékú, *Cultural Netizenship*, 53.

90. "Facebook Users in Malawi: November 2021," NapoleonCat, https://napoleoncat.com/stats/facebook-users-in-malawi/2021/11/.

91. Dickson Maseya, June 18, 2021, comment on "Facebook Love Part 13"; Facebook; Daniel Sibande, June 19, 2021, comment on "Facebook Love Part 13."

92. Mildda Aniettah Mussah, June 20, 2021, comment on "Facebook Love Part 13."

93. Sir Jim Chiona, "Facebook Love Part 8."

94. Sir Jim Chiona, "Facebook Love Part 11," "True Love Stories with Charity," Facebook, June 14, 2021, https://www.facebook.com/permalink.php?story_fbid=pfbid02bKvA2fEajskkUcC9M887Z5HAHNCue1cZwG2WES8zwryTZtG9VNofV1x9V88jXpwSl&id=1686883804911365.

95. "Announcing the Global Expansion of Professional Mode," Meta, Facebook, October 31, 2022, https://www.facebook.com/creators/expanding-professional-mode-for-profiles.

96. "About Us," Mzansi Stories, https://www.mzansistories.com/p/about-us.html (page removed). Ngwira says she was contacted by *Mzansi Stories* about

publishing her work and told them that she wanted to think about it. She says she was skeptical about having her work posted there since there are many people online who want to steal writers' content. It is unclear if she ever gave permission to the site to repost her work.

97. Thulani Lupondwana, "Honestly nothing sucks more," *Diary of a Cheating Husband*, Facebook, August 22, 2017, https://www.facebook.com/ShortstoriesbyLani/posts/pfbid0X9FgLnkdB5gzqQZJXdbFSkA9JdDM2PGjtKndM84RruC5h4FNvxtpND2ycF4YMVXVl.

98. Thulani Lupondwana, "I need to clarify some things," *Diary of a Cheating Husband*, Facebook, September 23, 2017, https://www.facebook.com/ShortstoriesbyLani/posts/pfbid02W1HkDvMVAkuqKcBWvJVg62AsjSpRVBzNm2qn5rwtNk6BGwDxfWxzEVorsBv6fTT6l.

99. A skeleton view of the site is visible on the Wayback Machine.

100. "About Wattpad," Wattpad, 2021, https://company.wattpad.com/press.

101. As Bold explains, these lists are updated daily and algorithmically determined according to readers' engagement with stories ("The Return of the Social Author," 121).

102. Lupondwana, "He Loves Me," *The Other Side of Love*, chapter 2, December 11, 2020, https://www.wattpad.com/994173230-the-other-side-of-love-he-loves-me.

103. "Copyright FAQ," Help Center, Wattpad, accessed October 14, 2023, https://support.wattpad.com/hc/en-us/articles/216192503; "Reporting Copyright Infringement," Help Center, Wattpad, accessed October 14, 2023, https://support.wattpad.com/hc/en-us/articles/204471770-Reporting-Copyright-Infringement.

104. "Copyright FAQ," Wattpad.

105. "Writer Programs and Opportunities," Wattpad, accessed December 2, 2021, https://www.wattpad.com/writers/opportunities/books/.

106. "Writer Programs and Opportunities: Wattpad Webtoon Studios," W Creators, Wattpad, accessed October 14, 2023, https://creators.wattpad.com/programs-and-opportunities/wattpad-webtoon-studios/.

107. "Home," Wattpad Creators, Wattpad, accessed October 14, 2023, https://creators.wattpad.com.

108. "Audience and Engagement," Wattpad Studios, Wattpad, accessed October 14, 2023, https://business.wattpad.com/studios/.

109. "Frequently Asked Questions," Wattpad Paid Stories, Wattpad, https://www.wattpad.com/paidstories/faqs-eng/ (page removed).

110. "How to Publish Your First Story," Creators 101, Wattpad Creators, Wattpad, accessed October 14, 2023, https://creators.wattpad.com/creators-101/getting-started-on-wattpad/how-to-publish-your-first-story/.

111. Ceci, "WhatsApp: Countries with the Highest Usage Penetration Q4 2020."

112. Makoza, "Analysis on Discourses on WhatsApp Coup Reported in the Media," 44.

113. See Omanga, "WhatsApp as 'Digital Publics'" on this phenomenon in Kenya and Makoza, "Analysis on Discourses on WhatsApp Coup Reported in the Media" on the Malawian context.

114. Makoza, "Analysis on Discourses on WhatsApp Coup Reported in the Media."

115. Kondowe, "Woman Charged for Sharing Video Clip 'to Ridicule President Chakwera.'"

116. "About Forwarding Limits," Help Center, WhatsApp, Meta, accessed October 14, 2023, https://faq.whatsapp.com/1053543185312573?helpref=faq_content.

117. Geuza and Wallis demonstrate the ways WhatsApp is used to organize book clubs in Dar es Salaam in "Reading Dar es Salaam's (Female-Led) Book Clubs as Paravirtual Networks."

118. "Hie, I'm planing [sic] to have a WhatsApp group," "Chichewa Stories Page 2," Facebook, August 17, 2019, https://www.facebook.com/permalink.php?story_fbid=pfbid02FiiJKWpVU8mLwR6DUHT29CtdwV2N3XiNfsX7FzkY7Es9UaqQhzrB84H1yBqLynivl&id=242179636144962.

119. Mike Maphoto, comment on "Origins of a Slay: Chapter 56," *Diary of a Zulu Girl*, September 29, 2020, diaryofazulugirl.co.za/2020/09/origins-chapter-56/ (page removed). Captured by the Internet Archive's Wayback Machine on May 17, 2022, https://web.archive.org/web/20220517051716/https://diaryofazulugirl.co.za/2020/09/origins-chapter-56/.

120. In October 2023, *A Ndebele Gay Diary* had 10,000 followers and *Diary of a Tswana Gay* had 6,200 followers.

121. McNamee, *Zucked*, 84.

122. McNamee, *Zucked*, 93.

123. Nuttall, "Reading in the Lives and Writing of Black South African Women," 98.

EPILOGUE

1. On December 14, 2021, the UK lifted the ban given the wide community spread of Omicron throughout its own population. The United States followed suit on December 31, 2021.

2. Achille Mbembe, "New Global Mobility Regime."

3. Mbembe, "Bodies as Borders," 9.

4. Mbembe, "New Global Mobility Regime."

5. Rugunanan, "'South Africa Belongs to All Those Who Live in It.'"

6. Rugunanan, "'South Africa Belongs to All Those Who Live in It.'"

7. Mbembe, "New Global Mobility Regime."

8. Mukumbang, Ambe, and Adebiyi, "Unspoken Inequality," 3.

9. Mukumbang, Ambe, and Adebiyi, "Unspoken Inequality," 4.

10. Mukumbang, Ambe, and Adebiyi, "Unspoken Inequality," 4.

11. Masina, "Malawi Mandates Quarantine for Returnees from South Africa."

12. Bara, "COVID-19 and the Future of Migration and Mobility in Africa," 16.

13. Crush, Skinner, and Stulgaitis, "Rendering South Africa Undesirable," 7.

14. Kateta, "Malawi Is No Longer Safe for Refugees."

15. "30 March 2021—Zimbabwe," *Detention Blog*, Global Detention Project, March 30, 2021, https://www.globaldetentionproject.org/30-march-2021-zimbabwe.

16. Abi Elkafi, quoted in Dietrich, "European Union Fortifies Is Mission on North African Frontline," 2.

17. Dietrich, "European Union Fortifies Its Mission on North African Frontline," 2.

18. Hu, *Prehistory of the Cloud*, xiv.

19. Hu, *Prehistory of the Cloud*, xv.

20. Hu, *Prehistory of the Cloud*, xvi.

21. Mbembe, "Bodies as Borders," 16.

Bibliography

ARCHIVAL SOURCES

Malawi
National Archives of Malawi, Lilongwe (NAM)
National Archives of Malawi, Zomba (NAM)
Society of Malawi Library and Archive, Blantyre
Times Group Newspaper Archives, Blantyre
University of Malawi Chancellor College Library, Zomba

South Africa
Bailey's African History Archive, Johannesburg (BAHA)

Zambia
Main Library at the University of Zambia Library, Lusaka

Zimbabwe
National Archives of Zimbabwe, Harare

United States
Schomburg Center for Research in Black Culture, New York Public Library
Beinecke Rare Book and Manuscript Library, Yale University Library, New Haven, CT

United Kingdom
The British Library, London
The British Library Newspaper Library at Colindale, London

PRIMARY AND SECONDARY SOURCES

Achebe, Chinua. "English and the African Writer." *Transition*, no. 18 (1965): 27–30.

Adejunmobi, Moradewun. "Abiola Irele and the Publicness of African Letters." *Journal of the African Literature Association* 14, no. 1 (2020): 72–89.

Adenekan, Shola. *African Literature in the Digital Age: Class and Sexual Politics in New Writing from Nigeria and Kenya*. Suffolk, England: Boydell and Brewer, 2021.

———. "Transnationalism and the Agenda of African Literature in a Digital Age." *Matatu* 45, no. 1 (2014): 133–51.

Adesokan, Akin. *Everything Is Sampled: Digital and Print Mediations in African Arts and Letters*. Bloomington: Indiana University Press, 2023.

Agyemang, Kofi. "A Repeat of Ghana-Must-Go." *Chimurenga Chronic*, *Chimurenga* 16, October 19, 2011.

Alexander, Jocelyn. "'Hooligans, Spivs and Loafers'?: The Politics of Vagrancy in 1960s Southern Rhodesia." *Journal of African History* 53 (2012): 345–66.

Alonso, Andoni, and Pedro J. Oiarzabal. "The Immigrant Worlds' Digital Harbors: An Introduction." In *Diasporas in the New Media Age: Identity, Politics, and Community*, edited by Andoni Alonso and Pedro J. Oiarzabal, 1–15. Reno: University of Nevada Press, 2010.

Anderson, Benedict. *Imagined Communities*. New York: Verso, 2006.

Andrade, Susan. *The Nation Writ Small: African Fictions and Feminisms, 1958–1988*. Durham, NC: Duke University Press, 2011.

Angolo, Shandrack. "Parade Is Read." *African Parade*, August 1961.

Apter, Andrew. *The Pan-African Nation: Oil and the Spectacle of Culture in Nigeria*. Chicago: University of Chicago Press, 2005.

Apter, Emily. "Untranslatability and the Geopolitics of Reading." *PMLA* 134, no. 1 (2019): 194–200.

———. "Untranslatables: A World System." *New Literary History* 39, no. 3 (2008): 581–98.

Armillas-Tiseyra, Magalí. "The African Novel at the Vanguard." *The Cambridge Journal of Postcolonial Literary Inquiry* 9, no. 2 (2022): 243–250.

Askew, Kelly. "Everyday Poetry from Tanzania: Microcosm of the Newspaper Genre." In *African Print Cultures: Newspapers and Their Publics in the Twentieth Century*, edited by Derek R. Peterson, Emma Hunter, and Stephanie Newell, 179–223. Ann Arbor: University of Michigan Press, 2016.

Aterianus-Owanga, Alice. "A Pan-African Space in Cape Town? The Chimurenga Archive of Pan-African Festivals." *Journal of African Cultural Studies* 32, no. 3 (2020): 251–69.

Backer, Ron. *Gripping Chapters: The Sound Movie Serial*. Albany, GA: BearManor Media, 2010.

Bady, Aaron. "Damning with Faint Prize: Stanley Kenani's 'Love on Trial.'" *The New Inquiry*, May 29, 2012. https://thenewinquiry.com/blog/damning-with-faint-prize-stanley-kenanis-love-on-trial/.

———. "The Varieties of Blackness: An Interview with Chimamanda Ngozi Adichie." *Boston Review*, July 10, 2013. https://www.bostonreview.net/articles/chimamanda-ngozi-adichie-americanah-varieties-blackness/.

Bakhtin, M. M. *The Dialogic Imagination: Four Essays*. Austin: University of Texas Press, 1981.

Balogun, F. Odun. *Tradition and Modernity in the African Short Story: An Introduction to a Literature in Search of Critics*. New York: Greenwood Press, 1991.

Banda, Paul Chiudza. "Ruling Minds: The Media and State Propaganda in British-Ruled Nyasaland, 1945–1964." In *Re-imagining Communication in Africa and the Caribbean: Global South Issues in Media Culture and Technology*, edited by Hopeton S. Dunn, Dumisani Moyo, William O. Lesitaokana, and Shanade Bianca Barnabas, 309–26. Cham, Switzerland: Palgrave Macmillan, 2021.

Bara, Anna. "COVID-19 and the Future of Migration and Mobility in Africa." International Centre for Migration Policy Development (ICMPD) Working Paper. October 2020. https://www.icmpd.org/file/download/54091/file/ICMPD_Working_Paper_COVID-190andotheoFutureoofoMigrationoandoMobilityoinoAfrica.pdf.

Barber, James, and John Barratt. *South Africa's Foreign Policy: The Search for Status and Security 1945–1988*. Cambridge: Cambridge University Press, 1990.

Barber, Karin. *The Anthropology of Texts, Persons and Publics: Oral and Written Culture in Africa and Beyond*. Cambridge: Cambridge University Press, 2007.

———. "Introduction: Hidden Innovators in Africa." In *Africa's Hidden Histories: Everyday Literacy and Making the Self*, edited by Karin Barber, 1–24. Bloomington: Indiana University Press, 2006.

———. "Introduction: I. B. Thomas and the First Yoruba Novel." In *Print Culture and the First Yoruba Novel: I. B. Thomas's 'The Life Story of Me, Segilola' and Other Texts*, edited and translated by Karin Barber, 3–75. Leiden, the Netherlands: Brill, 2012.

Barnard, Rita. *Apartheid and Beyond: South African Writers and the Politics of Place*. Oxford: Oxford University Press, 2007.

Barnes, Teresa. "'To Raise a Hornet's Nest': The Effect of Early Resistance to Passes for Women in South Africa on the Pass Laws in Colonial Zimbabwe." *Agenda* 5, no. 5 (1989): 40–52.

Barton, Frank. *The Press of Africa: Persecution and Perseverance*. New York: Africana, 1979.

Baucom, Ian. "Township Modernism." In *Geomodernisms: Race, Modernism, Modernity*, edited by Laura Doyle and Laura Winkiel, 227–44. Bloomington: Indiana University Press, 2005.

Bearak, Barry and Celia W. Dugger. "South Africans Take Out Rage on Immigrants." *New York Times*, May 20, 2008. https://www.nytimes.com/2008/05/20/world/africa/20safrica.html.

Behdad, Ali. "Postcolonial Theory and the Predicament of 'Minor Literature.'" In *Minor Transnationalism*, edited by Françoise Lionnet and Shu-mei Shih, 223–36. Durham, NC: Duke University Press, 2005.

Beukes, Lauren. "Is Science Fiction Coming to Africa?" BBC. The Documentary. June 17, 2012. https://www.bbc.co.uk/programmes/p00t4yn2.

Blum, Cinzia Sartini. *The Other Modernism: F. T. Marinetti's Futurist Fiction of Power*. Berkeley: University of California Press, 1996.

Boehmer, Elleke. "Stories of Women and Mothers: Gender and Nationalism in the Early Fiction of Flora Nwapa." In *Motherlands: Black Women's Writing from Africa, the Caribbean, and South Asia*, edited by Susheila Nasta, 3–23. New Brunswick, NJ: Rutgers University Press, 1992.

Bold, Melanie Ramdarshan. "The Return of the Social Author: Negotiating Authority and Influence on Wattpad." *Convergence: The International Journal of Research into New Media Technologies* 24, no. 2 (2018): 117–36.

Bollen, Katrien, and Raphael Ingelbien. "An Intertext That Counts? *Dracula*, *The Woman in White*, and Victorian Imaginations of the Foreign Other." *English Studies* 90, no. 4 (2009): 403–20.

Bond, Patrick. *Against Global Apartheid: South Africa Meets the World Bank, IMF and International Finance*. Cape Town, South Africa: University of Cape Town Press, 2003.

Bosch Santana, Stephanie. "From Nation to Network: Blog and Facebook Fiction from Southern Africa." *Research in African Literatures* 49, no. 1 (2018): 187–208.

———. "Review Essay: New Pan-Africanisms Online." *Wasafiri* 31, no. 4 (2016): 82–86.

———. "The Story Club: African Literary Networks Offline." In *Routledge Handbook of African Literature*, edited by Moradewun Adejunmobi and Carli Coetzee, 385–98. New York: Routledge, 2019.

boyd, danah. "Social Network Sites as Networked Publics: Affordances, Dynamics, and Implications." In *A Networked Self: Identity, Community, and Culture on Social Network Sites*, edited by Zizi Papacharissi, 39–58. New York: Routledge, 2010.

Bulson, Eric. *Little Magazine, World Form*. New York: Columbia University Press, 2016.

Bush, Ruth. "'Mesdames, il faut lire!': Material Contexts and Representational Strategies in Early Francophone African Women's Magazines." *Francosphères* 5, no. 2 (2016): 213–36.

Bush, Ruth, and Claire Ducournau. "Introduction: African Audiences: Making Meanings across Media." *Research in African Literatures* 51, no. 1 (Spring 2020): vii–xv.

———. "'Small Readers' and Big Magazines: Reading Publics in *Bingo*, *La Vie Africaine*, and *Awa: la revue de la femme noire*." *Research in African Literatures* 51, no. 1 (Spring 2020): 45–69.

Butler, L. J. "Britain, the United States, and the Demise of the Central African Federation, 1959–63." *Journal of Imperial and Commonwealth History* 28, no. 3 (2000): 131–51.

Bwelezani, I. J. "Kanthu Konama." *African Parade*, April 1955.

Bystrom, Kerry, and Joseph R. Slaughter, eds. *The Global South Atlantic*. New York: Fordham University Press, 2017.

Cagé, Julia. "The Economics of the African Media." In *Policies and Practices*, edited by Célestin Monga and Justin Yifu Lin, 605–26. Vol. 2 of *The Oxford Handbook of Africa and Economics*. Oxford: Oxford University Press, 2015.

Canana. "The Man with a Beard." *African Parade*, January 1954.

Cancel, Robert. *Storytelling in Northern Zambia: Theory, Method, Practice and Other Necessary Fictions*. Cambridge: Open Book, 2013.

Casanova, Pascale. *The World Republic of Letters*. Cambridge, MA: Harvard University Press, 2004.

Ceci, Laura. "WhatsApp: Countries with the Highest Usage Penetration Q4 2020." Statista, accessed December 3, 2021. https://www.statista.com/statistics/291540/mobile-internet-user-whatsapp/ (page updated). Earlier iteration available on the Wayback Machine, https://web.archive.org/web/20220215061608/https://www.statista.com/statistics/291540/mobile-internet-user-whatsapp/.

Chalamanda, Fiona Johnson. "'Pressing Literary Expressions': Reading Transitions in Malawian Press Poetry." *Interventions: International Journal of Postcolonial Studies* 3, no. 3 (2001): 376–90.

Chanda, Rudolph P. "Death of the Stranger." *African Parade*, February 1961–May 1961.

Chapman, Michael. *Southern African Literatures*. Pietermaritzburg, South Africa: University of Natal Press, 2003.

Charlton, Ed. "Jim in the Urban Jungle—South African Print Culture and Jungle Jim." *Africa in Words* (blog), December 4, 2012. https://africainwords.com/2012/12/04/jim-in-the-urban-jungle-south-african-print-culture-and-jungle-jim/.

Chayenda, Bob. "He Was Not among Them." *Malawi News*, May 18, 1974.

Cheah, Pheng. *What Is a World?: On Postcolonial Literature as World Literature*. Durham, NC: Duke University Press, 2016.

"Chichewa Stories HD." Facebook. https://www.facebook.com/ChichewastoriesHD/.

"Chichewa Stories Page 2." Facebook. https://www.facebook.com/profile.php?id=100066674672196.

Chidzulo, Ignatius V. "Chikondi Sachita Choumiliza." *Malawi News*, February 23, 1973.

Chikuni, Clara. "Ndaziona Mwana Wamasiye." In *Winning Stories from the 2008 Malawian Girls' Literary Competition*, edited by Stephanie Bosch and Sambalikagwa Mvona, 8–16. Blantyre, Malawi: Assemblies of God Press, 2009.

Chilima, Tiseke. "Be Careful What You Wish For." In *Winning Stories from the 2008 Malawian Girls' Literary Competition*, edited by Stephanie Bosch and Sambalikagwa Mvona, 17–22. Blantyre, Malawi: Assemblies of God Press, 2009.

Chimombo, Steve. *A Guide to Malawi's Literature*. Zomba, Malawi: Manchichi, 1996.

———. *Malawian Oral Literature: The Aesthetics of Indigenous Arts*. Centre for Social Research, University of Malawi, 1988.

Chimurenga Chronic. Chimurenga 16. Cape Town, South Africa: Kalakuta Trust, 2011.

Chinweizu, Onwuchekwa Jemie, and Ihechukwu Madubuike. *Toward the Decolonization of African Literature. Vol. 1, African Fiction and Poetry and Their Critics*. Enugu, Nigeria: Fourth Dimension, 1980.

Chiona, Sir Jim. *Facebook Love*. "True Love Stories with Charity." Facebook. https://www.facebook.com/profile.php?id=100063959019084.

Chirambo, Reuben Makayiko. "'All Men Do Is Love Love': The Politics of Women Liberation in Malawian Literature.'" In *Society and the Arts: Studies in Gender, Literature and Language*, edited by Brighton J. Uledi-Kamanga, 16–39. Zomba, Malawi: Kachere Series, 2014.

———. "Protesting Politics of 'Death and Darkness' in Malawi." *Journal of Folklore Research* 38, no. 3 (2001): 205–27.

Chirwa, Wiseman Chijere. "The Malawian Government and South African Labour Recruiters, 1974–92. *Journal of Modern African Studies* 34, no. 4 (1996): 623–42.

Chiume, M. W. Kanyama. "Commentary." *Federation of Rhodesia and Nyasaland. Africa Today Pamphlets*, no. 4 (1959): 23–6.

Cochrane, Thembisa. "San Junction." *Jungle Jim*, no. 23, March 17, 2014. Cape Town, South Africa: Afreak Press.

Cohen, Andrew. *The Politics and Economics of Decolonization in Africa: The Failed Experiment of the Central African Federation*. London: I. B. Tauris, 2017.

Coney, John, director. *Space is the Place*. North American Star System, 1974.

Cooppan, Vilashini. "World Literature and Global Theory: Comparative Literature for the New Millennium." "Globalism & Theory." Special issue, *symplokē* 9, no. 1/2 (2001): 15–43.

Coplan, David B. "The Power of Oral Poetry: Narrative Songs of the Basotho Migrants." *Research in African Literatures* 18, no. 1 (1987): 1–35.

Coppola, John, Interview with Theophilus Vincent. "African Writers Influence Society." *Malawi News*, September 17, 1978.

Coulon, Virginia. "Onitsha Goes National: Nigerian Writing in Macmillan's Pacesetter Series." *Research in African Literatures* 18, no. 3 (1987): 304–19.

Cowie, Alix-Rose. "Young South Africa : Jenna Bass and Hannes Bernard of Jungle Jim." *10and5*, June 9, 2014. 10and5.com/2014/06/09/young-south-africa-jenna-bass-hannes-bernard-of-jungle-jim/ (page removed). Available on the Wayback Machine, https://web.archive.org/web/20220702145753/10and5.com/2014/06/09/young-south-africa-jenna-bass-hannes-bernard-of-jungle-jim/.

Cowling, Lesley. "Echoes of an African Drum: The Lost Literary Journalism of 1950s South Africa." *Literary Journalism Studies* 8, no. 1 (Spring 2016): 7–33.

Cresswell, Tim. *On the Move: Mobility in the Modern Western World*. New York: Routledge, 2006.

Crush, Jonathan. "Vulcan's Brood: Spatial Narratives of Migration in Southern Africa." In *Writing across Worlds: Literature and Migration*, edited by John Connell, Russell King, and Paul White, 229–47. London: Routledge, 1995.

Crush, Jonathan, Caroline Skinner, and Manal Stulgaitis. "Rendering South Africa Undesirable: A Critique of Refugee and Informal Sector Policy (rep. i-35)." SAMP Migration Policy Series 79. Waterloo, ON: Southern African Migration Programme, 2017.

Daimon, Anusa. "Settling in Motion as Consciousness: Nyasa (Malawian) Informal Transit across Southern Rhodesia towards South Africa from the 1910s to the 1950s." *African Studies* 80, no. 1 (2021): 1–20.

Damrosch, David. *What Is World Literature?* Princeton, NJ: Princeton University Press, 2003.

de Certeau, Michel. *The Practice of Everyday Life*. Translated by Steven Rendall. Berkeley: University of California Press, 1984.

de Lange, Margreet. *The Muzzled Muse: Literature and Censorship in South Africa*. Amsterdam: John Benjamins, 1997.

Dee, Henry. "Central African Immigrants, Imperial Citizenship and the Politics of Free Movement in Interwar South Africa." *Journal of Southern African Studies* 46, no. 2 (2020): 319–37.

Deleuze, Gilles, and Félix Guattari. *A Thousand Plateaus: Capitalism and Schizophrenia*. Translated by Brian Massumi. Minneapolis: University of Minnesota Press, 1987.

Desai, Gaurav. *Commerce with the Universe: Africa, India, and the Afrasian Imagination*. New York: Columbia University Press, 2013.

Dietrich, Helmut. "European Union Fortifies Its Mission on North African Frontline." *Chimurenga Chronic*, *Chimurenga* 16, October 19, 2011.

Dimock, Wai Chee. "Genre as World System: Epic and Novel on Four Continents." *Narrative* 14, no. 1 (2006): 85–101.

Dlamanzi, Daniel. Makokoba Park Talk. *African Parade*, January 1959–October 1960.

Dlamini, Jacob. "The Death of Jacob Dlamini." *Chimurenga Chronic*, *Chimurenga* 16, October 19, 2011.

———. *Native Nostalgia*. Auckland Park, South Africa: Jacana, 2009.

Dodson, Don. "The Four Modes of Drum: Popular Fiction and Social Control in South Africa." *African Studies Review* 17, no. 2 (1974): 317–43.

Dombo, Sylvester. *Private Print Media, the State and Politics in Colonial and Post-Colonial Zimbabwe*. Cham, Switzerland: Palgrave Macmillan, 2018.

Driver, Dorothy. "*Drum Magazine* (1951–59) and the Spatial Configurations of Gender." In *Text, Theory, Space: Land, Literature, and History in South Africa and Australia*, edited by Kate Darian-Smith, Liz Gunner, and Sarah Nuttall, 227–38. London: Routledge, 1996.

Drum: A Magazine of Africa for Africa. Johannesburg: African Drum Publications, 1951–.

Dube, Angeline. "America as I Saw It." *African Parade*, July 1960.

Edjabe, Ntone. "Diagnosing the Chimurenga Chronic." *Rhodes Journalism Review* 32 (September 2012): 63.

———. "The Dour Rhetoric and the Don'ts of Nation-Building and the Hungry Eye of the Poet Revolutionaries." *Rhodes Journalism Review* 24 (September 2004): 60–61.

Edjabe, Ntone, in conversation with David Morris. "Performing Pan-Africanism." In *Curating after the Global: Roadmaps for the Present*, edited by Paul O'Neill, Simon Sheikh, Lucy Steeds, and Mick Wilson, 274–91. Cambridge, MA: MIT Press, 2019.

Edoro-Glines, Ainehi. "Unruly Archives: Literary Form and the Social Media Imaginary." *ELH* 89, no. 2 (Summer 2022): 523–46.

Edwards, Brent Hayes. *The Practice of Diaspora: Literature, Translation, and the Rise of Black Internationalism*. Cambridge, MA: Harvard University Press, 2003.

Eggan, Taylor A. "Regionalizing the Planet: Horizons of the Introverted Novel at World Literature's End." *PMLA* 131, no. 5 (2016): 1299–315.

Englund, Harri. "The Village in the City, the City in the Village: Migrants in Lilongwe." *Journal of Southern African Studies* 28, no. 1 (2002): 137–54.

Eshun, Kodwo. "Further Considerations of Afrofuturism." *CR: The New Centennial Review* 3, no. 2 (2003): 287–302.

Eshun, Kodwo, Avery F. Gordon, and Emily Pethick. "Navigating Pan-Africanisms: On the Chimurenga Library." *Afterall: A Journal of Art, Context and Enquiry* 43 (2017): 80–87.

Falola, Toyin, and Kwame Essien. Introduction to *Pan-Africanism, and the Politics of African Citizenship and Identity*, edited by Toyin Falola and Kwame Essien, 1–10. New York: Routledge, 2014.

Fanon, Frantz. *The Wretched of the Earth*. Translated by Constance Farrington. New York: Grove Press, 1963.

Fasselt, Rebecca. "Decolonising the Afropolitan: Intra-African Migrations in post-2000 Literature." In *Routledge Handbook of African Literature*, edited by Moradewun Adejunmobi and Carli Coetzee, 75–91. New York: Routledge, 2019.

Fawaz, Ramzi. "Space, That Bottomless Pit: Planetary Exile and Metaphors of Belonging in American Afrofuturist Cinema." *Callaloo* 35, no. 4 (2012): 1103–122.

Fenwick, Mac. "'Tough Guy, Eh?': The Gangster-Figure in *Drum*." *Journal of Southern African Studies* 2, no. 4 (1996): 617–32.

Ferguson, James. *Expectations of Modernity: Myths and Meanings of Urban Life on the Zambian Copperbelt*. Berkeley: University of California Press, 1999.

Fischer, Mia. "Trans Responses to Adichie: Challenging Cis Privilege in Popular Feminism." *Feminist Media Studies* 17, no. 5 (2017): 896–99.

Fleming, Tyler, and Toyin Falola. "Africa's Media Empire: *Drum*'s Expansion to Nigeria." *History in Africa* 32 (2005): 133–64.

Francis, Andrew. "'The Meanest Devil of the Pit': British Representations of the German Character in Edwardian Juvenile Spy Fiction, 1900–1914." In *The Foreign in International Crime Fiction: Transcultural Representations*, edited by Jean Anderson, Carolina Miranda, and Barbara Pezzotti, 153–64. New York: Continuum, 2012.

Fraser, Robert. "'Who No Know Go Know: An Interview with Ntone Edjabe.'" *Wasafiri* 22, no. 3 (2007): 62–67.

Frassinelli, Pier Paolo, and Lisa Treffry-Goatley, "Digital Media, Literacies, Literature, and the African Humanities." In *African Philosophical and Literary Possibilities: Re-reading the Canon*, edited by Aretha Phiri, 75–92. London: Lexington Books, 2020.

Ganguly, Debjani. *This Thing Called the World: The Contemporary Novel as Global Form*. Durham, NC: Duke University Press, 2016.

Gappah, Petina. "How Kenya Exploded in My Heart." *Chimurenga Chronic*, *Chimurenga* 16, October 19, 2011.

Gates, Henry Louis, Jr. *The Signifying Monkey: A Theory of African-American Literary Criticism*. Oxford: Oxford University Press, 1988.

Gathigira, H. S. "The African Parade Comes to Kenya." *African Parade*, September 1957.

Gbaffou, Marc. "The Spirit of May." *Chimurenga Chronic*, *Chimurenga* 16, October 19, 2011.

Geuza, Zamda R., and Kate Wallis. "Reading Dar es Salaam's (Female-Led) Book Clubs as Paravirtual Networks." *Eastern African Literary and Cultural Studies* 7, no. 1–2 (2021): 133–63.

Gikandi, Simon. "Contested Grammars: Comparative Literature, Translation, and the Challenge of Locality." In *A Companion to Comparative Literature*, edited by Ali Behdad and Dominic Thomas, 254–72. Chichester, England: Blackwell, 2011.

Gilbert, Melissa R. "'Race,' Space, and Power: The Survival Strategies of Working Poor Women." *Annals of the Association of American Geographers* 88, no. 4 (1998): 595–621.

Gilman, Lisa. *The Dance of Politics: Gender, Performance, and Democratization in Malawi*. Philadelphia: Temple University Press, 2009.

———. "The Traditionalization of Women's Dancing, Hegemony, and Politics in Malawi." *Journal of Folklore Research* 41, no. 1 (2004): 33–60.

Gilroy, Paul. *The Black Atlantic: Modernity and Double-Consciousness*. Cambridge, MA: Harvard University Press, 1993.

Godsman, Frank. "The Distant Place." *African Parade*, December 1957–March 1958.

Gomel, Elana. *Postmodern Science Fiction and Temporal Imagination*. New York: Continuum, 2010.

———. "Shapes of the Past and the Future: Darwin and the Narratology of Time Travel." *Narrative* 17, no. 3 (2009): 334–52.

Gondwe, Brighton. "When the Spirits Beckoned." *Malawi News*, October 3–9, 1981.

Gopnik, Adam. "Talk It Up: Damon Runyon's Guys and Dolls." *New Yorker*, February 22, 2009. https://www.newyorker.com/magazine/2009/03/02/talk-it-up.

Goyal, Yogita. *Romance, Diaspora, and Black Atlantic Literature*. Cambridge: Cambridge University Press, 2010.

———. *Runaway Genres: The Global Afterlives of Slavery*. New York: New York Universeity Press, 2019.

Graham, Shane. *Cultural Entanglements: Langston Hughes and the Rise of African and Caribbean Literature*. Charlottesville: University of Virginia Press, 2020.

Graham, Shane, and John Walters, eds. *Langston Hughes and the South African Drum Generation: The Correspondence*. New York: Palgrave Macmillan, 2010.

Gray, Stephen. "Third World Meets First World: The Theme of 'Jim Comes to Joburg' in South African English Fiction." *Kunapipi* 7, no. 1 (1985): 61–80.

Green-Simms, Lindsey. *Postcolonial Automobility: Car Culture in West Africa*. Minneapolis: University of Minnesota Press, 2017.

Greenberg, Cheryl. "The Politics of Disorder: Reexamining Harlem's Riots of 1935 and 1943." *Journal of Urban History* 18, no. 4 (August 1992): 395–441.

Grost, Michael. "Blue Bolt: A 1940's Comic Book Hero." Classic Comic Books, accessed October 14, 2023. http://mikegrost.com/bluebolt.htm.

Groves, Zoe R. *Malawian Migration to Zimbabwe, 1900–1965: Tracing Machona*. Cham, Switzerland: Palgrave Macmillan, 2020.

———. "Transnational Networks and Regional Solidarity: The Case of the Central African Federation, 1953–1963." *African Studies* 72, no. 2 (2013): 155–75.

Gunda, Warren. "Critique of 'The Jailbird.'" *Malawi News*, December 23, 1979.

———. "Joe's Replica." *Malawi News*, January 13, 1980.

Guvi, Tinos. "Malcolm the Man and His Ideas." *African Parade*, June 1965.

Gwande, Victor M. "The Political Economy of American Businesses in British Central Africa, 1953–1963." *Business History Review* 97, no. 1 (Spring 2023): 67–91.

Hamilton, Carolyn Anne. "'The Character and Objects of Chaka': A Reconsideration of the Making of Shaka as 'Mfecane' Motor." *Journal of African History* 33, no. 1 (1992): 37–63.

Hanke, Marvin. "Shut Up." *Malawi News*, March 9, 1980.

Hansen, Karen Tranberg. *Keeping House in Lusaka*. New York: Columbia University Press, 1997.

Harper, Donna Akiba Sullivan. *Not So Simple: The "Simple" Stories by Langston Hughes*. Columbia: University of Missouri Press, 1995.

Harris, Ashleigh. *Afropolitanism and the Novel: De-realizing Africa*. New York: Routledge, 2020.

Harris, Ashleigh, and Nicklas Hållén. "African Street Literature: A Method for an Emergent Form beyond World Literature." *Research in African Literatures* 51, no. 2 (Summer 2020): 1–26.

Harvey, David. "Spacetime and the World." In *The People, Place, and Space Reader*, edited by Jen Jack Gieseking and William Mangold, 12–16. New York: Routledge, 2014.

Hauya, Roy. "Imaginative Portrayal of Social Reality." *Malawi News*, January 20, 1980.

Hayles, N. Katherine. "Electronic Literature: What Is It?" *Electronic Literature Organization* 1, January 2, 2007. https://eliterature.org/pad/elp.html.

Hayot, Eric. *On Literary Worlds*. Oxford: Oxford University Press, 2012.

Helgesson, Stefan. "Shifting Fields: Imagining Literary Renewal in *Itinerário* and *Drum*." *Research in African Literatures* 38, no. 2 (2007): 206–26.

———. "Southern Africa: An Introduction." In *A Companion to African Literatures*, edited by Olakunle George, 197–211. Hoboken, NJ: John Wiley and Sons, 2021.

———. *Transnationalism in Southern African Literature: Modernists, Realists, and the Inequality of Print Culture*. New York: Routledge, 2009.

Helgesson, Stefan, and Christina Kullberg. "Translingual Events: World Literature and the Making of Language." *Journal of World Literature* 3, no. 2 (2018): 136–52.

Hobsbawm, Eric and Terence Ranger, eds. *The Invention of Tradition.* Cambridge: Cambridge University Press, 2012.

Hofmeyr, Isabel. "African History and Global Studies: A View from South Africa." *Journal of African History* 54 (2013): 341–49.

———. *Dockside Reading: Hydrocolonialism and the Custom House.* Durham, NC: Duke University Press, 2021.

———. *Gandhi's Printing Press: Experiments in Slow Reading.* Cambridge, MA: Harvard University Press, 2013.

———. *The Portable Bunyan: A Transnational History of "The Pilgrim's Progress."* Princeton, NJ: Princeton University Press, 2003.

———. "Transnational Circulation: Region, Nation, Identity and the Material Practices of Translation." *Current Writing: Text and Reception in Southern Africa* 15, no. 2 (2003): 1–16.

Hofmeyr, Isabel, Sarah Nuttall, and Cheryl Ann Michael. "The Book in Africa." *Current Writing: Text and Reception in Southern Africa* 13, no. 2 (2001): 1–8.

Hofmeyr, Isabel, and Derek R. Peterson. "The Politics of the Page: Cutting and Pasting in South African and African-American Newspapers." *Social Dynamics* 45, no. 1 (2019): 1–25.

Houston, Lynn Marie. *Food Culture in the Caribbean.* Westport, CT: Greenwood Press, 2005.

Hu, Tung-Hui. *A Prehistory of the Cloud.* Cambridge, MA: MIT Press, 2015.

Hughes, Langston. "Ball of String!" *Africa!* 1, no. 7 (September 1954): 40–41.

———. "Banquet in Honor!" *Africa!* 1, no. 3 (May 1954): 38–40.

———. *The Best of Simple.* New York: Hill and Wang, 1961.

———. "Explain That to Me!" *Africa!* 1, no. 11, January 1955.

———. "Feet Live Their Own Life." In *Simple Speaks His Mind*, 3–7. New York: Simon and Schuster, 1950.

———. "Here to Yonder: Conversation at Midnight." *Chicago Defender*, February 13, 1943.

———. "Here to Yonder: God, War, and Swing." *Chicago Defender*, June 5, 1943.

———. "Here to Yonder: Simple and Harlem." *Chicago Defender*, October 5, 1946.

———. "Here to Yonder: Simple Begs to Differ." *Chicago Defender*, October 11, 1947.

———. "Here to Yonder: Simple in the Hospital." *Chicago Defender*, December 9, 1944.

———. "Here to Yonder: Simple Looks for Justice." *Chicago Defender*, August 28, 1943.

———. "Here to Yonder: Simple Rocks a Rocket." *Chicago Defender*, January 24, 1948.

———. "Here to Yonder: Why and Wherefore." *Chicago Defender*, November 21, 1942.

———. "High Bed." In *Simple Speaks His Mind*, 102–8. New York: Simon and Schuster, 1950.

———. "House-Rent Parties Returning; Simple Sees Depression Coming." *Chicago Defender*, March 27, 1954.

———. "Landladies!" *Africa!* 1, no. 2 (April 1954): 20–21.

———. "Matter for a Book!" *Africa!* 1, no. 4 (June 1954): 58–59.

———. *Simple Takes a Wife*. Mattituck, NY: Amereon, 1979.

———. "A Toast to Harlem." In *Simple Speaks His Mind*, 31–35. New York: Simon and Schuster, 1950.

Hunter, Qaanitah. *Diary of a Guji Girl*. South Africa: Emerald Publications, 2015.

Idris, Abubakar. "Why Is Facebook Really Coming to Nigeria?" TechCabal, October 1, 2020. https://techcabal.com/2020/10/01/why-is-facebook-really-coming-to-nigeria/.

Iheka, Cajetan, and Jack Taylor. "Introduction: The Migration Turn in African Cultural Productions." In *African Migration Narratives: Politics, Race and Space*, edited by Cajetan Iheka and Jack Taylor, 1–15. Rochester, NY: University of Rochester Press, 2018.

Ikheloa, Ikhide R. "#Caineprize—The Thirteenth Caine Prize Shortlist: Love on Trial." Pa Ikhide, May 25, 2012. https://xokigbo.com/2012/05/25/caineprize-the-thirteenth-caine-prize-shortlist-love-on-trial/.

Jackson, Jeanne-Marie. "Reading for the Region in New African Novels: Flight, Form, and the Metonymic Ideal." *Research in African Literatures* 49, no. 1 (2018): 42–62.

Jackson, John L., Jr. *Harlemworld: Doing Race and Class in Contemporary Black America*. Chicago: University of Chicago Press, 2001.

Jaffu, Joyce F. *Kalata Yochokera Ku Joni*. Blantyre, Malawi: Assemblies of God Press, 2007.

Jaji, Tsitsi Ella. *Africa in Stereo: Modernism, Music, and Pan-African Solidarity*. Oxford: Oxford University Press, 2014.

James, Leslie. "The Flying Newspapermen and the Time-Space of Late Colonial Nigeria." *Comparative Studies in Society and History* 60, no. 3 (2018): 569–98.

Jones, Rebecca. *At the Crossroads: Nigerian Travel Writing and Literary Culture in Yoruba and English*. Suffolk, England: Boydell and Brewer, 2019.

Joyah, Charles S. "The Truth about Chapweteka's Fiction." *Muse* 32 (1979): 16.

Julien, Eileen. "Of Traditional Tales and Short Stories in African Literature." *Présence Africaine* 125 (1983): 146–65.

Kadzitche, Lawrence. "Mgodi Uvuta." In *Katakwe Zaka 10*, 4–6. Self-published, Graphic Elements, 2011.

Kadzuwa, Martin. "The Mask Fell Off." *Malawi News*, April 26–May 2, 1986.

Kahari, George P. *The Search for Identity and Ufuru: An Introduction to Black Zimbabwean Fiction in English, 1956–1980*. Gweru, Zimbabwe: Mambo Press, 2009.

Kahora, Billy. "Authority Stealing: The Business of Crime Writing in Kenya, India and Nigeria." *Chimurenga Chronic, Chronic Books*, March 2013.

Kalitera, Aubrey. "A Criticism of Yaya." *Malawi News*, December 25, 1977.

———. "Face Value." *Malawi News*, December 4, 1977.

———. "Face Value: Conclusion." *Malawi News*, December 11, 1977.

Kaliwo, George. "Face Value: An Appraisal." *Malawi News*, December 25, 1977.

Kalizga, Angeline Dudu. "The Wedding That Flopped." *Malawi News*, October 26, 1974.

Kalliney, Peter. "Modernism, African Literature, and the Cold War." *Modern Language Quarterly* 76, no. 3 (2015): 333–68.

Kalua, J. W. "The Mysterious Man That Never Was." *Malawi News*, April 6, 1974.

Kamkondo, Wisdom Dede. "Editorial." *Muse* 22 (1978): 1–2.

Kamwendo, Mike. "A Nation Indivisible." *Malawi News*, July 6, 1980.

———. "Yaya." *Malawi News*, October 2–November 27, 1977.

Kaspin, Deborah. "A Chewa Cosmology of the Body." *American Ethnologist* 23, no. 3 (1996): 561–78.

Kateta, Madalitso Wills. "Malawi Is No Longer Safe for Refugees." *Foreign Policy*, December 13, 2021. https://foreignpolicy.com/2021/12/13/malawi-africa-refugee-policy-relocation-dzaleka/.

Kato, Joshua. "45 Years of the Car Business in Uganda." Africa-Uganda-Business-Travel-Guide.com, January 26, 2012. https://www.africa-uganda-business-travel-guide.com/45-years-of-the-car-business-in-uganda.html.

Kaunda, Kenneth David. *Humanism in Zambia and a Guide to its Implementation. Part 1*. Lusaka, Zambia: Zambia Information Services, 1968.

Kemp, Simon. "Digital 2023: Global Overview Report." DataReportal, January 26, 2023. https://datareportal.com/reports/digital-2023-global-view-report.

———. "Digital 2023 July Global Statshot Report." DataReportal, July 20, 2023. https://datareportal.com/reports/digital-2023-july-global-statshot.

———. "Facebook Users, Stats, Data and Trends." DataReportal, May 11, 2023. https://datareportal.com/essential-facebook-stats.

Kenani, Stanley. "Love on Trial." In *African Violet and Other Stories: The Caine Prize for African Writing 2012*, 49–66. Oxford: New Internationalist, 2012.

———. "On the Gay Pardon." *Malawi News*, June 5–11, 2010.

Kennedy, Jenny. "Conceptualizing Social Interactions in Networked Spaces." In *Networked Sociability and Individualism: Technology for Personal and Professional Relationships*, edited by Francesca Comunello, 24–40. Hershey, PA: Information Science Reference, 2012.

Kholowa, Holyce. "Masamu atsikana ena." *Malawi News*, June 7–13, 2008.

Khunga, Cuthbert. "Criterion for Writing Should Be Competence in the Language . . ." *Malawi News*, June 24, 1979.

Kirschenbaum, Matthew G. *Mechanisms: New Media and the Forensic Imagination*. Cambridge, MA: MIT Press, 2008.

Kitchin, Rob, and Martin Dodge. "'Placing' Cyberspace: Geography, Community and Identity." *Information Technology, Education and Society* 1, no. 2 (2000): 25–46.

Kondowe, Russell. "Woman Charged for Sharing Video Clip 'to Ridicule President Chakwera.'" Malawi 24, September 10, 2021. https://malawi24.com/2021/09/10/woman-charged-for-sharing-indecent-video-clip-to-ridicule-president-chakwera/.

Kondowe, Zumani. "Gatehouse Man." *Malawi News*, March 6–12, 1993.

Kozain, Rustum. "La Puissance de Werewere Liking." Translated by Ninon Larché. *Chimurenga Chronic, Chronic Books*, August 2013.

Krishnan, Madhu. *Contingent Canons: African Literature and the Politics of Location*. Cambridge: Cambridge University Press, 2019.

———. *Writing Spatiality in West Africa: Colonial Legcies in the Anglophone/Francophone Novel*. Suffolk, England: Boydell and Brewer, 2018.

Kuntambira, Jonathan. "Namaluzi." *Malawi News*, December 4–10, 1982.

Kynoch, Gary. "Urban Violence in Colonial Africa: A Case for South African Exceptionalism." *Journal of Southern African Studies* 34, no. 3 (2008): 629–45.

La Hausse, Paul. *Brewers, Beerhalls and Boycotts: A History of Liquor in South Africa*. Johannesburg: Raven Press, 1988.

Laachir, Karima, Sara Marzagora, and Francesca Orsini. "Significant Geographies: In Lieu of World Literature." *Journal of World Literature* 3 (2018): 290–310.

Larmer, Miles. "Nation-Making at the Border: Zambian Diplomacy in the Democratic Republic of Congo." *Comparative Studies in Society and History* 61, no. 1 (2019): 145–75.

Lazarus, Neil. "The South African Ideology: The Myth of Exceptionalism, the Idea of Renaissance." *South Atlantic Quarterly* 103, no. 4 (2004): 607–28.

Lee, Christopher J. "Malawian Literature after Banda and in the Age of AIDS: A Conversation with Steve Chimombo." *Research in African Literatures* 41, no. 3 (2010): 33–48.

Levine, Caroline. *Forms: Whole, Rhythm, Hierarchy, Network*. Princeton, NJ: Princeton University Press, 2015.

Lewis, Wesley, Andrew Pauwels, Brian Underwood, and Adrianna Rodriguez. "John Lewis: Profile of a Civil Rights Legend." American Bar Association, January 22, 2021. https://www.americanbar.org/groups/communications_law/publications/communications_lawyer/fall2020/john-lewis-profile-a-civil-rights-legend/.

Ligaga, Dina. "Mapping Emerging Constructions of Good Time Girls in Kenyan Popular Media." *Journal of African Cultural Studies* 26, no. 3 (2014): 249–61.

———. *Women, Visibility and Morality in Kenyan Popular Media*. Grahamstown, South Africa: African Humanities Program, 2020.

Lindfors, Bernth. *Loaded Vehicles: Studies in African Literary Media*. Trenton, NJ: Africa World Press, 1996.

———. "Post-War Literature in English by African Writers from South Africa: A Study of the Effects of Environment upon Literature." *Phylon* 27, no. 1 (1966): 50–62.

Lionnet, Françoise, and Shu-Mei Shih. "Introduction: Thinking through the Minor, Transnationally." In *Minor Transnationalism*, edited by Françoise Lionnet and Shu-Mei Shih, 1–23. Durham, NC: Duke University Press, 2005.

Lipande, Gladys W. "To Kill or Not to Kill Is the Question." *Malawi News*, June 1, 1974.

Lipenga, Ken Junior. "Imagining the Malawian Urban Space in Lawrence Kadzitche's *Katakwe Kutauni*." *South African Journal of African Languages* 42, no. 2 (2022): 165–71.

London Committee of the United Central Africa Association. *Central African Federation: The Only Way to Partnership between the Races*. London: London Committee of the United Central Africa Association, 1951.

Lungu, Nora (née Ngoma). "Rumours . . ." *Malawi News*, October 8–14, 1988.

Lupondwana, Thulani. *Diary of a Cheating Husband*. Facebook. https://www.facebook.com/ShortstoriesbyLani.

———. *The Other Side of Love*. Wattpad. https://www.wattpad.com/story/250604644-the-other-side-of-love.

Lwanda, John Lloyd. *Kamuzu Banda of Malawi: A Study in Promise, Power and Legacy*. Zomba, Malawi: Kachere Series, 2009.

———. "Paper Tigers: The Rise and Fall of the Independent Media in Malawi, 1961–2001." *Society of Malawi Journal* 55, no. 1 (2002): 1–23.

Macharia, Keguro. "Blogging Queer Kenya." *Journal of Commonwealth and Postcolonial Studies* 1, no. 1 (2013): 103–18.

———. "Blogging Queer Kenya: A Reflection." *Journal of Commonwealth and Postcolonial Studies* 1, no. 1 (2013): 119–21.

Machingaidze, Victor E. M. "Agrarian Change from Above: The Southern Rhodesia Native Land Husbandry Act and African Response." *International Journal of African Historical Studies* 24, no. 3 (1991): 557–88.

MacPhee, Josh. "226: Small Press Africa, Part II: Judging Books by Their Covers." Justseeds. January 4, 2016. https://justseeds.org/226-small-press-africa-part-ii/.

MacViban, Dzekashu. "Q & A with Ntone Edjabe on Chimurenga, Fela, and Politics." *Bakwa*, August 18, 2012. https://bakwamagazine.com/2012/08/18/conversation-ntone-edjabe-by-breaking-the-divide-between-the-public-and-the-private-he-fela-expanded-our-vocabulary-of-resistance-the-musician-was-no-longer-simply-an-entertainer/.

Maganga, A. K. P. "Zufeyo Mwana Wokonda Kusaka." *African Parade*, December 1957.

Magaziner, Daniel, and Sean Jacobs. "The End of South African Exceptionalism." *Atlantic*, August 27, 2012. http://www.theatlantic.com/international/archive/2012/08/the-end-of-south-african-exceptionalism/261591/.

Mahmood, Shabnam. "The Most Beautiful Place." *Jungle Jim*, no. 4, May 25, 2012. Cape Town, South Africa: Afreak Press.

Makokha, J. K. S. "In the Spirit of Afropolitanism: Introduction." In *Negotiating Afropolitanism: Essays on Borders and Spaces in Contemporary African Literature and Folklore*, edited by Jennifer Wawrzinek and J. K. S. Makokha, 13–22. New York: Rodopi, 2011.

Makoza, Frank. "Analysis on Discourses on WhatsApp Coup Reported in the Media: The Case of Malawi." *International Journal of Social Media and Online Communities* 12, no. 2 (2020): 42–60.

Mala, Gammon. "Kwelani Galimoto Wa Ulere." *African Parade*, March 1955.

Mama, Amina. "Feminism or Femocracy? State Feminism and Democratisation in Nigeria." *Africa Development / Afrique et Développement* 20, no. 1 (1995): 37–58.

Mamdani, Mahmood. *Citizen and Subject: Contemporary Africa and the Legacy of Late Colonialism*. Princeton, NJ: Princeton University Press, 1996.

———. *From Citizen to Refugee: Uganda Asians Come to Britain*. 2nd ed. Cape Town, South Africa: Pambazuka Press, 2011.

Manase, Irikidzayi. "Making Memory: Stories from *Staffrider* Magazine and 'Testing' the Popular Imagination." *African Studies* 64, no. 1 (2005): 55–72.

Manda, Levi Zeleza. "Journalism Education and Training in Malawi: A Case for a National Policy." *Journal of Development and Communication Studies* 5, no. 2 (2017–2018): 35–53.

Manduli, M. N. "Kalata Ndi Kasumbalala." *African Parade*, November 1953.

———. "Kasumbalala and the Letter." *African Parade*, November 1953.

Mankhomwa, Elson. "Poking at Society." *Malawi News*, January 20, 1980.

Manus, Vicki Briault. *Emerging Traditions: Toward a Postcolonial Stylistics of Black South African Fiction in English*. Lanham, MD: Lexington Books, 2011.

Mapala, L. J. K. "Kodi mtsikanayo anali ku khitchini?" *Malawi News*, November 16, 1972.

Maphoto, Mike. *Diary of a Zulu Girl* (blog). http://diaryofazulugirl.co.za.

Marlin-Curiel, Stephanie. "Rave New World: Trance-Mission, Trance-Nationalism, and Trance-Scendence in the 'New' South Africa." *Drama Review* 45, no. 3 (2001): 149–68.

Marmon, Brooks. "Fallout from the Fallacious Accusation of Hastings Kamuzu Banda's West African Origins, 1960." *Society of Malawi Journal* 73, no. 1 (2020): 36–43.

Marten, Lutz, and Nancy C. Kula. "Zambia: 'One Zambia, One Nation, Many Languages.'" In *Language and National Identity in Africa*, edited by Andrew Simpson, 291–313. Oxford: Oxford University Press, 2008.

Masina, Lameck. "Malawi Mandates Quarantine for Returnees from South Africa." Voice of America, January 6, 2021. https://www.voanews.com/a/covid-19-pandemic_malawi-mandates-quarantine-returnees-south-africa/6200409.html.

Massey, Doreen. *For Space*. London: SAGE Publications, 2005.

Matlin, Daniel. "'Something Apart, Yet an Integral Part': Duke Ellington's Harlem and the Nexus of Race and Nation." *Modern Intellectual History* 19 (2022): 499–526.

Matsinhe, David Mario. "Africa's Fear of Itself: The Ideology of *Makwerekwere* in South Africa." *Third World Quarterly* 32, no. 2 (2011): 295–313.

Matthews, A. S. "The South African Judiciary and the Security System." *South African Journal on Human Rights* 1, no. 3 (1985): 199–209.

Mbalazo, Themba. "The Jailbird." *Malawi News*, November 25–December 9, 1979.

———. "Where Did We Go Wrong?" *Malawi News*, June 15, 1974.

Mbaluko, Cornex Kasuzi. "Interpretation of Chichewa Metaphors." MA thesis, University of Malawi, 2006.

Mbeba, Alfred David. *Ku Harare*. London: Lutterworth Press, 1950.

———. "Rhodesia Road." *African Drum*, March 1951.

Mbembe, Achille. "Afropolitanism." Translated by Laurent Chauvet. In *Africa Remix: Contemporary Art of a Continent*, edited by Simon Njami, 26–30. Ostfildern, Germany: Hatje Cantz, 2005.

———. "Bodies as Borders." *From the European South* 4 (2019): 5–18.

———. *Critique of Black Reason*. Translated by Laurent Dubois. Durham, NC: Duke University Press, 2017.

———. "The Idea of a Borderless World." *Chimurenga Chronic*, October 2018.

———. "The New Global Mobility Regime." Tanner Lectures on Human Values, Whitney Humanities Center, Yale University. March 27, 2018. YouTube video, 1:11:49. https://www.youtube.com/watch?v=o5PsV7JXBRY.

Mbembe, Achille, in conversation with Bregtje van der Haak. "The Way I See It: The Internet Is Afropolitan." *Chimurenga Chronic*, March 2015.

McClintock, Anne. *Imperial Leather: Race, Gender, and Sexuality in the Colonial Context*. New York: Routledge, 1995.

Mchombo, Sam. "Politics of Language Choice in African Education: The Case of Kenya and Malawi." *International Relations and Diplomacy* 5, no. 4 (2017): 181–204.

McLoughlin, T. O. "Zimbabwean Short Stories by Black Writers: Still-Birth or Genesis?" *Kunapipi* 12, no. 1 (1990): 76–89.

McNamee, Roger. *Zucked: Waking Up to the Facebook Catastrophe*. New York: Penguin Press, 2019.

Mgunda, Temwani. "This Is Man to Man." *Malawi News Weekender*, May 29–June 4, 2010.

Milanzi, Mary Matukuta. "Enmity in a Village Because of Education." *Malawi News*, October 19, 1974.

Milford, Ismay. "Federation, Partnership, and the Chronologies of Space in 1950s East and Central Africa." *Historical Journal* 63, no. 5 (2020): 1325–348.

Miller, Daniel. *Tales from Facebook*. Cambridge: Polity Press, 2011.

Miller, R. Baxter. "Reinvention and Globalization in Hughes's Stories." *MELUS* 30, no. 1 (Spring 2005): 69–83.

Milner-Thornton, Juliette. "Absent White Fathers: Coloured Identity in Zambia." In *Burdened by Race: Coloured Identities in Southern Africa*, edited by Mohamed Adhikari, 185–207. Cape Town, South Africa: UCT Press.

Mindano, Nixon. "Ndinali 'Che uje.'" *Tikambe*, supplement to *Malawi News*, October 13–19, 1990.

Mirani, Leo. "Millions of Facebook Users Have No Idea They're Using the Internet." *Quartz*, February 9, 2015. https://qz.com/333313/milliions-of-facebook-users-have-no-idea-theyre-using-the-internet.

Mithi, Pamela. "Nambewe the Heroine." In *Winning Stories from the 2008 Malawian Girls' Literary Competition*, edited by Stephanie Bosch and Sambalikagwa Mvona, 3–7. Blantyre, Malawi: Assemblies of God Press, 2009.

Mkhize, Khwezi. "'To See Us as We See Ourselves': John Tengo Jabavu and the Politics of the Black Periodical." *Journal of Southern African Studies* 44, no. 3 (2018): 413–30.

Mlenga, Maureen. "Bed no. 13." *Malawi News*, May 28–June 3, 1988.

Mogale, Arthur (pseud.). "Hot Diamonds." *Drum*, April 1953.

Mohutsiwa, Siyanda. "I'm Done with African Immigrant Literature." *Okayafrica*, February 8, 2016. https://www.okayafrica.com/im-done-with-african-immigrant-literature/.

Mokoena, Hlonipha. "An Assembly of Readers: Magema Fuze and His *Ilanga lase Natal* Readers." *Journal of Southern African Studies* 35, no. 3 (2009): 595–607.

Molamu, Louis. "Wietie: The Emergence and Development of Tsotsitaal in South Africa." *Alternation* 2, no. 2 (1995): 139–58.

Money, Duncan. "'Aliens' on the Copperbelt: Zambianisation, Nationalism and Non-Zambian Africans in the Mining Industry." *Journal of Southern African Studies* 45, no. 5 (2019): 859–75.

Mongia, Radhika. "Interrogating Critiques of Methodological Nationalism: Propositions for New Methodologies." In *Beyond Methodological Nationalism: Research Methodologies for Cross-Border Studies*, edited by Anna Amelina, Devrimsel D. Nergiz, Thomas Faist, and Nina Glick Schiller, 198–215. New York: Routledge, 2012.

Moore, David Chisoni. "Local Color, Global 'Color': Langston Hughes, the Black Atlantic, and Soviet Central Asia, 1932." *Research in African Literatures* 27, no. 4 (1996): 49–70.

Moretti, Franco. "Conjectures on World Literature." In *Debating World Literature*, edited by Christopher Prendergast, 148–62. London: Verso, 2004.

———. *Distant Reading*. London: Verso, 2013.

———. *Graphs, Maps, Trees: Abstract Models for Literary History*. London: Verso, 2005.

Morris, Rosalind C. "Style, *Tsotsi*-Style, and *Tsotsitaal*: The Histories, Aesthetics, and Politics of a South African Figure." *Social Text* 28, no. 2 (103) (Summer 2010): 85–112.

Mosiya, Dymon. "Why Are Men Driven into Crime and Women to Shame and Madness This Century?" *Malawi News*, September 21, 1974.

Motsisi, Casey. "Confessions of an Illicit Boozer." In *Casey & Co: Selected Writings of Casey "Kid" Motsisi*, edited by Mothobi Mutloatse, 64–66. Johannesburg: Ravan Press, 1980.

———. "Kid Hangover." In *Casey & Co: Selected Writings of Casey "Kid" Motsisi*, edited by Mothobi Mutloatse, 14–16. Johannesburg: Ravan Press, 1980.

———. "Kid Malalapipe." In *Casey & Co: Selected Writings of Casey "Kid" Motsisi*, edited by Mothobi Mutloatse, 44–46. Johannesburg: Ravan Press, 1980.

———. "Kid Newspapers." In *Casey & Co: Selected Writings of Casey "Kid" Motsisi*, edited by Mothobi Mutloatse, 33–35. Johannesburg: Ravan Press, 1980.

———. "Kid Playboy." In *Casey & Co: Selected Writings of Casey "Kid" Motsisi*, edited by Mothobi Mutloatse, 27–30. Johannesburg: Ravan Press, 1980.

———. "Mattress." In *Casey & Co: Selected Writings of Casey "Kid" Motsisi*, edited by Mothobi Mutloatse, 17–20. Johannesburg: Ravan Press, 1980.

———. On the Beat. *Drum*, April 1958–June 1962, November 1963, January 1974, March 1974.

"Mourir aux portes de l'Europe." *Chimurenga Chronic*, *Chimurenga* 16, October 19, 2011.

Mphahlele, Ezekiel (Es'kia). "Lesane." In *The Drum Decade: Stories from the 1950s*, edited by Michael Chapman, 132–61. 2nd ed. Pietermaritzburg, South Africa: University of Natal Press, 2001.

Mphande, Lupenga. "Dr. Hastings Kamuzu Banda and the Malawi Writers Group: The (un)Making of a Cultural Tradition." *Research in African Literatures* 27, no. 1 (1996): 80–101.

———. "Ngoni Praise Poetry and the Nguni Diaspora." Special issue in memory of Josaphat Bekunuru Kubayanda, *Research in African Literatures* 24, no. 4 (Winter 1993): 99–122.

Mponda, Felix. "Malawi Gays Pick Up the Baton to Fight for Rights." *Malawi News*, January 2–8, 2010.

Msowoya, Amin. "Writing Is a Contribution to Advancement of Our Country." *Malawi News*, August 1, 1972.

Mtepuka, Elias M. "Central African Federation: The Attack." *Africa South*, July 1957, 73–81.

Mtima, Billiard K. "Kuceza Kwanga Ku Rhodesia." *African Parade*, April 1955.

Mudeka, Ireen. "Gendered Exclusion and Contestation: Malawian Women's Migration and Work in Colonial Harare, Zimbabwe, 1930s to 1963." *African Economic History* 44 (2016): 18–43.

Mufti, Aamir. *Forget English! Orientalisms and World Literatures*. Cambridge, MA: Harvard University Press, 2016.

Mukumbang, F. C., A. N. Ambe, and B. O. Adebiyi. "Unspoken Inequality: How COVID-19 Has Exacerbated Existing Vulnerabilities of Asylum-Seekers, Refugees, and Undocumented Migrants in South Africa." *International Journal for Equality in Health* 19, no. 141 (2020): 1–7.

Mulera, Linda. "Mwana Wotayidwa M'chimbudzi." In *Winning Stories from the 2008 Malawian Girls' Literary Competition*, edited by Stephanie Bosch and Sambalikagwa Mvona, 52–56. Blantyre, Malawi: Assemblies of God Press, 2009.

Musodza, Masimba. "Here Be Cannibals." *Jungle Jim* 23, March 17, 2014. Cape Town, South Africa: Afreak Press.

Mwakikagile, Godfrey. *Ethnicity and National Identity in Uganda: The Land and Its People*. Dar es Salaam, Tanzania: New Africa Press, 2009.

Mwalwanda, Gospel. "It All Happened in Room 20." *Malawi News*, March 29–April 3, 1986.

Mwiyeriwa, Steve S. "Printing Presses and Publishing in Malawi." *Society of Malawi Journal* 31, no. 2 (July 1978): 31–53.

Nakao, Shuichiro. "Convivial Multilingualism as a Modern African Ethos: Cases of East African Non-Arab Arabophone Societies." In *Dynamism in African Languages and Literature: Towards Conceptualisation of African Potentials*, edited by Keiko Takemura and Francis B. Nyamnjoh, 19–45. Bamenda, Cameroon: Langaa RPCIG, 2021.

Namponya, Clemence R. "History and Development of Printing and Publishing in Malawi." *Libri* 28, no. 3 (1978): 167–81.

Namusanya, Dave Mankhokwe. "While Neighbors Rake in Awards." *Malawi News Weekender*, May 10–16, 2014.

Newell, Stephanie. "Corresponding with the City: Self-help Literature in Urban West Africa." *Journal of Postcolonial Writing* 44, no. 1 (2008): 15–27.

———. *Ghanaian Popular Fiction: "Thrilling Discoveries in Conjugal Life" and Other Tales*. Oxford, England: James Currey, 2000.

———. Introduction to *Readings in African Popular Fiction*, edited by Stephanie Newell, 1–10. Bloomington: Indiana University Press, 2002.

———. "Local Cosmopolitans in Colonial West Africa." *Journal of Commonwealth Literature* 46, no. 1 (2011): 103–17.

———. *Newsprint Literature and Local Literary Creativity in West Africa, 1900s–1960s*. Suffolk, England: Boydell and Brewer, 2023.

———. "'Paracolonial' Networks: Some Speculations on Local Readerships in Colonial West Africa." *Interventions: International Journal of Postcolonial Studies* 3, no. 3 (2001): 336–54.

———. *The Power to Name: A History of Anonymity in Colonial West Africa*. Athens: Ohio University Press, 2013.

Ndala, Lucy. "Wrestling with Fate." *Malawi News*, August 7–13, 1982.

Ndala, Rodrick. "Tchopa Dance—a Means of Expressing Love." *Malawi News*, April 27, 1974.

Ngara, Emmanuel, ed. *New Writing from Southern Africa*. Portsmouth, NH: Heinemann, 1996.

Ngoda, Tari. *Diary of a Harare Girl* (blog). https://diaryofahararegirl.wordpress.com.

Ng'omba, Dorothy. "The Prodigal Daughter." *Malawi News*, March 30–April 5, 1985.

Ngũgĩ wa Thiong'o. *Decolonizing the Mind: The Politics of Language in African Literature*. Oxford: James Currey, 1986.

Ngulube, Zulani Lance. "Malawian Women in Literature." *Malawi News*, October 19, 1980.

Ngwira, Juniah Sophie. *Diary of a Single Mum*. Facebook. https://www.facebook.com/diaryofasinglemum19892009.

Nixon, Rob. *Homelands, Harlem, and Hollywood: South African Culture and the World Beyond*. New York: Routledge, 1994.

———. *Slow Violence and the Environmentalism of the Poor*. Cambridge, MA: Harvard University Press, 2011.

Njakwa, D. F. Grey. "Dirika Gets Wages of Disobeying." *Malawi News*, June 22, 1974.

Nkhoma, Jonathan. "Chidamupha nchiyani mwamuna wakeyo?" *Tikambe,* supplement to *Malawi News*, August 28–September 3, 1993.

Nkosi, Lewis. "Obituary." In *The Will to Die: Can Themba*, by Can Themba, vii–xi. Selected by Donald Stuart and Roy Holland. London: Heinemann, 1972.

Nosy. "Low Down: On Rooms to Let." *Africa!* 1, no. 8 (October 1954).

Nothias, Toussaint. "Access Granted: Facebook's Free Basics in Africa." "Media, Culture & Society." Special issue, *Social Media and Democracy in Africa* 42, no. 3 (2020): 329–48.

Novosseloff, Alexandra, and Frank Neisse. "Walls Make Us Strangers, Not Stronger." *Chimurenga Chronic, Chimurenga* 16, October 19, 2011.

Nuttall, Sarah. "Reading in the Lives and Writing of Black South African Women." *Journal of Southern African Studies* 20, no. 1 (March 1994): 85–98.

Nxumalo, Henry. "The Birth of a Tsotsi." In *The Drum Decade: Stories from the 1950s*, edited by Michael Chapman, 18–23. 2nd ed. Pietermaritzburg, South Africa: University of Natal Press, 2001.

Nyamnjoh, Francis B. "Incompleteness: Frontier Africa and the Currency of Conviviality." *Journal of Asian and African Studies* 52, no. 3 (2017): 253–70.

Nyirongo, Stan. "Riches through Murder Foiled." *Malawi News*, March 30, 1974.

Odhiambo, Tom. "Inventing Africa in the Twentieth Century: Cultural Imagination, Politics, and Transnationalism in *Drum* Magazine." *African Studies* 65, no. 2 (2006): 157–74.

Ogbe, Yemisi. "Americanah and Other Definitions of Supple Citizenships." *Chimurenga Chronic, Chronic Books*, August 2013.

Ogude, James. "The Vernacular Press and the Articulation of Luo Ethnic Citizenship: The Case of Achieng' Oneko's *Ramogi*." *Current Writing: Text and Reception in Southern Africa* 13, no. 2 (2001): 42–55.

Ogundipe-Leslie, Molara. *Re-Creating Ourselves: African Women & Critical Transformations.* Trenton, NJ: Africa World Press, 1994.

Okorafor, Nnedi. "Africanfuturism Defined." *Nnedi's Wahala Zone Blog.* October 19, 2019. http://nnedi.blogspot.com/2019/10/africanfuturism-defined.html.

Omanga, Duncan. "WhatsApp as 'Digital Publics': The *Nakuru Analysts* and the Evolution of Participation in Country Governance in Kenya." *Journal of Eastern African Studies* 13, no. 1 (2019): 175–91.

Orel, Harold. *The Victorian Short Story: Development and Triumph of a Genre.* Cambridge: Cambridge University Press, 1986.

Ostrom, Hans. *Langston Hughes: A Study of the Short Fiction.* New York: Twayne, 1993.

Ouma, Christopher E. W., and Madhu Krishnan. "Small Magazines in Africa: Ecologies and Genealogies." *Social Dynamics* 47, no. 2 (2021): 193–209.

Owuor, Yvonne A. "Imagined Waters." *Chimurenga Chronic*, March 2015.

Paas, Steven. *English-Chichewa/Chinyanja Dictionary.* 3rd ed. Zomba, Malawi: Kachere Series, 2005.

Pambana, Mtandi. "A Race with Chance." *African Parade*, November–December 1954.

Parkes, George. "The Gub-Gub Peas." In *Jamaica Anansi Stories*, edited by Martha Warren Beckwith, 4–5. New York: American Folk-lore Society, 1924.

Peterson, Derek R., and Emma Hunter. "Print Culture in Colonial Africa." In *African Print Cultures: Newspapers and Their Publics in the Twentieth Century*, edited by Derek R. Peterson, Emma Hunter, and Stephanie Newell, 1–45. Ann Arbor: University of Michigan Press, 2016.

Peterson, Derek R., Emma Hunter, and Stephanie Newell, eds. *African Print Cultures: Newspapers and Their Publics in the Twentieth Century*. Ann Arbor: University of Michigan Press, 2016.

Pfalzgraf, Magdalena. *Mobility in Contemporary Zimbabwean Literature in English: Crossing Borders, Transcending Boundaries*. London: Routledge, 2022.

Phiri, D. D. (Desmond Dudwa). "It Happened Eighty Years Ago." *African Parade*, March–April 1954.

Phiri, Edward M. Kaperemera. ". . . Almost Home . . ." *Malawi News*, April 27, 1974.

Phiri, Grace. "Meet My Aunt." *Malawi News*, August 4–10, 1984.

———. "Sugar-Daddy's Style." *Malawi News*, March 24–30, 1984.

Phiri, Kings M. "Some Changes in the Matrilineal Family System among the Chewa of Malawi since the Nineteenth Century." *Journal of African History* 24, no. 2 (1983): 257–74.

Phwitiko, Elliot. "The Wedding That Never Was." *Malawi News*, December 14, 1974.

Pillay, S., V. Barolsky, V. Naidoo, N. Mohlakoana, and A. Hadland. *Citizenship, Violence and Xenophobia in South Africa: Perceptions from South African Communities*. Commissioned by the CEO of the Human Sciences Research Council, 2008.

Power, Joey. *Political Culture and Nationalism in Malawi: Building Kwacha*. Rochester, NY: University of Rochester Press, 2010.

Pressman, Jessica. "Electronic Literature as Comparative Literature." American Comparative Literature Association. *State of the Discipline Report*. June 28, 2014. https://stateofthediscipline.acla.org/entry/electronic-literature-comparative-literature-0.

Primorac, Ranka. "At Home in the World? Re-framing Zambia's Literature in English." *Journal of Southern African Studies* 40, no. 3 (2014): 575–91.

———. "Cosmopolitanism and Social Change in a Zambian Thriller." *Research in African Literatures* 41, no. 3 (Fall 2010): 49–61.

———. "Introduction: In/Visibility and African Thrillers." *Journal of Postcolonial Writing* 49, no. 1 (2013): 71–73.

———. "The Novel in a House of Stone: Re-categorising Zimbabwean Fiction." *Journal of Southern African Studies* 29, no. 1 (2003): 49–62.

Primorac, Ranka, and Stephen Chan. "*Gwebede's Wars*: Anglophone Black Novels in Southern Africa 1965–1989." *The Palgrave Handbook of Cold War Literature*, edited by A. Hammond, 551–69. Cham, Switzerland: Palgrave Macmillan, 2020.

Proferes, Nicholas, Naiyan Jones, Sarah Gilbert, Casey Fiesler, and Michael Zimmer. "Studying Reddit: A Systematic Overview of Disciplines, Approaches, Methods, and Ethics." *Social Media and Society* (April–June 2021): 1–14.

Quayon, Ato. "Kòbòlò Poetics: Urban Transcripts and Their Reading Publics in Africa." *New Literary History* 41, no. 2 (Spring 2010): 413–38.

Quinn, Mary Lou, and Eugene P. A. Schleh. "Popular Crime in Africa: The Macmillan Education Program." In *Mysteries of Africa*, edited by Eugene Schleh, 39–49. Bowling Green, OH: Bowling Green State University Popular Press, 1991.

Rabkin, David. "Drum Magazine (1951–1961): And the Works of Black South African Writers Associated with It." PhD diss., University of Leeds, 1975.

Rafapa, L. J. "South African Drum Writers of Fiction: The English Language and African Identity." In *English Language and Literature: Cross Cultural Currents*, edited by Mompoloki Mmangaka Bagwasi, Modupe Moyosore Alimi, and Patrick James Ebewo, 254–62. Newcastle upon Tyne, England: Cambridge Scholars, 2008.

Raftopoulos, Brian. "Nationalism and Labour in Salisbury 1953–1965." *Journal of Southern African Studies* 21, no. 1 (1995): 79–93.

Rampersad, Arnold. *The Life of Langston Hughes. Vol. 2, 1914–1967, I Dream a World.* 2nd ed. Oxford: Oxford University Press, 2002.

Ranger, Terence. *Bulawayo Burning: The Social History of a Southern African City 1893–1960.* Suffolk, England: James Currey, 2010.

Reid, Katie. "Q&A: (Pt 1) Jenna Bass—Editor and Co-founder of African Pulp Fiction Magazine Jungle Jim." *Africa in Words*, November 13, 2012. https://africainwords.com/2012/11/13/qa-editor-and-co-founder-of-jungle-jim-magazine-jenna-bass/.

———. "Q&A: (Pt 2) Jenna Bass—Editor and Co-founder of African Pulp Fiction Magazine Jungle Jim." *Africa in Words*, November 20, 2012. https://africainwords.com/2012/11/20/qa-jenna-bass-editor-and-co-founder-of-african-pulp-fiction-magazine-jungle-jim-pt-2/.

Rekacewicz, Philippe. "Les frontières les mieux gardées du monde." *Chimurenga Chronic, Chimurenga* 16, October 19, 2011.

Reuster-Jahn, Uta. "Newspaper Serials in Tanzania: The Case of Eric James Shigongo." *Swahili Forum* 15 (2008): 25–50.

———. "Sex and Relationship Education on the Streets: Advice on Love, Sex, and Relationships in Popular Swahili Newspaper Columns and Pamphlets in Tanzania." In *Popular Culture in Africa: The Episteme of the Everyday*, edited by Stephanie Newell and Onookome Okome, 69–92. New York: Routledge, 2014.

Roberts, Sarah R. "Digital Detritus: 'Error' and the Logic of Opacity in Social Media Content Moderation." *First Monday* 23, no. 3–5 (March 2018). https://journals.uic.edu/ojs/index.php/fm/article/download/8283/6649.

Robinson, Frank M., and Lawrence Davidson. *Pulp Culture: The Art of Fiction Magazines.* Portland, OR: Collectors Press, 1998.

Robolin, Stéphane. *Grounds of Engagement: Apartheid-Era African American and South African Writing.* Urbana: University of Illinois Press, 2015.

Robotham, Don. "Cosmopolitanism and Planetary Humanism: The Strategic Universalism of Paul Gilroy." *South Atlantic Quarterly* 104, no. 3 (Summer 2005): 561–82.

Roscoe, Adrian. *The Columbia Guide to Central African Literature in English since 1945*. New York: Columbia University Press, 2008.

Rugunanan, Pragna. "'South Africa Belongs to All Those Who Live in It,' COVID-19 Showed It Does Not." *openDemocracy*, July 2, 2020. https://www.opendemocracy.net/en/pandemic-border/south-africa-belongs-to-all-who-live-in-it-covid-19-showed-it-does-not/.

Sacks, Susanna L. "Moving Forms: Individuals, Institutions, and the Production of Slam Poetry Networks in Southern Africa." *ASAP/Journal* 5, no. 1 (2020): 153–179.

———. *Networked Poetics: The Digital Turn in Southern African Poetry*. Amherst: University of Massachusetts Press, 2024.

Said, Edward W. *Culture and Imperialism*. London: Vintage, 1993.

Saidi, William. Bits and Pieces from Harare. *African Parade*, December 1958–August 1962, October 1962.

———. "Copperbelt Capers." *Central African Mail*, October 25, 1963.

———. "How a Column Can Change Your Life." *Bill Saidi Memoirs* (blog), August 3, 2010. http://billsaidimemoirs.blogspot.com/2010/08/life.html.

———. Lusaka after Dark. *Central African Mail*, August 24, 1963–May 15, 1964.

———. "Nearly Killed in Combat." *Bill Saidi Memoirs* (blog), June 29, 2010. http://billsaidimemoirs.blogspot.com/2010/06/nearly-killed-in-combat.html.

———. "This Life." *Central African Mail*, May 15, 1964.

———. "Zimpapers: Ten Years of Turbulence." *Bill Saidi Memoirs* (blog), July 28, 2010. http://billsaidimemoirs.blogspot.com/2010/07/zimpapers-ten-years-of-turbulence.html.

Saint, Lily. *Black Cultural Life in South Africa: Reception, Apartheid, and Ethics*. Ann Arbor: University of Michigan Press, 2018.

Salima, Bertrand. "Rise and Fall of a Pretty Girl." *Malawi News*, November 9, 1974.

Samatar, Sofia. "Toward a Planetary History of Afrofuturism." *Research in African Literatures* 48, no. 4 (2017): 175–91.

Sampson, Anthony. *Drum: An African Adventure—and Afterwards*. London: Hodder and Stoughton, 1983.

Samuelson, Meg. "Coastal Form: Amphibian Positions, Wider Worlds, and Planetary Horizons on the African Indian Ocean Littoral." *Comparative Literature* 69, no. 1 (2017): 16–24.

———. "'Home and the World': The Contestation of Social Fictions in Three South African Women's Memoirs." *English Academy Review* 22, no. 1 (2005): 32–42.

Sandwith, Corinne. "Well-Seasoned Talks: The Newspaper Column and the Satirical Mode in South African Letters." *Social Dynamics* 45, no.1 (2019): 103–20.

Schwarzbach, F. S. "Newgate Novel to Detective Fiction." In *A Companion to the Victorian Novel*, edited by Patrick Brantlinger and William B. Thesing, 227–43. Malden, MA: Blackwell, 2002.

Scott, Peter. "Migrant Labor in Southern Rhodesia." *Geographical Review* 44, no. 1 (1954): 29–48.

Segar, Emma. "Blog Fiction and Its Successors: The Emergence of a Relational Poetics." *Convergence: The International Journal of Research into New Media Technologies* 23, no. 1 (2017): 20–33.

Semu, Linda. "Kamuzu's Mbumba: Malawi Women's Embeddedness to Culture in the Face of International Political Pressure and Internal Legal Change." *Africa Today* 49, no. 2 (2002): 77–99.

Sengendo, Hannington. "Urban Geography of Uganda." In *A Contemporary Geography of Uganda*, edited by Bakama B. BakamaNume, 131–58. Dar es Salaam, Tanzania: Mkuki na Nyota, 2010.

Sexton, Jared. "The Social Life of Social Death: On Afro-Pessimism and Black Optimism." *InTensions* 5 (Fall/Winter 2011): 1–47.

Shaw, Timothy M. "Zambia: Dependence and Underdevelopment." *Canadian Journal of African Studies / La Revue Canadienne des Études Africaines* 10, no. 1 (1976): 3–22.

Shepperson, George. "Pan-Africanism and 'Pan-Africanism': Some Historical Notes." *Phylon* 23, no. 4 (1962): 346–58.

Shili, Daniel G. From Cape Town to Pointe-Noir. *African Parade*, April–August 1957.

Shonga, G. H., and Jacob N. Zulu. *Matsotsi*. Lusaka, Zambia: Neczam, 1967.

Shringarpure, Bhakti. *Cold War Assemblages: Decolonization to Digital*. New York: Routledge, 2019.

Sidayiya, Douglas. "Ntombo Gets a Job." *Drum*, March 1952.

Silvey, Rachel. "Geographies of Gender and Migration: Spatializing Social Difference." *International Migration Review* 40, no. 1 (Spring 2006): 64–81.

Singano, Victor. "Ukatambatamba kumayang'ana kum'mawa." *Malawi News*, September 1–7, 2007.

Singh, Nikhil. "The Lonesome Ballad of Easter Jack." *Jungle Jim*, no. 1, June 1, 2011. Cape Town, South Africa: Afreak Press.

Slinn, Peter. "Commercial Concessions and Politics during the Colonial Period: The Role of the British South Africa Company in Northern Rhodesia 1890–1964." *African Affairs* 70, no. 281 (October 1971): 365–84.

Smethurst, James. "The Adventures of a Social Poet: Langston Hughes from the Popular Front to Black Power." In *African-American Poets, vol. 1*, edited by Harold Bloom, 49–70. New York: Infobase, 2009.

Smyth, Rosaleen. "War Propaganda during the Second World War in Northern Rhodesia." *African Affairs* 83, no. 332 (July 1984): 345–58.

Soja, Edward W. *Seeking Spatial Justice*. Minneapolis: University of Minnesota Press, 2010.

Sollors, Werner. *Ethnic Modernism*. Cambridge, MA: Harvard University Press, 2008.

Solomoni, Ester. "A Story by a Malawian Writer." *Malawi News*, October 5, 1974.

Somerville, J. J. B. "The Central African Federation." *International Affairs* 39, no. 3 (1963): 386–402.

Sosibo, Kwanele. "The Warm-Up." *Chimurenga Chronic*, *Chimurenga* 16, October 19, 2011.

Speke, John Hanning. *Journal of the Discovery of the Source of the Nile*. London: J. M. Dent, 1906.

Spencer, Lynda Gichanda, Dina Ligaga, and Grace A. Musila. "Gender and Popular Imaginaries in Africa." *Agenda* 32, no. 3 (2018): 3–9.

Spivak, Gayatri Chakravorty. "Three Women's Texts and a Critique of Imperialism." *Critical Inquiry* 12 (Autumn 1985): 243–61.

Stern, Lesley. "How Movies Move (between Hong Kong and Bulawayo, between Screen and Stage . . .)." In *World Cinemas, Transnational Perspective*, edited by Nataša Ďurovičová and Kathleen Newman, 186–216. New York: Routledge, 2010.

Stratton, Florence. *Contemporary African Literature and the Politics of Gender*. New York: Routledge, 1994.

Suhr-Sytsma, Nathan. *Poetry, Print, and the Making of Postcolonial Literature*. Cambridge: Cambridge University Press, 2017.

Swainson, N., S. Bendera, R. Gordon, and E. Kadzamira. *Promoting Girls' Education in Africa: The Design and Implementation of Policy Interventions*. Education Research Serial no. 25. London: Department for International Development, 1998.

Switzer, Les. "*Bantu World* and the Origins of a Captive African Commercial Press in South Africa." *Journal of Southern African Studies* 14, no. 3 (1988): 351–70.

———. "Introduction: South Africa's Alternative Press in Perspective." In *South Africa's Alternative Press: Voices of Protest and Resistance, 1880s–1960s*, edited by Les Switzer, 1–53. Cambridge: Cambridge University Press, 1997.

Tamale, Sylvia. "Gender Trauma in Africa: Enhancing Women's Links to Resources." *Journal of African Law* 48, no. 1 (2004): 50–61.

Themba, Can. "'Baby Come Duze.'" In *The Drum Decade: Stories from the 1950s*, edited by Michael Chapman, 109–13. 2nd ed. Pietermaritzburg, South Africa: University of Natal Press, 2001.

Toivanen, Anna-Leena. *Mobilities and Cosmopolitanisms in African and Afrodiasporic Literatures*. Leiden, Netherlands: Brill, 2021.

Tremayne, Mark. "The Facebook Agenda: Global Social Media News Characteristics." *American Communication Journal* 19, no. 1 (2017): 25–35.

Undie, Chi-Chi, Joanna Crichton, and Eliya Zulu. "Metaphors We Love By: Conceptualizations of Sex among Young People in Malawi." *African Journal of Reproductive Health* 11, no. 3 (2007): 221–35.

Uzoatu, Uzor Maxim. "The Impossible Death of an African Crimebuster." *Chimurenga Chronic*, *Chronic Books*, June 2014.

———. "Onitsha Republic." *Chimurenga Chronic, Chronic Books*, August 2013.

Vail, Leroy, and Landeg White. "Of Chameleons and Paramount Chiefs: The Case of the Malawian Poet Jack Mapanje." *Review of African Political Economy* 17, no. 48 (1990): 26–49.

———. *Power and the Praise Poem: Southern African Voices in History*. Charlottesville: University Press of Virginia, 1991.

Valley, Dylan, director. *Chimurenga: Who No Know Go Know*. Prince Claus Fund, 2013.

Vambe, Lawrence. "From Near the Bush to New York." *African Parade*, September 1957.

———. *From Rhodesia to Zimbabwe*. London: Heinemann, 1976.

Van der Westhuizen, Janis. "Popular Culture, Discourse and Divergent Identities: Reconstructing South Africa as an African State." *African Identities* 6, no. 1 (2008): 45–61.

Van Onselen, Charles. *Chibaro: African Mine Labour in Southern Rhodesia 1900–1933*. London: Pluto Press, 1976.

Van Wyk, Berte. "Indigenous Rights, Indigenous Epistemologies, and Language: (Re)construction of Modern Khoisan Identities." *Knowledge Cultures* 4, no. 4 (2016): 33–45.

Veit-Wild, Flora. *Teachers, Preachers, Non-Believers: A Social History of Zimbabwean Literature*. London: Hans Zell, 1992.

Wallis, Kate. "How Books Matter: Kwani Trust, Farafina, Cassava Republic Press and the Medium of Print." *Wasafiri* 31, no. 4 (2016): 39–46.

Wannamaker, William. "American Crisis." *African Parade*, September 1965.

Warner, Michael. *Publics and Counterpublics*. Princeton, NJ: Princeton University Press, 2005.

Warner, Tobias. *The Tongue-Tied Imagination: Decolonizing Literary Modernity in Senegal*. New York: Fordham University Press, 2019.

Watermeyer, Susan. "Afrikaans English." In *Focus on South Africa*, edited by Vivian de Klerk, 99–124. Amsterdam: John Benjamins, 1996.

West, Michael O. *The Rise of an African Middle Class: Colonial Zimbabwe, 1989–1965*. Bloomington: Indiana University Press, 2002.

White, Luise. *Speaking With Vampires: Rumor and History in Colonial Africa*. Berkeley: University of California Press, 2000.

Willcox, Walter F. "Statistics of Migrations, National Tables, South Africa, Southern Rhodesia, Swaziland, Tanganyika, Madagascar, French Somali Coast, Angola, Azores, Cape Verde Islands, Madeira, Cameroon, Togo." In *International Migrations. Vol. 1, Statistics*, edited by Walter F. Willcox, 1049–82. Cambridge, MA: NBER, 1929.

Williams, Paul. "Physics Made Simple: The Image of Nuclear Weapons in the Writing of Langston Hughes." *Journal of Transatlantic Studies* 6, no. 2 (2008): 131–41.

Williamson, Debra Aho. "Global Facebook Users 2019." EMarketer, December 12, 2019. https://www.emarketer.com/content/global-facebook-users-2019.

———. "Global Facebook Users 2020." EMarketer, December 8, 2020. https://www.emarketer.com/content/global-facebook-users-2020.

Wilson, Anika. "Of Love Potions and Witch Baskets: Domesticity, Mobility, and Occult Rumors in Malawi." *Western Folklore* 71, no. 2 (Spring 2012): 149–73.

Wyche, Susan, and Eric P. S. Baumer. "Imagined Facebook: An Exploratory Study of Non-Users' Perceptions of Social Media in Rural Zambia." *New Media & Society* 19, no. 7 (2017): 1092–108.

Yanes, Nicholas. "Graphic Imagery: Jewish American Comic Book Creators' Depictions of Class, Race, Patriotism and the Birth of the Good Captain." In *Captain America and the Struggle of the Superhero*, edited by Robert G. Weiner, 53–65. Jefferson, NC: McFarland, 2009.

Yékú, James. *Cultural Netizenship: Social Media, Popular Culture, and Performance in Nigeria*. Bloomington: Indiana University Press, 2022.

———. "Deference to Paper: Textuality, Materiality, and Literary Digital Humanities in Africa." *Digital Studies / Le champ numérique* 10, no. 1, 15 (2020): 1–27.

Yoshikuni, Tsuneo. "Notes on the Influence of Town-Country Relations on African Urban History, before 1957: Experiences of Salisbury and Bulawayo." In *Sites of Struggle: Essays in Zimbabwe's Urban History*, edited by Brian Raftopoulos and Tsuneo Yoshikuni, 113–28. Harare, Zimbabwe: Weaver Press, 1999.

Young, Robert J. C. "That Which Is Casually Called a Language." *PMLA* 131, no. 5 (2016): 1207–21.

Young, T. Cullen. "The 'Native' Newspaper." *Africa* 11, no. 1 (1938): 63–72.

Zander, Horst. *Fact-Fiction-"Faction": A Study of Black South African Literature in English*. Tübingen, Germany: Gunter Narr Verlag, 1999.

Zimmer, Michael. "'But the Data Is Already Public': On the Ethics of Research in Facebook," *Ethics and Information Technology* 12 (2010): 313–25.

Zingani, Willie. "Booked for Reading Pleasure." *Malawi News*, September 11–17, 1982.

Zizi, K. A. "The Man with Missing Fingers." *African Parade*, November 1953–March 1954.

Zuckerberg, Mark. "Building Global Community." Facebook, February 16, 2017, updated May 5, 2021. https://www.facebook.com/notes/3707971095882612/.

Index

Page numbers in *italic* refer to illustrations.

FLASHPOINTS

1. *On Pain of Speech: Fantasies of the First Order and the Literary Rant*, Dina Al-Kassim
2. *Moses and Multiculturalism*, Barbara Johnson, with a foreword by Barbara Rietveld
3. *The Cosmic Time of Empire: Modern Britain and World Literature*, Adam Barrows
4. *Poetry in Pieces: César Vallejo and Lyric Modernity*, Michelle Clayton
5. *Disarming Words: Empire and the Seductions of Translation in Egypt*, Shaden M. Tageldin
6. *Wings for Our Courage: Gender, Erudition, and Republican Thought*, Stephanie H. Jed
7. *The Cultural Return*, Susan Hegeman
8. *English Heart, Hindi Heartland: The Political Life of Literature in India*, Rashmi Sadana
9. *The Cylinder: Kinematics of the Nineteenth Century*, Helmut Müller-Sievers
10. *Polymorphous Domesticities: Pets, Bodies, and Desire in Four Modern Writers*, Juliana Schiesari
11. *Flesh and Fish Blood: Postcolonialism, Translation, and the Vernacular*, S. Shankar
12. *The Fear of French Negroes: Transcolonial Collaboration in the Revolutionary Americas*, Sara E. Johnson
13. *Figurative Inquisitions: Conversion, Torture, and Truth in the Luso-Hispanic Atlantic*, Erin Graff Zivin
14. *Cosmopolitan Desires: Global Modernity and World Literature in Latin America*, Mariano Siskind
15. *Fiction beyond Secularism*, Justin Neuman
16. *Periodizing Jameson: Dialectics, the University, and the Desire for Narrative*, Phillip E. Wegner
17. *The Practical Past*, Hayden White
18. *The Powers of the False: Reading, Writing, Thinking beyond Truth and Fiction*, Doro Wiese
19. *The Object of the Atlantic: Concrete Aesthetics in Cuba, Brazil, and Spain, 1868–1968*, Rachel Price
20. *Epic and Exile: Novels of the German Popular Front 1933–1945*, Hunter Bivens
21. *An Innocent Abroad: Lectures in China*, J. Hillis Miller
22. *Form and Instability: East Europe, Literature, Postimperial Difference*, Anita Starosta
23. *Bombay Modern: Arun Kolatkar and Bilingual Literary Culture*, Anjali Nerlekar
24. *Intimate Relations: Social Reform and the Late Nineteenth-Century South Asian Novel*, Krupa Shandilya
25. *Media Laboratories: Late Modernist Authorship in South America*, Sarah Ann Wells
26. *Acoustic Properties: Radio, Narrative, and the New Neighborhood of the Americas*, Tom McEnaney

27. *The New Woman: Literary Modernism, Queer Theory, and the Trans Feminine Allegory*, Emma Heaney
28. *Civilizing War: Imperial Politics and the Poetics of National Rupture*, Nasser Mufti
29. *Late Colonial Sublime: Neo-Epics and the End of Romanticism*, G. S. Sahota
30. *Globalizing Race: Anti-Semitism, Empire, and the Politics of Scale in Modern French and European Culture*, Dorian Bell
31. *Domestications: American Empire, Literary Culture, and the Postcolonial Lens*, Hosam Mohamed Aboul-Ela
32. *Behold an Animal: Four Exorbitant Readings*, Thangam Ravindranathan
33. *Capital Letters: Hugo, Baudelaire, Camus, and the Death Penalty*, Ève Morisi
34. *Immaterial Archives: An African Diaspora Poetics of Loss*, Jenny Sharpe
35. *Figures of the World: The Naturalist Novel and Transnational Form*, Christopher Laing Hill
36. *Imperfect Solidarities: Tagore, Gandhi, Du Bois, and the Forging of the Global Anglophone*, Madhumita Lahiri
37. *Fictional Environments: Mimesis, Deforestation, and Development in Latin America*, Victoria Saramago
38. *How to Read a Moment: The American Novel and the Crisis of the Present*, Mathias Nilges
39. *Secondhand China: Spain, the East, and the Politics of Translation*, Carles Prado-Fonts
40. *New World Maker: Radical Poetics, Black Internationalism, and the Translations of Langston Hughes*, Ryan James Kernan
41. *The Idea of Indian Literature: Gender, Genre, and Comparative Method*, Preetha Mani
42. *Concepts of the World*, Effie Rentzou
43. *Traces of the Unseen*, Carolina Sá Carvalho
44. *Cannibal Translation: Literary Reciprocity in Contemporary Latin America*, Isabel C. Gómez
45. *Entranced Earth: Art, Extractivism, and the End of Landscape*, Jens Andermann
46. *Dwelling in Fiction: Poetics of Place and the Experimental Novel in Latin America*, Ashley R. Brock
47. *Disoriented Disciplines: China, Latin America, and the Shape of World Literature*, Rosario Hubert